AF846441

Latine Lived Religions and Religious Identities in the United States

Latine Religion, Identity, and Culture

Series Editors: Edwin David Aponte and Miguel A. De La Torre

This series reimagines and advances Latine studies by publishing works that are innovative, cutting edge, and disrupt dominant, normative narratives. As an interdisciplinary series on Latine religion, culture, and identity, these works explore the intersectional dimensions of the Latine experience—such as religion, class, gender, ideology, and race—by engaging with lived identities, beliefs, and practices. Research will promote intersectional analysis as a critical tool, with work rooted in the Latine lived experience across the religious, theological, and spiritual landscape. Books in this series will move beyond the Christian experience, creating space for other faith traditions, which include Judaism, Islam, Santería/Lukumí/La Regla de Ocha-Ifá, Espiritismo, Curanderismo, and non-theistic experiences.

José Martí and the Intersection of Empires and Economics, by Miguel A. De La Torre

Making Face and Latine Neurodiversity: A Liberative Ethics, by Rudolph P. Reyes II

Latine Lived Religions and Religious Identities in the United States

¡Presente!

Edited by

MIGUEL A. DE LA TORRE AND EDWIN DAVID APONTE

BLOOMSBURY ACADEMIC
LONDON • NEW YORK • OXFORD • NEW DELHI • SYDNEY

BLOOMSBURY ACADEMIC
Bloomsbury Publishing Plc, 50 Bedford Square, London, WC1B 3DP, UK
Bloomsbury Publishing Inc, 1359 Broadway, New York, NY 10018, USA
Bloomsbury Publishing Ireland, 29 Earlsfort Terrace, Dublin 2, D02 AY28, Ireland

BLOOMSBURY, BLOOMSBURY ACADEMIC and the Diana logo are trademarks of Bloomsbury Publishing Plc

First published in Great Britain 2026

Series design by Jade Barnett
Cover image © Rui Almeida Fotografia / Getty Images

A catalogue record for this book is available from the British Library.

A catalog record for this book is available from the Library of Congress.

ISBN: HB: 978-1-3504-6022-5
PB: 978-1-3504-6021-8
ePDF: 978-1-3504-6023-2
eBook: 978-1-3504-6024-9

Series: Latine Religion, Identity, and Culture

Typeset by Newgen KnowledgeWorks Pvt. Ltd., Chennai, India
Printed and bound in Great Britain

For product safety related questions contact productsafety@bloomsbury.com.

To find out more about our authors and books visit www.bloomsbury.com
and sign up for our newsletters.

To the Latine communities: the living testimony of our history, the sustainers of our present, and the architects of our future.

Contents

Series Introduction ix

Introduction: How We Got Here 1
Edwin David Aponte

1 *What's in a Name?* 13
Edwin David Aponte

2 *Latine Jewish Identity, Religious Life, and Transnational Belonging in the United States* 25
Laura Limonic

3 *Thinking About Latine Islamicity or a Muslim* Latinidad/*Latinicity* 35
Biel Delgado Trabal

4 *Jesusito* 43
Rubén Rosario Rodríguez

5 *Full of the Spirit: US Latine Christian Pneumatologies and Religious Identities* 51
Albert Hernández

6 *The Permeability of Worlds: The Role of Spirits in the Latine Religious Landscape* 59
Elaine Penagos

7 *Latine Curación* 69
Damien Pascal Domenack

8 *Disabilities* 77
Rudolph P. Reyes II

9 *An Overview of Select Latin American Marian Devotions in the United States* 85
Sudabée Lotfian-Mena and Neomi De Anda

10 *Challenging the Patriarchy* 97
Isabela Leonor Rosales

11 *Shades of Inequality: Colorism at the Intersection of Society and Religion* 109
Alexandra Rosado-Román

12 *Our Fluidity* 117
Grego Peña-Camprubí

13 *Death or Salvation of a Planet* 127
Amanda J. Baugh

14 *Departing from the American Dream: Toward Visions of Collective Latine Human Dignity* 137
Francisco J. García Jr.

15 *Screwing with the System* 145
Miguel A. De La Torre

16 *Sacred Texts* 159
Jacqueline M. Hidalgo

17 *Sound, Cinema, and* Santería*: Listening to "Angelitos Negros" with Oyá* 167
Deborah De La Torre

18 "To Heal Every Little Wound": Reconnecting, Reclaiming, and Revitalizing Cultural Spiritual Traditions Among Indigenous Peoples of Mexico in the United States 175
Ramona Beltrán, Miriam Valdovinos, Olivia Hunte, My Ngoc To, and Tina Hulama

19 *Crossing Borders* 187
Noemi Vega Quiñones

20 *Nones and Alternative Paths* 193
José Francisco Morales Torres

Conclusion: Where Are We Going—Where Have We Been 201
Miguel A. De La Torre

Notes 209
Bibliography 253
Note on Contributors 277
Index 283

Series Introduction

Edwin David Aponte and Miguel A. De La Torre

Latine Religion, Identity, and Culture is a series that reimagines and advances Latine studies by publishing works that are innovative, creative, cutting-edge, and disrupt dominant, normative narratives. As an interdisciplinary series on Latine religion, culture, and identity, these works explore the intersectional dimensions of the Latine experience—such as religion, class, gender, ideology, and race—by engaging with lived identities, beliefs, and practices. Research will promote intersectional analysis as a critical tool, with work rooted in the Latine lived experience across the religious, theological, and spiritual landscape. Books in this series will move beyond the Christian experience, creating space for other faith traditions, which include Judaism, Islam, Santería/Lukumí/La Regla de Ocha-Ifá, Espiritismo, and non-theistic experiences.

Rooted in the experiences of Latine communities, these scholars will be asked to lean into the future to explore what Latine faith across traditions (Christian and non-Christian), religiosity, and spirituality has to contribute to the discourse. Whether framed from a descriptive or normative perspective, contemporary analysis will consider the increasingly complex issues of how all the constitutive elements of Latine identity interact. The books in this series will address the development of Latine personhood, discuss people's perception of the world, and consider whether, how, and why they understand themselves as religious and/or spiritual beings.

The vision of this book series on Latine religion, identity, and culture privileges and promotes intersectional analysis as a critical tool. The purpose is to reconsider the Latine social location by refracting what has come to be a normative vision into a collective one through which the prisms of embodied diversity (at the intersections of colorism, gender, class, sexuality to name a few) engages the interdisciplinarity of diverse academic discourses and methodological perspectives in this vast field of inquiry, study, and practice.

Each volume showcases scholars working at the intersection of disciplinary and transdisciplinary boundaries. The series will consist of volumes with exceptional authors who have knowledgeable understanding of the subjects they write about. The current list of volumes that will be published are as follows:

- *José Martí and the Intersection of Empires and Economics*
- *Latine Lived Religions and Religious Identities in the United States: ¡Presente!*
- *Making Face and Latine Neurodiversity*

Introduction: How We Got Here

Edwin David Aponte

A Pope in the Borderlands

On February 17, 2016, Pope Francis visited Ciudad Juárez opposite the Texas city of El Paso, across the Río Bravo del Norte, better known in English as the Rio Grande River, on the international border between the United States of America and los Estados Unidos Mexicanos, that is, the United Mexican States, a.k.a., México. At that northern point of the most northern Latin American country, in the borderlands sandwiched between two North American nations is where the religious and spiritual leader of an estimated 1.4 billion Catholics chose to be.

More than a geographic area flanked by Mexico and the United States, the borderlands are a multifaceted dynamic space where social, cultural, political, communal, religious, and spiritual dimensions intersect in multiple ways that impact not only the local frontier communities but also communities throughout the Americas of the Western Hemisphere and indeed around the world. Situated between two modern nation-states, this liminal zone is both a threshold and simultaneously a site of compound worlds, a place where multiple realities coexist, a distinct and ever-evolving experience characterized by hybridity, contestation, domination and resistance, negotiation, and creativity.

These living borderlands are shaped by both historical legacies and contemporary realities of politics, changing demands of capital and labor, shifting empires, hegemony and domination, fluid racial identities as well as prejudice and segregation, migration, and always by religion. Both official religions and the lived beliefs and practices are active in these threshold zones created by the 1848 Treaty of Guadalupe Hidalgo, which ended the US–Mexican War (1846–8), known in Mexico as La guerra de intervención estadounidense en México (the War of United States Intervention in Mexico), and the subsequent 1853–54 Gadsden Purchase.[1] National boundaries were redrawn through "manifest destiny" conquest as the United States took over 55 percent of Mexico, and the legal identities of Mexicans and Indigenous peoples were transformed. While the Treaty granted US citizenship to Mexican nationals in the newly occupied territory (which included people of European descent, African descent, and those of mixed heritage of European, Indigenous, and African), the political settlement did not address issues of citizenship or land rights of the many Indigenous populations of the vast region, which included Apache, Comanches, Kiowas, Navajos/Diné, the so-called Pueblo peoples, the numerous tribes in California including the Chumash, Gabrielino-Tongva, Ohlone, Pomo, Shasta, and peoples that the new international border separated the Yoeme-Yaqui and the Tohono O'odham.[2]

Various peoples now found themselves living in the territories newly annexed by the United States, transformed overnight into residents under US jurisdiction—some citizens (Article IX), others referred in the Treaty as "savage tribes" (Article XI)—with significant ramifications that continue to the present day.[3] The 1848 end of a war also marked a shift in imperialism that initiated long-standing tensions around citizenship, racialization, and national identities that continues to define the region, and impacts all of the Americas.

Emerging out of such a contested context are types of living and cultural production in a zone memorably characterized by Gloria Anzaldúa (1942–2004) as *Nepantla*, a state of in-betweenness and cultural mestizaje (mixture). In *Borderlands/La Frontera: The New Mestiza*, Anzaldúa theorizes not just a physical divide but also a site of cultural convergence and conflict, which also includes spiritual borderlands, a spiritual mix of in-betweenness. Anzaldúa asserts that "the Borderlands are physically present whenever two or more cultures edge each other, where people of different races occupy the same territory, where under, lower, middle, and upper classes touch, where the space between two individuals shrink with intimacy."[4] Reflecting further upon the borderlands complexity, philosopher Mariana Alessandri observes that "Anzaldua's writing addresses the difficulty of translating herself to monolinguals—we might also say mono-mundiales."[5] Living in-between reflects a reality in which monolinguals and mono-mundiales (one-world folk) share the same cultural spaces with folks who live in multiple worlds in multi-lingual ways, even if one group is ignorant of the existence of the other. Peoples of multiple borderlands live in several concurrent worlds, where they must engage others who occupy locations of social, cultural, political, and religious dominance, but simultaneously are monolingual, monocultural, and mono-world (mono-mundial) and yet who have little awareness of life in-between dealing with racial discrimination, war and revolutions, economic ebbs and flows, vigilantism, and increasingly draconian enforcement to control the flow of peoples that all contribute to overlapping crises not limited by the international demarcation of treaties: destruction of animal life and environment and the loss of thousands of human lives.[6] And it was in the borderlands that first Pope from the Americas showed up.

This Latin American who became the 266th pope of the Roman Catholic Church was born Jorge Mario Bergoglio (1936–2025) in Buenos Aires, Argentina, of Italian descent, reflecting yet another type of transnational migration from Europe to the Americas. Archbishop of Buenos Aires Bergoglio emphasized prophetical social justice drawing from the "theology of the people" of Argentina.[7] From the start of his papacy, and even in the choosing of his name, Francis emphasized care for the poor, active mercy, interfaith dialogue, as well as commitment to social justice and environmental stewardship, notably through his 2015 encyclical Laudato Si'.[8] And then on the last stop of a five-day trip to Mexico, Pope Francis went to the "in-between" space on the US–Mexico border.

In Ciudad Juárez at a large cross erected near the border in memory of migrants who died trying to cross into the United States, Pope Francis prayed in the in-between space merging mercy, spirituality, the prophetic, and political actions, confounding certain secularization theories and uninformed assumptions of what is religious. Pope Francis then celebrated a cross-border Mass for which thousands of people from both Ciudad Juárez and El Paso communities participated, with many people traveling to Juárez, while many others joined virtually from a remote location the Sun Bowl Stadium in El Paso, Texas.

Building his homily on a text from the book of Jonah in the Hebrew Bible, Pope Francis addressed the global humanitarian crisis:

> Here in Ciudad Juárez, as in other border areas, there are thousands of immigrants from Central America and other countries, not forgetting the many Mexicans who also seek to pass over "to the other side." Each step, a journey laden with grave injustices ... The human tragedy that is forced migration is a global phenomenon today. This crisis which can be measured in numbers and statistics, we want instead to measure with names, stories, families. They are the brothers and sisters of those expelled by poverty and violence, by drug trafficking and criminal organizations. Being faced with so many legal vacuums, they get caught up in a web that ensnares and always destroys the poorest. Not only do they suffer poverty but they must also endure all these forms of violence.[9]

In the borderlands, within the in-between space, Pope Francis spoke of the names, stories, families, and realities of Latin America and Latine peoples in the United States.

Latine: In-between and *Presente*

Being Latine in the United States like the shared geographic and cultural borderlands of the United States and Mexico is inconveniently complicated and cannot be reduced to one or two characteristics, especially when imposed identities and borders, individual and communal displacement, and ongoing racialization are part of the mix. Moreover, Latine religion and spirituality are complex, since living in the borderlands is an existential, multifaceted reality. For Latine peoples, the in-between experience is present throughout the United States, and it is very much *presente*.

In the United States, the phrase "say their names" often is used communally to honor persons, especially Black and Brown individuals, who have been brutally killed as a result of racial injustice, police, and vigilante violence.[10] In Spanish-speaking communities, there is a comparable way to "say their names" through *Presente*, translated into English as "present or to be present," but contextually there is a richer, deeper meaning. Emerging from Latin America, especially during the 1970s and 1980s protests against state violence and repression, people gathered in protest naming the individual victims of oppressions, and those assembled would respond to the naming by declaring "¡Presente!" honoring them and affirming the continued presence of those victims. Presente is a powerful call-and-response declaration of remembrance and solidarity, a testimony to justice in the face of everyday injustice, of resistance connecting past struggles to present ones. Latine religion and spirituality is presente in the United States.[11]

Presente and Lived Religions

Conceptually lived religion refers to the everyday religious and spiritual practices, experiences, commitments, and expressions of religion as embodied by individuals and communities, rather than a myopic focus solely on official doctrines, institutions, or texts. But a focus on lived religion and spirituality is not a binary choice since aspects of formal religion also are part of lived experiences, especially when notions of belonging and community are considered. Nancy Ammerman defines lived religion as the everyday religious and spiritual practices that people engage in as part of their ordinary lives, how religion is actually experienced, embodied, and expressed in daily routines, relationships, and social contexts. "Finding and understanding everyday lived religion is no less about studying religion in society, but it means paying attention to the nonexperts. It means looking for the ad hoc religious beliefs, practices, and communities that also constitute the presence of religion in society, and that means definitions and categories need to be expanded."[12] In his consideration of lived religion, Robert Orsi identifies what he calls intersubjective and interpersonal webs of experiences, emotions, and bodily practices that in addition to beliefs or theological positions challenge rigid boundaries between "religious" and "secular" life and reveals how diverse, complex, and adaptable religion really is in practice.[13]

As helpful as the lived religion approach is, we do well also to pay attention to the insights of Manuel A. Vásquez as he reminds us about the insights of religion and society in Latin America regarding the multilayered dimensions of what is going on in everyday or popular religion:

> Responding to the towering presence of Gramsci in Latin America, these studies show how popular religiosity, from "folk" Catholicism and liberation theology to Pentecostalism and African-based religions like Candomblé and Santería, is both powerfully lived at the personal and local levels and embedded in structural and systemic power arrangements reproduced and contested through class-, race-, and gender-based struggles. Amid these struggles, lived religion serves both to impose hegemony and animate resistance, sometimes simultaneously.[14]

In its interactions with both hegemony and resistance, lived religion and spirituality, like Latine identity, cannot be reduced to one or two neat convenient characteristics.

How We Got Here: Latine, Lived Religions, and *Presente*

Within the diverse religious and spiritual landscapes of the United States, and particularly within Latine contexts *lo cotidiano*, the everyday religion and spirituality of meaning-making, thriving, and survival is a one of many shared characteristics.[15] This volume provides a foundational exploration of the intersectionality of US Latine religious and spiritual experiences and practices, the variety of Latine religious and spiritual thought, and their connections to the construction of the multiplicity of Latine social locations. By exploring different cultural forms that will help to better grasp what it means to be a religious and/or spiritual Latine in the United States. By addressing facets of formal religion as well as lived religion and spirituality in varied contexts of Latine *lo cotidiano*, and thereby expand the definitions and categories of what is recognized as religion in society.

With my discussion in Chapter 1, *What's in a Name*, I explore some of the common threads that are woven together in shared Latine identities in the United States including nomenclature, self-identities, as well as imposed identities, and generational understandings. I interrogate the concept together when there is so much diversity, and how can it be that given so much diversity, distinct communities are lumped together as one monolith. Even with the ever-evolving diversity I argue that there is some sort of contextual unity to be recognized and explored.

Laura Limonic in Chapter 2, *Latine Jewish Identity, Religious Life, and Transnational Belonging in the United States*, discusses how Latine Jews in the United States are at the intersection of Jewish and Latine identities that complicate narratives that assume Jews in the United States only as White and Ashkenazi or Latines as only Catholic and Spanish-speaking. With histories rooted in migrations from Europe, the Middle East, and North Africa to Latin America, Latine Jews bring communal models centered on cultural and social institutions with distinct religious and cultural practices. Navigating religious and racialized concepts of belonging, Latine Jews reshape Jewishness and Latinidad, offering an inclusive and pluralistic vision of identity and lived religion in the United States.

In Chapter 3, *Thinking about a Latine Islamicity or a Muslim latinidad/Latinicity*, Biel Delgado Trabal examines Latine Muslims as a community shaped by several colonial legacies, Afro-Moro heritage, and activism rooted in civil rights and liberation movements. Tracing origins to organizations which connected Islam with anticolonial, Black, and working-class struggles, Delgado examines how Latine Muslims situate themselves in relation to African American Islam, Muslim Iberia (al-Andalus), and West African traditions, with the attendant challenges of Islamophobia, anti-Latine racism, lack of institutional support, pressures from larger Muslim communities, and different views regarding Latina women's central role, feminism versus "family-ism," and the need for culturally grounded spaces.

Through Chapter 4 *Jesusito*, Rubén Rosario Rodríguez conveys how common expressions of Latine faith embrace an intimate, compassionate Jesús who attends to everyday needs, producing a Christology rooted in lived experience, liberation theology, and cultural contexts that emphasizes the Incarnation as divine solidarity with the poor, oppressed, and marginalized. Distinct expressions of Latine Christology affirms a God of love, vulnerability, and intimacy who suffers with the community and empowers them to resist injustice, affirming a revelation through the lived faith of ordinary people, especially women. This Latine Christology recognizes God in daily struggles that include racism, political oppression, and dismissive theologies. Through lived faith and collective struggle God is revealed in the endurance, hope, and compassion of marginalized communities who dare to call on *Jesusito*.

With his Chapter 5 *Full of the Spirit: US Latine Christian Pneumatologies and Religious Identities*, Albert Hernández explores the central role of the Holy Spirit and Pentecost in shaping US Latine Christian identity. Through diverse cultural and historical experiences, the Spirit is understood as an indwelling, empowering presence that inspires renewal, hybridity, and social justice, drawing on Catholic and Protestant traditions while also incorporating Indigenous, African, and popular spiritual practices. Latine expressions of the Spirit emphasize heart, embodiment, and transformation, seen in movements like Pentecostalism, Charismatic Catholicism, and liberationist activism. Drawing on diverse theological voices and lived examples, US Latine Christian pneumatologies present a pluralistic, dynamic vision of the Spirit that challenges exclusionary paradigms and affirms the fullness of divine presence in everyday life, family, and community.

Examining other experiences of spirit in Chapter 6, *The Permeability of Worlds: The Role of Spirits in the Latine Religious Landscape*, Elaine Penagos surveys the importance of spirits in Latine religious thought and practice, highlighting three specific traditions with strong African influence: Santería, Palo, and Espiritismo. Within those contexts spirits are understood variously as interactive divine forces, ancestors, energies of nature, or beings that offer guidance, protection, healing, and interpretations of life. Rooted in diverse African, Indigenous, and European histories of colonization, enslavement, and migration, in these traditions spirits are active presences that daily interact with humanity as they cross borders, bind communities, embody resilience, creativity, and sustain daily life. Despite stigmatization and legal challenges, these spirit-based practices flourish within US Latine communities.

In Chapter 7, *Latine Curación*, Damien Pascal Domenack examines how Latine communities navigate healthcare disparities by drawing on both biomedical and traditional healing systems, highlighting the persistence and adaptability of spiritual and folk practices. Concentrating on three major influential traditions—Pentecostalism's divine healing, the Indigenous-rooted folk medicine of *Curanderismo*, and Cuban *Espiritismo*—Domenack demonstrates how each provides culturally resonant ways of addressing physical, spiritual, and emotional illness that fill cosmological gaps typically not addressed by Western medicine. These frameworks of belonging, ancestral continuity, and spiritual balance sustain resilience, mutual aid, and flourishing in the face of structural barriers and marginalization.

Focusing on *Disabilities* in Chapter 8 Rudolph P. Reyes II examines the intersection of disability, race, and spirituality in US Latine communities. Addressing racialized ableism and dominant models that individualize disability, stigmatize it, and render disabled Latines invisible, which in turn reinforces structural marginalization seen in poverty, education, violence, and incarceration disparities. However, a different approach is possible when the social model of disability shifts emphasis from individual bodies to systemic oppression, framing disability as a political identity and coalition for liberation. Connecting critical disability studies with Latine liberating spiritualities, Reyes highlights how spirituality, understood as a praxis of human flourishing and justice, can confront racialized ableism and affirm disabled Latines as vital agents in reimagining justice, belonging, and community.

In Chapter 9, *An Overview of Select Latin American Marian Devotions in the United States of America*, Sudabée Lotfian-Mena and Neomi De Anda summarize devotional Marian images within Latine communities, highlighting how these embody cultural identity, religious mixing, and diaspora practices. The authors discuss select Marian images that inspire devotional practices both in Latin America and in Latine diaspora communities: Nuestra Señora de Guadalupe (Mexico),who bridges Aztec traditions and Catholic devotion; Nuestra Señora de la Altagracia (Dominican Republic), rooted in Spanish origins but reshaped as a Dominican unifying symbol; Nuestra Señora de la Divina Providencia (Puerto Rico), tied to colonial history and national identity; Nuestra Señora de la Caridad del Cobre (Cuba), associated with *cubanidad* and exile communities; Nuestra Señora de la Leche y Buen Parto (Florida/USA), a devotion focused on fertility and family; and Nossa Senhora da Aparecida (Brazil), a Black Madonna linked to racial diversity and miracles.

Through *Challenging the Patriarchy* in Chapter 10, Isabela Leonor Rosales examines the nature of Mujerista theology, Latina feminism, Chicana feminism, and Queer Latine thought, situating them within broader struggles against patriarchy, colonialism, racism, anti-Blackness, and heteronormativity. Beginning with Mujerista theology's emphasis on *lo cotidiano*, Rosales traces both its liberative potential and the critiques from Latina feminism that incorporates Chicana perspectives and decolonial and community-rooted approaches. The work of particular scholars and activists explore how Queer Latine and trans perspectives advance the discourse while exposing internalized anti-Blackness, heterosexism, and the erasure of trans lives within Latine feminist and Mujerista thought. Rosales argues that genuine liberation requires an interdisciplinary, decolonial, and queer-inclusive approach that centers the "margins of the margins" in the pursuit of justice and solidarity.

Racialized social hierarchies are examined in Chapter 11 by Alexandra Rosado-Román with *Shades of Inequality: Colorism at the Intersection of Society and Religion*, which critically scrutinizes colorism as rooted in Eurocentric White hierarchies and colonial legacies in Latin American and Caribbean societies. Drawing on Afro-feminist and decolonial frameworks, Rosado-Román highlights how an anti-Blackness colorism is embedded in cultural practices, family dynamics, census categories, and religious imagery within marginalized communities. By raising awareness, challenging internalized biases, and fostering solidarity across skin tones and identities, communities can begin dismantling colorism's enduring hold and move toward justice, healing, and liberation.

Grego Peña-Camprubí in Chapter 12, *Our Fluidity*, discusses the trauma and resilience of queer Latines navigating transnational life. Through storytelling as both method and healing practice that features LGBTQ+ identity, Peña-Camprubí shows how migration, colonial legacies, and systemic oppression dismember identities across cultural, linguistic, religious, and racial lines. Through practices of heart remembering and reintegrating fractured selves, queer Latines transform trauma into healing, spirituality, and political resistance, showing how storytelling, ritual, and mysticism affirm identity, reclaim narratives, and envision liberating futures.

In Chapter 13, *Death or Salvation of a Planet*, Amanda J. Baugh sketches the history of Latine religious environmentalism, showing how Latine communities across time and place have integrated social justice, spirituality, and ecological ethics into their relationships with the land. Beginning with Ecuador's groundbreaking 2008 constitutional recognition of the rights of nature, rooted in the Indigenous philosophy of *buen vivir*, Baugh shows how Latine traditions have emphasized reciprocal, life-affirming relationships with the more-than-human world. Drawing on examples from Mexican American literature, Chicana/o activism, the United Farmworkers movement, grassroots environmental justice campaigns, and Catholic eco-theology, revealing that Latine communities are not only victims of environmental injustice but also leaders and agents of ecological care that center well-being, dignity, and social and ecological justice for both humans and nature.

In Chapter 14, *Departing from the American Dream: Toward Visions of Collective Latine Human Dignity*, Francisco J. García Jr. critiques the American Dream as an individualist and largely unattainable ideal for the majority of Latines and other working-class communities in the United States, as it obscures the exploitative realities of racial capitalism. While some Latine leaders invoke family success stories, such narratives mask the systemic inequalities that keep most Latines in precarious economic positions. In contrast to those prevailing narratives, García calls for instead embracing alternative visions rooted in liberatory Latine religious thought, labor organizing and activism, and communal models of justice, Latine traditions of faith and collective struggle offer a more just and cooperative framework for economic and spiritual well-being than the myth of individual upward mobility.

With Chapter 15, *Screwing with the System*, Miguel A. De La Torre unpacks the influence of his lived experiences of discrimination as a poor Latine in New York City and how movements like the Young Lords inspired a radical rethinking of ethics. De La Torre argues for a liberative, Latine-centered praxis rooted in disruption, trickster strategies, and the rejection of imposed notions of "the good." Drawing on cultural symbols like Pepito, Juan Bobo, and Eleggúa, alongside biblical tricksters, De La Torre calls for an ethics of "screwing with the system" as necessary, loving resistance against White supremacy and neoliberal oppression, insisting that justice for Latines requires destabilizing oppressive structures, a disruptive praxis that is both a survival strategy and an affirmation of human dignity.

Jacqueline M. Hidalgo in Chapter 16, *Sacred Texts* explains how Latine communities engage "texts" and "scriptures" in expansive, contested, and deeply communal ways that go beyond canonized forms. Latine lived religion treats a wide range of practices and media as sacred texts, from oral stories, *corridos*, and recipes to murals, protest manifestos, and rituals. These everyday scriptures are world-making tools, functioning as technologies of diaspora and utopian homing devices that orient communities, transmit memory, and imagine alternative futures amid displacement and oppression. Latine biblical scholars critically contest scripture, reframing its meanings through borderlands, decolonial, and queer hermeneutics that reclaim texts as sites of struggle, survival, and transformation. Scripture in Latine contexts involves an ongoing practice of meaning-making, identity formation, and contesting power, shaped through lived experience rooted in the everyday struggles, creativity, and resilience of Latine communities.

In Chapter 17, *Sound, Cinema, and Santería: Listening to "Angelitos Negros" with Oyá*, Deborah De La Torre explores the intersection of sound studies, Santería, and film through the lens of Oyá, the Orisha warrior of wind, and cemeteries. De La Torre argues that sound recording and filmmaking technologies share profound connections with Santería practices, particularly through Oyá's electrified communications. By examining Oyá's persona, her rattle (vaina), and her shroud, the essay offers new ways of hearing and interpreting cultural productions. De La Torre employs a Latine listening approach that invokes "de cierta manera" (a certain way) from Cuban film and literature, while also as a musician interpreting old songs, poems, and films through the spiritual power of Oyá.

In good *en conjunto* (collaborative) fashion, Ramona Beltrán, Miriam Valdovinos, Olivia Hunte, My Ngoc To, and Tina Hulama in Chapter 18, *To Heal Every Little Wound": Reconnecting, Reclaiming, and Revitalizing Cultural Spiritual Traditions Among Indigenous Peoples of Mexico in the United States*, listen to the stories and histories from US-based Indigenous peoples of Mexico, highlighting how communities reconnect, reclaim, and revitalize cultural and spiritual traditions in the wake of colonial violence, displacement, and erasure. They review how communities turn toward Indigenous spiritual practices such as ceremony and temazcal to restore belonging and collective healing. Maintaining and in many cases reclaiming ancestral practices—such as plant medicines, smudging, and Danza Mexica. Intergenerational transmission of knowledge and practices create spaces for identity, community belonging, and resilience while preparing future generations to inherit cultural continuity. These processes of remembering, relearning, and recreating Indigenous traditions embody resistance to colonial trauma and offer pathways of healing, flourishing, and hope for future generations.

In Chapter 19, *Crossing Borders*, Noemi Vega Quiñones describes the history, struggles, and resilience of Latine migrants in relation to borders, religion, and identity using the river Yanaguana (San Antonio River) as a central metaphor and a symbol of the erasure and resilience of Indigenous and Latine communities, connecting it to the broader experiences of border-making, migration, and survival. Vega Quiñones surveys how colonial logics of elimination, racial scripts, and immigration regimes sought to shape and impose identities and borders, while Indigenous and Latine peoples continued to live across them with creative fluidity. Through stories of displacement, forced crossings, and ongoing racialization, Vega Quiñones foregrounds the violence Latine migrants—especially women and queer communities—face, from feminicide to spiritual abuse, while also showing how religion, art, and community practices become sources of healing, remembrance, and sanctuary. Like Yanaguana's flowing waters, Latine migrants' religious and cultural expressions resist rigid categories, sustain networks of support, and shape visions of more just futures amid ongoing struggles against erasure, criminalization, and exclusion.

Chapter 20, *Nones or Alternative Paths* by José Francisco Morales Torres, examines the significant shift in Latine religious identity through growth of religiously unaffiliated "nones" and those following "alternate paths," which are both critical and creative movements within Latine religiosity. Morales Torres traces the sharp decline of Latine Catholic affiliation—especially among US-born Latines and youth. He also notes the complex spectrum of nones, from atheists to the spiritual-but-not-religious, unified by a rejection of institutional authority. It also broadens "alternate paths" to include Indigenous, African diasporic, and multiple-religious-belonging traditions that resist Eurocentric models of "world religions." Latine nones and followers of alternate paths reject institutional religion, confronting colonial religious narratives, and advancing progressive politics while also creatively generating new philosophical anthropologies, socialities, and communities rooted in Latine cultural inheritances. These movements represent both acts of resistance and imaginative reconstructions of spirituality, identity, and belonging.

Finally, but only in the sense of it being the last chapter of this volume, in the "Conclusion: Where are We Going," Miguel A. De La Torre discusses the ways Latines are subjected to Eurocentric historical narratives that marginalizes their own lived experiences and identities. De La Torre asserts that the dominant cultural myth of the "American Dream"—that anyone can succeed in life if they truly apply themselves through hard work—actually operates as a tool of assimilation and erasure, obscuring the structural forces of White supremacy and systemic inequality. Engaging thinkers like Hegel, Unamuno, and Walter Benjamin, De La Torre exposes how Eurocentric philosophies frame history as linear, progressive, and centered on Northern Europe, excluding Latines as inferior or invisible. As an alternative to such cultural domination and victimization, De La Torre calls for reclaiming Latine *historias* (stories) as a means of resistance, emphasizing the value of lived experience and everyday struggle over sanitized, progress-oriented histories. Finally, De La Torre declares that liberation cannot be found in Eurocentric systems but must emerge from within Latine communities through solidarity, self-definition, and storytelling.

Following the example of Pope Francis when he stood within the in-between place of the borderlands, we seek in this volume to name the families and communities called Latine, as well as the other designations people claim for themselves—even when such identities defy societal, governmental, religious, or academic norms.

Drawing insight from a comparable discussion in Brazil, Djamila Ribeiro observes about identity and power that

> our objective in confronting the norm is not merely to talk about identity but to unveil the ways that institutions use identity to oppress or to privilege. What we fundamentally hope emerges from this debate is an understanding of how power and *identities* work together, depending on context, and how colonialism not only creates but delegitimizes certain identities and legitimizes others... . Identities emerge out of a structure of oppression that privileges certain groups to the detriment of others, and to ignore this is to fail to understand how political systems function.[16]

Building on Ribeiro's insight, we assert solely not just politics but also religious and spiritual lives. Even if identities emerge out of oppressions, identities are reshaped, repurposed, and transformed, even in the midst of oppressions, and in counter-cultural ways for liberative goals. Through this volume, we resist erasure and marginalization, and we proclaim our solidarity with the pasts, presents, and futures of incredibly diverse peoples that also have a shared if always morphing identity. We know that we are different, and yet we also affirm that we have much in common. And by so naming them and sharing their stories, *historias*, practices, traditions, theologies, and deep-thinking, we declare that Latine peoples in the United States especially through their religions and spiritual practices are *presente*!

1

What's in a Name?

Edwin David Aponte

When considering both persons and populations in the United States that have some sort of connection through history and heritage to Latin America and Iberia, someone might think it odd, ironic, or perhaps even inappropriate to pose the question, "What's in a name?" Is it not self-evident who the peoples are and what groups we are talking about, so what more needs to be said? Indeed, one can argue "Let's agree on one all-inclusive racial, ethnic term that everyone will all use and then move on." But that is the challenge because in fact there is no general agreement about one common umbrella name, so are we still confronted with the basic question, what are we talking about?

Of course, the phrase "What's in a name?" evokes that famous line in the English language from William Shakespeare's *Romeo and Juliet*, "What's in a name? That which we call a rose by any other name would smell as sweet" (Act II, Scene II). Is it not the essence of something that really is important rather than a label? If that is true, do names, titles, or designations of any type really matter at all? What is the fuss about whether we use the word Hispanic, or Latino, or Latinx, or some other term to talk about some particular group? However, what if we allow for the possibility that "What's in a name?" is shorthand for substantive questions, concerns, and even disputes about core essence, identity, basic value, and even issues of power, oppression, agency, and liberation. When we are asking about names and the acts of naming might it be that actually we are talking about something more than mere labels?[1]

When naming something that initially might seem obvious, I am reminded of a piece of art that is also a visual philosophical and cultural commentary by the Belgian surrealist René Magritte (1898–1967), *La Trahison des images* (*The Treachery of Images*). This 1929 oil painting has an image of a pipe and below the image Magritte painted, "Ceci n'est pas une pipe," hence the painting's alternate name in French and

English. Mischievously, "This is not a pipe" invites us to consider that what initially is perceived as obvious may not be the actual reality but rather the representation of something else. As social creatures, the names we humans give to things and people may convey, or even assign meaning, history, social and cultural significance, but the various names may also just be pointing us in the direction of understanding and maybe even interpretation but not full comprehension and experience of the identity that the particular labels try to describe.

At the same time, embedded within labels and names are forms of power, whether for good or for ill, sometimes contested, especially whether or not the names are imposed or are a self-description, or even a type of hybrid combination of both. Names can shape perceptions and practices as well as influence how some people are treated by others. Sometimes a name—whether it's a person's name, a title, and even a product brand—might evoke certain ideas, attitudes, or associations. In particular cultural contexts, names can be symbols of tradition, family heritage, or even a perceived destiny that might be embraced or not. Names can hold deep personal meaning—a name can represent a connection to the past or aspirations for the future, or reflect perception of identity, either imposed or self-understanding, affirmation, or even aspiration. Assigned names might also be insulting and demeaning. Despite assertions to the contrary, US Hispanic-Latino-Latino/a-Latinx-Latinoax-Latine identity and culture is not one monolithic thing but rather constantly intersecting shifting realities of diverse ethnic, regional, national, and religious and non-religious peoples and communities. Marie Arana poignantly describes this complicated state of affairs about what is the collective term for people who have roots in what became Latin America and beyond:

> To tell the truth, we have no name. We never did. When we proliferated through these ancient lands in our countless varietals, we were simply tribes of this hemisphere, inheritors of a natural world, progenitors of a breed. We gave ourselves a multitude of names. Thousands of years later, when we were invaded and conquered, first by Spain, then by a battery of occupiers and usurpers, we became colonies to power—united by the boot, the sword, the crown, the cross, and the Spanish language. As time went on and history raveled, we became citizens of nineteen independent republics, admixtures of a crush of skin colors and cultures; we began to call ourselves by the names of our separate nations. Finally, when we found ourselves in the United States of America—some of us finding ourselves here without having left our native land—we ceased calling ourselves anything at all. We were amorphous, we were everyone, we were no one, we were invisible. We were chameleons, reflecting every color of man. When asked, we reached for the last turf we had occupied and the last label we had worn: we were Mexicanos, *Boricuas*, *cubanos*, *colombianos*, *dominicanos*, *peruanos*. Although we were no longer anything of the kind.[2]

Even with Arana's poignant observation in attempting to be inclusive of the varieties of peoples in the Americas, the presence of peoples in the United States with connections to Portugal, Brazil, and other former Portuguese colonies is still ignored. As described in the following chapters, US Latine religious expressions and experiences are multiracial, multiethnic, and multigenerational complex cultural mixtures that go far beyond any racialized pigeonholes.

Moreover, all of this is happening within the context of how race is constructed in the United States, to say nothing of the various concurrent constructions of racial identities throughout the world.[3] It is good to remind ourselves that the mandate to periodically count the population of the United States has its roots in the racialized context of the so-called three-fifth compromise reflected in the original language of the US Constitution (1787), "Representatives and direct Taxes shall be apportioned among the several States which may be included within this Union, according to their respective Numbers, which shall be determined by adding to the whole Number of free Persons, including those bound to Service for a term of years, and excluding Indians not taxed, three-fifths of all other Persons" (Article 1, Section 2, Clause 3). Those "three-fifths of all other Persons" were enslaved Africans and their descendants.

Adding to the grouping and naming complexity, there is the question of what does naming of peoples have to do with religion? Rather than being one small slice of life as some argue, examining what he calls "Latina/o religious politics," Felipe Hinojosa asserts that religion is at the heart of the Latina/o experience in the United States that motivates social and political action, including the ways in which Latina/o religious communities relate with efforts for social justice.[4] Elsewhere, Felipe Hinojosa, Maggie Elmore, and Sergio M. González develop this further in asserting that "we understand the 'religious' in Latino religious politics broadly as both a history of action and a shared culture, a way of understanding how injustice operates, and a belief that God is on the side of those who suffer, of those who struggle."[5]

This brings us back to the related questions at hand, "What's in a name?" and why did the editors of this volume and this series choose the name Latine? If names and labels are in some sense provisional and as Magritte reminds us only pointing us toward some deeper reality, then how did we get here to use Latine as an overarching term for the studies on lived religion of this collaborative volume? Realistically, the answer is not straightforward, since it is a story of multiple names before we come to Latine. Mike Davis helpfully summarizes part of the history of this naming conundrum:

> For half a century the designers of the U.S. Census have struggled to create a category that would successfully capture all the individuals, regardless of race or household language, who share distinctive Latin American cultural roots. After early vacillations over whether Mexicans were a "race" (yes in 1930; no in 1940), several alternate statistical universes, including the category of "Persons of Spanish Mother Tongue" (1950) and "Spanish Surname" (1960), were tried and abandoned because of heavy numerical leakage. In population sampling for the 1990 Census, census workers simply asked people if they identified with any of twelve national identities: Mexican, Puerto Rican, Cuban, and so on. Households with positive replies, independent of answers to other identity questions, were enumerated as

"Hispanic"—a category adopted in the 1970s by the Nixon administration and first deployed in the 1980 Census.[6]

Given over 50 years of official naming, let's discuss each pan-ethnic term. Up first is the label Hispanic—introduced by the US Census Bureau in 1970 as an effort to classify individuals and groups who were perceived by the government to have a shared common language, ethnicity, and cultural heritage. One of the assumptions was that the term Hispanic was readily acceptable common name to identify Spanish-speaking and ethnically related individuals and groups in the United States.

Even a seemingly straightforward explanation like that is embedded with bias that it accurately describes individuals and groups with a shared language, ethnic identities, and experiences that emerge out of the lived experiences of colonization. Yet, even the first criterion of a shared language is problematic in that not everyone who are identified as Hispanic or identified themselves as Hispanic spoke Spanish. Most notably, within the racialized context of the United States, the term Hispanic is not an apt descriptor for Portuguese-speaking people with roots in Brazil and Portugal. What is more Hispanic does not even begin to account for Indigenous groups for whom Spanish is a secondary language or is not spoken in daily life.

To press this point further, the question of whether or not Brazilians are Hispanic or Latino is at least ambiguous. The US Census Bureau's recent definition of Hispanic or Latino (March 28, 2024) states that the designation "includes individuals of Mexican, Puerto Rican, Salvadoran, Cuban, Dominican, Guatemalan, and other Central or South American or Spanish culture or origin."[7] The chosen ambiguity is that on the one hand "South American" geographically includes Brazil, but on the other hand, prior Census definitions focused on Hispanic/Latino as connected to Spanish-speaking countries in Latin America.

It might seem unnecessary to say that the term "Latin America" of course includes Brazil, which geographically is the largest nation in the continent South America. While not identical concepts, most of South America is considered part of the cultural region of Latin America, which is shaped by histories, imposed languages, religions, and cultural traditions that emerged from the sometimes violent encounters of Iberian colonization (Spanish and Portuguese empires), Indigenous civilizations (e.g., Aymara, Inca, Guaraní, Mapuche, and Quechua), African diasporic populations formed by the forced enslavement of millions of Africans through the transatlantic slave trade, and by the multiple types of mestizaje and mulatez or the mixing of Indigenous, African, European, and even Asian peoples and cultures. As South Americans, Brazilians are regionally, historically, linguistically, and culturally creators and participants in Latin American history, politics, economy, religious identities and practices, musical expressions, intellectual currents, and transnational networks across the Americas and the world. That being the case, Brazilians in the United States—both those who are part of Latin American migrations as well as those born in the United States—can be considered as Latine.

Once again, a person might think conclusion as the common sense end of the matter. However, the US Office of Management and Budget and the Census Bureau define the category of "Hispanic or Latino" as persons of "Spanish culture or origin," Portuguese-speaking, or Indigenous-language Latin Americans are not included under the name Hispanic. An institutional decision to not count Brazilians as "Hispanic/Latino" in US official statistics is a political and historical action to codify "Spanish culture or origin" and as such is another example of what's in a name does indeed matter. From a geographic–cultural and pan-Latin American perspective, Brazilians are Latinos; from the narrow administrative definition of US American bureaucracy, they are often not.

Moreover, government exclusion of Portuguese-speaking Brazilians from official definitions is a reminder that we should also consider how Brazilians in the United States actually self-identify. Beyond geography and history, some Brazilian migrants resist the "Hispanic/Latino" label because of the stigma associated with the pan-ethnic category in the United States and because they view the Portuguese language and Brazilian national identity as distinct from Spanish-speaking Latin America. At the same time, the US Census data reveal that when questions are phrased differently or when respondents interpret "Hispanic/Latino" to mean broadly "Latin American," significant number of Brazilians selected the category. In the 2020 US Census and the 2020 American Community Survey, a processing and coding irregularity resulted in approximately 416,000 Brazilian-born residents being classified as Hispanic or Latino—far exceeding prior counts—prompting researchers to reexamine how question design, social meaning, and institutional definitions shape responses. "In particular, the large number of Brazilians who self-identified as Hispanic or Latino highlights how their view of their own identity does not necessarily align with official government definitions." There appears to be a gap between official classifications and lived self-understandings that are not constrained by narrow governmental definitions.[8]

Second-generation Brazilians display further complexity, with many US-born combining Brazilian national identity with selective claims to Latinidad depending on context (e.g., solidarity with other Latin American communities or strategic self-presentation to access resources). Within the dominating white/Black racial binary studies indicate that some Brazilians in the United States reject Hispanic/Latino labels outright as inaccurate or stigmatizing, while others take advantage of the exclusion from Hispanic/Latino in order to embrace an inclusive "American" identity.[9] Other second-generation US Brazilians assert that limited census racial/ethnic labels fail to reflect their language (Portuguese), cultural specificity, and national origin.[10] They often self-identify in terms of Brazilian nationality rather than broad pan-ethnic terms: "They grounded themselves in their positive perceptions of the Brazilian culture (e.g., food, partying, clothing, and other elements), using their Brazilian identity to shield them from being associated with a racist America that they were not proud of, while also standing out among friends and schoolmates."[11] Deficiencies in US American racial categories become more apparent when it is remembered that Brazilians themselves are racially diverse—white, Black African descent, Indigenous, mixed, and multiple immigrant ancestries and different social constructions of race in Brazil. The dominant

US racial groupings (white, Black, and "Some Other Race") do not neatly map onto Brazilian racial categories.[12]

Despite the US Census Bureau's determination, conceptually, sociologically, culturally, and religiously, Brazilians in the United States belong within the collective category of Latinos/as or Latine if those terms are used to denote people of Latin American origin and belonging to Latin American cultural and historical formations. The persistent US federal linkage of "Hispanic/Latino" to Spanish-language origin produces a narrower, administrative category that excludes many Brazilians—often against their own self-understandings.[13] A fuller approach recognizes the multilingual, multiracial reality of Latin America and so that Brazilians' Latin American belonging is visible and its consequences accounted for.

The same prohibition of regarding US Hispanic/Latino is applied to people with origins in Belize (a multiracial nation that includes Maya, Mestizo, people of African, European, and Asian descent, where Spanish is one of the common languages), the Philippines (even though the Philippines was a colony of Spain for 333 years and administratively part of the Viceroyalty of New Spain, a.k.a., Mexico), and Portugal (which has an intermingled cultural, religious, linguistic histories with Spain in Iberia).[14] From 1565 to 1898, the Philippines archipelago was part of the Spanish imperial system and maintained deep cultural, religious, and institutional ties with Latin America. The connection between New Spain (the Spanish viceroyalty centered in Mexico) and the Philippines was deep, sustained, and foundational to early globalization, linking Asia, the Americas, and Europe. New Spain governed the Philippines from 1565 to 1821, making the islands administratively and economically part of Spanish America rather than directly ruled from Madrid. Manila was overseen by the Viceroy of New Spain in Mexico City, and Mexican silver financed colonial administration, military defense, and evangelization in the archipelago. This arrangement bound the Philippines to Mexico in everyday governance.

The linchpin of this relationship was the Manila–Acapulco Galleon Trade (1565–1815), the first sustained transpacific trade system. Silver mined in Mexico and Peru was shipped from Acapulco to Manila, where it was exchanged for Asian goods—silk, porcelain, spices, lacquerware, and textiles—from China, Japan, Southeast Asia, and India. These goods then traveled back across the Pacific to Mexico and onward to Europe. This trade made New Spain a central hub of the early modern global economy and integrated the Philippines into Latin American commercial networks.

The connection was also demographic and cultural. Thousands of people moved between New Spain and the Philippines, including Spanish officials, missionaries, soldiers, sailors, Indigenous Mexicans, Africans, and mixed-race peoples. Many Filipino sailors and migrants (often called Indios chinos in colonial records) settled in Mexico, particularly along the Pacific coast, while Mexican soldiers, clergy, and administrators shaped colonial life in the Philippines.[15] Catholic evangelization in the Philippines was largely carried out by religious orders trained or headquartered in New Spain, contributing to shared devotional practices, saints' cults, and baroque religious aesthetics.

Culturally, this transpacific exchange left lasting traces: Mexican crops such as maize, cacao, chili peppers, and tomatoes became staples in Philippine cuisine; linguistic borrowings, artistic styles, and folk religious practices crossed the ocean; and colonial racial and caste systems in the Philippines mirrored those developed in Spanish America. Even after Mexican independence in 1821 severed the formal administrative link, these cultural and economic legacies endured.

In short, New Spain and the Philippines were connected through governance, trade, migration, religion, and culture, forming a Pacific-facing extension of Latin America and making the Spanish Empire a truly global, transoceanic system centuries before modern globalization. And of course, as a result of the 1898 war, the Philippines became part of the US American empire.[16] Although the Philippines shares significant cultural heritage due to more than three centuries of Spanish colonial rule, Filipinos are not classified as Hispanic in contemporary US racial and ethnic categories, primarily the result of US bureaucratic definitions emphasizing Spanish-language origin, as well as the historical decline of Spanish in the Philippines, and not because Filipinos lack Spanish cultural influence.

Imposed Hispanic identity operates in a racialized way as a version of the melting-pot myth that all Hispanics shared the same cultural and social characteristics. Hispanic privileges one of the European powers that colonized parts of what became known as the Americas, while ignoring another European imperial power, that is, Portugal, whose major colonial legacy in the Americas is the nation of Brazil. As Steffano Montano insightfully observed, the so-called American melting pot,

> has served as a mask for the continued political and social stratification of racial and ethnic groups across the U.S. .... While immigrants who are white (coming from European ancestry) can easily assimilate into the culture and (eventually) enjoy financial and political benefits (i.e. the white Cuban community in Miami, with outsize representation in local and national politics as compared to other Latinx racial-ethnic groups), immigrants who bear the mark of race in their appearance will experience the same prejudices and implicit forms of discrimination that Native Americans and African Americans have always experienced since colonization.[17]

Ultimately, since there are significant differences among and between peoples and groups classified as Hispanic, this particular name can suppress the many linguistic, racial, ethnic, and cultural distinctions not only among the groups within the United States but also within nations of origin in the rest of the Americas.

Because of limitations with the name Hispanic, the alternate terms Latino/Latina surfaced, drawing on latinoamericano (Latin American) which emphasizes Latin America rather than Spain (Hispanic). Latino/Latina became common in the late twentieth century, referring to people from Latin America, and of course, it reflects the gendered language nature of both Spanish and Portuguese. Since its introduction, Latino/a is common in pop culture, such as with the Latino Grammy Awards or in politics and news media that discusses "the Latino vote" during elections.

Certainly, there is the gender issue with Latino/Latina, but there are other problems associated with the often-forgotten origins of the concept of "Latin America." The French term Amérique latine, or in Spanish América Latina, or in English Latin America, originated in the mid-ninetieth century in Europe. Michel Gobat contends that the idea of Latin America fused an anti-colonial idea of "America" (post-independence) with the French idea of a "Latin race" as seemingly incongruous complementary responses to both US expansionism and European imperialism.[18] Amérique latine was first popularized by French intellectuals and politicians during the rule of Napoleon III, Emperor of the French (reign: 1852–70), as part of the rationale for France's economic, cultural, and political intervention in the Americas, particularly in Mexico in the 1860s and the support given to the Emperor Maximilian by framing the Americas as part of a broader "Latin" family of nations, France, Spain, Portugal. This idea of a common "Latin" peoples was contrasted with "Anglo-Saxon" peoples of North America, to emphasize cultural and political differences between Southern Europe and Northern Europe's colonial legacies.

While embraced by some nineteenth-century intellectuals like Francisco Bilbao of Chile and José María Torres Caicedo of Colombia, actually the diverse peoples and lands had long histories before the nineteenth-century geopolitical invention of "Latin America" rooted in European politics and identity-making. Today, these historical roots are forgotten, and contemporary understanding of Latin American is seen as something distinct from European. Nevertheless, this leads to the irony that instead of avoiding the connection with Spanish colonialism associated with Hispanic, the legacy of European imperialism is simply masked with the use of Latino/a or its variants, which also contributes to racialized homogenization of the Indigenous, African, and mixed heritages of the millions of peoples. To be sure, the concepts of Latin America or Latin American are so deeply embedded that they will not be jettisoned despite their tainted origins, but we should be aware of the shortcomings.

Like other names, Latino/Latina may point to a reality but not is the thing itself. Although widely used in the United States, the binary nature and the historical deficiencies of Latino/a prompted the emergence of pan-ethnic term Latinx as a gender-neutral, inclusive alternative. Commenting on the newer name, Salvador Vidal-Ortiz and Juliana Martínez state that "Rather than seeing Latinx as a trend or a rupture in linguistic usage, we see it as a continuity of internal shifting group dynamics and disciplinary debates. We've gone from specific, nationality-based categories—some of them political (i.e., Chicano vs Mexican-American), to 'Spanish' (in certain regions), to 'Latin' (at certain time periods), to more pan-ethnic labels (like 'Latino'), to the @, a/o, e, and now 'x,' to denote the multiplicity of voices (silenced and invisible) in these umbrella terms."[19]

Latinx is seen as progressive and inclusive of LGBTQ+ and non-binary identities, signifying something more than a spelling choice.[20] Through traveling across the United States encountering many diverse individuals and communities, journalist and activist Paola Ramos concluded that

from coast to coast, I met people who couldn't see eye to eye on their identity—and at the end of the day, that's one of the main points of this story: It's okay to differ. It's okay not to see eye to eye. The point is that there is not one way to be Latino in the United States. There is not one way to feel Latino in this country. Not one way to look Latino or sound Latino. And at the moment, the only label that can honor that collective truth and accommodate that spectrum of ambiguity is the Latinx banner.[21]

Enthusiastic advocate Ed Morales opined that:

> the real power of the term and its true meaning, however, erupts with its final syllable. After years of Latin lovers, Latin looks, Latin music, and Latin America, the word describes something that is not as much Latin— a word originally coined by the French to brand non-English- and Dutch-speaking colonies with a different flavor—as it is an alternative America, the unexpected X factor in America's race debate.[22]

Despite such zeal, Latinx as a term is criticized by some as anglicized, hard to pronounce in Spanish, and imposed from outside communities.[23]

Given the shortcomings of Latinx, Latine appeared as an alternative gender-inclusive term. Developed in Latin America, Latine is used within Spanish-speaking communities in Latin America, and its use is spreading in the United States as a collective name for diverse peoples of Latin American descent (again Latin America understood broadly). Like Latinx, Latine is an alternative to binary gendered options of Latino/Latina that exclude non-binary people but avoid the deficiencies of Latinx.

While Latine has a stronger linguistic fit in Spanish, it appears that its use is still limited both within Latin America and the United States. An additional critique of Latine is that it is yet another imposition by a small elite without connection to everyday folk. However, some supporters see Latine as an improvement and an intentional non-binary alternative to the awkward pronunciation of Latinx, the product of US Spanglish/Espanglish. Its advocates view Latine as a grassroots alternative from Spanish-speaking communities that is easier to pronounce in Spanish, slowly gaining traction, especially in Queer, youth, and Spanish-speaking communities who prefer something pronounceable in Spanish.

Social media has accelerated the spread of Latinx in the United States and Latine in Spanish-speaking countries. Latine in the United States shows up in grassroots and online communities, such as Groups on social media like AfroLatine Theology Project, Latine con Orgullo, and groups like San Diego Pride and the Latine Coalition that sponsors together a LGBTQ+ Latine Coalition annual Latine Pride Event.[24]

With all this advocacy for inclusive alternative names, it should not be forgotten that in the United States the term Hispanic is still widely used, especially in government, media, and demographics (e.g., Hispanic Heritage Month, annually September 15–October 15, an official US celebration). At the very least, it appears that there are two impulses regarding pan-ethnic labels for various cultural, religious, political, media, and identity purposes: to classify people with an umbrella term what groups that have in common due to overlapping characteristics and secondly to name the shared commitments of possible coalition partners.

Pew Research Center reports that as of late 2023, about 47 percent of US Hispanic/Latino adults say they have heard of the term Latinx; however, as a term of self-identification, only about 4 percent of US Hispanic/Latino adults say they have used the term Latinx to describe themselves. Regarding the use of newer term Latine, in 2023, about 18 percent of US Hispanic/Latino adults have heard of Latine. When asked which term they prefer as a pan-ethnic term, 52 percent prefer Hispanic and 29 percent prefer Latino/a. Among those who identify as LGBTQ+ Hispanic/Latino persons, they are more likely to use or accept Latinx, for example, 13 percent of lesbian, gay, or bisexual Latinos say they have used Latinx. When language is considered, persons who are predominantly English speakers or bilingual are much more likely to be familiar with the term Latinx than those who are Spanish dominant. Survey results show that Latine is largely unknown among United States, whereas 15 percent of those asked have no preferred term.[25]

"What's in a name?" A great deal, especially within contexts of growing oppression, racism and racial profiling, social and political polarization, growing economic disparity, and wars and rumors of wars. The peoples in the United States called Hispanic-Latino-Latino/a-Latinx-Latinoax-Latine are subject to all of that and more. Presently, there is no single pan-ethnic name that is fully accepted by the communities such terms are intended to describe. Moreover, even when a particular group name is used, there is the risk that any pan-ethnic identity may compromise the cultural integrity and self-identity of the respective communities classified together. As noted elsewhere in this volume by many of the contributors, as well as everyday people, despite all the well-intended arguments in its favor, the term Latine is a contested one in the United States. And yet as co-editors, Miguel A. De La Torre and I chose to call this collaborative work *Latine Lived Religions and Religious Identities in the United States*. There are some things that the diverse peoples share in common concurrent with all the differences, and one of the major ways that is manifested is in religion and spirituality. The following chapters help us explore the overlapping and shared realities through the lived religious and spirituality, practices, orientations, and thinking of diverse peoples in the United States sometimes unite under one or a variety of names.

How do the peoples describe themselves? For scholars and activists committed to the people, *el pueblo*, and the community *la comunidad*, the question must be regularly asked. In Latin America, when asked people emphasize their country, culture, or Indigenous/African-descendant identity first, and pan-ethnic labels are secondary, a practice also appearing in the United States when people are given the opportunity to self-identify, for example, Dominican, Mexican-American, Salvadoran, Cuban, Chilean, Puerto Rican, Venezuelan, and so on. This is the case whether a person is a recent arrival or going back generations in the same way that third- and fourth-generation Americans of European descent may still refer themselves as Irish, Italian, or Swedish. That is not to say that pan-ethnic umbrella terms are totally a myth. Pan-ethnic terms definitely describe the reality of the social construction of race in the United States, especially where there is an additional overlay of racism and oppression. All can be true at the same time.

But we made the choice to use Latine because of the many present options it is the most inclusive. Additionally, it must be admitted that the use of a collective name for peoples is not a simply grammatical decision but rather it is a political, cultural, social, and possibly a religious declaration. For some, it is a decolonial strategy that seeks to push back against colonial, patriarchal, and heteronormative norms embedded not only in language but also in all spheres of life in the hope to be more comprehensive and to reflect the realities of all people.

When we look at René Magritte's *La Trahison des images* (*The Treachery of Images*), we are reminded that "This is not a pipe," but it gives us a good idea of what a pipe looks like, even as we are simultaneously reminded that the image is still only a representation. Through the use of Latine, we try to describe, to represent, and to encompass the diversity of many communities and peoples from various countries, regions, and cultural backgrounds within Latin America who make their home in the United States. They speak many language communities: Spanish, Portuguese, Zapotec, Mixtec, Creole (of many types), Spanglish, English, and so on, often bilingual, and in many cases trilingual. Latine as a collective representation gets us close to what this collective community looks like, but we recognize that the name is not the real thing. We have chosen to use Latine, knowing that there are many challenges with this name as well as other names. We know Latine is not the full reality, but it points us in the right direction of better understanding of the peoples, their religions, their spiritualities, and the multiple distinct and concurrent identities of those who are named Latine in the United States.

2

Latine Jewish Identity, Religious Life, and Transnational Belonging in the United States

Laura Limonic

Latine Jews in the United States occupy a unique and often underrecognized space within both the American Jewish community and the broader US Latine population. Their lives are shaped by multiple, intersecting trajectories of migration, ethnic identification, and religious practice. As Latin American Jewish immigrants or descendants of immigrants from Latin America, Latine Jews straddle two diasporic legacies—that of global Jewry and of the Latin American diaspora—and, as a result, often find that their racial, ethnic, and religious identities do not seamlessly fit into the contours of US ethnoreligious structures and groups.[1]

Latine Jews challenge the racial, ethnic, and religious boundaries that define both Latinidad and Jewishness in the US context. Their experiences complicate dominant narratives that frame US Jews as white and Ashkenazi, and Latine individuals as Catholic and Spanish-speaking. Latine Jews in the United States comprise a diverse and complex population shaped by intersecting factors, including national origin, class background, racialization, religious affiliation, and migration trajectories. In this chapter, I trace the historical contours, cultural practices, and social positioning of Latine Jews, examining how they navigate the American racial and religious landscape, construct hybrid identities, and expand the contours of Jewish life and communal identity.

Drawing on historical scholarship, recent sociological research, and my own ethnographic work, I explore how Latine Jews maintain transnational connections, recreate communal ethno-religious life in their new country, and negotiate inclusion and exclusion in both Jewish and Latine spaces. I argue that Latine Jews are not simply assimilating into existing Jewish or Latine categories but are actively remaking the boundaries of both. Through processes of cultural reimagination and community building, they construct identities that are rooted in their cultural practices of their home countries while adapting to the ethnoreligious landscape of their new one.

Jewish Migration to Latin America

The Jewish presence in Latin America dates to the colonial period, an era that coincides with the Spanish and Portuguese Inquisitions of the late fifteenth century. The Inquisition prohibited adherence to and practice of any religion other than Catholicism. Jews and Muslims were required to convert to Catholicism or face expulsion, exile, or death. Many Jews who migrated to territories under Iberian control, including those in present-day Latin America and the Caribbean, were forced to convert. Among these *conversos*, some continued to practice Judaism in secret, risking persecution, while others assimilated fully into Catholic life. While it is unlikely that a majority of the *conversos* clandestinely practiced Jewish faith and rites—suspicion surrounding the faithfulness of former Jews abounded. Charges of "Judaizing"—accusations of clandestinely observing Jewish customs—led to arrests, imprisonment, and executions. In Lima, Peru, for example, converted Jews were publicly tried and, in some cases, burned at the stake.

Nonetheless, there were moments and places of relative tolerance for Jews. Under Dutch rule, for instance, Jews were able to establish communal life and religious institutions in parts of Brazil, Suriname, Curaçao, Haiti, Jamaica, Barbados, and St. Croix by the mid-seventeenth century. From these early enclaves, Jewish families eventually spread to the Spanish-speaking Caribbean and Central America—including to Costa Rica, the Dominican Republic, and Puerto Rico.[2] However, due to centuries of persecution and erasure under Spanish colonialism, relatively few Latin American Jews today trace their ancestry to this early period.

The majority of contemporary Jewish communities in Latin America originate from more recent migration waves. During the late nineteenth and early twentieth centuries, Jews fled pogroms, antisemitism, economic collapse, and political upheaval across Eastern Europe, North Africa, and the Middle East. While many intended to settle in the United States, the passage of the 1924 Johnson-Reed Immigration Act—which sharply restricted immigration from Asia and Southern and Eastern Europe—curtailed these plans. Latin American countries such as Argentina, Mexico, Cuba, and Colombia became alternative destinations. In many cases, families were divided across hemispheres: one sibling arriving in New York, another in Buenos Aires or São Paulo.

Jewish Communities Across Latin America

Jewish populations are found throughout Latin America. The following section highlights the communities most prominently represented among Latin American Jews in the United States today.

Argentina

Argentina is home to the largest Jewish community in Latin America. Jewish migration to Argentina began in earnest in the late 1800s, facilitated by national immigration policies that actively encouraged European settlement. In the late 1800s, Argentina was a key site for the Jewish Colonization Association, a philanthropic project led by Baron Maurice de Hirsch that sought to resettle Eastern European Jews in agricultural colonies. These settlements—known as *Colonias de Baron Hirsch*—offered Jews the opportunity to become landowners and farmers, some even adopting the role of *gauchos*, or Argentine cowboys and creating rural communities outside of the urban centers.

Over the subsequent decades, Jewish immigrants increasingly left the countryside for the urban center of Buenos Aires, where they settled and formed vibrant urban communities. There they founded synagogues, community centers, Yiddish newspapers, credit unions, and schools. Sephardic Jews, particularly from the Ottoman Empire, arrived later and formed their own communal infrastructures. Together, these groups forged a distinctly Argentine Jewish identity, characterized by both integration into the larger Jewish community and strong ethnic communal boundaries. Today, Argentina's Jewish population numbers approximately 200,000. Buenos Aires remains a hub of Jewish life, home to over 100 synagogues, a robust network of day schools, Jewish cultural and athletic institutions, and a growing Orthodox and Chabad presence.[3]

Mexico

Mexico was not initially a primary destination for Jewish immigrants, especially during a time when church and state remained heavily intertwined. Prior to 1917, Jews in Mexico lacked legal protections for religious freedom, limiting their ability to establish synagogues, cemeteries, and schools. It was only after the Mexican Revolution and the 1917 Constitution—which established a secular state—that Jewish communal life began to take root.

Most Jews settled in Mexico City, creating close-knit neighborhoods anchored by mutual aid societies, synagogues, burial organizations, and cultural centers. Early Jewish migrants—primarily Ashkenazi Jews fleeing Eastern Europe and Sephardic Jews from Syria, Turkey, and the Balkans—faced economic and professional restrictions and often worked as small-scale merchants or peddlers. As these limitations diminished, Jewish families achieved upward mobility and entered the middle and upper classes. Today, Mexico's Jewish community numbers between 40,000 and 50,000 and is known for its cohesion, maintained through separate but interconnected subethnic communities, strong educational institutions, and an active Jewish public sphere.

Venezuela

Jewish life in Venezuela dates to the seventeenth century, when Jews arrived via Curaçao (one of the original Dutch colonies where Jews were allowed to live and practice in relative safety). However, the contemporary Venezuelan Jewish community was shaped primarily by twentieth-century migrations, particularly Moroccan Jews in the early 1900s and Eastern European Jews following World War I. Subsequent waves included Holocaust survivors, Jews from North Africa, and Middle Eastern Jewish communities. Caracas, the capital, became the focal point for Jewish life.

Over time, Jews in Venezuela built a thriving communal infrastructure, including synagogues, day schools, and cultural centers. Many ascended economically, entering the professions and middle-to-upper classes. However, the rise of Hugo Chávez and the political and economic crises of the early twenty-first century led to a dramatic demographic shift. The Jewish population has dwindled from a high of 25,000 to fewer than 6,000.[4] Emigration, primarily to the United States and Israel, has strained the viability of Venezuela's Jewish institutions. Attendance at synagogues, schools, and the Jewish community center in Caracas has sharply declined.

Cuba

Jewish migration to Cuba followed patterns seen across the Latin American region. While a small number may have arrived during the colonial period, organized communal life began in the early twentieth century, with the establishment of the first synagogue in 1906 by American Jews residing on the island. Over the following decades, Ashkenazi and Sephardic Jews from the United States, Eastern Europe, Turkey, and the Middle East made their way to Cuba, drawn by economic opportunity and the island's strategic location in the Caribbean. As in other Latin American contexts, Jewish migrants built communal institutions, found success in commerce, and experienced upward mobility. By the time of the Cuban Revolution in 1959, the Jewish population numbered around 15,000, with many situated in the middle and upper classes. The revolution triggered a dramatic rupture: approximately 95 percent of Cuban Jews left the country. While concerns about religious repression were present, it was the nationalization of property and the loss of economic security that played a more decisive role in the mass exodus. Most resettled in Miami, where they went on to form a vibrant Cuban Jewish enclave, complete with its own synagogues and cultural institutions.

Latin American Jews in the United States

Jewish migration to Latin America peaked during the early twentieth century, a period in which vibrant Jewish communities were established across the region. These communities developed robust infrastructures: synagogues, day schools, philanthropic associations, and cultural institutions. Many Jewish families experienced significant upward mobility and became integrated into the national fabric.

Yet beginning in the mid-twentieth century, Latin America was plagued by political instability, authoritarian regimes, economic crises, and social upheaval. These developments sparked renewed waves of emigration—this time from Latin America to the United States. Cuban Jews were among the first to arrive, facilitated by Cold War immigration policies that classified them as political refugees. The passage of the 1965 Hart-Celler Act further opened US immigration to previously restricted regions, enabling greater numbers of Latin American Jews to settle in the United States.

Today, an estimated 300,000 Jews in the United States identify as Hispanic or Latino.[5] Many are immigrants or the children of immigrants who fled political violence or economic collapse in their countries of origin. Others are the product of intermarriage between Hispanic and Jewish families, including both patrilineal and matrilineal lineages. Latine Jewish Americans reflect the broader diversity and transnationality of Jewish life in the Americas—navigating dual identities shaped by language, migration histories, religious affiliation, and community belonging.

Religious Life and Cultural Practice in the United States

When Latin Jews arrive to the United States, their expectations of Jewish life are shaped by their experiences of communal Jewish life in Latin America. In countries such as Argentina, Mexico, and Venezuela, Jewish identity is often expressed through participation in cultural institutions—schools, athletic clubs, and mutual aid societies—rather than synagogue membership alone. For example, many Latin American Jews send their children to Jewish day schools or summer camps while rarely attending synagogue services. Cultural, social, and familial networks define Jewishness as much as (and sometimes more than) formal ritual or religious observance.

This model contrasts sharply with the American Jewish landscape where synagogue membership is often the primary marker of formal Jewish engagement. For Latine Jews accustomed to centralized communal structures, the reliance on religious institutions as the markers of community building makes it difficult for them to find an entryway into American Jewish life.

One way that Latine Jews incorporate into the American Jewish landscape is by creating or changing Jewish institutions. This is particularly true in cities with significant Latin American Jewish populations. In Miami, for example, institutions such as Beth Torah Benny Rok Campus and Temple Moses have embraced a Latin American sensibility, offering services in Spanish, programs rooted in Latin Jewish traditions, and cultural events that reflect the food, music, and holidays of countries like Venezuela, Argentina, and Mexico. Youth groups, modeled after the Hebraica system of Latin America (a cultural and athletic space for the Jewish community that offers programming and inclusion throughout the life cycle), allow Latine Jewish children to grow up in institutions where their language, rituals, and social norms are normalized and valued.

These adaptations reflect a broader trend in which Latine Jews hybridize religious and cultural practices. For instance, Shabbat dinners might feature *matzah ball soup* infused with Mexican chiles, or Argentine *empanadas* prepared for Purim. In some congregations, prayers are sung in Ladino or Spanish, and religious school curricula incorporate Latin American Jewish history. These hybrid practices not only foster belonging but also constitute acts of resistance against dominant narratives that equate American Jewishness with Ashkenazi whiteness.

Panethnicity and Identity Formation

Latine Jewish identity in the United States cannot be reduced to a single category or experience. While national origin (e.g., Argentine, Cuban, and Mexican) plays a significant role in shaping identity, the experience of migration and diasporic life fosters panethnic solidarities. In cities like Miami and Los Angeles, Jews from across Latin America—many of whom would have belonged to separate institutions in their home countries—form associations, share institutions, and forge common identities as "Latine Jews." This process reflects what sociologists describe as *panethnicity*: the shaping of collective identity among individuals from diverse national origins who share common experiences of marginalization and migration.

Panethnic identity among Latine Jews reflects real cultural convergence, especially in the second generation. In South Florida (the area with the highest concentration of Latine Jews), children of immigrants from Venezuela, Mexico, and Argentina often attend the same synagogues and schools, form social networks, and develop a shared inventory of cultural symbols—Spanish-inflected liturgy, Latin Jewish food traditions, and communal memory of emigration. In these contexts, national differences recede, and a broader Latine Jewish identity emerges.

This identity is both affirmational and strategic. It affirms the cultural richness of Latin American Jewish traditions while also providing a collective platform for negotiating inclusion within the broader American Jewish community. Latine Jews may draw on this identity to assert visibility in Jewish communal organizations, challenge racialized assumptions about Jewishness, and create spaces for mutual recognition and solidarity.

Race, Racialization, and the Boundaries of Belonging

In the United States, Latine Jews encounter a different kind of race and racialization structure than that of their home countries. While some Latine Jews identify as white or are read as such, many are of mixed or non-European heritage and do not experience the protections of whiteness in the same way. Even those who appear phenotypically white often encounter racialized otherness in American Jewish spaces—marked by accent, surname, cultural expression, or the perception of foreignness. At the same time, in Latine communities, their Jewishness is frequently misunderstood, rendered invisible, or treated as an anomaly—underlining the porous and shifting nature of racial and ethnic categories in the American racial context.

These experiences highlight the racialized boundaries of American Jewishness. Scholars such as Eric Goldstein[6] and Karen Brodkin[7] have argued that Jews in the United States became "white" over the course of the twentieth century, a process that involved upward mobility, suburbanization, and assimilation into dominant cultural norms. However, this racialization primarily benefited Ashkenazi Jews of European descent. Latine Jews—particularly those with darker skin or non-European ancestry—often remain outside this framework.

Moreover, Latine Jews challenge dominant US racial categories that treat "Latino" and "Jewish" as mutually exclusive. In surveys, Latine Jews may be forced to choose between identifying as "white," "Latino," or "Jewish," obscuring the intersectionality of their identity. In Jewish spaces, they may be asked to "prove" their Jewishness, explain their origins, or downplay their Latine heritage to fit in. These dynamics of questioning and exclusion reflect broader systemic issues of racism and ethnocentrism within American Jewish institutions.[8]

In response, many Latine Jews engage in cultural and political work to redefine the boundaries of Jewish belonging. They write, teach, and lead in ways that center their experiences and affirm the legitimacy of non-Ashkenazi, non-white Jewish identities. Organizations such as Jews of Color Initiative, Latine Jewish student groups, and independent minyanim (prayer groups) all contribute to this transformation. As Latine Jews gain visibility and voice, they are reshaping what it means to be Jewish in the twenty-first-century United States.

Transnational Ties and Diasporic Continuity

Latine Jews in the United States maintain strong transnational ties to their countries of origin—cultural, familial, spiritual, and institutional. Some families maintain relationships with their Latin American synagogues, participate in holiday observances via livestream, and travel for major life cycle events such as weddings, bar and bat mitzvahs, and funerals. Additionally, many Latine Jews assist in upholding the financial security of family members as well as Jewish institutions in home communities. Those that are able send remittances to family members in countries experiencing political and economic crisis such as Venezuela, whereas others contribute to Jewish schools, cemeteries, and religious institutions. Latin American Jewish day schools often receive financial support from alumni now living in the United States. In turn, these schools host alumni events in places like Miami or New York, reinforcing the affective and institutional linkages that bridge the hemispheres.

These practices demonstrate that religious and communal belonging for Latine Jews is not confined by national borders. Latine Jews inhabit both transnational social spaces and what anthropologist Peggy Levitt terms "transnational religion," where individuals maintain simultaneous attachments to multiple religious communities and sites of practice across borders.[9] These attachments are particularly strong in cities with established Latin American Jewish diasporas, such as Miami and Los Angeles, but they can also be sustained in smaller communities through digital media, family networks, and cultural memory.

Institutional Inclusion and the Struggle for Recognition

Despite their deep involvement in Jewish communal life in their home countries, in the United States, Latine Jews often remain institutionally underrepresented and socially marginalized within mainstream Jewish organizations. National Jewish institutions—including federations, seminaries, and advocacy groups—have historically centered Ashkenazi norms, often sidelining Sephardic, Mizrahi, and Latine voices. Until recently, Latine Jews were largely absent from leadership pipelines, survey research, and strategic planning within Jewish communal frameworks.

This exclusion is not accidental. It reflects long-standing assumptions about who "counts" as Jewish, what Jewish culture should look like, and how resources should be allocated. Many Latine Jews report encountering barriers to participation, including language obstacles, cultural misunderstandings, and financial expectations that do not account for immigrant or first-generation realities. In interviews and community surveys, Latine Jews have described being treated as guests, outsiders, or novelties in predominantly white Jewish institutions.[10]

However, in recent years, there has been a growing movement toward institutional inclusion and recognition. Organizations such as the Jews of Color Initiative have produced important reports, convenings, and leadership programs that highlight the experiences of racially and ethnically diverse Jews, including Latine Jews. Synagogues and federations in cities with large Latin American populations have begun hiring Spanish-speaking staff, offering bilingual materials, and redesigning programs to be more accessible and culturally affirming.

Importantly, Latine Jews themselves are at the forefront of this transformation. Young leaders are creating new communal models—whether through independent minyanim, cultural collectives, digital media, or grassroots organizing—that reflect their identities and commitments. Latine Jewish artists, educators, and scholars are producing work that reshapes public narratives and expands the catalogue of Jewish thought and culture. These efforts are not simply about inclusion within existing structures but about redefining what those structures can be.

Redefining Jewishness: Latine Jews and the American Jewish Future

As Latine Jews become increasingly visible within American Jewish life, they are reshaping the meaning of American Jewish identity. Through their presence, practices, and institutional involvements, Latine Jews challenge the assumption that American Jewishness is white, Ashkenazi, English-speaking, and middle or upper-middle class. They bring with them experiences shaped by migration, linguistic plurality, and cultural hybridity expanding the boundaries of what Jewish life can be in the United States. Latine Jews introduce new cultural practices that diversify Jewish communal experiences. And they also challenge exclusionary narratives—questioning who "counts" as Jewish in the United States, what does an "authentic" practice look like, and how power is distributed within and across Jewish institutions. They underscore the ways in which race, language, and class intersect with religious identity and demand accountability from the organizations that claim to serve all Jews.

The Latin American Jewish experience is instrumental in the scholarship on diaspora, displacement, and identity.[11] Living at the intersection of Latine and Jewish worlds—often at the margins of both—offers a distinct lens through which to think about home, memory, and sacred inheritance. Rather than treating hybridity as a challenge to overcome, Latine Jewish thinkers are developing frameworks that see migration, diversity, and cultural exchange as central to Jewish life. In doing so, they push back against narrow constructions of identity and open space for more expansive understandings of Jewish peoplehood.

Intergenerational Change and the Future of Latine Jewish Identity

The children and grandchildren of Latine Jewish immigrants are forging new paths in American society. Many are bilingual, bicultural, and deeply embedded in both Jewish and Latine social worlds. While some may marry outside the faith or move away from formal religious affiliation, others are reclaiming and reconstructing their Jewish identity in novel ways. For this generation, Jewishness may be expressed through activism, cultural production, digital media, or new forms of spiritual practice. For example, the Mexican-Jewish painter Aliza Nissenbaum uses elements from her Mexican cultural heritage as well as Jewish thinkers in her work on visual identity and immigration.

Importantly, these younger Latine Jews are less likely to accept the dichotomy between Jewish and Latine identities. For them, the experience of hybridity is not a source of tension but of creativity. They may attend a Latine Jewish Hanukkah party that includes *arepas* and salsa dancing or host a Passover seder that incorporates both Ashkenazi blessings and Spanish-language poetry. These expressions are not seen as erosions of tradition but an extension of it—adaptations that reflect the realities of transnational lives and the pluralism of contemporary Jewish American identity.

But new generations also bring new challenges. As community ties to Latin America grow more distant, questions of cultural continuity arise. Will younger Latine Jews maintain the language, culinary traditions, and communal norms of their immigrant parents and grandparents? Will they sustain the transnational connections that defined earlier generations? The answer depends in part on whether American Jewish institutions are willing to invest in spaces that nurture these identities—not as temporary or transitional but as integral to the future of American Jewish life.

Conclusion

Latine Jews in the United States are not simply navigating the boundaries of Jewish and Latine identity—they are redrawing them. Through migration, community formation, cultural production, and religious practice, they are constructing new frameworks of belonging that challenge assumptions about race, religion, and ethnicity in America. Their identities are transnational, plural, and dynamic—grounded in both continuity and change.

This chapter has traced the historical trajectories, institutional landscapes, and cultural practices that define Latine Jewish life in the United States. It has shown how Latine Jews maintain transnational ties, construct hybrid forms of religious expression, and negotiate complex systems of inclusion and exclusion. In doing so, they offer a powerful model of diasporic resilience and religious innovation—one that expands the possibilities of Jewish life and affirms the multiplicity of the Latine experience. In a moment when American Jewish communities are reckoning with their diversity, Latine Jews provide crucial insights into what it means to belong across boundaries. Their stories invite us to imagine a Jewish future that is more inclusive, more pluralistic, and more attuned to the lived realities of migration, memory, and cultural hybridity.

3

Thinking About Latine Islamicity or a Muslim *Latinidad*/Latinicity

Biel Delgado Trabal

There was a bit of irony to having grown up in a Section 8 apartment building in northern New Jersey, directly across the street from a statue of Christopher Columbus. While Columbus never set foot in New Jersey, he did spend quite a bit of time traversing Cuba, the Dominican Republic, and Puerto Rico—homelands to the overwhelming majority of low-income, working poor families that comprised my neighbors. The man whose statue stared directly at us was part of a European imperial, colonial, and civilizational project that began in 1492 with the expulsion of Jews and Muslims from the Iberian Peninsula, the conquest and decimation of the Caribbean's indigenous civilization, and the enslavement of scores of West Africans. We were the direct descendants of those peoples who first faced "imperialist white supremacist capitalist patriarchy,"[1] and a few of us, upon awakening to this reality, elected to embrace Islam.

Muslim Latines, in their religious and racial composition, combine the two communities that political scientist Samuel P. Huntington (1927–2008) singled out, respectively, as the greatest foreign and domestic threats to the United States. The US policy has, since the 1990s, embraced Huntington's proposals and transformed his vulgarity into a hellish reality. In this chapter, I will answer the following questions: Is there a Muslim Latinicity? From where does it originate? What is its current state? In what directions is it developing? After a brief discussion of Latine Muslims' population size, I will examine the ways in which a Muslim Latinicity is entangled with communities from majority-Muslim countries and other convert or revert communities. I then proceed to an examination of Muslim Latinicity according to three dimensions: (1) Muslim Latinicity in relation to its social and ethical dimensions; (2) Muslim Latinicity in relation to political dimensions; and (3) Muslim Latinicity in relation to its cultural dimensions. I conclude that while the potential for a flourishing, deep, and complex Muslim *Latinidad* exists, it is stifled by a lack of external or internal community support, particularly in the form of establishing spaces and places where Latine Muslims themselves are in charge. Such institutions and organizational control are necessary for this vulnerable community to repel both Islamophobia and anti-Latine racism.

Latine Islam "By the Numbers"

In 2017, a survey concluded that the US Latine Muslim population numbered somewhere "between 50,000 and 70,000,"[2] almost three-quarters of which are women, a figure that ought to make the good historian or sociologist wonder about its significance. More than half of Latine Muslims in the United States were either Mexican (31 percent) or Puerto Rican (22 percent). Considering that Latines of Mexican descent represent over half of all Latines in the United States, while Puerto Ricans in the United States are less than half a quarter of the Latine population, Puerto Ricans have an outsized representation in the Latine Muslim community. This is a result of the early history of Latine Muslims in the United States being rooted in the movement work of New York Puerto Rican activists in the 1970s and 1980s. And it was from within that movement that the idea of a distinctly *Latine* Muslim lifeway was most thoroughly embodied.

Latine Muslims Across Abiayala and the Black-Moorish Atlantic

Alianza Islamica has been described as "the best-established Latino Muslim organization ... founded in 1975 by a group of Puerto Rican converts who discovered in Islam the principles of universal brotherhood and equality that were so prominent in the civil rights activities of the era."[3] That activism from which the founders of Alianza sprang forth was internationalist, third-worldist, and in solidarity with Chicano movements, Black nationalist movements, American Indian movements, and anti-racist, working-class white radical movements like the Young Patriots Organization. We now turn to an overview of the relationships between a Muslim *Latinidad* and the wider Muslim population and how it has proceeded forth from this earlier movement of solidarity.

The Muslim heritage of Iberia has been the starting point for many conversations between Latine Muslims in the United States and white/Anglo or Euro-American Muslims as well as with white Muslim reverts in the rest of the American hemisphere and in Spain. Canadian–American Professor T. B. Irving (1914–2002),[4] also known as Al-Hajj Taʿlim ʿAli, was an early advocate for the burgeoning Latine Muslim community. His writings on Islam in Iberia marked the beginnings of a Latine *dawah* (calling) that claimed moral and symbolic links between Latine Muslims and pre-modern al-Andalus.

Today, annual conferences and retreats organized around figures such as the white American convert Dr. Umar Faruq Abd-Allah are held in Granada in Southern Spain, seeking to connect themselves to the much-lauded legacy of coexistence in Islamic Iberia. That "Latino identity could be shown to be rooted in an Islamic past"[5] is then tempered by the fact that not only Europeans and Euro-Americans but also African Americans citing the Afro-descendant Moors, as well as Arab Muslims from the Southwest Asian and North African (SWANA) diaspora, all claim Golden Age Muslim Iberia as their inheritance.

With the Latine Muslim community's origins in the urban spaces of the greater New York metropolitan area, its historical ties are closest to African American Muslim communities.[6] Some estimates state that over one million enslaved Africans brought to the United States were Muslims.[7] That number would conceivably be much higher were it to include enslaved African Muslims brought to those parts of what is now the United States that were previously parts of Mexico and/or the Spanish and French empires. Enslaved African Muslims were brought to every corner "of the Americas, leaving Arabic writings in Panama, Colombia, Trinidad, Mexico, and especially Brazil, where Muslim slaves led the great revolt of 1835 in Bahia"[8] preceded by other Muslim-led revolts in the Caribbean and elsewhere. "After Malcolm X's assassination," Rahim Ocasio, one of the four founders of the Alianza Islamica, recounts how he and fellow Puerto Rican activists embraced the martyred revolutionary's view of Islam "as an answer to oppression: an activist religion of liberation, justice, and human rights."[9] They responded to the racialization of Caribbean Latines in the Eastern United States by embracing an *Afro-Moro* heritage.

Latine Muslims and Afro-Moro Political Thought

In the 1990s, Samuel Huntington, the former National Security Advisor for the Reagan Administration, declared the religion of Islam and its adherents in the Global South the greatest foreign threat to the United States.[10] The greatest domestic threat to the United States, on the other hand, was "Hispanization."[11] Every presidential administration since has followed Huntington's anti-Latine and Islamophobic policy playbook without fail, whether Republican or Democrat. Proof of this abounds—from Obama's having ordered more drone attacks throughout the Muslim world and more deportations from the United States than his predecessor Bush, to Muslim bans, ICE raids and the equating of Puerto Ricans and Mexicans with dirtiness, poverty, drugs, crime, and rape being the order of the day under Trump, to Biden's support of the extermination campaign against the people of Gaza. In this regard, any attempt to define a politics of *Islamidad* within the constraints of a Republican–Democrat binary would be misrepresenting the facts.[12] The original griots of *Islamidad* promoted a far more expansive, decolonial, Afro-Moro, political platform.

"We're a colonized, broken people," said co-founder and emir of Alianza Islamica, Yahya Figueroa. This understanding tied the leaders of Alianza to movements for Black lives, to Palestinian liberation, to the plight of political prisoners, whether Puerto Rican or not, and to educational, economic, and physical upliftment and psychological well-being as a Muslim civic duty just as important as theology.[13] It was this awareness of the damaging impact of colonialism upon the peoples of the Global South that cautioned the leaders of Latine Muslims away from taking the Muslim immigrant community as infallible mentors. How, Yahya asked, could Latine Muslims be expected to "cower to another oppressed people suffering from the same political situation and expect them to guide us?"[14]

Egyptian American scholar of Islamic law Khaled Abou El Fadl has stated "that religious institutions in dictatorial and despotic countries are marred in hypocrisy. Their credibility does not stand up to scrutiny. We, Muslims in the West, must not look to these institutions for authority or guidance."[15] Abou El Fadl calls upon Muslims in "the west" to free themselves from Islamic thought produced under a "colonized, dominated, and subjugated Middle East."[16] A Muslim *Latinidad*, were it to have any efficacy at all in addressing the brokenness from colonization that Figueroa identifies, would profess to build up that which has been broken down by colonialism. A Muslim *Latinidad* would have to be an anticolonial, decolonizing, and Afro-Indigenizing *Latinidad*.

When Figueroa refers to "a colonized people,"[17] he does not intend only US colonization of Puerto Rico, although the "decolonization of Puerto Rico was a major issue"[18] for Alianza. He is also referencing the centuries of enslavement[19] that form a history shared by all Afro-descendant people of the African diaspora throughout the American hemisphere from the Southern United States to South America. Latine Islam's genealogy begins in what Ella Shohat calls the Moorish Atlantic, its inquisitions and expulsions,[20] and the Afro-Atlantic with its trafficking in Black bodies. Among them were "educated Muslims and scholars of Islam. We need a non-Eurocentric version of our history,"[21] says Figueroa, and from that cosmovision, a politics can be developed. Figueroa, Ocasio, and Hajj Yusuf Padilla from New York and New Jersey in the early 1970s "became Muslims because of Malcolm,"[22] El-Hajj Malik Shabazz, who had linked a militant anticolonial international solidarity with a religious discipline of strict sobriety.

For Ocasio, the result of a Western Marxist revolutionary ideology, of the kind which had informed the Young Lords politics, was that "not enough attention was being paid to the development of character."[23] The illegal FBI counterintelligence program, COINTELPRO, exploited such failings, ultimately putting an end to the Young Lords although not to its spirit. The revolutionary politics made them aware of the systemic white supremacy at the root of their condition in Latine ghettos: the police brutality, dilapidated housing, and the lack of basic services. A spiritual discipline and lived religious community were believed to have the capacity to withstand the other aspects of systemic racism's genocidal indifference and neglect: heroin and crack epidemics, violent crime, and an AIDS epidemic, the death toll of all of which was disproportionately higher in communities of color.

Latine Muslims, Social Ethics, and an Islamic Latina Family-ism

Social ethicist Miguel De La Torre cites an "underlying problem with Eurocentric ethics" being that it is "less concerned with 'what you do' than 'how you think.'"[24] This holds resonance with the case of Latina Muslims living in a larger Latine Muslim community that rejects mainstream (white) feminism with critiques which parallel that of women of color feminists.[25] At the center of present discussions on Latine Muslim social ethics are Latina Muslims, being as they are three-quarters of the US Latine Muslim community, this community being defined within the framework of an ethics of Islamidad as a family of families.

In 2017,[26] a conference that invited some of the founders of Alianza Islamica to speak about its history was held at New York's Mosque of Islamic Brotherhood, "a descendant of Malcolm X's Muslim Mosque, Inc."[27] A question was posed to the panel about the role of Latina Muslims in the organization. In response, Figueroa and others argued that feminism, presumed to be the ideology informing the question posed, was a "Caucasian issue" the application of which upon communities of color has been cause "for the destruction of our families."[28] Sister Yasmine, a female leader of Alianza, added, "I want to honor her questions about where's the female voice ... we weren't feminists there. We weren't [male] chauvinists there. Alianza Islamica, my experience is that we were family-ists there."[29] Family-ism is an intriguing notion, and it is in conjuncture with larger critiques of (white) feminism by women of color.

The work of Sylvia Marcos on pre-colonial Latin Abyiayala and Oyèrónkẹ́ Oyěwùmi on Africa has gone far in problematizing assumptions of a universal and ahistorical patriarchy.[30] Precolonial cultures in Mesoamerica and West Africa have been shown not to adhere to the patriarchal gender norms that, for all its warmongering on behalf of women's rights, are the products of imperialist, white supremacist, and capitalist patriarchy. French Algerian scholar-activist Houria Bouteldja writes "My body does not belong to me. No moral magisterium will make me endorse a law conceived by and for white feminists ... I belong to my family, my clan, my neighborhood, my race; I belong to Algeria, to Islam. I belong to my history and God willing, I will belong to my descendants ... France wants to tear my body away from them, colonize it."[31] These words can, with good reason, be related back to the concept of family-ism. When Sister Yasmine rejects feminism in favor of a social ethics rooted in a Muslim, Afro-Moro family-ist *latinidad*, she is rejecting that feminism, which is indifferent to the multiple forms of oppression she endures: racial, religious, class, and gender oppression. When she rejects chauvinism, she is rejecting a *machismo* that originates as a white European colonial imposition masquerading as a tenet of Latine identity.[32]

Latine Muslims and Afro-Moro Culture

"One salient finding is the tendency for Latino Muslims to place a high emphasis on the historical connection between Latino culture and Islam ... a product of the 800–year-long presence of Islamic culture and civilization in Spain."[33] In the case of Latine Muslims, this tendency comes with the added belief that one is most likely returning to the faith of one's ancestors, a faith that had been violently ripped away due to forced conversions and the Spanish Inquisition. "The process by which Latino Muslims identify with pre-Columbian Islamic Spain is fairly similar to the way in which many African-American Muslims have identified with the role of Islam in African history"[34] writes Barzegar. Instead of making a "faulty translation from one failed society to another when we are, as a minority, already the most vulnerable," and here Figueroa is referring to the Islamic movements of the Middle East and South Asia whose representatives were proselytizing in the United States, Muslim Latines are encouraged to inculcate an "Andalusian spirituality."[35] The attainment of this spirituality, this "conscious awakening," "true knowledge," and a 900–year "true history," suppressed by an imperial Catholic-dominated education system in Latin America, depends on a program that includes the philosophical, legal, and mystical writings of "Ibn Hazm, Ibn Rushd, Ibn Arabi" and "Ibn Abbad of Ronda."[36]

The list of publications available for download on the website of the largest Latine Muslim organization today, La Asociación Latino Musulmana de América (LALMA), suggests that they have taken seriously Alianza's call to center the Islamic tradition of al-Andalus. Among them is Muhammad Asad's English translation and commentary of the Qur'an, translated into Spanish by LALMA's imam, César Domínguez. In Imam César's online library one also finds a Spanish translation of Khaled Abou El Fadl's *The Great Theft*, a refutation of Saudi-sponsored Sunni fundamentalism.[37] Abou El Fadl, like the late Asad (1900–1992), champions the intellectual and literary inheritance of Muslim Iberia. An example of this is his recommendation to read *al-ʿIqd al-farīd* (*The Unique Necklace*) by the Andalusī scholar-poet Ibn ʿAbd al-Rabbih (d. 328/940) "to see how much of its poetry is about valuing nature, loving animals, and loving human beings."[38] This he contrasts with the epistemological framework of modern Muslims who "seem to think that you can claim to love God but be neutral about God's creation or indifferent to who suffers, who lives, and who dies."[39] It is this indifference as a quality of a modern, perhaps Constantinian, Islam that a project of Latine Muslim cultural education would confront, necessitating a perspective of "non-indifference and responsibility, both of which presuppose listening to the cry of the condemned" as Nelson Maldonado-Torres describes it, a perspective that Yomaira Figueroa-Vásquez has linked to Chela Sandoval's concept of decolonial love.[40] Islamidad requires an education in the history of the American hemisphere, before and after 1492, connecting the Christian Crusader ethnic cleansing of Spain and Portugal's Jewish and Muslim populations to the holocaust of the Caribbean's natives and other indigenous populations as well as the transatlantic slave trade, the witch hunts on behalf of patriarchy, and the 500 years of resistance that followed.[41]

Imam Domínguez's latest project is "Vivir el Islam" (Living Islam), a Spanish translation of an essay by Dr. Umar Faruq Abd-Allah, whose summer programs in Granada represent one form of Islamic revival in America that is also rooted in the tradition of *al-Andalus*. A future direction for LALMA to take is to give greater attention to the cultural productions that linked the Moorish Atlantic to the Afro-Atlantic. This would entail incorporating those parts of Muslim West Africa's classical curriculum which, via the city of Timbuktu's attracting of Iberian intellectuals exiled by the conquering kingdoms of Castile and Aragon, included a great deal of al-Andalus's intellectual output. Credit must go to Imams Yusuf Rios and Hamza Perez of Pennsylvania, who by their "authority to teach and transmit the revered works of Shaykh Uthman Dan Fodio and the esteemed scholars of the Sokoto Caliphate"[42] of nineteenth-century West Africa, are the Latine Muslims most dedicated to centering an Andalus-cum-Timbuktu Afro-Moro Islamic tradition in the United States.

Alianza leaders' emphasis on the Ibero-Islamic "classics of antiquity" was not for the sake of "dwelling on the past" as Figueroa writes in his 2017 essay "Reclaiming Our Heritage."[43] It was instead for the sake of guiding not only Latines "on the road to New Andalusia" but also those suffering "in traditional Muslim homelands and minorities in Europe." But are there cultural spaces in the Latine United States, fitting Ibn Hazm's description of Muslim Iberia's Sufi lodges, the zawiyas, and their "*hospitalidad generosa*,"[44] that would provide such Latine-led guidance and cultivation?

There is seemingly little to no support from the wider Muslim community for such a space. LALMA has in the past been pressed by the far more numerous, mostly West and South Asian immigrant Muslim community to accept a non-Latino male Muslim scholar as their sponsor[45] or "handler." Even after the passing of their non-Latine imam, Fathi Osman, in 2010, not much has changed. Imam César shares duties with an Egyptian teacher, and their physical meeting space is an assimilationist-oriented Indonesian Islamic center in Los Angeles, Indonesian being an ethnic identification that—like Bosnian or that of other nationality-based Islamic centers—does not receive the same scrutiny or criticisms for being schismatic and unknowledgeable as do Latine Muslims.

Imagining the Future of a Latine Muslim Identity

"The Muslims do not care about supporting Hispanics because Hispanics are looked at as a people without money" said the former imam of one of the largest Islamic centers in the country, in criticism of much of SWANA-American Muslim leadership.[46] Since 2016, only one Latine Islamic center is up and running, the IslamInSpanish community center of Houston, Texas. LALMA, the largest Latine Muslim organization in the United States has no physical presence save for some space and time allotted to them within an Indonesian Islamic center in Southern California. A Muslim Latinicity in the United States would necessitate Latine-led Islamic centers in all areas of the United States where large populations of Latines are concentrated. These centers would need to take seriously the proposals presented by the elders of Alianza Islamica and build from there. The IslamInSpanish center, as one physical space in Houston, does not have the capacity to cater to the needs of an estimated 70,000 Latine Muslims across the United States, even if it wanted to. Other organizations, like the Latino American Dawah Organization (LADO) whose slogan is "Puro Latino. Puro Islam. A su LADO," live only in cyberspace.

While LALMA and all or most other Latine Muslim organizations center al-Andalus as their inheritance, expanding upon the earlier work of Alianza Islamica would require serious investigations into and engagements with the knowledge and wisdom traditions formed and spread from historical al-Andalus to West African cultural epicenters. It would require a political, ethical, and cultural education that decenters the European and recenters the Red, Black, and Moorish Atlantic. Finally, it would require a decentering of white patriarchy and white feminism, and a Latina Muslim-led development of concepts like family-ism.

Muslim Latines have the dubious distinction of combining the "two groups most negatively stereotyped in American media today."[47] They confront popular culture and policies that are Islamophobic as well as anti-Latine, most often in the form of anti-immigrant rhetoric and legislation. Both major political parties in the United States have been complicit with Samuel Huntington's vulgar vision of a violent foreign and domestic policy for preserving an imperialist Anglophilic white-supremacist capitalist heteropatriarchy threatened by populations at its southern border. For a Muslim *latinidad*, or Islamidad, to thrive, not only under conditions such as those imposed by Western modernity and its universalism but also to embody an alternative and pluriversal vision for the hemisphere, it almost feels like it would take a miracle.

4

Jesusito

Rubén Rosario Rodríguez

Recently, an Anglo colleague confidently stated that one ought to never pray to God for a better parking space or for their favorite sports team to win. I cannot speak to the latter, but the former immediately evoked a powerful childhood memory with profound Christological implications. As a child, I suffered from years of gastric distress and internal bleeding that confounded all my doctors (turns out I suffered from an undiagnosed duodenal ulcer). I was scheduled for an endoscopy at the nearest children's hospital about an hour's drive from our home. My father was out of town since his job often required travel, so my mother—whose English fluency allowed for basic communication at best—drove me to the appointment even though she was sick with bronchitis. Unknown to me at the time, the coughing from her bronchitis was so severe that it had fractured one of her ribs. That morning my mother looked pale, glassy-eyed, and physically exhausted. After a long drive, we pulled up to the hospital and could not find a parking space on the street, so she drove into the parking garage and level-by-level searched for an open space. As she scanned for the coveted space, she uttered a prayer to Jesús for a parking space—preferably one close to the elevator so she would not have far to walk.[1]

Despite my Anglo colleague's proclamation, the Jesus I got to know and love in my Latine home welcomed such prayers, especially those that spoke to our everyday needs and concerns; our Jesús encouraged this intimacy, reassuring us that any need, no matter how insignificant, would be heard. Did my mother's prayer cause the vacant spot we found so close to the elevator? Or was her prayer of petition, followed by a heartfelt prayer of thanksgiving, more a reflection of her trust in a God who provides for our needs and responds to our suffering? Either way, this memory exposes in my view deficiencies in my Anglo colleague's Christology and affirms a Latine faith in a fully incarnated God who encourages the kind of intimacy that enabled us to call him our "little Jesus"—*Jesusito.*

Sketches of a Biblical Christology

Christology is that subdiscipline of theology that reflects on the person and work of Jesus Christ guided and informed by the Word of God, Christian praxis, and Christian worship. While Christian theology cannot be reduced to Christology, understanding the person and work of Jesus the Christ provides the focal point from which to understand what Christians say and believe about God and humanity. Recalling the words of Jesus to his disciples, the principal task of Christian theology is to answer the question, "But who do you say that I am?" (Mt. 16:15; Mk 8:31; Lk. 9:20).

For Western Christianity, the first seven ecumenical councils provide a doctrinal framework within which to talk about the person and work of Christ so that most Christologies reflect the dogmatic formula of the Council of Chalcedon (451 CE) that Christ is fully human and fully divine: "two natures without confusion, without change, without division, without separation—the difference of the natures being by no means taken away because of the union, but rather the distinctive character of each nature being preserved."[2] But Jon Sobrino contends, while "it has been customary to start with the dogmatic formulation of the Council of Chalcedon," for a church in solidarity with the world's poor, "it hardly seems suitable or adequate as a point of departure."[3] Latine theologians in the United States, influenced and nurtured by Latin American liberation theology, begin their theological reflection on the person and work of Christ with Jesús's earthly life and ministry rather than the abstract theological formulations of the early church councils, thereby placing the historical liberation of the poor and oppressed at the center of their understanding of Christ's salvific mission. If the Christology of the creeds affirms that in the person of Jesús we most fully discover what it means to be both human and divine, a Christology originating within the Latine experience of God argues that speaking of Jesús as the "Christ" of God is a foundational statement that orients Christian theology toward liberation.

Jesus of Nazareth is identified in the New Testament by the Greek term *ho christos*, the Christ, from the Hebrew *Ha-mashiach*, the Messiah, the anointed one. For the earliest Christians, the conviction that Jesus was the Christ, the Messiah expected by Israel, led to an understanding of the Hebrew Bible term *Ha-mashiach* as an agent of divine deliverance. As Messiah, Jesus proclaimed the imminent kingdom of God (Mt. 12:28; Mk 1:15; Lk. 11:20); Jesus worked miracles that were signs of God's impending reign (Mk 3:22-30; Jn 10:31-38); Jesus embraced his Davidic descent (Mk 11:1-11; Mt. 21:1-11; Lev. 19:28-40; Jn 12:12-19); and Jesus accepted his mission as the Messiah/Christ of God empowered by the Spirit to bring good news to an afflicted people (Isa. 61:1-3; Mk 8:27–30; Lk. 6:20-21; 9:18.21; Mt. 5:3.12; 16:13.20; Jn 4:25. 26). The political was an aspect of first-century Jewish messianic expectations, and Jesus' own self-understanding as Son of David and Messiah created political consequences for the earliest (Jewish) Christians, who were nurtured and formed by these same expectations. The title "Christ" carries the meaning "one anointed to rule," yet the life and ministry of Jesus of Nazareth, universally acknowledged by early Christians to be the Christ, can be interpreted as a rejection of precisely those political expectations in which the Messiah comes to overthrow Israel's oppressors and reestablish a *temporal* order. Standing before Pilate, the embodiment of temporal political power in first-century Jerusalem, Jesus was accused of political sedition for claiming to be "King of the Jews," to which Jesus answered, "My kingdom is not from this world. If my kingdom were from this world, my followers would be fighting to keep me from being handed over to the Jews. But as it is, my kingdom is not from here" (Jn 18:33-36).

While Jesus defines his kingdom as "not from this world," this does not mean that followers of Jesus should disengage from the concerns of this world, as demonstrated by the consistently political themes in Jesus' preaching: poverty (Mt. 23:14; Mk 10:17-27; Lk. 6:20-25), taxation (Mt. 9:10; 17:24-27; 22:15-22; Mk 12:13-17), leadership (Mt. 20:24-28; Lk. 22:24-30; Jn 13:1-5, 12-14; 15:12-17), and wealth (Mt. 19:16-26; Lk. 16:10-13; 18:18-27). Jesus' self-understanding as the Christ of God references Isaiah's suffering servant: "Then he began to teach them that the Son of Man must undergo great suffering, and be rejected by the elders, the chief priests, and the scribes, and be killed, and after three days rise again" (Mk 8:31). Temporal powers dragged Jesus to the criminal's cross, but God raised Jesus from death and glorified him at the right hand of the Father; temporal powers tried to take the life of the early church martyrs, yet God raised them to eternal life; temporal powers continue to legislate life and death today, but Jesus' teaching still stands as a relentless force for countercultural transformation: "For those who want to save their life will lose it, and those who lose their life for my sake, and for the sake of the gospel, will save it" (Mk 8:35); "No one has greater love than this, to lay down one's life for one's friends" (Jn 15:13); "Let the same mind be in you that was in Christ Jesus, who, though he was in the form of God, did not regard equality with God as something to be exploited" (Phil. 2:5–6). Although the New Testament presents a range of moral instruction, it also contains a consistent unifying narrative grounded in the moral judgment that Jesus Christ brings liberation from every kind of bondage.

Sketches of a Latine Christology

One major insight of a Latine Christology is the centrality of the Incarnation for understanding the person and work of Christ from the perspective of a marginalized and oppressed people. Archbishop Romero emphasized this incarnational aspect of a liberative Christology in his preaching: "Had Christ realized his incarnation today, in 1978, he would be a man thirty years old, a peasant [*campesino*] from Nazareth, looking like any one of the peasants from our surrounding cantons so that the Son of God would be in the flesh and we would not recognize him. He would so resemble us!"[4] The Latine experience allows us to see "that in the face of suffering, in the struggle of life and death, God is present with us. Just as God is present sacramentally in the Eucharist, God is present in the lives of those who suffer and agonize."[5] Accordingly, one of the earliest loci for a Latine Christology, as articulated in the work of Fr. Virgilio Elizondo, was Jesus' Galilean identity as a racially and ethnically marginalized "other" in the context of imperial domination. Elizondo writes, "The God of Jesus cannot be known unless Jesus is known (Jn 12:44-45, 14:9). And we cannot really know Jesus of Nazareth unless we know him in the context of the historical and cultural situation of his people. Jesus was not simply a Jew; he was a Galilean Jew, throughout his life and his disciples were identified as Galileans."[6]

Accordingly, Latine Christologies do not begin with abstract speculation but with the concrete experiences of Latine people to argue that "anyone who takes the Incarnation seriously truly" cannot separate "Christ or Christianity from its cultural and historical matrix."[7] This vital insight, that all aspects of human experience are embedded in particular cultural matrices and that both divine revelation and theological reflection occur *within* culture, leads Latine theologians to conclude that all theologians interpret Christ through the lens of their distinctive culture. Understanding "Christ through culture" presumes two things: (1) Jesus is not a mere creation of human culture, though born into a particular culture and (2) God's revelation never occurs separate from culture (i.e., there is no unmediated experience of the divine). Given this understanding, the theologian's task is not to abstract Christ from culture to uncover some kernel of transcendent truth free from cultural distortions but to discern how Christ is known in and through human cultures. The mystery of the Incarnation is that God chooses to become human in a particular—Galilean and Jewish—context for the purposes of universal salvation. Understanding "Christ through culture" does not negate the reality of divine revelation. Rather, it forces theology to become fully incarnational by accepting culture as a central source of divine revelation, meaning that when we encounter God, it is always within a particular historical and cultural context. Not only do theologians have to work hard to discern the meaning of theological symbols in their original sociocultural context—for example, the task of biblical theology in locating the life and ministry of Jesus of Nazareth within the context of first-century Israel—they must also interpret and translate these symbols for their contemporary context.

For *mujerista* theologian, Ada María Isasi-Díaz, the popular beliefs and practices of the Latine people become a unique locus of divine action in the world, specifically, the lived experience of Latinas: "Hispanic women's experience and our struggle for survival, not the Bible, are the source of our theology and the starting point for how we should interpret, appropriate, and use the Bible."[8] Accordingly, Isasi-Díaz views divine revelation as ongoing, not "completed and closed when the canon of Christianity was determined," but taking place "through the faith and religiosity of the poor and oppressed of this world."[9] In other words, the praxis of liberation manifest in the popular faith of marginalized peoples is the continuation of the divine act of Incarnation, which requires "that theology today be done not just by being attentive to where we once encountered God's work—the Exodus, the Incarnation, the cross, and the Resurrection—but also by being attentive to where God continues to work today."[10]

A Latine Christology broadens traditional conceptions of the Incarnation to encompass Christ's ongoing work for human liberation:

> Through those who suffer at the hands of others, God becomes incarnate as the object and recipient of the very real consequences of our sin. Through those who struggle on behalf of life, who act out of love and compassion for others, God becomes incarnate as a subjective agent of history, working to transform human history into God's kingdom, where love and justice reign.[11]

Therefore, the story of salvation does not end at the cross, for "together, the cross and the resurrection promise us that life and love will triumph over death and hatred by confronting them and enduring in spite of them.... The promise of life in spite of death emboldens and empowers us to live and to confront evil."[12] These words take on new meaning as elected leaders act to criminalize Latinidad and exploit the populist drive for immigration reform to further marginalize and silence Latine voices in the United States. The creation of an internment camp in the Florida Everglades, ostensibly for deporting undocumented immigrants, reveals the underlying racism and xenophobia driving these politicians: "Alligator lives matter. The good news is, alligators are guaranteed at least 65 million meals if we get started now."[13]

Latines are the largest community of color in the United States, and while this demographic bloc represents a great number of different national and cultural identities, people of Latine heritage in the United States are treated as a single minority population and viewed as recent immigrants despite the fact that the Latine presence in North America predates the founding of the United States by hundreds of years. Furthermore, Latines are often portrayed as criminals or lazy welfare cheats while simultaneously accused of stealing American jobs. Consequently, Latine identity is a political choice to resist integration into the dominant white Anglo culture and its hollow promises of material prosperity, which has enchanted many Latine voters who continue to support the GOP and President Trump even as they face arrest and deportation.[14] This tragic reality demands a hermeneutics of suspicion since "we all create Jesus in our own image," it is vital to counteract how "Jesus has been constructed throughout history by those wielding political power."[15] Miguel De La Torre asks, "Can Jesus be saved from Jesus?"[16] Then concludes, "There is no one true Jesus that can be objectively known; there only exists subjective interpretations of Jesus. The social, cultural, political, and global economic power of Euroamericans allows them to impose their subjective interpretation of Jesus as the objective Truth (with a capital *T*) for everyone else."[17] In much the same way that James H. Cone has argued for a black Jesus, De La Torre contends in *The Politics of Jesús* (2015) that "Jesús is Hispanic because the biblical witness of God is of one who takes sides with the least among us against those who oppress them."[18]

In *Jesus Is My Uncle* (1999), Luis Pedraja identifies several important tensions in Latine Christology. Concerning the doctrine of the Incarnation, Pedraja affirms that

Christ is incarnate *historically* in the person Jesus of Nazareth and incarnate *in the present* through our acts of love: "God's incarnational power cannot be limited to a single historical event. God also works within humanity in all ages through God's love for us, empowering us to do God's will and receive God's revelation. Thus, through the power of the Holy Spirit, God's love can become concretely incarnate through us, acting in us to reach others."[19] Affirming that Christ is incarnate "through us" poses a challenge to more traditional understandings of the person of Christ that emphasize the uniqueness of the Incarnation, so Pedraja reinterprets the doctrine by arguing that humanity encounters God in the midst of humanity—Christ revealed through culture. Encountering Christ *through* culture, he navigates the poles of divine transcendence and divine immanence while affirming both: "In love, God's transcendence does not negate God's immanence in any respect. Most Hispanics believe in an immanent God who is accessible to them and who stands with them. But they also believe in a transcendent God who can empower them. The God of the Incarnation is also the God of the Resurrection and of the Ascension."[20]

Given this cultural matrix within which to interpret and understand the person and work of Christ, Latine Christologies tend to emphasize certain culturally specific images of the Christ.[21] As Eduardo Fernández contends, popular representations of Jesús in Latine households—especially those that reveal the suffering and broken Christ—"not only evoke some aspects of Christ as experienced in these believing communities but also highlight three key characteristics related to him: his vulnerability, brokenness, and divine love."[22] These three pervasive images promote certain devotional practices while nurturing an ethos of intimacy and closeness to the immanent God who has chosen to manifest as helpless infant and crucified victim, before being revealed as Risen Lord. Similarly, Latine Protestant hymnody (specifically *coritos*) displays a Jesús "whose love is embodied in intimacy, closeness, caress, and embrace. The power of Christ against evil is channeled through an imagery of tenderness and intimacy, not conflict and warfare."[23]

For some Latine theologians the emphasis on liberative praxis puts them in conflict with the dominant institutional church, but others, like Roberto Goizueta, choose to navigate the straits between repudiating the most repressive aspects of the institutional church while fully participating in the church's liturgy and sacraments: "As a self-consciously Catholic theologian, however, I theologize from within the context of the larger Roman Catholic tradition as this is lived out in our Hispanic communities."[24] If the lived faith of the Christian community (the *sensus fidelium*) is the key locus of God's revelation in history, the central function of popular Catholicism as an expression of that *sensus fidelium* calls for a reexamination of the relationship between the official tradition and the popular traditions of the people—what Alejandro García-Rivera has called the relationship between the "Big Story" and the "little stories."[25] Goizueta's main conversation partner is Western Catholic Christianity, which, notwithstanding the reforms of the Second Vatican Council, has failed to fully appreciate the importance of popular practices in the prayer and worship life of most Catholics. Ironically, the willingness by many Latine people to incarnate their faith as part of the institutional

Roman Catholic Church stems from the very popular beliefs and practices the institutional church so often resists, like the Guadalupan Marian devotion, or Holy Week reenactments of Christ's Passion: "It is no accident, therefore, that the crucified Christ plays such a central role in Latino/a popular Catholicism."[26]

Embracing the Incarnational aspect of Latine Christology, Goizueta articulates a theology of accompaniment and sacramental encounter in which the crucified Christ accompanies believers in their struggles: "Jesus is, first of all, a flesh-and-blood human being who is with us today."[27] To belong to the church is to participate in the body of Christ, which in the analysis of Latine theologies cannot be reduced to just Eucharistic participation but involves "participation in the lives of those peoples who are themselves crucified victims, those whose wounded bodies are the mirrors of our souls."[28] Thus, so long as the institutional church—despite all its shortcomings—embraces Christ's ministry of compassion and accompaniment among the most powerless and destitute, believers are assured that Christ is present in the church.

Conclusion

Perhaps in jest, an Anglo colleague dismissed petitionary prayers that ask God to intervene in trivial matters, like praying to God for a better parking spot. Yet, in my experience, the God revealed in Jesús is primarily a God of love and compassion, and for the person trapped in an unjust situation—or the victim of innocent suffering—a God who fails to respond to human suffering, no matter how "trivial," fundamentally lacks empathy and therefore falls short of authentic divinity. Like Cornel West, I am convinced that Christianity "is first and foremost a theodicy, a triumphant account of good over evil."[29] Yet, I am unmoved by traditional theodicies that provide rational arguments for resolving the question of evil. Latine theology, firm in the belief that God triumphs over evil, recasts the conversation by breaking free from the bonds of logical argumentation toward an understanding of evil *as it is experienced*. More to the point, by understanding evil and suffering as it is experienced by the oppressed and marginalized of the world, liberation theology offers an incarnational and existential response to the problem of evil and innocent suffering that remains focused on Paschal joy, firm in the belief that Christ suffers with us.

A Latine theodicy does not seek to refute the inherent logical contradictions articulated by the problem of evil. Rather, it seeks to nurture a collective spirituality whose focus is incarnating the earthly ministry of Christ, embodying the good news of the kingdom by working to establish a foretaste of God's kingdom in the world. The hope that grounds and motivates the Latine Christian community despite the wretched realities of this world constantly threatening its belief in the goodness and compassion of God, is the lived faith of those who, in the face of overwhelming injustice and suffering, remain "participants in Christ's ongoing work"—the *abuelitas*, school teachers, church members (lay and clergy), and elected officials—"who toil in the obscurity of their homes, neighborhoods, and communities" to establish a more just and compassionate common good.[30] Their lives and their sacrifices give response to the problem of evil and innocent suffering. It is not the rationality of theological and philosophical arguments that overcome the moral objections raised by the problem of evil and keep the victims of injustice within the Christian faith, "but the beauty of those lives in which that faith is incarnated and made visible and palpable."[31] Because God is known amid the suffering of a crucified people, not as theological abstraction but as a fellow sufferer, Latine Christians are emboldened to approach God in the most intimate terms, without pretense, without standing on ceremony. As Luis Pedraja emphasizes, for many of us "Jesús" is an uncle, brother, or friend, and to the person in pain, for whom a closer parking spot means the alleviation of real suffering, God is properly and faithfully named *Jesusito*, our little Jesus.

5

Full of the Spirit: US Latine Christian Pneumatologies and Religious Identities

Albert Hernández

As recounted in the New Testament teachings about Jesus of Nazareth, and as embodied in the Trinitarian Doctrine of divinity as Three Persons in one God, Christianity presents a distinctive set of beliefs and practices for personal salvation through one's relationship with God, Jesus Christ, and the Holy Spirit. As Father, Son, and Holy Spirit, the Persons of the Trinity are separate yet coequal, acting in full unity with one other. Without diminishing the power and majesty of God, the Father, or of Jesus Christ as the Son of God, the Third Person of the Trinity, *the Holy Spirit*, represents a crucial link between God and each human individual. Jesus promised the Spirit specifically as intermediary by using the word Paraclete, meaning the advocate, helper, comforter, or counselor: "You will receive power when the Holy Spirit comes upon you; and you will be my witnesses in Jerusalem, and in all Judea and Samaria, and to the ends of the earth" (Acts 1:8).[1] Both in the individual and communal areas of life, Christians believe the Spirit actively and mysteriously nudges all people and all things to their embodied and spiritual *fullness*. Consequently, Christians across different cultural, sociopolitical, and historical contexts have given continual witness to the presence and guidance of the Holy Spirit.

Although US Latine Christian religious identity is highly variable, this chapter asserts that a particular emphasis on the Holy Spirit and Pentecost is a persistent theme. Latine Christians have been drawn toward the most Spirit-focused aspects of existing Christianities and have folded their local and ethnic traditions of Spirit into them. Among the widespread diversity of US Latine Christians—whether Roman Catholic,

Protestant, or Pentecostal—the Holy Spirit's mystical power and abiding presence is most often known in *the heart*, the affective and emotional center of the human person. This is not to imply that Latine religious identity is incapable of appreciating the Spirit's capacity to be known in *the mind*, a person's intellectual and rational center. Rather, our claim is that the Euro-American post-Enlightenment emphasis on scientific rationalism has obscured the importance of spiritual experience and ethnic identity among US Latine Christian persons and groups.

Pneumatology is the branch of theology concerned with the formal study of the Holy Spirit. This includes traditions, dogmas, practices and rituals, and miraculous manifestations of Spirit in the collective life of churches and in the private life of individuals. Fire, water, mighty winds, and a white dove are common Biblical metaphors for the Holy Spirit. The phrase "Gifts of the Spirit," or *"los Dones del Espíritu"* in Spanish, are given for the fullness and empowerment of individuals and the community.[2] Among these gifts are wisdom, understanding, counsel, fortitude, knowledge, piety, and fear of the Lord (signifying "respect" for God). The lived experience behind these spiritual gifts is amplified by use of the phrase *"los frutos del Espíritu"* meaning "the fruits of the Spirit." Among these fruits are love, joy, peace, patience, kindness, goodness, gentleness, faithfulness, and self-control.[3] Together, these Gifts and Fruits are tangible signs of the Holy Spirit's abiding presence moving individuals and communities towards the *fullness of the Spirit*.

This chapter's title, *Full of the Spirit,* invokes this important characteristic of Christian theology and religious experience. It is also a direct allusion to the many Biblical verses about *the fullness of the Spirit* that witness to the early Christian community's faith in God's promise of empowerment through the Holy Spirit's indwelling in their hearts and minds. To date no contemporary scholar has written a comprehensive study detailing the immense variety of US Latine Christian traditions and practices focused on the Third Person of the Trinity, or an extensive study documenting the wide-ranging Latine interpretations and commemorations of Pentecost.[4] Rather than a comprehensive treatment of such a vast subject, this chapter summarizes major concepts and threads in contemporary religious thought about the Holy Spirit and Pentecost alongside brief examples illustrating these in US Latine Christian contexts.

The story of Pentecost in Acts (2:1-21) is considered the birthday of *Jesusito's Iglesia* (Jesus' church) charged with spreading the good news of his ministry and resurrection. Pentecost literally means "the fiftieth day" as the disciples were huddled together in the upper room of a house in Jerusalem for forty-nine days after the Romans crucified Jesus. They were gathered for Shavuot, the Jewish Festival of Weeks, consisting of a fifty-day cycle honoring God's giving of the Torah and Ten Commandments to Moses on Mount Sinai. Thus, the seven times seven weeks of forty-nine days concluding on Pentecost Sunday, the fiftieth day after Easter. Acts recount the outpouring of the Holy Spirit at Pentecost, starting with a mighty wind; then amplified by the miraculous tongues of fire descending on the heads of those present; and culminating in the phenomenal manifestation that those present were endowed with knowledge to speak and hear the Word of God in the languages of the Roman Empire. Hence, this story also alludes to Christianity's evangelizing mission in the social and political arenas.

Considering the violence, oppression, and economic marginalization Jews experienced as Roman subjects, the story in Acts is all the more remarkable. These first Christians were spiritually empowered to spread Jesus' message of healing and human dignity across the Hellenistic-Roman world and beyond. Among US Latine Christians, there is ambivalence toward the traumatic colonial past inherited from Spanish imperial dominance since 1492 and followed by centuries of Euro-American and Protestant supremacy. For Latine Christians, Spain's historical, religious, and cultural legacies bequeathed two enduring elements. The strongest is linguistic, the Spanish language. The second is the pervasive influence of Catholic traditions and practices. This is true whether a person or family arrived in the United States as Roman Catholics or as Protestants. And just as true if, after living here, they converted from Catholicism to Protestantism or from either one of these to Latine Pentecostalism. Given the cultural, intergenerational, political, and economic disruptions among many Latine family origin stories, the persistent affinity of the Pentecost narrative and its implications for social justice activism among US Latine Christians is understandable.

In her study of popular religiosity among Mexican-American descendants of Tejanos since the sixteenth century, the late Anita de Luna stated: "Spirituality is mediated through lived experience, and experience is contextualized in culture."[5] Thus, cultural hybridity, or the mixing of various ethnic elements to form new cultural identities and spiritual expressions, is also persistent across these social and religious landscapes. Until recently, such appraisals of Latine religious synthesis and spiritual diversity were not met with respect. In the nineteenth and twentieth centuries, books were published extolling the civilizing agenda of "the White Man's Burden" through the British Empire or the virtues of "the American mind" and Manifest Destiny. Such nationalistic and racialized works praised the achievements of Euro-Christian and Euro-American culture against those of the peoples and nations that emerged from the breakup of Spain's Empire. Often referred to as "mongrel nations," the ancestors of today's US Latine population were considered too racially mixed and denigrated as inferior to the North Atlantic, Western European, and Protestant peoples.

This style of social analysis was typified in the American anthropologist and eugenicist Madison Grant's book: *The Passing of the Great Race: Or the Racial Basis of European History* (1916). By stressing the superiority of the Nordic races and scientific racism, Grant's work influenced the Nazis and ideologies of white supremacy. Another example was French writer Frédéric Hoffet's *Protestant Imperialism* (1948), which romanticized the socio-political merits and rationalism of Northern European Protestantism against the political deficits and religious superstitions of Southern European Catholicism. Such an ideology belittles the cultural hybridity and lived-religious expressions of Latine Christianity.

However, recent Euro-Christian pneumatology is embracing the inherent experiential nature of Spirit and its natural hybridizing effects when operating in diverse cultural contexts. This reassessment has important implications for a more effective, holistic, and respectful understanding of US Latine Christianity as lived religion. The German Protestant theologian Jürgen Moltmann (1926–2024) wrote: "Whatever we may say in general about ourselves and other people in the light of eternity, the Spirit of life is present only as the Spirit of this or that particular life."[6] Building on his ideas, a further reassessment comes from today's most prolific writer about the Holy Spirit, the Finnish Lutheran theologian Veli-Matti Kärkkäinen. He suggests shifting away from the older "*unitive paradigm* in which only one Spirit (of God) is considered, while the rest of the spiritual realities are being dismissed, to a *plural paradigm*" that "accounts for the Spirit of God in a highly pluralistic cosmology with many spirits, powers, and spiritual realities. In the *plural cosmology*, the Spirit of God is also related to the (great and smaller) spirits of other religions."[7]

The US Latine Christian pneumatologies, with their local inflections and regional variations, contain many of these same cosmological and earth-based continuities and discontinuities "with many spirits, powers, and spiritual realities" from other religious traditions. Catholic theologian Orlando Espín's recent study about the Virgin of Guadalupe, *Pentecost at Tepeyac: Pneumatologies from the People*, reassess his earlier ideas about the Holy Spirit and cultural hybridity among Mexican and Mexican American religious expression marginalized by the dominant society. Espín's reappraisal of the "maternal" in US Latine Christian spirituality as lived religion is the conviction that "we can affirm that the *Virgen de Guadalupe* is a culturally authentic symbol expressing God's Holy Spirit, even if today there are many who are still not allowed (or are afraid) to use *Madre* to name the One who is one with the Father and the Son."[8] This not simply about devotion to Mary, as the Mother of Jesus, but a keen discernment of the Spirit's tendency to subvert dominant paradigms by transforming ethnic symbols and realities into new life-giving Latine Christian expressions.

Comprehending US Latine Christianity requires a humble acceptance of the pervasive influence the Holy Spirit wields on a person's religious identity in combination with other complementary spirits or *Santos* among the people. A wide-ranging study of common themes found among Latine Christians is Edwin David Aponte's, *¡Santo!:Varieties of Latino/a Spirituality,* which provides insightful descriptions of religious practices regarded as intimately sacred. Aponte surveys Latine multiple consciousness and cultural hybridity overlapping with wider theological inflections of the Holy Spirit. Looking beyond official forms of Christian doctrine, he reminds us that: "Although some concepts of *santo* have regional or ethnic roots as well as urban and rural manifestations, the growing national Latine 'cultural reality is such that these different understandings of *santo* extend beyond regional boundaries and are in contact with other traditions.' "[9]

It might be objected that claiming a particular US Latine Christian religious character regarding the Holy Spirit necessitates caution against slipping into romanticized or essentialist stereotypes about the presumed national, ethnic, racial, patriarchal, or spiritual characteristics of any particular group's religiosity. As shown previously, however, the intercultural comingling of the Holy Spirit and the story of Pentecost with particular local and ethnic spiritual expressions that transcend formal dogmas and doctrines is precisely a fundamental feature observed by theologians and scholars across the long history of Christianity, and this feature is particularly present in the cultural hybridity of US Latine Christianity.

Given this inherently experiential and contextual nature of the Holy Spirit, how can we more broadly characterize the activity of the Spirit across the multiplicity of lives that it touches? The rest of this chapter offers a framework first developed for understanding the Spirit's intercession in lived-religious contexts across global Christianity and then discusses several US Latine examples within this framework. Historically and theologically, the Holy Spirit's intercession exhibits four interrelated characteristics or predispositions inspiring revitalization and action. Each of these tendencies left its mark on all branches of Christianity as well as in the lived-religious experience of US Latine Christians.[10]

The first is a creative tension between remembrance (*anamnesis*) and forgetfulness (*amnesia*) in the people's relationship with God and Christ toward the *fullness of the Spirit*. This accounts for the many reform movements, revivals, and church revitalization efforts among historic and contemporary examples of Latine Christianity, such as the enormous growth of Latine Pentecostalism since the 1906 Azusa Street Revival in Los Angeles and the spread of Catholic Charismatic groups from the 1970s to the early 2000s advocating renewed devotion to the Sacred Heart of Jesus. This is what is meant by the *imagination of Pentecost* or by the high-voltage potentiality and outpourings of the Spirit during annual remembrances of Pentecost whenever the churches and the people are perceived as afflicted with spiritual amnesia.

Another example of this imaginative tendency in pneumatology is the story of Saint Ignatius of Loyola's (1491–1556) inspiration establishing the Jesuit Order. Before beginning his priestly studies, Ignatius was a knight seeking military honor and glory. While defending the city of Pamplona from an invading French army, he was severely wounded by a cannonball that nearly ripped off both his legs. The date was May 20, 1521. Providentially for him and his life's work, it was the day after Pentecost. During his convalescence, Ignatius read books about the saints and was inspired by Jesus' earthly life and relationship with God and the Holy Spirit. However, it was contemplation about Jesus' relationship with his mother, and a vision of the Virgin Mary in heavenly majesty with Jesus, which sparked his decision to abandon serving the state as a knight and dedicate his life and service to Christ and *Nuestra Señora* (Our Lady) by founding an order of spiritual knights, the Society of Jesus (the Jesuits). More about their influence on US Latine Christianity in a moment.

The second predisposition is the close association between the Holy Spirit and Nature throughout Christianity. We find this in St. Francis of Assisi's (1181–1226) devotion to Pentecost in the spring time of each year; in his reverence for animals, trees, and birds; and in his calls for stewardship of natural resources as the patron saint of ecology. We find it too in the Cuban comingling of West African Yoruba religious traditions with Roman Catholic saints known as Santeria. For example, as the god of wisdom and destiny among the pantheon of Seven African Powers, Orula is linked with St. Francis for their respective stewardship of plants and animals. Moreover, to the extent that Christian liturgical calendars are aligned with the earth's seasons, many localized feast days and venerations of the Virgin Mary recall earlier pre-Christian, indigenous traditions alongside remembrance of local saints and fertility rites as found in parts of New Mexico, Arizona, and southern Texas. Some of these commemorations, such as the Feast of Corpus Christi, or the Feast of Pentecost, originated from biblical sources inflected through Christian Spain or Latin America; and others have more localized origins encoded into the liturgical calendar.

The third tendency is the *subversive* function of Spirit-inspired movements and their advocates who challenge preconceived notions of authority, religious exclusivity, economic exploitation, and all forms of violence, oppression, and exclusion, including racialized and gendered discrimination. Closely related is the fourth and final pneumatological predisposition: the empowerment of individual believers for prophetic leadership, church revitalization, and social activism promoting the *fullness of the Spirit* for all peoples. These are the liberative ethics and prophetic leaders ignited by *the imagination of Pentecost* advocated in Luke's gospel: "The Spirit of the Lord is upon me, because he has anointed me to preach good news to the poor. He has sent me to proclaim release to the captives. And recovering of sight to the blind, to set at liberty those who are oppressed, to proclaim the acceptable year of the Lord" (4:18-19).

An example of these third and fourth tendencies is the ubiquitous link between contemporary US Latine Christians and the influence of Roman Catholic religious orders on spiritual formation and education. Founded in Europe between the Medieval and Reformation periods, clerics from these groups arrived with the Spanish conquistadors at the beginning of Euro-Christian colonization serving continuously as teachers, counselors, spiritual guides, and social activists across Latin America, the Caribbean, and the United States. The greatest impacts in US Latine contexts are the Franciscans, Augustinians, Dominicans, Jesuits, and Discalced Carmelites, especially with their respective teachings about the Holy Spirit and putting "contemplation into action" on behalf of the poor. Their social activism is not limited to Roman Catholic spaces because their respective institutions and community centers serve other Christian and non-Christian groups suffering economic necessity. As a result, across the inner cities and working-class neighborhoods of cities like New York, Philadelphia, Miami, Chicago, and Los Angeles, including the densely populated urban centers of Northern New Jersey, significant numbers of Latine immigrant children and teenagers (among them Protestants, Baptists, Evangelicals, Pentecostals, and increasing numbers of Latine Muslims) are influenced by the pneumatological piety, teachings, and charisms of these religious orders.

The most prolific contemporary scholar specializing in Christian history, Cuban-born theologian and historian Justo González, has written extensively about US Latine Christian expressions of the Holy Spirit and the meanings of Pentecost. González grew up in Cuba as a minority Protestant surrounded by a Roman Catholic majority. As an ordained United Methodist minister, he understands the Spirit's presence and agency not only on that first Pentecost but across the entire range of past, present, and future Christianities: "The basis for Christian spirituality is the Spirit, the Holy Spirit of God."[11]

González opens his two volume international bestseller, *The Story of Christianity*, by stating: "the theme of the book commonly called the Acts of the Apostles is not so much the deeds of the apostles, as the deeds of the Holy Spirit through the apostles (and others)." This account is thus "much more than the history of an institution or of a movement. It is a history of the deeds of the spirit in and through the men and women who have gone before them in the faith."[12] These "deeds" further exemplify the Spirit's subversive role moving faith into action in the sociopolitical arena.

González also edited the fourteen-volume, Spanish-language edition of Methodist founder John Wesley's collected works. It is worth noting, the reverence John Wesley (1703–1791), his brother Charles Wesley (1707–1788), and their English *familia* held for the Holy Spirit and Pentecost. Charles' conversion occurred on Pentecost Sunday, May 21, 1738, while John's famous "warmed heart" experience at Aldersgate Street in London happened three days later on Wednesday May 24, 1738. The Wesleyan movement they founded, with its emphasis on the Spirit's indwelling, the ideals of Methodist holiness and personal sanctification, and ministries of outreach and healing, was embraced by US Latine Christians in the mid-1800s; and is considered a precursor of twentieth-century Latine Pentecostalism.

From my social location as a first-generation Cuban-American, I offer this self-portrait as a closing example of US Latine lived-religion and identity formation regarding the Holy Spirit and cultural hybridity. In the aftermath of the 1959 Cuban Revolution, my parents and several extended family members came to the United States as political refugees. I was raised by my maternal grandmother, Abuela Maria, who was a feisty, self-determined Cuban *campesina* or *guajira* (peasant woman) with a fourth-grade education. Her ancestors were from Galicia in northern Spain; then immigrated to the Canary Islands; and then to Cuba after nearly starving to death in the Canaries. She was born a subject of the Spanish Empire and often told stories about violence committed against mixed-race Cubans born under colonial rule, against Indigenous Tainos and African slaves. She was living proof of the Latine ambivalence about Spanish colonialism and official Catholic doctrine discussed earlier. Her religious identity was a mixture of Roman Catholicism, African Cuban Santeria, and personal devotion to Jesus' mother, Mary, in her local Cuban form as *Nuestra Señora de Caridad del Cobre* (Our Lady of Charity of Copper, after the copper mines in Oriente Province). She practiced *curanderismo* in the styles of Santeria and Jesus' ministry of "sacred touch" through the Holy Spirit. She made medicinal elixirs from her cherished assortment of herbs and roots. She kept these traditions and practices very private, especially when interacting with clergy.

Growing up poor in small apartments necessitated lots of sharing, so Abuela Maria and I shared a bedroom together where we slept in two separate beds until her death when I was sixteen. The formation of my religious identity happened in that spiritual space. It was there that I first heard about the Santeria deities and *santos* and their connection to Roman Catholic figures and saints. It was there that I learned about the Holy Spirit and Pentecost. Although I received a Roman Catholic education, it was in that intimate space that I learned about healing and prayer; and about paying attention to the Spirit's mysterious presence in the winds and waters; about the spirits of Nature and the spirits of Santeria; and about noticing my dreams as nudges from the Holy Spirit.

Years later, upon learning about Wesleyan holiness relating to the Holy Spirit and Pentecost, I joined the Methodist Church but remained active in Catholicism with the Franciscans and the Jesuits. For a time, I was an administrator in an inner-city Catholic high school serving the urban poor in Paterson, New Jersey. The majority of students there were not Roman Catholic, but Latine or African American Protestants, Baptists, Pentecostals, and Latine Muslims. "From this perspective," as Edwin David Aponte states, "self-identified spiritual traditions and practices, can be seen as central to Latino/Hispanic worldviews and activity in the world as self-initiated agents of transformation and empowerment."[13]

Abuela Maria was my "live-in-minister" for as Kat Armas writes, "Abuelita theology stems from the reality that in Latine religious culture matriarchal figures such as abuelitas preserve and pass along religious traditions, beliefs, practices, and spirituality...but we continue in an ongoing and communal effort to critically discern aspects of our inherited traditions that have been colonized."[14] Such examples of complex Latine pneumatological interpretation and experience attest to the Holy Spirit's indwelling as a vital aspect of the Trinitarian God's spiritual embodiment in the human person. Thus connecting the Divine Spirit with the particular; the ancestral with the contemporary; and the mind with the heart. As embodied in Abuela Maria's earthy wisdom, and as stated in Moltmann's academic wisdom: "Therefore, the experience of the Holy Spirit is as specific as the living beings who experience the Spirit, and as varied as the living beings who experience the Spirit are varied."[15]

In conclusion, as lived-religion, US Latine Christian expressions of the Spirit are not just pluralistic syntheses of long forgotten ethnic practices or of colonized Spanish–American traditions. They are examples of a multiracial, multiethnic, and multigenerational cultural hybridity often overlooked and misunderstood in the racialized stereotypes of the dominant Euro-Christian and Anglo-American paradigms of superiority and exclusion. Furthermore, these continuities and discontinuities, yearning across the centuries for integration and belonging, are integral to understanding how the *fullness of the Holy Spirit* and the *imagination of Pentecost* animate US Latine Christian religious identity in contemporary hearts and minds and in the social contexts of *la familia* and *la comunidad.*

6

The Permeability of Worlds: The Role of Spirits in the Latine Religious Landscape

Elaine Penagos

What are the qualities and characteristics of spirits? What type of entities do our minds gravitate toward when we hear the word "spirits?" Within Latine religious worldviews, the concept of spirits is varied. For some, the singular "spirit" is shorthand for the Christian Holy Spirit. For others, spirit refers to some sort of unnamed, universal, sentient energy; an immaterial intelligence with the power to deliver messages to humanity and make itself and its will known. Yet, for many Latines, to think of "spirit" is to simply focus on a single entity within a larger configuration or pantheon of incorporeal beings. Spirits can refer to the animated souls of the dead; consciousnesses present in nature, objects, or specific locations; unembodied energies or vibrations; or to powerful ethereal beings with abilities to interact with humanity and, in some cases, manifest via bodily inhabitation. In short, the notion of spirits for Latines is far-reaching and encompasses a variety of metaphysical and ontological orientations.

The array of religious traditions practiced by Latines explains the various conceptions of spirits held by this ethnically and racially diverse group. With roots and routes stretching across numerous national origins and cultural traditions, spirits are necessarily border-crossers in the Latine worldview. Spirits are not confined by walls or geopolitical lines on a map; they are not hindered by immigration policies or border patrol agents. Spirits can also navigate between visible and invisible realms, often traversing from metaphysical to corporeal manifestations. Indeed, boundaries of any kind are porous and permeable, especially for the variety of spirits that dot the diverse religious landscape shaped by Latine communities in the United States. These varied religious practices extend beyond Catholicism and numerous other Christian denominations and fall into the camp of what Charles H. Long calls "extra-church orientations."[1]

The practice of African heritage religions and popular forms of Spiritism by Latines reveals an ongoing, perhaps unresolved entanglement between histories of colonization, oppression, enslavement, and ancestral traditions. Indeed, colonialism, various Christianities, and the transatlantic slave trade profoundly shaped the development of many African and Indigenous religious practices in the so-called New World. The forceful interactions between the Christianities of the fifteenth through nineteenth centuries and colonized and enslaved peoples' struggles for survival, freedom, and independence led to unique poetic strategies, often qualified as syncretism, that depended on a host of spirits and ritual practices. In this chapter, I explore three of the most well-known resulting religious systems: La Regla de Ocha, popularly called Santería; Reglas Congas, colloquially called Palo; and Espiritismo, a distinct Caribbean and Latin American expression of Kardecian Spiritism. Central to each of these traditions is a deep engagement with the invisible world, where metaphysical manifestations of a variety of entities dubbed "spirits" play crucial roles in the lives of practitioners.

Spirits in Santería, Palo, and Espiritismo profoundly shape the cosmological worldviews of Latines who practice these religions and even those who misconceive and warn against them. These beliefs contribute to an orientation in the world where the spiritual and material realms are interconnected and permeable. In Santería, the orishas are deities representing divine forces that govern the natural world and human affairs, while *egún* are ancestors that embody the wisdom and guidance of the past. Palo cosmology centers on the power of *nfumbe* and *kimpungulu*, spirits of the dead and nature, respectively, who can be engaged with for various purposes. Espiritismo posits a universe populated by spirits at different stages of evolution, with whom communication is possible for guidance and healing. Espiritismo also aligns with Indigenous-Latine beliefs about life after death and complements African heritage religions and other ancestor veneration traditions like Día de los Muertos.

In addition to the histories that contribute to and shape the practice of extrachurch traditions, the varied origins of the US Latine population suggest that how Santería, Palo, and Espiritismo are received and practiced can differ considerably among national, ethnic, and cultural subgroups. Given that Latines are not a monolith and that distinct national groups such as Cubans, Puerto Ricans, Mexicans, and Venezuelans possess their own unique histories and cultural traditions, the location-specific historical roots of Santería and Palo in Cuba, and Espiritismo in Europe, the Caribbean, and Latin America become particularly relevant. Santería and Palo, with their Afro-Cuban roots, are prevalent among Cuban Americans, but their practice has expanded to other Latine groups and even non-Latines in the United States. Espiritismo has a strong following among Puerto Ricans, Dominicans, Cubans, and Brazilians who each brought their unique traditions to the United States. Regional variations also exist in the United States, with cities like Miami and New York serving as major centers for practicing and adapting these Afro-Caribbean and Latin American religions. Consequently, Latines' adoption, adaptation, and practice of Santería, Palo, and Espiritismo are influenced by geography as well as their national origin, any preexisting spiritual beliefs they may hold, and even political, ethical, and racial identities.

It is also crucial to acknowledge the wide breadth of religious and spiritual beliefs within the Latine community, which extends beyond Santería, Palo, and Espiritismo—practices like Curanderismo, Vodou, and countless other spiritual healing modalities. Many people participate in multiple religious traditions, codeswitching between Santería, Palo, and Espiritismo with Catholicism or other Christian denominations depending on their particular needs. Engagement with spirits in many of these traditions is often related to health, well-being, and coping with life's challenges, with individuals seeking guidance and intervention from spiritual entities in matters of illness, relationships, and personal difficulties. Indeed, scholars of African heritage religions and other forms of popular religion assert the pedagogical and healing natures of these traditions.[2]

Belief in spirits provides a fundamental framework for understanding and interacting with the unseen world, offering Latines a sense of agency, control, and connection to ancestral and divine forces. Traditions such as Santería, Palo, and Espiritismo offer explanations for life's events and provide means to influence them through established relationships with spiritual entities. For immigrants navigating new environments and feelings of displacement, spirits can provide comfort, a sense of continuity with their cultural heritage, and a culturally congruent way to address problems when other resources might be limited or feel less relevant.

Santería

Santería traces its origins to West African Yoruba Orisha religion. It is a religion reshaped in Cuba by enslaved Africans during the island's colonial era due to the transatlantic slave trade. Under the oppressive conditions of bondage and Spanish colonialism, enslaved Africans and their descendants devised strategies to preserve their ancestral traditions. Through a process that Mercedes Cros Sandoval calls "logico-structural integration," the Yoruba associated their deities called orishas, with Roman Catholic saints, allowing them to continue their traditional practices under the guise of the religion of their oppressors.[3] However, prior to the arrival of significant numbers of captive Yoruba in the nineteenth century due to the collapse of the Oyo Empire, a substantial number of the enslaved Africans brought to Cuba were from the Kongo region of the continent. Cuban artist and Palo Monte initiate José Bedia believes that the Kongo peoples devised the "syncretic" associations between their African deities and Catholic saints in Cuba using their knowledge of medieval Catholicism. Bedia argues that it would have been impossible for the late-arriving Yoruba to develop a detailed system of associations/equivalents that would take such a stronghold within Cuban culture within the relatively short time between their enslaved arrival on the island and abolition. Given the reign of a Catholic king in the Kongo since 1491, Bedia's theory is highly plausible and substantiated by historian John Thornton, who argues in favor of the idea of "the syncretic nature of Christianity in Kongo."[4] Regardless of where precisely the associations between Catholic saints and African deities came from, clearly, the worldviews of Africans in Cuba drew on a detailed knowledge of Catholic aesthetics. Nonetheless, it is important to note that African knowledge of Catholic aesthetics includes both European Catholicism and African Catholicism, given the orthopraxic leeway that the Portuguese permitted in the Kongo. This knowledge enabled and undergirded the process of "logico-structural integration," which some refer to as syncretism.[5] Thus, religious borrowing and exchange processes facilitated the survival, growth, and expansion of Yoruba religious practices in the Caribbean and throughout the Americas.

Santeria's arrival and subsequent spread in the United States occurred largely through Cuban immigration, particularly after the Cuban Revolution, when a mass exodus of the island's population fled. Today, Afro-Cuban religions like Santería and Palo are practiced by individuals of various ethnic backgrounds in the United States. However, they often maintain a strong connection to the Afro-Cuban roots of these religions. Santería practice in the United States includes a range of rituals and ceremonies such as divination using the Ifá oracle to communicate with the orishas; offerings such as fruits, flowers, and sometimes animal sacrifices to feed the deities; initiations such as *kariocha* to activate the connection with a tutelary orisha, and ceremonies known as *bembes* or *toques de santo* involving drumming, singing, and dancing. The religion is typically organized around *ilés*, or religious houses, which are kinship-based communities led by experienced *santeros/babalochas* or *santeras/iyalochas* (priests), or *babalawos*, who specialize in Ifá divination.

In the United States, Santería has undergone certain adaptations, reflecting its practitioners' unique environments and experiences. For example, in the absence of easily accessible rivers in Miami, Florida, many practitioners are taken to canals used to mitigate flooding and divert water to and from the Everglades to begin their initiation process. *Botánicas*, shops selling religious articles, herbs, and candles, have become important community hubs in cities with significant Latine populations.[6] However, Santería has also faced legal challenges and public scrutiny in the United States, particularly concerning the practice of animal sacrifice, which is frequently misrepresented on television in police procedurals and other forms of popular culture and was notably addressed by the Supreme Court in the case *Church of the Lukumi Babalú Ayé v. City of Hialeah*.[7]

The survival strategy used by the earliest practitioners of Santería, in which enslaved Africans and their descendants in Cuba used Catholic elements to disguise the practice of their traditional religion, likely played a role in the religion's measured acceptance by the Latine community. When Santería was brought to the United States by Cuban immigrants, the associations between Yoruba orishas and Catholic saints facilitated understanding and perhaps even adoption by some Latines from other nationalities already familiar with Catholicism. However, the growing emphasis on "Yorubanization" within some Santería communities, similar to Yoruba revivalism among African Americans in the mid-twentieth century, indicates an ongoing negotiation and reevaluation of the religion's African origins and colonial history among its practitioners.[8]

Orishas

Among the core beliefs of Santería is the existence of a salient mystical power known as ashé. Practitioners believe that ashé is a divine force that permeates all of existence and is necessary to maintain balance in the world. The source of ashé is the supreme creator deity called Olodumare. In addition to Olodumare are Olorun and Olofi, two other aspects of the supreme being tasked with responsibility over the heavenly realm, the orishas, and earthly affairs, including humanity. Beneath the triune supreme deity is a pantheon of orishas who themselves are focused concentrations of Olodumare's ashé that govern different facets of nature and human life. Because Olodumare is a remote deity that does not interact directly with humanity, practitioners access ashé through a reciprocal relationship with the orishas.

The orishas are powerful supranatural beings associated with specific natural elements, human attributes, and dominions or spheres of influence. The total number of orishas in Africa prior to the transatlantic slave trade is unknown; estimates range from 401 to over 1,000. Of the innumerable orishas in pre-colonial West Africa, a relatively small number took hold in the Caribbean and Latin America.[9] While the orishas are not spirits in the sense of being metaphysical manifestations of the dead, they are sometimes considered spirits, similar to how practitioners of Haitian Vodou refer to their relationship with the *lwa*, the deities of that religion, as "serving the spirits."

The grouping of orishas collectively known as "*las siete potencias Africanas*," the seven African powers, is particularly popular among US practitioners, evidenced by the ease with which votive candles dedicated to them can be found in Latine grocery stores around the country.[10] These seven orishas are not only well-known but are also associated with Catholic saints that figure prominently in Latine religiosity. For instance, Elegguá is a trickster orisha who owns all roads and crossroads and is associated with St. Anthony and the Holy Infant of Atocha. Ogún is the orisha of iron, war, and endless work associated with St. Peter. Oshún, a fluvial orisha with dominion over fresh waters, often associated with love and sensuality, is affiliated with the Virgin of Charity. Yemayá is the orisha of universal motherhood and the sea and is associated with the Virgin of Rules. Shangó is another warring orisha with dominion over thunder and lightning and is affiliated with St. Barbara. Obatalá, the orisha of the white cloth and sculptor of the human form, is associated with the Virgin of Mercy. Finally, Orula is the orisha of divination, knowledge, and wisdom affiliated with St. Francis. The orishas' powers are vast and include providing protection and guidance to their devotees in times of need. Practitioners cultivate relationships with specific orishas through various means, including divination, where the messages of the orishas are interpreted; sacrifice, which involves offerings to appease and honor the deities; initiations, rituals for protection and of commitment to particular orishas; and manifestation, where practitioners may experience bodily inhabitation by an orisha during drumming ceremonies.

Egún

Beyond the orishas, Santería practitioners place great importance on *egún*, ancestral spirits that include deceased blood relatives and those connected through religious lineage. Similar to the orishas, *egún* offer advice, guidance, and even warnings. These spirits are intermediaries between the living and the invisible realm, and their approval is sought before major rituals or ceremonies. The popular phrase "*Iku lobi ocha*," roughly translated to "the dead give birth to the orisha," demonstrates the importance of *egún* in Santería. Practitioners utter this saying to signal the importance of the ancestors in all rituals, but especially *kariocha*, the initiation into the Santería priesthood. The spirits of the dead must be consulted and concur that everything is in place in both the invisible and the visible realms before a practitioner's seven-day initiation ceremony begins. In this way, the spirits of the dead are the ones who clear the way for the ashé of an orisha to be placed on the head of a practitioner through initiation and for a new orisha priest to be born.

Egún influence the lives of the living, and, therefore, must be acknowledged prior to any serious ritual undertaking. The *moyugba*, a prayer that invokes the names of a practitioner's *egún*—the deceased in their blood and religious families—is the most common way adherents honor and remember their ancestors. Recited at the beginning of all rituals, including divination sessions, the *moyugba* reaffirms links between a practitioner's past and present. Some Santería practitioners also participate in *misas espirituales,* spiritual seances, a ritual that connects practitioners of the Afro-Cuban religion to Espiritismo, to communicate directly with specific ancestral spirits to obtain their messages or address their needs.

Palo

Las Reglas Congas, known popularly as Palo, has its roots in the Kongo region of Central Africa and arrived in Cuba through the transatlantic slave trade, even earlier than the Yoruba traditions that formed the basis of Santería. This Afro-Cuban religion also has influences from Catholicism and Spiritism in varying degrees. Palo is divided into several distinct branches or *ramas*, including Briyumba, Kimbisa, Mayombe, and Monte, each with its own nuances in practices.[11] The spread of Palo within the Latine community has often occurred alongside or intertwined with Santería, particularly among Cuban and other Caribbean immigrants who seek the more immediate assistance of the dead. Palo practices revolve around the ritual object of the *nganga* or *prenda* and a practitioner's ability to communicate with and command the spirits within it. The *nganga* is a consecrated cauldron, clay pot, bag, or urn that typically contains different types of earth, sticks, and, significantly, human remains, along with other sacred objects.[12] Within the "spiritually-charged" *nganga,* a microcosm of the Palo world is represented, hosting a variety of spiritual entities related to ancestors and nature, such as animals, minerals, and plants.[13] Due to its misassociation with "dark magic," including practices that can be perceived as harmful and the use of human remains, Palo practitioners often operate with a high degree of secrecy, fueling negative perceptions and misunderstandings of the religion. As with Santería, *botánicas* are important sources for obtaining the necessary materials for Palo rituals.[14] While Palo is often linked with Santería, it possesses a distinct cosmological framework deeply rooted in Kongo traditions. This framework emphasizes a different relationship with spirits, particularly the *nfumbe,* spirits of the human dead residing in the *nganga,* and the potent forces of the natural world represented by the *kimpungulu,* Kongo-descended deities of the religion.[8] This distinctiveness offers Latines drawn to Palo's focus on ancestral power, protection, and direct engagement with the spirits of the dead, an alternative to the more broadly practiced Santería.

Nfumbe

The spirits of the dead are crucial to Palo. Central to Palo practice is the *nfumbe,* the spirit of the dead, who is sometimes an ancestor and resides within the *nganga.* According to Bárbaro Martínez-Ruiz, "the *nfumbe* organizes the other spirits [in the *nganga*] and enables the priest using the *prenda* to access its energy...Although only one spirit is the controlling force..., the others may be called upon as needed."[15] The *nfumbe* possesses considerable power and can offer protection, healing, and even cause harm. These spirits are directed and commanded by the palero/a or *tata/yaya,* gendered terms for Palo priests.

Kimpungulu

In addition to the *nfumbe,* Palo practitioners venerate the *kimpungulu,* Kongo deities known as *mpungu* in the singular. Palo practitioners engage with *mpungu* through offerings and reciprocal agreements and seek their assistance in various aspects of life. The *kimpungulu* are forces or energies of the natural world, similar to the orishas in Santería, and are akin to divinities. Many *kimpungulu* have associative relationships with orishas from Santería and Catholic saints, reflecting the co-informing nature of these traditions in the African diaspora. Examples of some *kimpungulu* include Lucero Mundo, the spirit of roads and travel associated with St. Anthony; Sarabanda, associated with metal and war is affiliated with St. Peter; Siete Rayos, representing lightning and fire is associated with St. Barbara; Madre Agua, the spirit of the seas associated with the Virgin of Rules; Mama Chola Wenge, associated with love and money and affiliated with the Virgin of Charity; and Pata Llaga, the spirit of diseases is associated with San Lázaro.

Espiritismo

Espiritismo, meaning "Spiritism" in Portuguese and Spanish, broadly refers to the belief that spirits of the deceased can influence human life. This tradition originated in nineteenth-century France with the ideas about Spiritism defined by Hippolyte Léon Denizard Rivail, a French pedagogue known as Allan Kardec. With the exchanges between Europe and its colonies, Kardec's ideas about spirits subsequently spread throughout Latin America and the Caribbean, influencing African diaspora religions and forming distinct modes of practice throughout the region. Espiritismo was introduced to the United States primarily by Latine immigrants in the early twentieth century, particularly Puerto Ricans and Cubans. However, some of the ideas espoused by *espiritistas* (practitioners or Espiritismo) were not novel in the United Statesand had been circulating since the mid-1800s, thanks to the development of Spiritualism by the Fox sisters in New York. In Cuba, several approaches to Espiritismo evolved, including scientific Espiritismo, which emphasizes the study of Kardec's writings; Espiritismo de cordón, an approach in which practitioners hold hands to form a figurative cord through which healing is effectuated; and Espiritismo cruzado, which blends African heritage and Spiritist elements.[16]

The tenets of Espiritismo include a belief in a supreme God, a spirit world inhabited by evolving discarnate entities, reincarnation as a process of spiritual growth, and communication between the living and the dead. Communication with spirits in Espiritismo occurs in various ways. Mediums, individuals with heightened sensitivity to the spirit world, play a central role in channeling messages and facilitating interaction. Dreams and intuition are also important avenues through which spirits can convey messages or offer guidance. Spiritual gatherings known as *misas espirituales* or séances provide a communal setting for connecting with spirits. Practitioners utilize tools such as the *mesa blanca* (a white-clothed table), candles representing spiritual light, glasses of water symbolizing clarity, incense or perfume for purification, and photographs or the personal belongings of spirit guides or deceased loved ones to create an environment conducive for spiritual connection. Spirit manifestation can also occur in Espiritismo, where a spirit temporarily inhabits the body of a medium to communicate directly with other practitioners.

Several practices are recognized across the various approaches to Espiritismo. Spiritual masses are held to communicate with spirits and receive their guidance. Many practitioners create home altars called *bóvedas* to honor ancestors and spirit guides and enhance communication with them. The term *bóveda*, unironically the

Spanish-language word for a burial vault or sepulcher, refers to an arrangement of glasses of water, typically on a small table, through which spirits are remembered and given offerings. *Bóvedas* often include photographs, statuettes of Catholic and folk saints, Indigenous figures, black baby dolls, and other figural representations that correlate with the identities of a given practitioner's spirit guides.

Spiritual cleansings, or *limpias/limpiezas*, are performed to remove negative energies and influences. Healing rituals are also a significant aspect of Espiritismo, often involving the channeling of spiritual energies in cordón-associated practices. As with Santería and Palo, *botánicas* also serve as vital community resources for Espiritismo practitioners, providing access to herbs, candles, and other essential items used in rituals. Differing from religions of African heritage, Espiritismo centers can often be found in some major cities throughout the United States, Latin America, and the Caribbean. These more institutionalized centers lend a certain amount of credence to Espiritismo that is often withheld from practices of African heritage. To be sure, Espiritismo rituals are also held in practitioners' homes. However, formalized centers for study and practice speak to a public tolerance toward Espiritismo practitioners that is a different reality than that experienced by those who adhere to Santería or Palo.

Espiritismo, with its focus on communication with spirits for guidance and healing, holds a significant place within the Latine community. This resonance can be attributed to the strong cultural values of family that are prevalent among Latines, which aligns with the emphasis on ancestor veneration in Espiritismo.[17] Furthermore, the accessibility of spiritual assistance through Espiritismo, occurring outside the confines of traditional church settings in homes, *botánicas*, or centers, makes it a more approachable and culturally congruent spiritual path for many Latines in the United States, particularly immigrants with varying documentation statuses, seeking support,guidance, and connection to their ancestors.

Espíritus de Luz and Muertos Oscuros

A key aspect of Espiritismo is the belief in spirits with differing levels of evolution and that less evolved spirits—or those clinging to the material world—can be helped up the spiritual ladder, sort of speak, by the living's interactions with them. According to Ennis Edmonds and Michelle Gonzalez, "Spirits exist in a hierarchy: the lower spirits remain attached to the material world, are ignorant, and try to do harm to human beings; the highest level of spirits, called *espíritus de luz* (spirits of light), protect humanity through their higher state of spiritual perfection."[18] These spirit guides are morally upright, evolved beings whose purpose is to assist the living from the invisible realm. *Espíritus de luz*, often ancestors or elevated spirits, provide protection, wisdom, and direction on one's spiritual path. There are various types of spirit guides, each with distinct areas of expertise or connection to the practitioner.

Conversely, lower spirits, sometimes referred to as *muertos oscuros* (literally, the dark dead) or *enviaciones* (spirits that are sent to do harm), are discarnate beings who offer little in terms of assistance or guidance and instead haunt or torment the living. Practitioners must work to either help these spirits move up the evolutionary spirit ladder by "giving light" to them, a term that refers to ushering spirits towards goodness often through the use of candles and prayers, or what anthropologist Diana Espírito Santo refers to as "ghostbusting," the removal or vanquishment of these negative entities from a person's life.[19] The belief in spirits such as *enviaciones* or *muertos oscuros* reflects the intersection between the abilities of the *nfumbe* in Palo and Espiritismo.[20]

Conclusion: The Enduring Role of Spirits in Latine Religious Life

The host of spirits in the religious practices discussed earlier help foster a strong sense of community among Latines through various forms of collective engagement. In Santería, *ilés* serve as extended religious families, and Palo communities often center around a particular *nganga* and the *palero/a* who cares for it. Espiritismo gatherings, such as *misas*, bring together like-minded believers for spiritual communion and support. Religious leaders, including *santeros/as*, *babalawos*, *paleros/as*, and *espiritistas*, play crucial roles in guiding practitioner communities, performing rituals, and offering spiritual counsel. Santería and Palo have demonstrated remarkable resilience in the face of stigma, misunderstanding, and even legal challenges within the United States. These traditions have continuously adapted and innovated, incorporating new elements and evolving in response to their practitioners' experiences and specific needs. Espiritismo, with its fluid and adaptable nature, has also found a significant place within the US Latine spiritual landscape, offering comfort, connection, and guidance to many. What these three religious traditions show is that spirit-based beliefs and practices are not static remnants of the past but dynamic forces that play a significant role in shaping identity, community, and resilience within complex and often challenging social environments.

The role of spirits is central to the religious thought and life of Latines. Santería, Palo, Espiritismo, and other extrachurch traditions offer a unique and fuller understanding of the invisible world. Spirits are not abstract concepts but are actively engaged with by practitioners seeking guidance, protection, healing, and connection to their ancestral and religious lineages. Spirits profoundly shape the religious imagination of Latines, influencing their cosmologies, practices, and approaches to life's challenges. The spirit world remains an active and dynamic presence in the religious landscape of Latine communities, and continues to evolve and adapt to the unique experiences and needs of its adherents within the confines of the United States.

7

Latine Curación

Damien Pascal Domenack

Latine communities in the United States often experience delayed care and health disparities due to various barriers in biomedical care. Multiple factors, such as mistrust in Western food systems and healthcare, influenced by socioeconomic differences, provider bias, limited interpretation services, cultural beliefs, and xenophobia, contribute to healthcare avoidance.[1] As a result, Latine communities rely on folk medicine alongside Western medicine to address gaps in care. Research shows that 70 percent of the US Latine population across all ages sought healthcare services from folk healers at least once between 2000 and 2020 for a wide range of physical, mental, and emotional illnesses. This chapter examines Latine healing practices in Pentecostalism's divine healing narratives, the folk medicine of *Curanderismo*, and Cuban *Santería Espiritismo*. It explores their approaches to wellness by highlighting how these methods fill the cosmological gaps left by Western healthcare and tracing the historical roots of their contemporary applications in the United States. For Latine Pentecostals, healing narratives become resounding testimonies that affirm the power of prayer and reorient believers to a new cosmological reality of being born again.

Divine Healing in Latine Pentecostalism

Latine Pentecostalism operates within a mixed demographic of intergenerational English and Spanish speakers, US and international-born members that face economic and cultural barriers to biomedical care. Built across generations of Latine believers, Latine Pentecostal healing ministries sustain a resourceful social landing pad for Latine communities in need and are the fastest-growing group of US evangelical Protestants. Pentecostalism is a Protestant movement within evangelical Christianity emphasizing "an active presence of the Holy Spirit in the lives of its adherents."[2] As of 2022, 15 percent of Latines self-identify as evangelical Protestants, the fastest-growing group of US evangelical Protestants.[3] What sets Pentecostalism apart from other mainline US Protestant denominations and Catholics is faith in divine healing, prophecy, and a second immersive baptism of the Holy Spirit. The largest Pentecostal denomination, Assemblies of God USA (AG), emphasizes that all ordained or licensed ministers must have experienced speaking in tongues as the initial evidence of baptism in the Holy Spirit. These experiences affirm Pentecostalism as a part of the early Apostolic lineage and tradition of divine healing.

The spirit-centered epistemology of divine healing and the movement that became Pentecostalism is based on scripture, the prophecy of an overflow of the Spirit before the *eschaton*, and reviving prayer as "a power, a force, an answer–sufficient to prove that Christ is a Savior of the body as well as the soul."[4] For the AG, the experiential blessing of divine healing is one of the nine gifts (*charisms*) of the Holy Spirit, which include words of knowledge, discerning spirits, words of wisdom, prophecy, faith, speaking in tongues, interpreting tongues, and miracles (Acts 2:38, 8:20, 10:45, 11:17). The gift of divine healing from physical, spiritual, mental, and emotional ailment is salvation and deliverance from demonic oppression through the atonement of Christ (Rom. 8:23). It includes redemption from sin, prosperity, abundance, wholeness, and reconciliation of relationships with the human and spiritual worlds.[5] Divine healing is administered by placing hands, Bibles, or handkerchiefs on the sick, anointing them with oil, and praying over their bodies while speaking in tongues. The Biblical foundation for divine healing is the Feast of Pentecost, fifty days after the resurrection of Jesus (Acts 2:1-31), in which the Holy Spirit filled the house and tongues of fire appeared over the Apostles' heads and began to speak various languages.[6] *Glossolalia*, or speaking in tongues, offers a vulnerable and embodied experience of sacred prayer articulated through divine communication.

From its inception in the United States, Pentecostal healing ministries have generated widespread reach through the accessibility and mobility of its oral liturgy and the integral discipleship of Spanish-speaking Latine migrant laity and clergy. During segregation in 1906, African American evangelist and student of Charles Parham, William J. Seymour, led the Azusa Street revival in downtown Los Angeles and the US Pentecostal movement. Seymour's healing ministry specified that "Medicine is for unbelievers. The acceptable remedy for the saints of God involved prayer and the anointing of the sick with oil, as detailed in James 5:14."[7] His message was largely embraced by a socially underserved, non-English-speaking Latine migrant labor force that faced economic, cultural, and structural barriers to institutional healthcare. The revival converted Catholic Latine families to lay ministry and dedicated their lives to service, "We want to be used for the salvation and healing of both soul and body. I am a witness of His wonderful promise and marvelous miracles by the Holy Ghost."[8] By 1909, Seymour ordained Latine ministers Abundio López and Juan Navarro Martínez, and together with lay ministers Rosa Lopez and Susie Villa Valdez went on to build Pentecostal mutual aid missions that functioned as spaces for community, belonging, and healing.[9] A decade later, future Latine AG leaders spread healing ministries throughout Mexico, Puerto Rico, Latin America, and abroad.

Latine Pentecostal healing ministries continue to be the main catalyst for conversion from Catholicism to Protestant Christianity. From 2017 through 2022, thirty migrant caravans journeyed from Central America to the Mexico–US border to seek refuge and asylum from violence, poverty, and political repression.[10] A testament to Latine healing ministries is that by 2022, about three in ten US Latine immigrants from Central America—31 percent—identify as evangelical Protestants, a higher percentage than the combined percentages of US Latine descendants from Puerto Rico (15 percent) and Mexico (12 percent).[11] For Latine migrants in the United States, the conversion experience serves as a process of acculturation that offers social belonging and the psychological space to share the complex trauma and hardships of migration. Latine converts gain a sense of belonging to the Apostolic lineage as brothers and sisters in Christ and to evangelical Protestant Christian society in the US Conversion is a radical reorientation to the world of both past and present and creates a temporal-spatial distancing as a marker of Pentecostal belonging.[12] This orientation often means rejecting relationships with nonbelievers, Catholic, and Indigenous material culture and language that inhibit Pentecostal spiritual empowerment and development. Healing narratives become testimonies of being born again and away from a lost and worldly past to a new life of daily prayer, Bible study and meditation, fasting, and discipleship classes. This transformative experience informs shared Latine healing narratives and testimonies of salvation and recovery from physical, spiritual, mental, and emotional traumas and illness.

Curanderismo

In 1848, eighty thousand people of Mexican, Central American, and Spanish descent from Mesoamerican communities (including Mayan, Toltec, Aztec, Zapotec, Mixtec, and Yaqui) became residents of new American territories following Mexico's cession of 55 percent of its prewar territory in the Treaty of Guadalupe Hidalgo.[13] Their embodied culture, worldviews, values, and centuries-long healing tradition of *Curanderismo* now resided under US governance, yet it was not the first time they encountered a disorienting reality. *Curanderismo* is a healing practice and product of sixteenth-century Spanish Catholic colonialization—the terms *curanderismo* and *curandero/a/e stem* from the Spanish verb *curar*, meaning to cure and heal. The amalgamation of peoples, philosophies, merged values, and religious and spiritual beliefs resulted in *mestizaje* and the syncretic process of merging Spanish Catholicism with Native and Indigenous worldviews. In coloniality, the Indigenous medicinal expertise, ritual practices, knowledge, and unifying worldview of the Nahua *tícitl*, the Huastec *ilalix*, the Tzeltal *h'lojel*, the tzotill *hill*, the Mayan *h-men*, and the Pokoman *ah cut* over became homogenized and referred to as folk healers or *curanderes*.[14] Contemporary curanderes reclaim the practice in the Mesoamerican episteme by invoking the pre-colonial pantheon and Aztec gods to allow for personal, historical, and collective healing that recognizes cultural woundedness.

Curanderismo encompasses a variety of healing and shamanistic practices that take a multidimensional approach to treating illness and disease. Multiple historical influences helped shape *curanderismo,* yet its basic principles, ritual practices, and cosmological framework derived from the Indigenous peoples of the Americas. *Curanderes* are called by their ancestors to follow a spiritual healing path and apprentice their elders for decades until they are given the title by the community they serve. As traditional healers who provide plant-based folk medicine, care, and support for Mexican Americans, Latines, and Indigenous peoples of Mesoamerica and Latin America they are considered a "*med-dica* in the classic sense of one who knows how to manifest the measure (med) suitable to restore a multidimensional equilibrium."[15] Healing implies the restoration of wholeness through a balanced relationship with the self (physical, spiritual, emotional, psychological, and environmental). By the eighteenth century, plant-based ethnomedicine and cures from European medicinal herbs became standardized home remedies when Jesuit lay missionary Juan de Esteyneffer published his three-volume work *Florilegio Medicinal.*[16] While folk medicine is generally thought to be an exclusive practice of less educated people, current research trends indicate that *curanderismo* is practiced and sought out across all economic, social, and ethnic groups that use a combination of folk medicine and Western medicine.[17]

Today, *curanderismo* is widely known as a synergetic practice that integrates healing, divination, shamanic journeying, root medicine, soul retrieval, spirit repair, physical healing, medicinal plants, and herbs to treat physiological, psychological, spiritual, relational, or environmental disharmonies. Curanderes specialize in improving the health of their clients with plant-based folk medicine as *sobadores*, *yerberos/hierberos*, *ensalmador*, *hueseros*, *parteras*, and *espiritistas.*[18] *Sobadores* administer massage therapy to treat *empacho*, indigestion, constipation, and digestive issues, whereas *hueseros* are physiotherapists who reset dislocated or broken bones and address sprains and pulled muscles. *Ensalmadores* are folk Reiki healers and *yerberos/hierberos* or herbalists prescribe medicinal herbs, teas, and baths to improve physical and mental health illness. *Parteras* function as doulas and *espiritistas* or spiritists apply Catholic, spiritism, and ancestral veneration rituals for *limpias* or spiritual cleansing rituals, spirit mending, and soul retrieval. *Curanderes* are known for treating everyday illnesses: *mal de ojo* (evil eye); *susto* (trauma, fright, or spirit loss); *nervios* (panic attacks); *caida de mollera* (fallen fontanel); *empacho* (indigestion); *mal aire* (upper respiratory illness and colds); *desasombro* (higher grade of *susto* or spirit loss); *cólico* (colic); *espanto* (the most severe form of spirit loss); *bilis* (excessive bile); *muina* (anger sickness); *latido* (palpitations or throb); *nervios* (panic attacks); *embrujado* (being hexed); *envidia* (envy); and *mal puesto* or *maleficio* (a physical disorder caused by envy).[19] These definitions are useful for understanding the significant psychospiritual role *curanderes* play in filling the gap in health services in Latine communities in the United States.

For *curanderes* who situate their healing practice within folk Catholicism, dualism and equilibrium is also a prevalent biblical theme of light/darkness, good and evil, health and illness, and life and death.[20] When the most popular *curanderes* of the early twentieth century, Teresita Urrea, Don Pedrito Jaramillo, and Niño Fidencio transitioned to the spirit world, their followers began to venerate them as folk saints and called upon their blessings for healing. However, unlike Juan Diego Cuauhtlatoatzin and La Virgen de Guadalupe's image on his *tilmàtli* (Nahua cloak) are both canonized by the Catholic church, these *curanderes* are not recognized or canonized by the Catholic Church. At the time, psychic healing and European spiritism, especially the works of its French founder H. Leon Denizard Rivail, who wrote under the pen name Allan Kardec influenced Mexican American communities to build spiritual temples as healing centers for rituals, prayers, and incantations.[21] Spiritism emphasizes a theory of multiple souls in which an individual spirit afterlife can reside in the spiritual realm/invisible world and be reborn after death. *Curandere* spiritists engage with spirits of the dead through séances and often function as spirit mediums to communicate information and guidance for those seeking messages from individuals, ancestors, Saints, or spiritual guides. Followers of Niño Fidencio or *Fidencistas* built temples in the United States to form a link of communication with el Niño through entranced mediums that invited the spirit of el Niño to descend upon them to offer cures like protection, guidance, and perform *limpias* or spiritual cleansing, *despojos* or dispossession of negative energy by connecting the material and spiritual realm.[22] Moreover, the Kardecian spiritual system provides a structure to affirm a *curandere's* spiritual development by facilitating ancestral connections and energetic prescriptions that reinforce core beliefs about spiritual presence and ancestral guidance.

Cuban Espiritismo

Kardecian Spiritism is also a core component for Latine *espiritisas* in Cuban Santería and Palo Monte. *Espritismo* provides access to spiritual integration by inviting protective and elevated energies of ancestral and guardian spirits to offer information and guidance for spiritual balance. *Espritistas* or practitioners provide economically accessible therapeutic services like spiritual consultations, card readings, and divination in *botánicas*, or spiritual pharmacies, where practitioners play a dual role as religious leaders and spiritual advisers. *Botánicas* are generally owned and operated by practitioners of Afro-diasporic religions who import and sell material specialty spiritual goods to fellow practitioners and clients. In 1942, Botanical Gardens became the first documented *botánica* in New York City by Cuban pharmacist and ethnographer Rómulo Lachatañeré.[23] These *farmacias invisibles* or invisible pharmacies cater to a Latine population, often uninsured and undocumented, who seek healing herbal remedies and effective spiritual solutions to a wide range of problems. *Espiritisas* that practice within the Cuban Santería religion have an African Indigenous cosmological perspective that understands the universe as a fluid, active, and impressionable space, with agents from the visible (living) and invisible (spiritual) realms working together toward balance and spiritual harmony.[24]

The ancestral veneration practices of Cuban *Santería espiritistas* are composed of creolized elements from West African Yoruba Egungun, folk Catholicism, Central African Kongolese Palo Monte, and European Kardecian Spiritism practices of the Caribbean.[25]Throughout the eighteenth and into the twentieth century, Afro-Latine communities in the Caribbean and Latin America developed Afro-diasporic spiritual practices through a process of syncretism between African and Indigenous traditions and Catholicism. These spiritual practices derive from enslaved and creolized Yoruba, Igbo, Kongo, Ewe, Fon, and other West and Central African groups that were housed by Spanish colonialists without regard to differences in language, culture, or spiritual practice. The broad similarities between Catholic saints and sub-Saharan traditional deities/gods served as the connective fabric that wove polytheistic African belief systems with Catholicism.

By the late nineteenth century, Cuban *Cabildos* were registered as African mutual aid networks of religious and linguistic preservation that supported creating social, economic, and political outcomes for the benefit of African descendants.[26] Soon after, Kardecian Spiritism arrived through the European-educated Cuban elites who read his writings and were soon embraced by the masses. Kardec systemized a hierarchy of spirits, where lower spirits are linked to the material world and may influence humans, while higher-level spirits, known as *espíritus de luz* (spirits of light), exist in a state of spiritual perfection and protect humans.[27]At the turn of the century, civic scrutiny dismantled Cabildo networks and led African religious leaders to establish new institutionalized *Casas de Ocha* and Black Atlantic religions. During this period, the arrival of eminent Yoruba priests, including Mama Monserrate, Octavio Sama, Timotea Albear, and Ferminita Gomez, marked the culmination of the Black Atlantic episteme in Cuba. In 1954, Lydia Cabrera published *El Monte*, an encyclopedia of Afro-Atlantic healing rituals and herb remedies, a decade of ethnographic field research on Black Atlantic herbalism and medicine. Cabrera documented over five hundred creolized Yoruba and Kongo herbal remedies according to the spirits that oversee their healing powers in Afro-Cuban terms to represent the oral traditions of African-diasporic religions in their Cuban context.[28] For Afro-Cuban religion practitioners, *El Monte* served as a guide and handbook for Black Atlantic medicine and worked with an adapted version of Kardecian Spiritism for mediumship development as *Espritismo Crusado* or mixed spiritism alongside Santería and Kongo-based Palo Monte.

In pre-colonial times, the Yoruba would bury their deceased beneath the family home and build a shrine above the burial site for loved ones to pay their respects today, a corner of an area in the home is designated to serve as an ancestral altar known as an *egun* shrine.[29] A consecrated *Opa Egun* or Egun staff is utilized to call in ancestral guides and sits at the shrine. The staff is decorated with nine colorful ribbons and bells to represent the costumes of *Egungun* masquerades, along with glasses of water, cigars, food offerings, photos of ancestors, images of spiritual guides, and candles.[30]

Santería's espritismo crusado or mixed method adapted Kardec's white table ritual to a *bóveda* or home shrine, where an odd number of glasses of water, a white candle, and a rosary and cross are placed on top of a white tablecloth to create a ritual site for communication with the invisible world.[31]

Espiritistas begin their spiritual work or consultations by cleansing themselves with a *baño*, a mixture of Holy water, flowers or herbs, colognes, and Florida water, before reciting prayers from Kardec's *Collection of Selected Prayers* to mediate messages from the spirit guides and ancestors of their clients. *Espiritistas* view individual symptoms as spiritual imbalances caused by disruptions in the client's social and spiritual world, often triggered by negative energies in the environment. The terms *trabajo* and *obra* refer to spiritual work, while *limpieza, rompimiento,* and *despojo* are often used interchangeably to describe the cleaning, breaking, and clearing of negative spiritual or psychic energy. *Espiritistas* use two types of herbs: sweet herbs to attract positivity and balance and bitter herbs to protect against imbalance and repel negativity. The most common therapeutic practices from consultations and invocations relate to client spiritual maintenance and are addressed through at-home prayer practice with *belóns* or spiritual candles and sweet or bitter botanical baths. For *espiritistas,* the healing process is facilitated and sustained through a relationship with the invisible world that guides the spiritual work of balancing spiritual, physical, mental, and environmental energies.

Conclusion

Latine communities in the United States are inherently diverse, and healing is a complex process shaped by the dynamic interplay between Western institutional medicine and traditional folk medicine. While approaches to health and wellness vary, from Pentecostal healing testimonies of belonging to the reclamation and integration of embodied ancestral guidance and the wisdom of Indigenous and African folk medicine, these healing traditions center relational mutual aid networks of care. Healthcare providers are increasingly recognizing and incorporating the therapeutic benefits of spiritual care and traditional folk medicine into their practices within Latine healthcare. This integration has the potential to enhance the well-being of Latine communities, moving beyond basic survival toward collective flourishing.

8

Disabilities

Rudolph P. Reyes II

Arnaldo Rios Soto, a Latino Autistic man, walks away from his group home in North Miami. He sits in the street and plays with a toy truck. A passerby mistakes this toy truck for a gun and calls the police. Charles Kinsey, an African American man and Soto's behavioral therapist, approaches Soto to get him off the street. Shortly after, the police arrive. They position themselves behind telephone poles with M4 rifles. Kinsey lies down with his hands up, trying to get Soto to do the same. Kinsey tells police that he is Soto's behavioral therapist and that Soto only has a toy truck. Police shoot three rounds at Soto but hit Kinsey instead, wounding him. This shooting occurs at the intersection of racism and ableism.

Disability is often treated as a personal tragedy. When disability is individualized, it obscures the marginalization of disabled people. Disabled Latines experience higher rates of marginalization than their non-disabled Latine peers. Disabled Latines have a higher rate of poverty than non-disabled Latines.[1] In education, only 10 percent of disabled Latines have a Bachelor's degree compared to 17 percent of non-disabled Latines.[2] The rate of violence against disabled Latines is triple that of their non-disabled peers.[3] Disabled Latines are overrepresented in the US prison system, where they account for half of the Latine population in state and federal prisons.[4] These statistics are not aimed at downplaying the marginalization that all Latines face but rather to point out that the invisibility of disability prevents understanding and combating the full scope of Latine marginalization. This chapter explores the intersection of disability studies and Latine spirituality by examining how models of disability contribute to the invisibility of disabled Latines and provide a lens for combating this invisibility.

Critical Disability Studies and Latine Spirituality

Critical disability studies and Latine spirituality are linked in the pursuit of justice. As disability scholar Julie Avril Minich argues, critical disability studies is an approach that "involves scrutinizing not bodily or mental impairments but the social norms that define particular attributes as impairments, as well as the social conditions that concentrate stigmatized attributes in particular populations."[5] For Minich, this approach recognizes that not everything written about disabled people counts as disability studies. While some activists' movements do not name or claim disability, they are engaging in critical disability approaches.[6] This approach, as disability scholar Dan Goodley writes, starts "with disability [but] it never ends with it, remaining ever vigilant of political, ontological and theoretical complexity."[7] Critical disability studies place disability into a broader matrix of social identities.

Disability justice is central to this perspective. Disability justice, as critical disability studies scholar Mia Mingus writes, involves

> moving away from an equality-based model of sameness and "we are just like you" to a model of disability that embraces difference, confronts privilege and challenges what is considered "normal" on every front. We don't want to simply join the ranks of the privileged; we want to dismantle those ranks and the systems that maintain them.[8]

Disability justice seeks justice for disabled people as disabled people and their myriad complexities. When disability justice is placed within a broader context, the link between disability and racial justice is inextricable.

Disability justice offers a connection between critical disability studies and Latine spirituality. Spirituality, as Latino ethicist Christopher D. Tirres argues, is a way of actively engaging with a quality of human experience that is oriented to an ultimate concern.[9] In this way, spirituality is not a separate type of experience nor is it tied to a religious tradition. Furthermore, Tirres defines liberating spiritualities as "one in which this consistent and habitual pattern of living incorporates a *critical consciousness* and measures ultimate concern in terms of *redressing oppressive situations* and *promoting human flourishing*."[10] This expansive definition of spirituality and liberating spirituality provides the means to understand redressing the oppressive situation of racialized ableism and promoting the flourishing of disabled Latines as deeply spiritual. Liberating spirituality acts as an aid in understanding the work to combat racialized ableism and the invisibility of disabled Latines as spiritual praxis.

This chapter provides an orientation to connect disability studies and Latine spirituality in spiritual praxis. This praxis acknowledges the invisibility of Latines and the challenge of combating racialized ableism in pursuit of human flourishing. Models of disability provide a means of understanding the invisibility (individual models) and combating it (social models) as a spiritual praxis.

Individual Models of Disability

Disability is often viewed as a natural category, but it is, in fact, a social construction. There is a diversity in human embodiment. Disability is frequently used to categorize certain forms of embodiment. How disability is defined and valued, as well as which bodily diversity is classified as a disability, is constructed within specific times and places. There are various approaches to disability. Disability studies frame these approaches as models of disability. Models of disability serve as heuristics and keys for discerning different approaches and interventions to disability that operate within societies.[11] While these models are analytically distinct, in practice, people often combine models in their approach to disability or employ specific models for particular disabilities or categories of disabilities. For example, a person may view a mobility impairment through the medical model but depression through the religious model. The models covered here are not comprehensive but selected to highlight approaches to disability that make the marginalization of disabled Latines invisible.

Disability as Spiritual Condition (Religious Model)

Religion can either hinder or aid human flourishing. Religion hinders human flourishing when disability is viewed through the lens of the religious model. In the religious model, disability is associated with a spiritual state that necessitates religious intervention. This model is often called the moral model of disability; however, it is important to separate the religious model from other forms of moralizing disability due to the distinctiveness of religion as an area of study.

This view takes parental blame or the individual's moral failure as responsible for disability. The religious model operates in the exchange between Jesus and the disciples in the Gospel of John. The disciples ask Jesus, "Rabbi, who sinned, this man or his parents, that he was born blind?" (Jn 9:2). For the disciples, the man's blindness is the result of sinfulness. Jesus replies to the disciples: "Neither this man nor his parents sinned; he was born blind so that God's works might be revealed in him" (Jn 9:3). The disciples understand disability through this religious model, where blindness is viewed as a consequence of sin.

This moralizing of disability is present within Latine culture. Latine parents of Autistic children report encountering these cultural attitudes when discussing the relationship between disability and religion, specifically, cultural blame for parents, where disabled children are a "negative sign from God."[12] One mother remarked: "Many people think that it's the mother's fault ...I say this because I know people from my culture [who believe this]. I respect my family, but they don't know about what this [having a child with a disability] is like."[13] Religious theories about the origin of disabilities have a stigmatizing effect and blame disabled people and their families for their disability.

Regardless of the cause of disability, there is an expectation that a disabled person wants healing. Amy Kenny notes that the disabled body in religious spaces is often viewed as an invitation for strangers to approach a disabled person for prayers of healing.[14] If a person is not healed, one response is to attribute the lack of healing to their lack of faith in God to heal them. Another is to view disability as a test of their faith in God. Like religious theories of the source of disability, the act of healing or absence is viewed as residing in the individual.

Last, disability is viewed as closer to the sacred. This closeness can be positive or negative. Disability can be associated with mysticism, where a disabled person has a connection with the holy because of their disability.[15] Similarly, disabilities can be associated with malevolent forces. These versions of the religious model not only cause stigma and harm to disable people but can also have deadly consequences. An eight-year-old autistic boy died when a church performed an exorcism to cure him of his Autistic.[16] When disability is closeness to the sacred, disabled people become religious objects for others to exercise their religious beliefs.

All these notions hold in common that disability is the result of a spiritual condition—sin, closeness to God, testing of faith, lacking faith, or malevolent forces. The intervention becomes spiritual, involving repentance, seeking forgiveness, exorcism, or belief in healing. The accumulated result of the religious model is to hinder disabled human flourishing and obscure their marginalization.

Disability as Unfitness (Eugenics Model)

The eugenics model of disability defines disability as unfitness.[17] The origins of this model date back to the nineteenth century, with the emergence of the Eugenics movement, which sought to control populations. The Eugenics movement created a binary between "the fit" and "unfit," with disabled people, people of color, LGBTQ people, and others as being "unfit." "Fit" or "unfitness" was understood as individual and hereditary.[18] Therefore, the eugenicist model used interventions to promote birthrates among "the fit" and eliminate "the unfit." Two methods of the latter were controlling immigration and forced sterilization.

Latines, both disabled and non-disabled, were targets of eugenicist measures. Eugenists used immigration laws and enforcement to prevent people of Latin American descent from entering the United States. The 1882 US Immigration Act excluded disabled people from migrating to the United States and was expanded in 1891 to include those "*likely* to become a public charge."[19] Immigration officials used disability and disease to prevent migrants from entering the country, whether or not an immigrant was disabled. Between 1882 and 1924, Mexican immigrants were able to cross the US–Mexico border more freely because they were primarily seen as manual laborers. Concern over Mexican immigrants shifted in 1924. The Immigration Act of 1924 greatly restricted immigration from Europe and Asia but did not impose quotas on immigration from the Western Hemisphere. As Natalia Molina writes, "With the cessation of the flow of southern and eastern European immigrants, brownness came to signify the most important new threat to the racial hegemony of white native-born Americans."[20]

It was medicalized nativism, Molina notes, that targeted Mexicans as carriers of the disease to enact quotas.[21] Eugenicists restricted those who they deemed "unfit" from entering the country by banning disabled immigrants and associating immigrants and minoritized populations with illness and disability.

Force sterilization was another tool for eugenicist. In 1927, the US Supreme Court, in *Buck v. Bell,* ruled that state programs of forced sterilization were constitutional. The state of California had one of the most active eugenics programs in the United States; where from the 1920s to 1950s, the state sterilized 20,000 people, accounting for a third of forced sterilizations in the country.[22] The California program targeted people who were deemed "unfit," people categorized as having "feeble-mindedness." While this term was used "to describe the same symptom complex of low IQ score, economic status, and social deviance," it was "much more reflective of the ableism, racism, sexism, and classism of the time than the disability status of the person in question."[23] In California, "feeblemindedness" was used to justify the institutionalization and forced sterilization of Latines, primarily made up of Mexican and Mexican Americans. Latino men had a 23 percent greater risk of sterilization, and Latinas had a higher risk of 59 percent than their non-Latine peers.[24] As Natalie Lira writes, "disability in the form of feeblemindedness legitimized subjective judgements about Mexican-origin youth as racially and socially inferior, and justified violating the bodily and reproductive autonomy."[25] Eugenicists target Latines by labeling them disabled to reduce the Latine population in the country.

This dark history of eugenics continues to haunt the present. The racialized ableist construction of Latine inferiority led to the disavowal of disability by Latine combating anti-Latine racism. This disavowal only serves to uphold ableist values and obscure the marginalization of disabled Latines.

Disability as Medical Condition (Medical Model)

The medical model of disability defines disability as a medical condition. Disability, in this model, is an impairment or loss of functioning compared to a "normal" body. The medical intervention then is to restore the person to "normal" functioning or as close as possible. The notion of "normal" did not emerge until the 1830s.[26] This model operates out of normalization by "attempting to modify, repair, or relocate individuals with disabilities until they are congruent with societal expectations of normalcy and acceptability."[27] This medical model is not simply about the use of medicine but rather a model that focuses on maintaining dominant notions of embodiment. Like the religious model, which is not merely a religious perspective on disability but moralizing informed by religion, the medical model is not the use of medicine but rather the use of medicine to normalize embodiment through the elimination of disability.

For example, the Trump Administration exemplified the medical model with efforts to transfer the oversight of special education from the US Department of Education to the US Department of Health and Human Services (HHS). The Office for Special

Education Programs (OSEP) supports states and school districts to comply with IDEA, the Individuals with Disability Education Act. IDEA is a civil rights act that mandates that disabled students have the same education as their non-disabled peers. If disability is only a medical condition, it would make sense for OSEP to fall under HHS. However, OSEP oversees disabled students' rights to free and less restrictive education, not the medical needs of disabled students. This move further marginalize disabled Latine students who often do receive special education services they qualify for.

The medical model is used in instances of prophetic temptation. The prophetic temptation is the temptation to sacrifice marginalized members of one's own community and other marginalized communities to achieve justice for one's own community. The prophetic model leverages a shared dominance because of its explanatory power and political expediency.[28] This prophetic temptation is exercised in the fight for racial justice when deploying ableist values to raise consciousness or make arguments for combating injustice. For example, efforts to raise awareness of environmental racism by focusing on the cause of impairment risk making disability itself an injustice rather than the violence itself. This use of disabled Latines makes them hypervisible while making their marginalization invisible.

These models fall under the umbrella of individualizing models. While different in many respects, they share that disability solely resides in the individual. In all these models, but one possible instance, the goal of these models is to eliminate disability through religion, state, or medical intervention. These models make disability invisible, stigmatize it, and prevent a better understanding of disabled Latines marginalization.

Social Model

The social model emerged out of the disability rights movement and disability studies. Disability activists' critique individual models for conceptualizing disability as a personal tragedy or a fate worse than death. The social model shifts the locus of disability from the individual to society. Various other emancipatory models oppose individual models of disability.[29] The insights of these other models augment the social model presented here. The social model allows for the recognition of the marginalization of disabled people and the ways it intersects with different forms of oppression like anti-Latine racism, xenophobia, and nativism.

The social model makes a pragmatic distinction between disability and impairment. *Disability* is a positive political identity for individuals who experience social barriers due to embodied differences. *Impairment* refers to limits in functioning due to embodied differences. *Ableism* refers to the oppression of disabled people. Disability is a positive political identity. As a political identity, it is confessional. Disability scholar Mia Mingus makes the helpful distinction between being descriptively disabled and politically disabled. *Descriptively disabled* for Mingus is "someone who has the lived experience of being disabled,."[30] while *politically disabled* is "someone who is descriptively disabled but also has a political understanding about that lived experience."[31] This political understanding is a commitment to disability liberation. There are several barriers for Latines who are descriptively disabled to identify as politically disabled. The stigmatization of disability is amplified for Latines as they encounter a double stigma. There is a lack of resources for understanding disability within Latine cultural contexts and an erasure of Latine's role within disability activism.

Disability is a coalitional identity with many disability communities. There are distinctive disability communities. These communities include different disability groups, such as Deaf, chronically ill, neurodivergent, and Mad, as well as other orientations to disability culture. Disability is coalitional in that disability identity emerged as an umbrella term for those with embodied differences or limits. While not all those within these disability communities understand themselves as disabled, they fall under the disability umbrella.

This pragmatic distinction between disability and impairment needs to be teased out to avoid several pitfalls in understanding the aims of disability liberation.[32] Disability and impairment are historically and culturally constructed. As noted in the previous section, disability is socially constructed. Equally, impairment is socially constructed. Impairment is an embodied limit. The naming of these limits is value neutral and informed by Debbie Creamer's limits model of disability. All humans have limits. Creamer uses the example of flying. Humans cannot fly, which is an embodied limit. To use the definition of impairment above, the human embodied limit, which cannot fly, is not considered an impairment because this limit is not viewed as a limit according to normative views of human embodiment.[33] Therefore, impairment is not all human limits but those culturally defined. Recognizing disability and impairment as socially constructed avoids mapping on a natural/constructed distinction into impairment/disability with disability as culturally constructed but impairment as natural.

Another pitfall is associating a totalizing understanding of impairment. Not all disabled people understand their disability as an impairment. Some neurodivergent individuals may not perceive their embodied differences as a limitation or impairment. Nevertheless, they are marginalized due to their embodied differences. Similarly, some disabled people experience their embodied limit as painful. Those with chronic illness provide a more nuanced understanding of medical intervention and resisting ableism. As feminist disability philosopher Susan Wendell writes, some with chronic illness "very much want to have their bodies cured, not as a substitute for curing ableism, but in addition to it."[34] People can have different relationships to their embodiment, but they may still experience ableism due to social structures and systems.

The social model reverses the traditional approach to disability intervention. The problem is not located in embodiment but in a society that oppresses disabled people. Racialized ableism is a system of power that oppresses disabled Latines and other people of color. This system of power results in a higher poverty rate, lower education attainment, greater risk of victimization, and overrepresentation in prisons for disabled Latines. The social model shifts the focus to disability liberation from an ableist society.

This shift of focus allows for a connection with liberating spirituality. Latine spirituality operates in the religious model as a moralizing and stigmatizing force. However, a liberating Latin spirituality can aid human flourishing through spiritual praxis. Critical disability studies provide the avenue to raise one's critical consciousness of the invisibility of disabled Latines to redress the oppressive situation of racialized ableism to promote human flourishing. This liberating spirituality is intentionally discussed at the level of human spirituality without the grammar of a specific Latine religious tradition. Latine spirituality can take many forms, including both theistic and nontheistic expressions. Focusing on the level of human spirituality reveals that spiritual praxis against racialized ableism extends beyond any one religious tradition and those traditions that do not choose to employ religious language.

9

An Overview of Select Latin American Marian Devotions in the United States

Sudabée Lotfian-Mena and Neomi De Anda

This chapter provides a very basic overview of a few Marian images[1] with their devotional history followed by a brief discussion of marianismo as a concept that affects Latine peoples culturally in daily life.[2] The following snippets on Marian scholarship in the United States of America come after years of research by many people. This first part of this chapter grew out of a project that was originally modeled after *Pokémon Go!*, a mobile smartphone game that fuses the virtual and the real-world experience through a sort of scavenger hunt for fantasy creatures. But instead of Pokémon, our project was focused on Mary in the real-world of everyday religion, popular devotions, and culture. The original version of this interactive tool was a collaboration of almost eighty people.[3] The authors have chosen to highlight only a few of the Marian images which members of the Latine communities may have connections and devotions. Attention to an image from each country of America Latina would take much more space than the parameters of this volume permits. The images chosen have to do with the largest populations in the United States as well as the levels of expertise of the authors.[4]

Nuestra Señora de Guadalupe: México

On December 9, 1531, ten years after the Spanish Conquest of Tenochtitlan (the capital of the Azteca empire), Nuestra Señora de Guadalupe appeared to Juan Diego

Cuauhtlatoatzin (1474–1548) on a hill in north of Mexico City called Tepeyac. Speaking the indigenous language Nahuatl with the newly baptized Juan Diego, it is reported that Mary requested a church be built for her upon that spot. Some sources say she appeared three times, others four.[5] Whatever the case, the Archbishop Juan de Zumárraga (1468–1548) only finally heeded what Juan Diego was telling him on the last visit, when Juan Diego opened his tilmatli (cloak) and roses tumbled out of it revealing an image of the Guadalupe imprinted on the rough fabric. Juan Diego told the Archbishop that Mary had ordered him to pick the roses in an area that Juan Diego knew nothing was able to grow, but when he arrived it was overgrown with roses native to the bishop's home area in what is now Spain.

The legend was not officially recorded until the mid-seventeenth century first by Mexican born Oration priest Miguel Sanchez (1549–1674) connecting this event with the woman of Revelations 12 then six months later in the Nican Mopohua, which translates to "here it is told," with contested authorship by the priest Luis Lasso de la Vega.[6] The oral tradition of this story today follows the latter account, originally scripted in Nahuatl. The shrine, however, has been rebuilt several times, over the years since the earliest erection in 1530s, the most recent construction project to transform it into a basilica.[7] The image holds pride of place above the altar depicting a veiled young woman with native features wearing an open crown on her dark hair, her hands raised before her in prayer, and standing upon a crescent moon. She is one of the few patronas of Latin America who are not Madonna with Child; however, the black belt or cinta across her belly communicates that she is pregnant.

Interestingly, the hill that Mary favored had once been the site of a temple to Tonantzin (Mother Goddess), an Azteca goddess associated with the moon. While the question of María de Guadalupe being a goddess is regularly raised and very contested by Catholic scholars, Kroger and Granziera solidly affirm the claim, "while considered a saint by the Catholic Church, has become nothing less than a goddess to the people of Mexico."[8]

Spanish missionary Friar Bernandino de Sahagún (1499–1590) writes that for years after the Spanish conquest, the natives continued to pilgrimage to Tepeyac as they had done before, referring to Nuestra Señora de Guadalupe as Tonantzin. Sahagún also notes that though there are churches bearing Mary's name everywhere, the natives bypassed them, preferring to pilgrimage to Tepeyac.[9] Kroger and Granziera argue that Marian images and shrines allowed native peoples in what is now Mexico to continue practicing their own traditions related to various goddesses while outwardly using the symbols presented by the Spanish colonizers. The ability to decipher the deep code switching occurring at Tepeyac which became the place for Guadalupe because it was also the place for goddess mother of Nahua peoples. Catholic missionaries feared idolatry, and some say that both the bishop of the time and the Franciscans were not fond of the Guadalupe cult in the early days.[10]

Scholar Eric R. Wolf sees in the image of Guadalupe a dual function that, despite "the bitter theological and political" debate between colonizing factions in the New World that sought to exploit the natives, the Guadalupe validated the native's rights before the Spanish system to both supernatural salvation as children of God and equal citizenship before Spanish law.[11] "The campaign to legitimize Guadalupe as the primary Virgin Mary in New Spain" began early, in 1648, with "scores of treatises and published sermons [revealing a] mixture of nationalism and fervent *guadalupanismo*."[12]

Popular Devotions

Nuestra Señora de Guadalupe, as patroness of Mexico, has remained a strong representative figure for the nation of Mexico through the centuries. More than ten million people visit her Mexican shrine each year, making it the second most popular in the Catholic world after Saint Peter's Basilica. Some people make pilgrimage to this site in thanksgiving for prayers answered. People can often be seen miles away walking on their knees in completion of a promise made for healing or some other answered prayer.

Guadalupe is also the patroness of the continental Americas and is celebrated in other Latin American countries on her feast day—December 12—as well. Her fiestas patronales in Mexico, as is to be expected, are the most elaborate and the most expressive of her unique syncretic cultural and religious history. However, here in the United States, there are celebrations in areas with large Mexican American populations, including the National Cathedral Shrine of Nuestra Señora de Guadalupe in Dallas, Texas; the thirty-foot Guadalupe and Juan Diego at St. Mark Catholic Church in El Paso, Texas; or the Shrine of Our Lady of Guadalupe in La Crosse, Wisconsin. Guadalupe as a pregnant Marian image has been used arguably to forward an anti-abortion political agenda in the United States, which is not part of either the oral tradition from Mexico or the early written accounts about Guadalupe. This anti-abortion rhetoric can be found scripted into novena devotions to Nuestra Señora de Guadalupe,[13] in videos discussing "the crime of abortion" as part of shrines,[14] and Our Lady of Guadalupe for Life billboards.[15]

Nuestra Señora de la Altagracia: Dominican Republic

The Dominican Republic boasts two patronesses: Nuestra Señora de la Altagracia and Nuestra Señora de las Mercedes. Dating to 1495, the latter's cult is the first and, therefore, the oldest of the so-called New World.[16] However, Nuestra Señora de la Altagracia has been given precedence over the centuries and remains the most beloved and the most celebrated image of Mary in the country. There are two stories associated with the origins of the Altagracia. The more prosaic version of the story is that the image was brought from Estremadura, Spain, in the early 1500s and became a focal point for the community in Higüey at the time. The second, more widely known story also places the origin of the cult in the early 1500s but tells of a merchant traveling home to Higüey who was having difficulties finding a picture of Nuestra Señora that his little daughter had requested of him. Confiding his troubles to a stranger he met on his travels, the stranger removed an image on canvas from his knapsack, gave it to him and then went on his way. The orange tree associated with the legend marks the spot where the father gave the image to his daughter and is the same place where the basilica to Mary stands today.[17]

The image is a small paint-on-canvas depicting a young woman with her hands raised before her in prayer as she stands before the manger where the Christ child lies. Upon her head is an open crown, and she is enveloped in a midnight blue cloak embroidered with stars over a white dress and a red underdress. The stars on her cloak seem to float into a halo that surrounds her. Hovering in the background, taking in the scene, is Joseph entirely arrayed in bright red.

In his investigation of Marian devotion in Latin America, scholar Stephen Holler contends that most Latin American Marian devotions' founding legends are rooted in the indigenous cultures.[18] The cult of the Altagracia is one exception. The Taíno indigenous people of Quisqueya were not allowed the chance to be, as Holler states, "the major influence in safeguarding the Catholic and Marian culture from the secularization of the dominant cultures."[19] By 1519, most of the indigenous were decimated from either disease or mistreatment or both.[20] In 1537, too late for the Taínos from the renamed Hispañola, Pope Paul III promulgated the bull *Sublimis Deus* (1537), forbidding the enslavement of indigenous peoples.[21] The few indigenous that remained mixed in with the population of Europeans and Africans, a mestizaje that gave rise to the Dominican people of today. Though the cult of Nuestra Señora de la Altagracia was Spanish at its inception, it has morphed along with the people of the island to become a universal image for all Dominicans.

Popular Devotions

The feast day of Nuestra Señora de la Altagracia is January 21, which coincides with the anniversary of the victory of Spanish troops over the French in 1691 in the Battle of Sabana Real de Guarico, the confrontations between the Spanish and the French for control of the island are myriad and never-ending.[22] Her chapel, then her church and later her basilica, which remains in the Eastern province of Higüey, has been a place of pilgrimage for centuries. The fiestas patronales of la Altagracia in the Dominican Republic last for two weeks and are a rich expression of folkloric culture. In the United States, scholar Thomas Weyr believes that Dominicans celebrating their patrona have "set the tone for New York's Marian cults."[23] Seeing in this celebration a way to bind Dominicans in diaspora together, Weyr describes how the fiesta has become institutionalized to the point where a Dominican bishop is customarily flown in to preside over Mass at Patrick's Cathedral, where the Dominican ambassador to the UN and the consul general are in regular attendance. Weyr also makes sure to mention that the experience is an intense one.[24] A more recent example of Altagracia Marian devotion at St. Patrick's Cathedral—January 14, 2024—was mass celebrated by Bishop Espaillat, a Dominican-American who is Auxiliary Bishop of the Archdiocese of New York.[25]

Nuestra Señora de la Divina Providencia: Puerto Rico

The cult of the *patrona* of Puerto Rico, Nuestra Señora de la Divina Providencia, originated in Italy in the thirteenth century, where it was associated with the Order of the Servants of Mary. The earliest miracles associated with la Divina Providencia were of providing food and material assistance to those in dire need. The image, however, did not emerge until the seventeenth century when the Barnabites, who had adopted the cult, received the gift of a Madonna and Child. They requested and received permission from Pope Benedict XIV (1675–1758) to associate the image with the cult of the Divina Providencia, and the cult began to grow.[26]

Monsignor Gil Estévez y Tomás (1798–1858), a Servite who had been introduced to Nuestra Señora de la Divina Providencia in Cataluña, brought the cult to Puerto Rico in 1853. Upon his arrival, he found San Juan Bautista Cathedral in poor condition and undertook a restoration of the edifice. When the work was completed, a sculpted image commissioned from artisans in Barcelona was placed in the cathedral by Monsignor, which he dedicated to Nuestra Señora de la Divina Providencia, placing the cathedral and the people of Puerto Rico under her protection.[27] The image has changed over the centuries. The one that most are familiar with today depicts a fair woman with light brown hair and a brilliant silver halo radiating from behind her veil. Her hands are raised, clasping the hand of the Christ child who is sleeping peacefully in his mother's lap. Her gaze is cast downward onto his face, watching him sleep. Her white veil matches her dress, which is covered by a gold-trimmed light blue cloak.

Popular Devotions

The original feast day of Nuestra Señora de la Divina Providencia was November 2, which marked the day the image arrived on the island. This was changed when Pope Paul VI declared her patroness of Puerto Rico and decreed her new feast day would be November 19, which coincides with Puerto Rico's date of so-called discovery. And so, the cult of Mary in the small island nation is fused with its particular history in a colonial context. In the diaspora, there are two places of worship, both in New York where Nuestra Señora de la Divina Providencia is on permanent display: the Church of Barbara in Brooklyn and Lucy in East Harlem.[28] Her feast day is celebrated with a modest procession that ends with Mass at Patrick's Cathedral.

Nuestra Señora de la Caridad del Cobre: Cuba

La patrona of Cuba is Nuestra Señora de la Caridad del Cobre or, as she is referred to by way of endearment, simply "Cachita." Her origin story takes place in a small mining village outside of Santiago de Cuba in the 1600s.[29] Three men—brothers Rodrigo and Juan de Hoyos and Juan Moreno—set out on the Bay of Nipe in El Cobre with the intent to gather the salt required for meat preservation. Though there are many stories to be told about exactly what happened out on the water, we will look at the two most common here.

The first is a very short story; that the image made its way over to the men, and that it was dry despite having been in and on the water.[30] The second, more well-known story is that the men were sailing back to El Cobre when a fierce storm hit. They were in a very small boat that was in danger of capsizing, and so the men, under the direction of Juan Moreno, who was devotee of the Virgin, began to pray to her for salvation. The storm passed as suddenly as it had appeared. As the clouds dissipated, the men saw a bit of driftwood floating toward them. There, on top of the bit of flotsam, was a small carved wooden image of a dark-skinned Madonna cradling the Christ child in her arms. Written on the driftwood was the declaration, "Yo soy Nuestra Señora de la Caridad." As in the first story, neither the bit of wood nor the statue was wet despite the sea and the rain. The men collected the statue and took it back with them to Cobre, where it was placed in a small chapel that took the name of la virgencita.[31]

Nuestra Señora de la Caridad del Cobre is a unique image in that the legend behind it begins in the so-called New World and is very representative of the Cuban land, people, and history. There have been attempts to trace the cult of la Cachita back to Europe, for example, scholar I. A. Wright contends that she is one and the same as Our Lady of Charity of Illescas, Castille. However, Cobre defies such simplification. She is an emblem of the sort of Caribbean and, really, Latin American mentality adopted by our *gente* who have suffered under colonial subjugation for centuries. As religious scholar Miguel A. De La Torre encapsulates rather succinctly when quoting his parents: "*Somos católicos romanos, y apostólicos, creemos a nuestra manera.*"[32] The statement is very Latin American. The intransigent "pero" is there, but it is not given voice. It is not passive aggression; it is quiet acknowledgement of one's own God-given dignity and freedom. De la Torre sees this dignity as a gift from la Cachita, along with "the birth of Cuban identity, the birth of *cubanidad*."[33]

Popular Devotions

Though the Cuban Revolution brought with it a shift in Cuban religiosity, "beliefs, practices, and traditions were kept alive through the years as integral parts of people's ways of thinking, feeling, and dreaming."[34] It was only in the 1990s that popular expressions slowly reentered the Cuban public sphere on the Island. An underground

Christianity has morphed into a particularly "Cuban" Catholicism, as scholar Ana Celia Perera Pintado tells us, with the Church in Cuba demanding "a recovery of national identity through reconciliation" with the *exilados*.[35] It is a lovely nod to the unifying role Nuestra Señora de la Caridad del Cobre plays in the life of the Cuban people that the bishops in La Havana, on her feast day on September 8, 2003, made a plea for "all paths toward reconciliation."[36] For their part, the Cuban exiles in Miami built a small conical shrine to Mary in Bay Biscayne on the Atlantic Ocean facing in the direction of Cuba and the Caribbean Sea, where they housed a small replica smuggled out of a parish church in Guanabo Beach in La Havana. The shrine was consecrated in 1973 and has since been the center of religious celebration of Nuestra Señora de la Caridad del Cobre on her feast day for those in exile.[37]

Today, Ermita de la Caridad in Miami, Florida, is an active national Marian shrine with fourteen Eucharistic Liturgies or Masses celebrated each week, a confraternity or group of people dedicated to this Marian image, and regular prayer opportunities. The National Shrine of La Cachita was designated as a special place for prayer during the Jubilee year of 2025 marking for Roman Catholics a Jubilee of Hope.

Nuestra Señora de la Leche y Buen Parto: United States of America

Nuestra Señora de la Leche y Buen Parto arrived in Saint Augustine, Florida, between September 8, 1565 (feast of Mary's birth), and the year of 1606 when the first shrine was built for the image. A copy of this little statue of a nursing Mary was believed to have been brought over with the mariners in one of the ships that docked in Augustine. Mary is known as the Star of Sea, protector of mariners. Many times, these Marian images were nursing Madonnas. A small area of land on Mission Nombre de Dios, now known as Americas most Sacred Acre, was the home to this devotion by those Spaniards as well as the indigenous who were converted to Christianity and lived on and away from the mission. According to narratives from the archives of the Diocese of Augustine, "The arrival of the statue at Nombre de Dios coincides with the beginning of a time of unprecedented success for the missionaries in the area."[38]

The original statue has been lost. Some believe it to be in Cuba, where it was sent due to impending British invasion, since Saint Augustine, Florida was part of the Cuban Archdiocese at the time. The original chapel was destroyed by the British; however, some of the stones were left intact. Except for about eighty years when the British colonized this land, the devotion to Nuestra Señora de la Leche y Buen Parto has remained at Mission Nombre de Dios. A new statue was placed in the chapel in the 1930s. The 1930s image was replaced by another image of a similar size in the 1950s. The image in the chapel until the canonical coronation, a special designation granted by the pope for Marian images who bring great numbers of people to Jesus Christ, was placed in the alcove of the chapel in the 1970s. Until the canonical coronation, the breast of Nuestra Señora de la Leche had been covered more and more in the three iterations created for the chapel in the twentieth century.

During his tenure, Bishop Felipe de Jesús Estévez, declared Nuestra Señora de La Leche y Buen Parto the Patron Saint of the Diocese of Augustine, Florida. Although he was mostly raised in the United States, he brought his devotion to this Mary from Cuba, his homeland. Nuestra Señora de la Leche y Buen Parto was the image used for the 2012–13 Year of Faith prayer cards in this diocese. Historically, other prayers have been written for "Time of War" and for seeking assistance with conception of a child.

Popular Devotion

The number of families who visit the shrine and the many indigenous people who converted to Catholicism because of this image gave Bishop Estevez of Augustine the impetus to seek Canonical Coronation, which began with a letter to Pope Francis in 2012. On March 11, 2020, commemorating the 150th anniversary of the establishment of the diocese of Augustine as its own diocese and a place of devotion for over 450 years, Pope Francis declared that Nuestra Señora de la Leche y Buen Parto of Augustine, Florida would receive a canonical coronation. Cardinal Carlos Osoro Sierra, Bishop of Madrid, Spain, was sent as Pontifical Legate for the coronation on October 10, 2021. A new statue was commissioned from an artist in Italy. This statue now sits with both Mary's head and Jesus' head adorned with a golden crown.

Nossa Senhora da Conceição Aparecida: Brazil

One day in 1717, three fishermen named Domingos Garcia, Filipe Pedroso, and João Alves cast their nets on the Paraiba River where it flows alongside the small city of Guarantinqueta near the Port of Itaguaçu.[39] Of late, the fishermen of the region were having bad luck with their fishing, so they had been praying to Our Lady of the Immaculate Conception in hopes God would grant a good catch. To his surprise, the fisherman pulled up a headless wooden statue. When two other fishermen cast their nets beside him, they brought up the statue's head and, finally, some fish. Legend has it that the parts were so heavy that the fishermen could not lift it from the water, so they set aside those nets and kept casting because the water was suddenly full of fish. Once back on shore, the fishermen cleaned the sculpture and reassembled it, only to discover that it was an image of the Immaculate Conception. Because the image appeared from nowhere followed by a miraculous catch, the fisherman decided to name the statue Nossa Senhora da Conceição Aparecida (literally, Our Lady of the Conception who Appeared).[40] Story of the miracle soon spread, and people began to visit the small city to venerate the statue. Devotion to the image caused Nuestra

Señora de Aparecida's cult to grow and the first chapel dedicated to her was built in 1737.

The little exquisitely worked dark clay statue of Nossa Senhora da Aparecida is a very humble image of a young woman with her hands raised before her heart in prayer. A large round golden open crown was placed over a colorfully embroidered navy mantle. She is not only popular for her representation, as a Black Madonna, of the racially diverse people of Brazil, but because of the miracles people have attributed to Mary over the centuries. Eventually, due to the growth of her cult, work began in 1834 on the construction of a denominated New Basilica in her honor. Prior to the inauguration of the New Basilica in 1955, Pope Pius XII (1876–1958) proclaimed Nossa Senhora da Conceição Aparecida the principal patroness of Brazil and approved the devotion to her image.[41]

Popular Devotions

The feast day of Nossa Senhora da Conceição Aparecida is October 12. In Brazil, the celebration is week long, with entire parades filling the street. The little statue is taken out on procession and returned to her basilica for a solemn Mass. Interestingly, Japan immigrants in Brazil attend the Buddhist Church Nambei Yugazam Jyomiyoji, a Shingon Shugundo temple, where Nossa Senhora "is venerated alongside Fudo Myo and other Shingon deities."[42] These Buddhists go on pilgrimage to Aparecida three times a year to honor Nossa Senhora.

In the United States of America, James Church in Newark, New Jersey, holds an interesting celebration, where Nossa Senhora is venerated alongside the Portuguese patroness Nuestra Señora de Fátima. It is the result of an intentional effort by the parish pastors to bring their Brazilian, Portuguese, and English parishioners together to form one community.[43] Through the selection of hymns and symbols that reflect a common "Lusophone Catholic identity," and through liturgical actions like carrying replicas of the Madonnas side-by-side, the pastors hoped to "bridge social boundaries."[44]

Conclusion

While the first part of this chapter has provided an overview of some of the specific Marian images to highlight differences among Latines, especially Latine Catholics in the United States of America, the concluding part of this chapter highlights some ways Marian devotion has been criticized and even reworked, especially Guadalupe through artistic expressions.

The authors wonder what the reasons may be for the ability to play with Guadalupe's imagery far more than that of, for example, La Divina Providencia or La Cachita. For instance, might there be some sort of political influence at work here? Or is it merely reflective of demographic realities?

The attention to Mary and Marian devotions in Latin American culture as have grown out of Spanish and Portuguese colonization brings many critiques around binary gender roles and particularly what is termed "marianismo" or gender roles constructed out of arguable understandings of Mary of Nazareth as virginal, pure, family-centered, and submissive to men.[45] Sometimes, the notion of marianismo is understood through multiple dimensions of family, with women placed at the center; silencing of self to maintain harmony; and spiritual leader who is responsible for the family's and therefore community's spiritual growth.

Two recent studies regarding the notion of marianismo questions this cultural phenomenon's relationship with Latine's physical, mental, and communal health.[46] While both studies listed multiple limitations to the generalizations of their findings, they nevertheless identified culturally critical findings. Nuñez et al. found that marianismo is significantly associated with negative cognitive–emotional factors with particularities of study participants marking different levels of relationship between marianismo and negative cognitive–emotional factors.[47] The strongest relationship between marianismo and higher levels of negative cognitions and emotions was found in the spiritual pillar and silencing self to maintain harmony subscales.[48] Gallegos and Segrin studied the relationship between Latinas, loneliness, and marianismo. Part of their hypothesis states, "Because loneliness has pathogenic effects on health (Hawkley and Cacioppo, 2010), marianismo may indirectly protect Latina health by reducing loneliness."[49] They found that the family (the authors add spiritual) pillar of marianismo "may have health-protective benefits through reduced loneliness."[50]

Much remains to be explored and developed. Questions about cultural impacts of these Marian devotions call for longitudinal ethnographic research. The need for additional research alone marks the strong impact Marian images of the American continents have on Latine cultures and peoples.

Appendix: Reference of Other National Marian Devotions

Virgencita	Country of Origin (A-Z)	Fiesta
Nuestra Señora de Lujan	Argentina	May 8
Nuestra Señora de Copacabana	Bolivia	October 9
Nuestra Señora del Monte Carmel	Chile	July 16
Nuestra Señora del Rosario de Chiquinquirá	Columbia	July 9
Nuestra Señora de los Ángeles	Costa Rica	August 2
Nuestra Señora de Quinche	Ecuador	November 21
Nuestra Señora de la Paz	El Salvador	November 21
Nuestra Señora del Rosario	Guatemala	October 7
Nuestra Señora de Suyapa	Honduras	February 3
Nuestra Señora de la Inmaculada Concepción	Nicaragua	December 8
Nuestra Señora de la Antigua	Panamá	September 9
Nuestra Señora de los Milagros	Paraguay	December 8
Nuestra Señora de la Candelaria	Perú	February 2
Nuestra Señora de los Treinta y Tres	Uruguay	November 8
Nuestra Señora de Coromoto	Venezuela	September 11

10

Challenging the Patriarchy

Isabela Leonor Rosales

The sun rises on corn fields in northeastern, rural Iowa. I, a daughter of a Mexican immigrant, am the only little girl with a name the teachers struggle to pronounce. I do not see the differences between myself and the other young girls in school. They have light blonde hair, blue eyes, and pink skin, while I have dark brown hair, brown eyes, thick eyebrows, and a slight shadow over my lip. Still, developing alongside these girls, I never questioned my place until the first week of sixth grade when we had to change for our weekly physical education class. Standing next to a teal green locker, I begin removing my school uniform for a pair of Nike shorts and T-shirt. As my top flies over my head, I hear a disgusted gasp escape a classmate's mouth as she cries, "Ew! Look at Isabela's back!" A swarm of giggling and pointing ensues as hot tears spill out the corner of my eyes. Unlike the other girls, my skin is covered in a peach-fuzz layer of dark brown hair. The shame of being different is overwhelming. I feel as uncomfortable as I feel undesirable. Growing up is hard enough.

Now, I am grown and still establishing confidence with my differences and healing the pieces I have molded to assimilate with Euro-American culture. With my epistemological privileges, I can speak to the unique shape of patriarchal sexism and ethnic/racial discrimination Latinas face in a predominantly white, rural Midwest context.[1] My experience as a light-skinned Latina in a rural Midwestern white community will be distinct from a dark-skinned Latina's experience in a large city like Chicago. It would be harmful to equate the experiences as the particularities of each inform a crucial analysis of the Latina experience in the United States. Additionally, I lean on other Latine experiences within and beyond Mujerista thought and Latina feminism to inform a critique of anti-Latina systems while also exploring the tension between the two major approaches for Latina-based responses to patriarchy. My personal story illustrates the lived experience of navigating differences as a Latina in Euro-American society, setting the foundation for understanding the frameworks of Mujerista theology and Latina feminism. These approaches, while distinct, can be enriched and moved beyond a perceived dichotomy through a commitment to anti-Latina frameworks, decolonial methods, and inclusivity of queer experiences.

Beginning with Mujerista thought, Mujerista theology intends to provide a voice for Latinas living in the United States. It is a source for understanding grassroots Latina-led movements struggling against daily oppression. Ada María Isasi-Díaz references Mujerista theology as a framework for "thinking with" instead of "thinking about" the Latina experience and starts using the term in academic settings to distinguish the ideological concept of gender unique to a Latina moving through departments of theological and gender studies.[2] In this way, Mujerista thought is a direct response to the flaws in the Euro-American feminist movement, which prioritizes the needs of white women in a heteronormative, patriarchal society. As my personal testimony revealed at the beginning of this chapter, white feminism possesses the danger of perpetuating the same hegemonic structures it claims to oppose.

Because of these realities, Isasi-Díaz defines a Mujerista as someone who makes a preferential option for Latina women and for their specific struggle for liberation in an ethnically racist, white supremacist, heteronormative, and patriarchal society.[3] The term began as a title in religious circles and as a branch in liberation theology. As the term became more popular, community organizers began using it as an affinity marker. Today, based in Miami, there is an Instagram account dedicated to "The Mujerista" with nearly 100,000 followers.[4] Mujerista thought, while perhaps less prominent in academia, continues to be used on social media as a signifier for Latinas seeking gender justice and liberation.

While theological vocabulary is not as explicit in popular uses of Mujerista ideology, Mujerista thought originated out of a need for a theological lens catered toward the Latina lived experience and effort for liberation. For Isasi-Díaz, Mujerista theology includes both ethics and systemic theology in its engagement with questions of moral agency and interpretation of biblical scripture for current, ongoing social issues.[5] The term arises from similar theological ideologies and sense of identity as the terms "mestizaje" and "mulatez." These two latter terms have been used by US Latine liberation theologians and scholars to illustrate the racially and culturally mixed nature of Latine identities in what is now the Americas. In Isasi-Díaz's words, "Mestizaje refers to the mixture of white people and native people living in what is now Latin America and the Caribbean. Mulatez refers to the mixture of black people and white people."[6] Her claiming these labels for entire groups of people who had not necessarily claimed them for themselves created a problem of social location awareness for Isasi-Díaz, and she faced great criticism for her use of these terms without the epistemological privileges of belonging to either group or engaging sufficiently in these communities to inform her research.[7]

For Isasi-Díaz, using the Latina experience as a source of knowledge is nonnegotiable for understanding the struggle in liberation. She understood that even the discourse on decolonization was not free from dominant thinking just as she understood a certain level of engagement with dominant thinking as necessary for structural change. Her approach reveals that although Mujerista theology has used the language of liberation, it understands liberation as an impossible project within modern power structures. Rather, Isasi-Díaz would argue the Mujerista theological project has radical structural changes as its goal.

Latinas are just one group of oppressed people, but for Isasi-Díaz, theirs are the lived experiences that need to shape social ideas of liberation. She writes, "[A]n ongoing option for the oppressed is an option for Latinas, and a commitment to value *lo cotidiano*—the everyday of Latinas." Mujerista theology is deeply rooted in the experiences and struggles of Latinas in the United States, offering a theological framework that centers *lo cotidiano* (daily life) as a source of knowledge. Isasi-Díaz writes, "*lo cotidiano* steers Mujerista theology away from any essentialism that would obscure precisely what is at the core of *lo cotidiano*: difference," and "As an epistemological category *lo cotidiano* goes well beyond adding another perspective and points to the need to change the social order by taking into consideration the way Latinas see and understand reality."[8] Isasi-Díaz prioritizes what W.E.B. Du Bois calls the "double-consciousness"[9] of the oppressed. Referring to five different modes of oppression: exploitation, marginalization, ethnoracism, powerlessness, and structural violence, Isasi-Díaz claims to center Latinas in her analysis of these modes and names the oppressed as those who are conscious of their oppression, struggle for their liberation, and take into consideration their communities.[10]

This double-consciousness of daily reality, or *lo cotidiano* as articulated by Isasi-Díaz, carries profound hermeneutical value. It encapsulates the tension between experiencing oppression and actively fighting for liberation, a dynamic embodied in the lived reality of Latinas. For Isasi-Díaz, *lo cotidiano* is more than the material reality of life; it encompasses the ways individuals relate to their realities, cultural practices, and historical memories. The embodied practices and beliefs passed down through generations are a core aspect of *lo cotidiano*. For instance, a parent blessing their child with the sign of the cross before the child leaves for school illustrates how these rituals, grounded in everyday life, carry theological and cultural significance. As Isasi-Díaz emphasizes, "It is the diversity made present by and in *lo cotidiano* and the particularity and specificity of *lo cotidiano* that makes it possible to highlight differences and generate shared meanings as the basis for creating liberating societal structures."[11] This perspective reframes the lived experiences of impoverished Latinas as sites of socially informative epistemologies and radical social transformation.

However, Isasi-Díaz warns against romanticizing *lo cotidiano* or reducing it to essentialist understandings of Latina identity. She critiques practices that exploit oppressed identities for personal gain, such as scholars using subjugated knowledge for recognition without truly committing to the communities they study - notably, something for which she, herself, has been criticized. Isasi-Díaz writes, "The lack of value given to Latinas' *cotidiano* goes hand in hand with the lack of appreciation for the epistemology of all oppressed people. Ignorance about the value of subjugated knowledge contributes to the oppression of the vast majority of the people in the world."[12] The day-to-day experiences of oppressed Latinas are central to Isasi-Díaz's contribution to Mujerista thought, which is ultimately an expression of these daily lived experiences. For Isasi-Díaz, the recognition of Mujerista epistemologies is intrinsic to both the liberation of Latinas and the flourishing of all life. In other words, liberation for all is contingent upon Latina liberation.

Despite efforts to articulate the significance of *lo cotidiano* and the particularities of Latina oppression, Mujerista theology has faced significant critiques, particularly from Latina feminist scholars like María Pilar Aquino. Aquino rejects Mujerista as a title, arguing that it essentializes womens' experiences and obscures the sociopolitical origins of "Mujerista" as a signification. Highlighting how "Mujerista" was initially coined in Peru during the 1970s by women who distanced themselves from mainstream feminism due to its failures in addressing local realities, Aquino critiques the abstraction of Mujerista into a mythical subject detached from these historical and political roots. She writes, "We cannot by virtue say that because one is Hispanic and one is a woman, they are immediately moving us towards liberation."[13] Instead, she calls for a theology deeply rooted in the movements and lived realities of the people, asserting, "If you're not doing theology rooted from these movements, you're not doing liberation theology."[14] This critique highlights the tendency of liberation theologians to subject their communities associated with their identities to a monolithic category and for understanding oppression and liberation without actually being a member of that community.

The tension between Mujerista theology and Latina feminism highlights critical distinctions in their approaches. Mujerista theology addresses the lived experiences of Latinas in a United States context, while Latina feminism often adopts a broader, more contextually colonial lens that considers the lingering impacts of colonialism beyond the United States in Latin America. Aquino's critique resists essentialism while maintaining a commitment to liberation that is grounded in the material realities of Latina lives. Although Isasi-Díaz attempts to resist essentialism in her application of *lo cotidiano*, her critics claim this results in romanticizing daily experiences of oppression under one Spanish language label.

Within the context of theology, María Pilar Aquino, Daisy L. Machado, and Jeanette Rodriguez introduce themselves as Latina feminists, which is an intentional signifier and distinction from "Mujerista." To address multiple realities in a US context, Latina feminism seeks to represent multicultural voices experiencing racism, sexism, devaluation, and exclusion. With special attention to Latina religious experiences, Latina feminists engage theological reflection to move in liberating directions.[15] The vocabulary of liberation is common within the liberation theological movement arising from Latin America in the twentieth century in response to economic, political, and racial/ethnic oppression. Latina feminist theologians have arisen out of a need to confront gender norms and sexism within the liberation theological movement and its vocabulary. More specifically, Latina feminist theologians seek to articulate and examine "the 'in-betweenness' of Latinas" who live in the United States.[16]

Still, without ignoring the larger sociopolitical context, Latina feminist theologians insist their theology is not based on something existing "only in one's mind" but as a product of a religious reflection on oppression and vision for better social living.[17] Within the context of liberation theology and Latina experience, Latina feminist theologians intentionally choose to separate themselves from Mujerista theology. The main argument for this distinction from Ada María Isasi-Díaz's theological perspective "is that there are no Mujerista sociopolitical and ecclesial subjects or movements in the United States."[18] In other words, the descriptor "Mujerista" arose out of the academy whereas "Latina" comes from social and ecclesial movements and community. In this move away from a Mujerista theology, Latina feminist theologians seek to develop their "theological languages in dynamic conversation with the plural feminist experience and thought of Latinas/Chicanas."[19] Ultimately, in order to discuss Latina feminism in a US context, Chicana feminism[20] and its contributions and shortcomings must be included in the discourse.

While faith and liberation vocabularies make up Latina feminist theology, Latina feminism has functioned as a larger umbrella for theologies and non-white gender studies. Nancy Pineda-Madrid argues for an integration of a Chicana feminist epistemology into the development of Latina feminism because of the unique distinction of the Chicana lived experience in the United States.[21] Within a US context, "Latina" is often an umbrella term used to represent a variety of realities of "Chicanas (or Xicanismas), Puertorriqueñas, Cubanas, Mexicanas, and Sur Americanas."[22] Pineda-Madrid argues that because of the unique origin of "Chicana" in a strictly US context, their epistemological insight is necessary to "uncover and analyze gender, racial, and class hegemonies operative in the work of U.S. Latino theologians in particular and in theology in general."[23] Aquino would agree with Pineda-Madrid, stating that the Latina feminist theological project is an "intercultural activity." In her chapter, "Latina Feminist Theology: Central Features," Aquino writes "Latina/Chicana feminism" throughout the essay, thus grouping the two together while still sharing space for the distinction between the two signifiers. Pineda-Madrid calls attention to the tendency within Latina feminist theologies to generalize experiences - interestingly, this is the same critique Latina feminists share for Mujerista thought. Pineda-Madrid writes, "Unarticulated epistemological assumptions often shape how theological debates proceed and where they ultimately settle."[24] Because "Chicana" arises out of a specific historical moment in the United States where race, class, and gender were critically engaged within the Latin American migrant community, it presents itself as a critical epistemological lens.

Where Mujerista thought, in Isasi-Díaz's articulation of it, does not engage with Chicana feminism, Latina feminism does address Chicana feminists because "Chicana" is a label arising out of a specific community in a specific political moment in the US history. Again, the lack of specificity is exactly what Latina feminists like Aquino are critiquing in Mujerista theology. Latina feminism has been critiqued by Chicana feminists and all the aforementioned lines of feminist ideology have been heavily critiqued by both antiracist and queer frameworks. By addressing critiques within both

Mujerista and Latina feminist approaches, an understanding can emerge that uplifts all Latinas, regardless of skin pigmentation, sexual orientation or gender identity.

With more attention to community praxis, race, and decolonial methods, Xhercis Méndez draws from her Puerto Rican geographical context to discuss coalition across Latina feminisms with special attention to pervasive anti-blackness in the dominant Latina feminist discourse. Méndez views anti-blackness as an act of "counteridentification" occurring within her community in an effort to distance themselves from white supremacist narratives of black people as " 'lazy,' 'ignorant,' and 'inherently criminal.' "[25] According to Méndez, these identifiers are "(re)deployed in relation to Puerto Rican communities both on the island and on the mainland."[26] Méndez calls these "antiblack colonial logics," which have been internalized by Latine communities and "create obstacles to our building complex coalitions."[27] Due to her own African ancestry, Méndez is concerned with confronting her own privileges as a light-skinned Latina within the discourse on Latina feminism and employs decolonial feminist methods in the process.

Engaging decolonial methods, Méndez seeks to push the discourse on Latina feminism beyond the relationship between men and women, toward an analysis of colonization. She argues, "gender works to entice a series of complicities from racialized folks with colonial logics as well as to undermine our efforts to organize coalitionally across deep differences."[28] Méndez acknowledges the history of dehumanization of colonial racial categories and how this simultaneously complicates gender as a concept and creates barriers in cross-cultural connection. Critically, she asks, "[I]n what ways do racialized folks have to shift how they understand gender in order to identify and activate a communally oriented liberatory politic that does not mimic Western (neo) colonial and settler colonial arrangements of bodies and power?"[29] In other words, gender as a concept was created out of a worldview that only saw the gender of white people. Therefore, the question is when dark bodies claim gender, how can they do so without repeating or mimicking the same colonial logics that attempted to strip them of their humanity in the first place?

Considering colonization's role in the construction of gender, Méndez introduces the "wages of gender." Arising from her decolonial lens, this concept is her "effort to make explicit 'gender's' grounding in colonial relations of power and the impact that has on the racialized communities produced as the constitutive outside of gender."[30] Because the bodies of Africans who were enslaved were "sexed," not "gendered," they were able to be viewed and sold as chattel "because the 'sex' of their bodies only matters to the extent to which they serve breeding practices and the purposes of capital accumulation."[31] This level of critical racial awareness has been missing from the dominant discourses in both Mujerista thought and Latina feminism, which in its efforts to participate in a dialogue on race has also mistakenly ignored its own internalized anti-blackness and complicity in uplifting colonial concepts of race and gender.

In understanding the colonial framework in which the concept of gender emerged, Méndez argues that "gender is intimately tied to those who are structurally produced and recognized as human over and against those structurally produced as a degeneration of humanity, a subhumanity with various degrees of nonhumanness."[32] Ultimately, "The wages of gender can be understood as the economic, social, political, legal, psychological and affective privileges/benefits one gets for being systematically recognized as an individual who fits into light-side gender and gender arrangements."[33] With this understanding, Méndez could be calling other Latina feminists, Mujerista theologians, and Chicana feminists who fall into the colonial category of "light-side gender" to acknowledge their own racial privileges within a colonial context.

To disrupt anti-blackness and colonial conceptualizations of gender within Latina feminisms, Méndez engages community-praxis and ritual, specifically in her affinity with and research on Santería.[34] By engaging the concept of "spiritual seniority" in Afro-Cuban Santería, Méndez explores how "ritual enactments introduce explicitly non-Western formulations of the body that include non-gendered/non-racialized logics, culturally specific modalities of empowerment, and an alternative system of valuation for what it means to be human."[35] For Méndez, Santería offers alternative epistemologies and systems of human classification wherein humans are not already and always defined in white, colonial terms. By engaging ritual practices, Méndez rejects neocolonial concepts of self and gender, which have historically functioned to dehumanize dark-skinned people. In recentering race in Latina feminism, Méndez demonstrates how anti-blackness can be confronted within Latine communities without dismissing the unique integrity of Latina experience in sexist systems of oppression.

With decolonial methods and anti-racist ideologies, Latina feminism has the capacity to reveal the priorities and needs of women from vastly diverse colonial, ethnic, and racial contexts. The incommensurability of experiences amongst Latinas is paramount. Through an interdisciplinary approach with decolonial methods, Latina feminism and Mujerista theology have the ability to forge new epistemologies without imposing universality or colonial logics which seek to uplift one racialized experience over another. Latina feminists and Mujeristas are obligated to not recreate the same methods of colonial and hegemonic oppression from which they seek liberation. This is possible as long as both prioritize an interdisciplinary approach that also prioritizes queer Latine perspectives.

Queer Latine thought is a continually evolving field as well as an indispensable conversation partner for Latina Feminism and Mujerista thought. Returning to a Chicana context, Cherríe Moraga is often quoted among contemporary queer folks as a formative voice in the ongoing discourse. In her essay, "Queer Aztlán[36]: the Reformation of Chicano Tribe," Moraga offers a critique of both the Chicano Movement and Chicana feminisms. With clear commitments to upholding the notion of Chicano as a nation, Moraga argues that by centering Aztlán in the movement, a new nationalism arises that centers the indigenous connotation of a Chicana identity, "and heterosexism and homophobia are no longer the cultural order of the day" as they are products of European colonization.[37] Moraga upholds "nation" because she notices trends within the academy dismissing the existence of Chicanos. She explains, "without specific naming of the nation, the nation will be lost (as when feminism is reduced to humanism, the woman is subsumed)."[38] In an effort to sustain the radicalism of the

Chicano Movement, Moraga intentionally maintains nationhood but pushes it into a broader space to include queerness.

By integrating "Aztlán," Moraga speaks to a cultural worldview that acknowledges the presence of Indigenous peoples in the contemporary geographical Southwest of the United States. On this, Moraga writes:

> Chicano Nation is a mestizo nation conceived in a double-rape: first, by the Spanish and then by the Gringo. In the mid-19 century, Anglo-America took possession of one-third of México's territory. A new English-speaking oppressor assumed control over the Spanish, Mestizo, and Indian people inhabiting those lands. There was no denying that the United States had stolen Aztlán from México, but it had been initially stolen from the Indians by the Spanish some 300 years earlier.[39]

Within the Chicano Movement, Aztlán functioned to honor an ancestral belonging to the lands of the Southwest region in the United States and highlighted a sense of nationality integral to the Chicano Movement. Moraga seeks to queer Aztlán by suggesting that, as a nation, Aztlán has less to do with ancestral claims to land and more to do with the indigenous life that persists in México and the US Southwest.[40] With this reverence for all forms of life, Moraga argues that Aztlán, unlike the Chicano Movement, is accepting of "gay and lesbian" ways of living. For Moraga, Aztlán is more symbolic of acceptance than of indigenous claims to land.

Moraga reveals the hypocrisy of veteran heterosexual men in the Chicano Movement that fought for freedom all while oppressing women and queer folks. Regarding these men, she writes, "Twenty years later, they move into 'elderhood' without having seriously grappled with the fact that their leadership in *El Movimiento* was made possible by all those women who kept their '*plumas planchadas*' at every political event."[41] Moraga highlights this utter disregard for womens' participation in order to effectively demonstrate just how invisibilized queerness had become in the Chicano Movement. Without support from either heterosexual men or women, Moraga engages Aztlán as an "imagined homeland" for queer Chicanos.

In this "queer Aztlán," Moraga ensures that there would be no discrimination against queerness and the contributions of "lesbians and gay men" would be upheld in the "new Chicano movement."[42] Drawing from indigenous models of egalitarianism and acceptance of "two-spirit" peoples, Moraga intentionally intersects her lesbian identity with her sense of Indigenous ancestry and affinity by queering Aztlán.[43] While Moraga's work in Queer Latine thought is an essential part of the canon of Latina/Chicana feminism in calling attention to generalized homophobia in the Chicano Movement, it lacks a distinct decolonial lens. A decolonial method would be critical of appropriating Aztlán as a romanticized version of Indigenous past when the Indigenous present and Indigenous *presence* tell a different story. Additionally, Moraga blatantly leaves non-binary, gender-queer, and transgender experiences out of the dialogue.

Outside of a Chicana context, Mariana Ortega writes on her experience as a Latina and as a lesbian in the United States, building on José Esteban Muñoz's scholarship in *Cruising Utopia: The Then and There of Queer Futurity*. Through an analysis of Alma Lopez's image of *Lupe and Sirena in Love* in conversation with Muñoz's understanding of "melancholic longing," Ortega offers a critical analysis of "Queer Latinidad" as Latina lesbian desire.

Like Muñoz and Moraga, Ortega acknowledges the "normativity of whiteness" in US queer culture and studies. In response to images of queer folks that are upheld in the dominant discourse, Ortega expresses a longing to find "visual representations of Latinas who love and desire women."[44] For Ortega, the lack of these images demonstrates a history of intolerance within both white and Latine culture. Lopez's image of Our Lady of Guadalupe and the Sirena from the *Lotería* game in an intimate embrace confronts this intolerance. Engaging this image with Muñoz's understanding of melancholia, Ortega beholds Lopez's depiction of the two popular female figures in Latine culture with simultaneous excitement for the possible opening to new worlds and a "state of ambivalence, because they prompt both uneasiness and longing." In other words, not only do the two women create new epistemologies, but they also represent a grief for a kind of love and life that has been lost due to systemic homophobia. This interpretation references what Ortega calls "melancholic longing"[45] or Muñoz's "queer utopian hermeneutic" which he defines as an unsettling of the present, looking beyond the here and now, and hoping for a queer future.[46]

The engagement between Muñoz and Lopez's art encourages Ortega to consider a "Queer Latinidad." For Ortega queerness and "Latinidad" are expansive and "thus need to go beyond the polarities of lesbian and gay, homosexuality and heterosexuality."[47] While Latinidad can be criticized for attempting to universalize Latine experience into a generalized reality, Ortega intentionally confronts this potential criticism and likens "Latinidad" with queerness as two lenses that question "the very practices and systems that have attempted to define" what it is to be Latine and queer.[48] Ortega pays special attention to Latine queerness in art to explain "queer Latinidad." According to Ortega, Lopez's piece is disruptive in understanding queerness and Latinidad because it displays more than just lesbian desire and subverts popular female figures in Latine society. On *Lupe and Sirena in Love*, she writes:

> It is about recognizing the different possibilities of Chicanas and other Latinxs, whether lesbian identified or not, to desire or love other women; questioning the narrow religious construction that Guadalupe may represent; problematizing the geographies and borders that suppress immigrant Latinas; countering hegemonic instantiations about what it means to be a good Latina; recognizing the multiplicity of desires that have a place in our visual imaginary; and finding new desires, even in the face of erasure.[49]

Returning to Muñoz's use of melancholia, Ortega acknowledges the lived reality of erasure, loss, and death in LGBTQIA+ lives. In this way, "melancholic longing" also functions to draw new possibilities without erasing the pain of living in heteronormative, homophobic social structures. Ortega explains how in their efforts to create new paradigms accepting of all forms of desire, queer people construct worlds where we "will carry our dead with us but in which we can also *be* who we want to be."[50] Here, Ortega takes a significant step away from Moraga's idyllic Aztlán because she acknowledges the unshakeable grief within a community of historically invisibilized and systemically murdered individuals.

Although she is writing from her perspective as a lesbian, Ortega does not impose her experience of sexuality and desire on all queer experiences. Unlike Moraga, Ortega intentionally includes trans folks in her imagination of "queer futurity." Pushing Muñoz, Ortega highlights how most of the examples in his imagination of queer futurity are centered on artistic productions of gay men and their particular experiences of loss and mourning. Therefore, her mourning is directed toward the object of "Latina desire, lust, and love for women and the visual representation of such desire, lust and love." For Ortega, "Latina desire for women has been erased from dominant culture and dominant culture's artistic production; it has also been minimized from gay/lesbian culture but also from queer culture/history/art as the latter centers the experience of the queer white male and sometimes the queer male of color."[51] Ortega's "Queer Latinidad" presents itself as a disruption in the understanding of queerness in Latine communities with special attention to a Latina/queer experience.

Ortega is careful to include other experiences of queer identity in her analysis but is still hyper-fixated on female-gendered desire and her own experience as a lesbian. Like Moraga, Ortega's perspective is a necessary conversation partner in Latina feminism and Mujerista thought as she indicates generalized intolerance of queer experience in both contexts and specific lack of awareness of lesbian desire in Queer Latine thought. Although both Moraga and Gloria Anzaldúa[52] identify as lesbians, and advocate for uplifting lesbian desire in Queer Latine thought, their understanding of queerness does not offer queer experiences outside of the lesbian/gay binary and are also wrapped up in a nationalist cultural worldview embedded in the Chicano Movement. On the other hand, Ortega seeks a broader understanding of queerness in a Latine context including, but not limited to, the Chicana experiences of lesbianism.

If Latina feminists and Mujeristas are more concerned with distinguishing themselves from each other rather than looking inward to unravel their own hegemonic tendencies through internal community racism, anti-blackness, and homophobia, it will be difficult to move beyond a perceived dichotomy between the two approaches. For this reason, the ways in which decolonial methods and Queer Latine thought push the discourse on gender and sexuality in Latina feminism and beyond must continue to be a priority. Francisco J. Galarte, a trans Chicano, is currently pushing the discourse in both Latina feminism, specifically Chicana feminism, and Queer Latine thought. Galarte notes the term "Chican@" is entirely different and distinct from "Chicana/o." He explains how "Chican@" is often viewed as a shorthand for Chicana/o but argues that "Simply regarding Chican@ as a shorthand alternative to get around post-1980s gender-inclusive formulations is quite possibly the resurgence of heteronormative patriarchal disciplining."[53] Like Méndez, Galarte is concerned with confronting racialized gender and engages "Chican@" "as a visual citational code for racialized gender outside the regularized categories of male and female as well as a direct resistance to heteronormative patriarchal disciplining."[54] Because trans identities have long been ignored by Latina feminist, Mujerista, and Queer thought, Galarte is invested in inscribing trans lived experiences into the discourse by integrating "Chican@" as a separate term and point of entry for creating necessary social paradigm shifts.

According to Galarte, this integration follows a legacy of self-advocacy within Latine movements. Just as Chicana feminists pushed back against the patriarchy in the Chicano Movement and queer Chicanas fought against the heteronormativity in both the movement and the feminist projects, Galarte seeks to push back against the canon that has not adequately dealt with trans experiences.[55] For Galarte, the failure to acknowledge and uplift the existence of trans folks in the discourse has relegated transgender Latine people "to a subordinate position wherein discourses of transphobia, homophobia, and racism enact themselves upon transgender bodies, repeating the violence of disavowal."[56] Here, Galarte is specifically grappling with Moraga's complicated inclusion of the trans experience in the fight against colonial heteronormative patriarchy.

Reading Moraga's *Xicana Codex of Changing Consciousness*, Galarte notes Moraga's acknowledgement of transness within the Chicano Movement while also adamantly privileging the female consciousness. For example, Moraga writes to the trans community, "Should you choose to transition to a man's body, you must still hold on desperately to your womanhood in the shaping of that masculinity. You must know that there is something in being born female from a female in a female-hating world that still matters."[57] Galarte sees this as both an acknowledgement of trans existence and an imposition of subordination on trans lives as this text "forces transgender folks to bear the burden of proving loyalty to a nation as well as being the figure that is the exemplar of race, sex, and gender abjection and liberation."[58] Within the field of Queer Latine studies, Galarte insists that queer and transgender cannot be "mutually antagonist terms."[59] On the contrary, Galarte's perspective actively asserts and defines queerness or "jotería as a family to which transgender Chican@s belong."[60] Moving forward, the inclusion of all forms of queerness and gender expression like Galarte's will only enrich the discourse and further complicate notions of gender, sex, and sexuality.

Finally, if Latina feminism and Mujerista thought do not center the narratives of queer folks, particularly our trans siblings, in analyses of eurocentric moral thinking, they risk ignoring the margins of the margins. In our pursuit of authentic solidarity and liberation, we must prioritize these voices in any critical analysis of power structures. An interdisciplinary dialogue between Latina/Chicana feminism, Mujerista thought, decolonial methods, and Queer Latine thought reveals the complexity of lived experiences in any given Latine context. Critical engagement across all fields will resist monolithic categories of identity and encourage contextually sensitive practices in our collective pursuit for justice and liberation.

11

Shades of Inequality: Colorism at the Intersection of Society and Religion

Alexandra Rosado-Román

I did not always have the words for it, but I felt its weight early on. The subtle silences, the sideways compliments, the unspoken standards of beauty and belonging. Colorism works like that: quietly, insistently, and often invisibly, shaping lives and communities from within. It is a legacy of colonialism that lives on in language, skin, and memory, reinforcing hierarchies even within the marginalized communities. This essay draws from an Afro-feminist decolonial framework to critically examine how colorism functions not only as a form of interpersonal bias but as a systemic force that cuts across social location, language, religious imagination, and practices of solidarity. By tracing its presence in everyday life and institutional structures, I seek to make visible what has long been normalized—and to imagine how confronting colorism might open pathways toward liberation, accountability, and radical communal healing.

What Is Colorism?

Colorism is a direct consequence of racism, defined as discrimination or prejudice based on race or ethnicity, and serves as a mechanism that reinforces social hierarchies within racialized communities. Rooted in colonial and Eurocentric standards, it favors lighter skin tones over darker ones, perpetuating inequalities in beauty, value, and social status.[1] Far from simply reflecting the contours of racism, colorism also intensifies intra-community divisions and embeds internalized forms of bias. Its influence extends beyond skin tone, shaping societal attitudes toward physical features such as hair texture and facial structure and intersecting with socioeconomic markers like education, class, and income.[2]

In the Americas—spanning North, Central, South, and the Caribbean—the roots of colorism can be traced to the period of *la Conquista*, when European colonizers instituted rigid racial hierarchies to secure and legitimize their dominance over Indigenous and African populations. Though these structures have transformed over time, their legacy endures through the ongoing logic of coloniality, which continues to shape multiple dimensions of life, including being, knowledge, power, and gender.[3] Although race is understood today as a social construct and not as an ontological reality, colorism persists as a pervasive and often invisible ideology deeply embedded across all facets of society.[4]

Examining colorism through these interconnected dimensions reveals its pervasive impact, deeply rooted in the colonial systems that shaped the Americas. By understanding this history, we can confront its enduring effects and work toward dismantling its influence on contemporary society. The persistent historical and intercultural tensions within Latin American communities underscore colorism as a significant source of inequality, demanding critical examination, deconstruction, and active efforts to eliminate it.[5]

Social Location: Cotidianidades Coloristas

Cotidianidad refers to the routine aspects of life that often go unnoticed due to familiarity and repetition. This concept allows us to examine subtle yet pervasive instances of colorism that may feel familiar, whether experienced personally or observed in others. To illustrate this, I present several cultural examples that highlight how colorism is performed and materialized in everyday cultural expressions and practices. For instance, being advised by family members about the need to *mejorar la Raza*—or "improve your race"—by marrying a white or lighter-skinned person with light-colored eyes and straight hair to produce "better" offspring exemplifies colorism. Likewise, being encouraged to straighten one's hair because it is deemed more beautiful or professional than curly, Afro, or dreadlocked hair reflects colorist ideals.

Compliments such as *eres una negra perfilá,* which imply that certain features are atypical of a Black person and therefore more desirable, also underscore the impact of colorism in daily life. In a similar vein, being affectionately called *negrita, canelita, azúcar morena, piel morena, prieta, trigueña, mulata, café con leche, color oliva,* and *negra* is noteworthy. Interestingly, these endearments are not often explicitly tied to racial discourse, adding to the complexity of our colorist discourse. Finally, hearing someone described in a beauty contest as "pretty or "well-expressed" for a Black or brown woman is a clear example of colorism.

Colorism operates on a spectrum, affecting both darker-skinned individuals and lighter-skinned people, particularly in the Caribbean and Latin America, who may be deemed "too light" to claim or engage with their Afro-descendant heritage and traditions fully. Additionally, colorism affects family interactions, shaping children's self-perceptions and the expectations they feel compelled to meet in order to gain parental approval.[6] All the previous examples reveal how deeply ingrained colorism is in Caribbean and Latin American societies, often remaining unacknowledged yet continuously reinforcing anti-Black racism within families and communities.

Far from being confined to academic or religious contexts, colorism impacts many aspects of daily life. Its internalized effects shape the dynamics of belonging and influence an individual's self-esteem and self-concept.[7] There is also significant discomfort when Caribbean or Latin American individuals decline to identify themselves within a racial category, as, due to the blending of cultures and identities, they often perceive themselves through their ethnicity rather than their skin color. Much of this rejection can signify several things: a rejection of the US racial binary paradigm, the assertion of an anti-Black racist understanding formed through colonial socialization, or simple ignorance.

My initial understanding of colorism as a Caribbean woman was shaped by the dominant rhetoric in Puerto Rico surrounding *la gran familia puertorriqueña*. This discourse promotes an image of harmonious integration among Indigenous, European, and African ancestries in the Caribbean and broader Latin America, fostering the illusion of a racially egalitarian society. However, this idealized portrayal often masks the pervasive realities of racial hierarchies and discrimination that persist beneath the surface.[8]

Deep-seated anti-Blackness permeates nearly every aspect of life, from personal relationships to broader sociocultural and spiritual practices. Colorism as an ingrained bias not only perpetuates intracultural and intercultural violence but has also historically impeded the development of just and equitable practices of solidarity within Caribbean and Latin American communities. Anti-racist activists are often criticized as overly sensitive or problematic, even as racial prejudice continues to erode community solidarity. This tension highlights the challenge of confronting deep-seated societal biases. Addressing these complexities demands sustained effort, as greater awareness and activism are essential for building more just and politically educated societies.

Colorism and Language

The exploration of colorism, often centered around skin tones and social advancement, rarely delves into the role of language. These privileges serve as a form of *"epidermal capital,"* enhancing opportunities for lighter-skinned individuals and for those who attain a normalized or higher status in education, economics, marriage, social status, culture, religion, citizenship, and mobility.[9] Puerto Rico's colonial history, first under European powers beginning in 1493 and later under the United States after 1898, makes it essential to examine language within the context of colorism. The ethnocentric ideologies and racial hierarchies established during these periods persist today. For instance, the United States attempted to impose English as the national language in 1902, shortly before imposing US citizenship on Puerto Ricans.[10]

In this context, language operates as a marker of colorism, with English linked to upward mobility within an imperialist hierarchy of privilege. While all dark-skinned individuals face discrimination, those who lack English proficiency and belong to lower social classes often experience compounded forms of marginalization. The connection between language and colorism is further reflected in colonial-era racial classifications, which established a Eurocentric hierarchy based on skin tone and racial mixture, thereby reinforcing systems of social stratification.[11]

This means that Spaniards born in the Caribbean with different ancestries were considered *Criollos.* At the same time, Europeans mixed with indigenous peoples were called *mestizas/os*, Europeans mixed with Africans were called *mulatas/os*, and First nations mixed with Africans were called *zambas/os*. At the top of the hierarchy in any union was the centrality of a white European person.[12] In discussing the repercussions of this racial stratification and its sociopolitical, cultural, religious, and citizenship consequences, individuals experience *colonial heterogeneity*—the multiple forms of violence articulated and materialized around race.[13] This dehumanization, rooted in colorism in the Caribbean, fuels intra- and intercultural conflicts, intensifying racism and obstructing anti-racist efforts. Expanding on these considerations, the relevance of representation when discussing colorism and language lies the fact that:

> Discussions on representation bring to the table analysis of how imperialism and colonization, as it is greatest expression, were embedded in social structures, ideological imperatives, cultural systems, and their value creations, as well as in language.[14]

This means that language within political movements and identity categories is critical to promoting or detracting from change. In the case of Latin American communities in the United States, this stratification is further codified through mechanisms such as the census.[15] An examination of this process, particularly regarding Puerto Rico, reveals how these classifications reinforce colorist hierarchies and maintain colonial legacies.

2010 Census[16] **Population: 3,725,789**	**2022 Census[17]** **Population: 320,000**
White 75.8%	White 59.97%
Black or African American 12.4%	Black or African American 11.30%
Other Race 7.8%	Other Race 18.68%

2010 Census[16] Population: 3,725,789	2022 Census[17] Population: 320,000
Asian 0.2%	Asian 0.18%
American Indian Alaskan Native 0.5%	Native American 0.17%

Notes
a. Percentages are based on racial self-identification reported in the US Census.
b. The increase in the "Other Race" category reflects shifting patterns of racial self-identification in Puerto Rico.

Recent demographic trends reveal three key shifts: (1) a decline in overall population numbers, (2) a decrease in individuals identifying as white, and (3) a reduction in those identifying as Black. At the same time, there is an increase in people selecting the "Some other race" category, suggesting a distancing from white identity. This shift may reflect ongoing adherence to the *la gran familia puertorriqueña* narrative or a growing acknowledgment of Afro-descendant heritage. For Latin American communities participating in the US census, selecting a category that accurately reflects ethnicity and race is complex. While broadly categorized as Hispanic or Latino, Caribbean communities like Puerto Ricans struggle to find a racial category that fits their multifaceted identities. Many avoid identifying as African American due to its US-centric association and reject the Black category due to racial mixing and internalized colorism. This reluctance complicates racial identification within census frameworks.

Examining the complexities of racial categorization for Puerto Ricans in the United States highlights significant challenges. For example, the native "Hawaiian or Other Pacific Islander" category is problematic, as Puerto Ricans are Caribbean islanders, not Pacific islanders, each with distinct ethnicities and cultures. The "American Indian or Alaska Native" category also presents issues, as Puerto Rico's colonial history and the near eradication of its Indigenous population have led to the misconception that these communities were completely eliminated during the conquest. However, genetic studies show that Puerto Ricans retain substantial Indigenous Latin American ancestry, a fact often overlooked in Puerto Rican identity. Consequently, the "American Indian or Alaska Native" label is typically reserved for Indigenous populations within the continental United States. These rigid categories fragment Puerto Rican and Latin American identities, fueling confusion and reinforcing white supremacy within these communities.

Black and Afro-descendant *Latiné* American communities have worked to expose their invisibility within both local and US contexts, challenging prevailing definitions of "Hispanic" and Latinidad. This movement, framed by *Afro-Latinidades*, underscores the urgent need to reclaim Afro-descendants as a core component of identity. It also highlights how racial classification in the United States is often tied to access to federal funding and economic resources, affecting the structural treatment of communities. These rigid racial categories fragment and homogenize identities, reinforcing confusion and perpetuating white supremacy within Latin American communities.[18] For those who argue race is not a pressing issue, the pervasive influence of colorism across social, cultural, and political domains proves otherwise. Colorism, like all ideologies, adapts to shifting social conditions and systemic pressures, necessitating ongoing analysis and contextualization in order to address these issues in our present realities.

In summary, like the spectrum of skin tones, colorism is a layered construct, with each layer revealing a distinct way in which it shapes lives. Understanding identity requires more than exploring cultural traits; it also demands a critical examination of the colonial ideologies that colonized communities have internalized and perpetuated among themselves. Racial stratification is not solely based on skin tone but also on phenotypic traits such as hair texture, nose width, and lip thickness—traits that, when closer to European standards of whiteness, are often associated with greater social mobility and privileges.[19] In this framework, lighter skin is granted higher value,[20] while darker skin is deemed less valuable. These categorizations are further complicated by intersecting factors such as educational attainment, socioeconomic status, gender, sexual orientation, and religious beliefs, each adding nuance to how colorism operates within society.[21]

Colorism and Religion

Colorism remains a neglected topic in religious curricula due to the persistent dominance of Eurocentric perspectives and the marginalization of issues related to race and ethnicity within theological discourse as well as the continued reliance on a binary and segregated view of race that obscures the complex realities of Afro-descendant and mixed-race identities. This reliance on such binaries, reinforced within academic settings, often limits critical conversations about the subtleties of racial and color-based discrimination, particularly within religious communities. As a teaching assistant under an African American male professor, I was once confronted by an African American female student who told me I was neither "a man, a reverend, a Christian, nor Black enough" to teach the class.

This personal experience highlights how colorism manifests within religious education, where individuals with lighter skin or perceived marginal identities face invalidation. Such instances reflect how colorism, often overlooked, serves as a source of interpersonal and institutional conflict, which, if left unaddressed, perpetuates systemic inequities and hinders the development of inclusive and culturally competent religious education. Addressing colorism within academic curricula is essential for promoting justice, solidarity, and equitable representation in faith-based and educational institutions. Nevertheless, colorism in religion is evident in the depiction of religious figures with lighter skin, the preference of lighter-skinned individuals for leadership positions, the demonization of darker-skinned cultural practices, and the association of moral superiority with lighter skin. Yet where do these entrenched practices and understandings originate from?

As this essay outlines, *limpieza de sangre* (blood purity) is deeply rooted in colonial history, where it shaped social mobility within rigid caste systems.[22] Used to "cleanse" Jewish and Muslim converts, it primarily served to subjugate African and Indigenous communities. Racialized groups were forced to conform to Christian orthodoxy, renouncing "heterodox" beliefs as part of a broader racial and religious assimilation.[23] This practice reinforced social hierarchies, solidifying the dominance of European-descended elites by equating racial purity with moral and cultural superiority. In many other parts of the world influenced by colonial histories, portrayals of religious figures predominantly feature European phenotypic traits, often propagating the idea that lighter skin is synonymous with purity and sanctity.[24]

Similarly, there are verses in the Bible that use the binary white-versus-Black.[25] This entrenched colorism within religious iconography, which often portrays Jesus closer to the lighter end of the colorist spectrum of privilege, implicitly reinforces racial hierarchies and the marginalization of darker-skinned individuals. However, artistic expressions, particularly in music, often challenge these entrenched views by reimagining religious figures in more inclusive forms. A poignant example comes from the Puerto Rican salsa artist Roberto Angleró, who envisions a world where divine figures mirror those often marginalized in society. Roberto Angleró's song "Si Dios fuera negro" imagines a world where divine figures, including God and Jesus, are Black. The chorus states: "Si Dios fuera negro, mi compay, todo cambiaría, fuera nuestra raza, mi compay la que mandaría. Negro fuera el Papa y negro el ministro, los ángeles negros, negro Jesucristo, compay."[26] These lyrics challenge traditional religious depictions, suggesting that if these figures were Black, it could disrupt societal norms and power structures. Angleró's song serves as a counter-narrative, interrogating the theological foundations of racial inequality, including colorism.

Moreover, James Cone, a Black liberation theologian, developed a Black theology in response to the Black people's historical and ongoing oppression, particularly in the United States. He asserted that "God is Black" to challenge the dominant Eurocentric, white supremacist images of God and to affirm God's solidarity with the oppressed, especially Black individuals.[27] For Cone, God's identification with the marginalized was central to liberation theology, empowering Black people, affirming their dignity, and confronting the racialized theology used to justify their oppression. Similarly, the devotion to the Black Christ of *Esquipulas*, originating in Guatemala, has become a powerful symbol of resistance and identity for marginalized communities across Central America, Mexico, and the United States.[28] Sculpted by Quirio Cataño, the Black Christ is a religious figure who counters the Europeanized image of Christ imposed by colonial powers. In a region with a history of racial hierarchies, the Black Christ affirms the humanity, dignity, and spiritual worth of Afro-descendant communities, offering a divine representation that aligns with their lived experiences.

Colorism and Solidarity

Colorist practices contribute to inequalities in areas such as media representation, marriage prospects, income, employment, education, healthcare, employment opportunities, religious affiliation, and criminal justice.[29] Similar to racism, colorism involves prejudice and discrimination among people, often upheld by societal institutions, and exists within marginalized communities such as Black, Latin, Caribbean, Native American, and Asian groups.[30]

Frantz Fanon's concept of "atmospheric violence" highlights how colonialism stifles awareness of these dynamics, limiting opportunities for solidarity.[31] He argues that the colonial narrative, which favors the colonizer, permeates society, creating racialized identities that subordinate communities, foster dependency on the colonizer, and perpetuate internalized racial narratives. Consequently, discrimination based on shade of color is not only external but also occurs within many marginalized communities. Like epidermal capital or upward mobility, these privileges afford lighter-skinned individuals greater educational opportunities, employment, marriage prospects, social standing, cultural acceptance, religious affiliation, citizenship rights, and physical mobility.[32]

Understanding colorism requires a multifaceted approach, starting with introspection and expanding to collective action. This involves examining personal histories, challenging inherited biases, and dismantling systemic structures that perpetuate colorism. Beyond focusing solely on "white supremacy," we must deconstruct the Black-and-white racial binary. Prioritizing conflict transformation within communities is vital, as conflicts offer opportunities for listening, reflection, and accountability. It is also crucial to address the errosion of solidarity when lighter-skinned individuals within marginalized communities downplay the violence of colorism, as this disregard deepens conflict and entrenches societal separation. Colorism manifests in everyday life through microaggressions, such as compliments about "light skin" being more desirable or assumptions that lighter-skinned individuals are more capable.

Finally, key practices include raising awareness through education, amplifying diverse media representation, and promoting critical pedagogy on race and identity. Creating inclusive spaces that celebrate all skin tones, engaging in self-reflection, and holding individuals accountable remain essential for both personal and collective growth. Solidarity from lighter-skinned individuals and advocacy for institutional change are vital steps toward broader transformation. By fostering interracial and intercultural solidarity, communities can challenge colorism and move closer to justice.

12

Our Fluidity

Grego Peña-Camprubí

Tú tienes en los recuerdos profundos que en mi alma forman lo más alto y sublime, una luz inmortal.

—RUBÉN DARÍO[1]

***Recordar** (Spanish) (v.): from the Latin 'recordari', which is composed by the prefix "re-," indicating repetition, and "cordis," meaning 'heart'.[2] Together, these roots form a concept that can literally be interpreted as 'to pass through the heart again'.*

Luisa was born in a coastal town in Colombia. From a young age, she remembers her grandmother telling her, "Oh, my butterfly! Don't stay trapped on this branch." Luisa would smile, chalking up the nonsensical phrase to the ramblings of a woman who, for as long as Luisa could remember, had sported gray hair. At the age of twenty, Luisa emigrated to New York, invited by her cousin. In the United States, she discovered a new world full of spots where she could celebrate her identity as a trans woman. However, Luisa could not shake a sense of disconnect from the people around her. It felt like wearing crimson red to a party where everyone else wore white, yet only herself could notice the difference. The routine visits of Aunt Aurora to her parents' house, the coastal Colombian jargon, the closeness of friendships—all of them seemed to have been left behind and trapped among the palm trees of her childhood village.

In the Bronx, Luisa worked as a waitress. It was there that she met Clara, a Mexican trans woman with whom Luisa forged a beautiful friendship. Clara spoke to her about Mexico, about her native Oaxaca, filled with colors, music, and life in the streets; about feeling far from that warm, familiar home of her childhood, where life seemed more human and simpler; and about the nostalgia that comes from building bridges that simultaneously distance and connect us to the worlds we inhabit. Clara spoke of the price one pays to truly be oneself.

"You don't have to choose, Luisa," Clara told her. "You're like a butterfly that migrates and flies through the skies of different worlds." Over the years, Luisa began spending more time between her native Colombia and New York. Slowly, running barefoot along Colombia's beaches felt as natural as soaring through the skyscrapers of the Big Apple. With each journey between her two homes, Luisa carried a piece of the place she was leaving behind, bringing with her—like butterflies do—the essence needed to find her way back home.[3]

This vignette illustrates the challenges and fluidity of living between the Global North and the Global South. Luisa's story is powerful, both in its content and in its method of transmission. Storytelling is a potent tool for communication. Storytelling is likely the most ancient mechanism through which human beings have conveyed ideas, cosmologies, worldviews, myths, and histories that have given meaning to our existence since the advent of oral language. The transmission of information and ideas through stories is as old as our species. Its power lives in the fires of the first *Homo sapiens*, resonates in medieval epic songs, and moves us on the big screen. Storytelling is an intrinsic part of the human DNA—its value is immense. In this chapter, I use storytelling as a method of healing. I utilize storytelling, often used to harm LGBTQ+[4] people, as a tool to reclaim our own narratives. Storytelling can affirm identity and visibility, celebrate cultural intersectionality, and provide meaning and context for the queer Latines who live in fluidity between the Global North and the Global South.

The Global North and the Global South: A Tale of Fluidity

To contextualize the fluidity experienced by LGBTQ+ Latine individuals between the Global North and the Global South, it is necessary to begin this argument by discussing nomenclature. Terms such as *queer*, *LGBTQ+*, *homosexual*, and *genderfluid* respond to specific contexts. These concepts are products of sociological, cultural, and historical realities rooted in Western frameworks. The dominant discourse of LGBTQ+, particularly in academia, originates in the Western paradigm of thought, which includes phenomena such as the nineteenth-century medicalization of homosexuality and the emancipatory struggle for the rights of non-heterosexual individuals.[5] When it comes to queer discourses, the case of Latin America is unique. These narratives are informed by the genocide and epistemicide of Indigenous perspectives,[6] while simultaneously imbued with Western epistemologies. The permeability of its borders—both physical and metaphysical—renders Latin America a complex context in which essentializing the idiosyncrasies of the Global North and the Global South is challenging,[7] particularly in the case of Latine lived experiences.

Despite this fluidity, there are ontological and epistemological differences between the Global North and the Global South. Ontology focuses on the study of being, reality, and existence. In the Global North, LGBTQ+ reality is expressed through an individualistic and universalist lens. The term *LGBTQ+* is understood primarily in political and medical terms. The Global North emphasizes the individual rights of queer subjects, often divorced from other aspects of identity such as ethnicity, race, religion, or spirituality. Sexual identities like gay and lesbian are viewed as fixed categories, and inclusion is approached institutionally as exemplified by same-sex marriage laws in modern nation-states.

In the Global South, particularly in the Americas, queer ontology is understood differently. In general, queerness is approached from a more relational and contextual perspective. Queer identities are less static and are more closely tied to community, historical, and spiritual factors. As such, LGBTQ+ experiences are often intersectional and intertwined with culture, family, religion, and more. Within this framework, queer identities do not exist as separate categories but are inseparable from the larger whole. Examples include the *muxes*[8] in Mexico or the *chacha-warmis*[9] in Aymara Andean culture.

Epistemologically, there are also significant differences between the Global North and the Global South within the Americas. Epistemology concerns itself with how we come to know reality, focusing on the origin, evolution, and limits of knowledge. In the Global North, a scientific, secular, and rationalist approach dominates the inquiry into knowledge. This is evident in milestones like the depathologization of homosexuality by the American Psychological Association (APA) in 1973 and subsequent changes to the DSM (Diagnostic and Statistical Manual of Mental Disorders). LGBTQ+ rights movements in the Global North are framed within a universal understanding of human rights, often assuming an essentialist and homogenous nature of queer experiences. This can lead to the decontextualization of local queer experiences and the imposition of Western normative frameworks.

In contrast, the Global South's approach to knowledge is more localized than universal and often rooted in oral and spiritual traditions. Generally, cosmologies and worldviews in the Global South are more collectivist, and LGBTQ+ activism takes an intersectional form, addressing issues such as poverty and the lack of social and political recognition alongside sexual and gender diversity.

Trauma: Beyond the Individual Psique

To understand the fluidity experienced by queer Latine individuals straddling the Global North and Global South, it is essential to address trauma—both individual and collective. Indeed, assessing the role of trauma is the central focus of this chapter. The word *trauma*, derived from the Greek verb meaning "to pierce or wound," etymologically signifies "injury or damage."[10] In Latin and Germanic languages, the term *trauma* was initially used in medical contexts. With the development of psychology and psychiatry in the nineteenth century, *trauma* began to describe emotional or psychological wounds with lasting impacts on the psyche. Originally conceptualized in psychology, trauma was largely understood in individualistic terms.

Today, there are many definitions of trauma. For this chapter, I adopt the definition offered by Dutch psychiatrist Bessel van der Kolk, who describes trauma as something that "leaves an imprint on mind, body, and brain."[11] I am fully aware that van der Kolk's definition of trauma is far from perfect. The fields of psychology and psychiatry, inherently rooted in Western epistemological contexts, can pose significant challenges when applied to decolonial queering processes. Nevertheless, van der Kolk's definition highlights the centrality of the body in assessing trauma, expanding the conversation beyond the trauma's psychological effects. The element of embodiment is a crucial factor, particularly in decolonial approaches to evaluating, processing, and healing trauma. To provide a more holistic and accurate approach within a decolonial framework of Global North–Global South fluidity, a spiritual dimension to van de Kolk's definition of trauma should exist.

From a decolonial perspective, trauma takes on a collectivist and holistic dimension, where the individual is situated within the constellation of their community rather than as an independent subject. Moving away from the individualistic view of Western ontology, trauma can be understood as a wound in the equilibrium of being. This imbalance affects not only the individual but also their connection with their community, ancestors, natural environment, and cosmos. Healing trauma requires restoring the body, physiology, collective relationships, and spirituality—not just the psyche. The dismemberment of queer LGBTQ+ identities occurs on both individual and collective levels. Migration or the colonization of Indigenous spaces can uproot the self geographically and culturally. This spatial disintegration can lead to emotional dismemberment, severing familial or group ties through border policies—both physical and symbolic—persistent coloniality, and diaspora.

Another source of trauma for Latine individuals in the United States is linguistic and cultural fragmentation. Spanish, Portuguese, or Indigenous languages are often displaced in linguistic contexts dominated by English or another language.[12] Stripped of their mother tongue, Latine individuals are not only deprived of words but also of a worldview that situates them in a familiar location. In an unfamiliar linguistic context, individuals lose agency in their new society. One consequence of the rampant individualism of the Global North is the inability to affirm a holistic identity fully. The internalization of multiple oppressions leads to the disintegration of the complete self into atomized identities. In other words, the power systems of the Global North fragment the Latine subject into someone who may experience homophobia, racism, xenophobia, and so on but who is forced to struggle to conceive the intersectionality and overlapping layers of these systems of oppression.

The Latine context has a complex history concerning its religious and spiritual thought. The Christianization of the Americas and the subsequent collapse of Indigenous religious and spiritual forms created an epistemological and ontological rift. The emergence of hybrid forms of spirituality and religious thought permeates the Americas, expressing itself uniquely in queer contexts, such as the *muxes* in Mexico and the *chacha-warmis* in Andean cultures. While there are multiple types of traumas manifesting in the lives of queer Latine individuals, this chapter focuses on six: (1) structural and systemic trauma, (2) intersectional trauma, (3) cultural and historical trauma, (4) spiritual and religious trauma, (5) racial trauma, and (6) complex trauma.

According to Norwegian sociologist Johan Galtung, structural and systemic trauma is characterized by the harm caused by social structures that prevent individuals from meeting their basic needs or reaching their full potential.[13] Galtung further explains that this structural trauma is often invisible and lacks a single identifiable perpetrator, making it multilayered. In her book *Trauma and Recovery*, Judith Herman suggests that trauma is best understood not only as an individual psychological experience but also as a deeply social phenomenon interconnected with and shaped by systems of power and oppression.[14] Although her book does not specifically focus on trauma, Vivian May's *Pursuing Intersectionality* can help us understand trauma as an intersectional experience. May's analysis of intersectionality highlights systemic oppression as a source of trauma and the erasure of marginalized individuals' voices.[15]

Gloria Anzaldúa's renowned book *Borderlands/La Frontera* is an excellent resource for exploring cultural and historical trauma among individuals who live between the Global North and the Global South. Using autoethnography, Anzaldúa demonstrates how US Latines inhabit an interstitial space where different cultures, identities, and oppressions intersect. She suggests that existing in this space, because of identity dismemberment and re-memberment, creates a "new mestiza consciousness."[16] Marcella Althaus-Reid's *Indecent Theology* seeks to disrupt the constraints of "decent theology," which marginalizes and silences those living outside the boundaries of decency and respectability. While rooted in Christian theology, *Indecent Theology* is a fascinating resource for addressing religious and spiritual trauma from a queer Latine perspective. The book challenges the sacred-secular binary that divides the sacred from the profane in "decent theology," contributing to religious trauma and spiritual alienation.[17]

Although not centered on religious thought, Melissa Harris-Perry's *Sister Citizen: Shame, Stereotypes, and Black Women in America* explores the role of shame in personal and communal contexts. In Chapter 6, titled "God," Harris-Perry highlights faith as a source of resilience for Black women. Her analysis of shame as a political tool also applies to religious spaces, where shame can be used to enforce conformity within religious communities, generate spiritual alienation, and separate LGBTQ+ individuals from their communities, thus preventing them from accessing God collectively.[18] Racial trauma is a reality for many queer Latines living in the Global North. In her book *Ain't I a Woman?*, the multifaceted American writer bell hooks examines the intersectionality of oppression faced by Black women in America. Hooks argues that racism is rarely experienced in isolation; rather, oppression creates layers of trauma that impact individuals and communities. She emphasizes that the indissolubility of race and gender is key to understanding how oppression manifests in the lived experiences of people of color.[19] Complex trauma results from repeated or cumulative exposure to traumatic events, including microaggressions. Cathy Caruth's book *Unclaimed Experience: Trauma, Narrative, and History* deeply engages with the concept of complex trauma, which is typically understood as embedded in relational or systemic contexts. In cases of complex trauma, survivors often grapple with fragmented memories (i.e., dis-membering) and experience these as deeply intersectional wounds.[20]

Re-member and Recordar

The value of *recordar* and re-membering serves as the central thread that contextualizes this chapter. These processes of reconstruction and reevaluation can only occur after experiences of dis-membering. Dis-membering is crucial and necessary for any act of re-membering to take place. Re-membering recognizes the body as the locus of change. It becomes an embodied act of political resistance and a narrative of reconstruction that is communal, relational, theological, and spiritual. The Spanish term *recordar* (to remember) is etymologically rooted in "to pass through the heart again." This concept of *recordar* underscores that dismembering is not just important but a necessary prerequisite for re-membering. This is not to suggest that colonization, genocide, and oppression are justified but rather is to present them as inescapable realities in the lives of Latines.

Dismembering and re-membering permeate the religious thoughts, stories, and myths of people across the Americas. As Wendy Doniger explains in *Other People's Myths*, myths are not static but dynamic and fluid entities that narrate the stories of the societies and individuals that create and interpret them. For Doniger, myths are both universal and specific—they address fundamental human concerns while reflecting cultural, societal, and historical particularities.[21] For example, in many Native American traditions, maize is considered a sacred gift from the gods.[22] The processes of planting, harvesting, dormition, and regrowth symbolize a cycle of breaking apart (dismembering) and regeneration (re-membering). The kernels of corn must be separated from the cob to grow into new plants, offering a powerful symbol of renewal and transformation rooted in the earth. In Aztec mythology, the Moon Goddess Coyolxauhqui was dismembered by her brother Huitzilopochtli, the Sun God, during a cosmic battle. After her dismemberment, her body parts were cast down the mountain, and her head became the moon, illuminating the night. Coyolxauhqui's story is one of transformation and motion. Each lunar cycle reenacts her dismemberment, symbolizing death, rebirth, and renewal.

In Christianity, the death of Christ represents the ultimate act of dismembering. During his crucifixion, Jesus's body is literally broken, and the hope and joy of his followers are shattered. However, the resurrection of Christ is a profound act of re-membering, restoring hope and unity within Christian communities and symbolizing the emergence of new life and wholeness from suffering and fragmentation.

The universal theme of dismembering and re-membering is expressed through another deeply human universal—storytelling. Storytelling is both a tool for meaning-making and a medium for cultural, psychological, and spiritual healing. Myths often serve as vehicles for shared values, cosmologies, and moral lessons. Through oral tradition, storytelling reveals profound truths about human existence, such as the inevitability of fragmentation and the promise of healing. For Latines, storytelling frames experiences of grief, crises, resilience, and renewal, offering opportunities for continuity in identity formation and allowing fragments to be pieced together to create a cohesive present and future. Since dismembering occurs in relational and social contexts, re-membering must also be interrelational. Trauma isolates individuals from themselves and their communities. Therefore, healing is the work of restoring and rebuilding the "social body," which sees the individual as embedded within a particular social context.

Audre Lorde's perspective on self-care in *A Burst of Light* offers an inspiring lens: "Caring for myself is not self-indulgence, it is self-preservation, and that is an act of political warfare."[23] For LGBTQ+ Latines, self-care is indeed an act of resistance—a reclamation of agency over one's body and life in a world that often devalues and discards them. Self-care is a deeply embodied process engaging the mind, heart, and spirit. It is also an act of *recordar*—to revisit joys and tribulations in the heart to move toward wholeness. Lorde's concept of self-care extends beyond the individual to the community. Just as wounding and dismemberment occur in relational contexts, healing and wholeness must also take place between people. Honoring one's story and the stories of others becomes a way to re-member and mourn collective struggles. Through *recordar* and re-membering, collective healing practices transform pain into power. Spaces of *hermandad*[24] enable communities to recraft narratives and re-member fractured selves, gaining tools for resistance and survival. To bring memories to the forefront is an active, transformative process—accepting both past and present realities while laying the groundwork for future acts of political resistance, as Lorde describes. In this way, *recordar* becomes the cornerstone for imagining and building future pathways for queer Latines.

Latine Queer Theologies, Spiritualities, and Mysticism

It would be a disservice to discuss stories of disintegration, dismemberment, and reconstruction for LGBTQ+ Latines without mentioning the spiritual and mystical dimension. Meza Santos reminds us that "mystical experiences are always perceived as new forms of religiosity, new spiritual paths … emergent approaches through which the full integration of humanity is sought."[25] Mysticism is a fluid form of religiosity because it is simultaneously anchored in the center and at the periphery. It is central because it addresses the most intimate metaphysical aspects of being. At the same time, mysticism in organized religion inhabits a constellation of spirituality that overflows established normative frameworks. In this part of the chapter, I argue that queer theology and mysticism, as well as the spiritual experiences of LGBTQ+ individuals, exist within this paradoxical and fluid duality of center and periphery.

This mystical space is shaped by mystical practices and experiences and encompasses the physical, the metaphysical, and the imaginative. This multidimensional space is also polyphonic, molded by the plurality of queer Latine voices.[26] These voices do not exist in a vacuum; rather, they share lived experiences represented by "common religious identities, existential realities, cultural contexts, searches, and questions ..."[27] Dismembering represents a fragmentation, exile, and uprooting of the queer subject and their community. As Santos Meza highlights, religious institutions have systematically marginalized mystics who challenge cis-heteropatriarchal norms.[28] This is particularly evident for queer individuals who are profoundly affected by certain theological principles, such as the duality of body and soul in traditions like Christianity. The body, gender expression, and sexual orientation—intrinsically connected to spiritual life—are relegated to the realm of the indecent and the heterodox.[29] These are often labeled as "sinful" or "immoral," thus fracturing a sense of unity with the self, the community, and the divine.

Re-Membering as Reconstruction, Embodiment, and Reintegration

The process of re-membering involves a theological and spiritual effort of reconstruction, where what is fragmented is reintegrated, creating a new sense of wholeness. This is a key concept in queer mysticism, which seeks to validate, heal, and present the mystical experiences of queer individuals as orthodox. Re-membering and reconstruction can be sacred acts of calling one's soul back. For queer Latines, spiritual fragmentation can be the product of colonial inheritance. By re-membering, the soul can retrieve its parts scattered by trauma, diaspora, and isolation. This act can be a step in mending the double rupture caused by the exile of body and spirit.

Reconstruction is a ritual of constant becoming. Rituals have that power—they can be restorative. Wearing an *awayo* bracelet, putting on eyeliner, dancing to Bad Bunny, or making *arroz con leche* can be restorative practices for many queer Latines because they hold spiritual, cultural, and emotional relevance. Far from constituting formal practices, these rituals are embodied, improvised, and sacred in their repetition. Following the legacy of theologians like Marcella Althaus-Reid, a focus on the body and embodiment informs queer religious thought, spiritualities, and theologies, as they challenge heteropatriarchal notions of spirituality and access to the divine. In Christianity, queering the body of Christ can transform and redeem the queer individual as a living member in an eschatological process of salvation, which can be both individual and collective. In an Indigenous context, the recovery of peripheral practices and narratives associated with animist traditions can play a central role in the process of re-membering. These practices, which often defy binary categories of gender and sexuality, may prioritize the restoration of a divine and/or cosmic balance disrupted by the fragmentation of the individual self, the collective entity, their cosmologies, and the earth. Celebrating both Día de Muertos and Queer Remembrance Day or pouring *chicha* or tequila on the land as an ofrenda are examples of how queer Latines can embody this restorative logic. From this perspective, syncretism is not confusion but wisdom. Spiritual reintegration is not about "mixing" but about honoring these practices by making a home for them across worlds.

Recordar can be conceived as a spiritual act of mourning, reconciliation, healing, and reconstruction. Beyond being a cerebral exercise of memory, *recordar* takes on a dimension as a multitemporal theological movement encompassing the past, present, and the radical potential of a future liberation. *Recordar* can also be approached as an act of mystical resistance for LGBTQ Latines. Santos Meza describes mysticism as a radical openness to reality that challenges hegemonic structures.[30] This vital and spiritual openness allows the experiences of exclusion and violence to be brought into the present through an act of vital and spiritual discernment. This exercise of multidimensional cartography—exploring vertical, horizontal, and intersectional axes of the subject's relationships with their surroundings and the divine—can acquire a healing dimension. Our wounds are diverse. Some examples include exclusion, family pressure to meet dating expectations, the burden of social, academic, and career achievement as a child of immigrants who sacrificed so much, the murder of queer spiritualities committed by religious leaders, shame, the need to become a parent to one's younger siblings or even one's own parents—whether for linguistic reasons or simply to survive, etc. While these experiences may not amount to capital-T Trauma, they constitute what we know as complex trauma[31]—a thousand cuts that leave both body and spirit scarred. The ointment for these cuts is spiritual discernment, understood not as a victimizing reaffirmation, but as a form of resistance and repair, which can transform pain into liberation and a commitment to justice. In this sense, forgiveness does not need to mean reconciliation or forgetting. It becomes a way of freeing the spirit so it can witness its own liberation—its own journey to wholeness.

At the same time, memory takes on an eschatological character. After the metaphorical death of the unliberated Latine queer subject, memory finds meaning and significance in the becoming of God and the divine. The act of passing through the heart once again (*recordar*), in its dimensions of resistance, discernment, and liberation, opens a horizon of meaning, hope, and transformation for both the individual and the collective self, where queer Latine lives are valued and celebrated.

13

Death or Salvation of a Planet

Amanda J. Baugh

On September 28, 2008, Ecuador became the first country in the world to enshrine the rights of nature into its constitution. Drawing from the Andean philosophy of *buen vivir* (living well), an Indigenous outlook that prioritizes harmony with nature and views nonhuman nature as a subject with its own intrinsic value, the new constitution established a legal framework that empowers ordinary citizens to represent and defend nature regardless of personal damage.[1] In direct opposition to Western legal codes that separate humans from the rest of the environment and treat nature as inert property, Ecuador's constitution affirms that nature has a right to exist regardless of its usefulness for humans.[2] At the same time, the constitution recognizes that humans are part of nature and rely on the natural world for their survival.[3] The constitution further establishes that defending Mother Earth is a matter of both necessity and religion. It expressly invokes the name of God and recognizes that "diverse forms of religion and spirituality" can enrich society by supporting struggles against colonialism and domination.[4]

While Ecuador's constitution is noteworthy for establishing a legal framework that recognizes the inalienable rights of nonhuman nature, its underlying set of religious environmental values is far from unique. Scholars of Latine history, culture, and religion have identified a similar set of ecological values among Latine communities in a variety of historical and geographical contexts, although these values are not always recognized as religious or environmental.[5] Rather than aligning with dominant environmental narratives that prioritize relationships with nature based on leisure and recreation, Latine ecological values often integrate social and environmental concerns and center on productive relationships with the land.

This chapter introduces readers to scholarship from within and beyond the study of religion in order to identify a long and often overlooked tradition of Latine religious environmentalism. While stories of environmental values among minoritized communities generally focus on environmental racism and injustice, this chapter emphasizes that Latine communities are not merely victims of environmental problems; they are also environmental leaders and agents. The inclusion of *buen vivir* philosophy in Latin American legal frameworks offers one example among many, where Latin American and Latine communities enact religious environmental values that are oriented toward well-being, dignity, and justice for the entire community—including both humans and the more-than-human world. Identifying and uplifting these stories can strengthen our understanding of earth care from a Latine perspective and advance the aims of social and environmental justice.

Life-Affirming Ethics and Relationships with the Land

The Andean philosophy of *buen vivir*—living well— is a plural concept whose meaning varies depending on the ecological, cultural, and historical context. But in general, writes Uruguayan ecologist Eduardo Gudynas, *buen vivir* (or *vivir bien*, as it is better-known in Bolivia) "are the Spanish words used in Latin America to describe alternatives to development focused on the good life in a broad sense."[6] The concept is further associated with "both material and spiritual wellbeing and is identified with a life of fullness."[7] The origins of *buen vivir* can be traced to cultural revitalization movements in Bolivia and Ecuador in the 1970s and 1980s, when Indigenous leaders and allies reacted to the rise of neoliberal policies by seeking alternative futures grounded in visions of the good life. By the 1990s, the idea increasingly became detached from its original Indigenous context as it was popularized among Latin American intellectuals. The idea of "living well" has since been adopted by both Indigenous and non-Indigenous activists and intellectuals, as a constantly evolving vision for the future that draws wisdom from the past.[8] According to anthropologist Robert Albro, *buen vivir* typically encompasses "a community-centric, ecologically balanced, economically sustainable, socially harmonious, and culturally meaningful set of commitments, where 'society' also includes people's reciprocal obligations and responsibilities to 'nature.' "[9]

Numerous scholars invested in environmental politics among Latine communities have identified a related set of community-centric environmental commitments that involve reciprocal relationships with nonhuman nature. Among the scholars and activists who have emphasized the promise of *buen vivir* for addressing a variety of global environmental issues, Peruvian American theologian Theresa Yugar argues that Latine "environmental resisters" in the United States and Latin America—including Indigenous leaders in Latin America, grassroots organizers in the United States, and Latin American leaders in the global Catholic Church—have often engaged in struggles for social and environmental justice "in the spirit of *buen vivir*."[10] Literary scholar Priscilla Solis Ybarra finds a related set of environmental values through analysis of Mexican American literature dating back to the mid-nineteenth century. Through a genre that she calls "goodlife writing," Ybarra illustrates how Mexican Americans have long maintained reciprocal relationships with the land through practices such as small-scale agriculture, curanderismo, backyard gardening, and recycling. Similar to the philosophy of *buen vivir*, these sustainable practices offer a dynamic vision for the future that draws wisdom from the past. While narratives of modern environmentalism center on a desire to repair unhealthy, exploitative human relationships with the environment, Ybarra writes, "goodlife writing shows how the Mexican American and Chicana/o culture enacts values and practices that include nature all along."[11] While Ybarra does not dwell on the religious or spiritual elements that shape this genre, she does emphasize that it maintains connections with pre-colonial practices and epistemologies, and rejects modernity's anthropocentric vision of humans as separate from the rest of nature.

If Ybarra is correct that Mexican American culture contains deeply rooted environmental values, then why is it that Mexican American communities do not figure more prominently in dominant narratives of American environmental history? Scholars have noted that a combination of philosophical and epistemological differences, overt racism within the environmental movement, and historical conflicts have alienated many Latines from modern environmentalism. Historian Sara C. Fingal traces this disjuncture to the rise of the conservationist movement (a precursor to modern environmentalism) in the late-nineteenth and early-twentieth centuries. In that era of rapid urbanization in the United States, affluent white Americans began worrying that they were destroying the last remnants of untouched nature that made the nation so exceptional. They wanted to ensure there would always be places where they could escape the artificialities of city life and experience the beauty and wonder of nature. In response, conservationist leaders such as Theodore Roosevelt, John Muir, and Gifford Pinchot began creating protected areas such as wilderness preserves and state and national parks.[12]

But in order for uninhabited wilderness to be preserved, conservationists first had to *create* unpeopled landscapes by forcibly removing Indigenous inhabitants and other people who relied on the land for their survival.[13] In the Southwestern United States, conservationist priorities affected the livelihoods of Mexican farmers, hunters, and fisherman whose homelands became part of US territory with the Treaty of Guadalupe Hidalgo in 1848. Fingal notes that these communities had "developed a sustainable relationship with their surrounding landscapes and their culture was closely tied to knowledge of forests, mountains, and other 'wild spaces.'" Yet conservationist priorities "turned local residents into trespassers and poachers on property they viewed as their homeland."[14] A sense of resentment over these restrictions represents one factor that has led Latine communities to feel ostracized from the ensuing environmental movement.

Environmental Justice and Civil Rights

A sense of alienation from the modern environmental movement continued shaping Latine environmental politics in the Chicana/o Civil Rights movement of the 1960s and 1970s. In that era, literary scholar Randy Ontiveros notes that Mexican Americans shared broader societal concerns about the growing environmental crisis. But they were hesitant to join forces with national environmental organizations such as the Sierra Club or Greenpeace due to past animosities with conservationists and also because they felt those organizations prioritized concern for nonhuman nature *above* concerns for struggling human communities. Chicana/o leaders instead began cultivating their own distinct approach to Chicana/o environmental politics, "one that drew on Mexican American traditions and that joined ecological concerns with social concerns."[15] In particular, Ontiveros sees the makings of a distinct Chicana/o environmental politics in "*El Plan Espiritual de Aztlán*" (The Spiritual Plan of Aztlán), a cultural nationalist document which called on Chicano/as to mobilize and realize their own independent nation. The document's preamble states: "We, the Chicano inhabitants and civilizers of the northern land of Aztlán, from whence came our forefathers, reclaiming the land of their birth and consecrating the determination of our people of the sun, *declare* that the call of our blood is our power, our responsibility, and our inevitable destiny."[16] By describing Chicana/os as "people of the sun" who are "reclaiming the land of their birth," Ontiveros suggests that *El Plan Espiritual de Aztlán* "makes a powerful link between the human domain of Chicana/o politics and the larger natural order of the universe."[17] Similar to the philosophy of *buen vivir*, this vision recognizes humans and nature as part of the same integrated whole and emphasizes humans' reciprocal responsibilities toward nature. Ontiveros further finds an environmentalist critique of consumer capitalism in the plan's plea for Chicano/as to reject the "gringo dollar value system" in favor of a Chicana/o "cultural background and values which ignore materialism and embrace humanism" and "sustain an economic base for healthy growth and development."[18]

Considerations of humans' reciprocal relationships with the land also shaped Latine involvement with United Farmworker (UFW) activism in the civil rights era and beyond, but in this case, the activism had explicit ties to organized religion. Beginning in the 1960s, labor organizers César Chavez and Dolores Huerta organized a series of boycotts and strikes against grape growers in order to demand fair wages, the right to unionize, and the right to a clean, safe environment for farmworkers. UFW campaigns to regulate pesticide use can be seen as precursors to the modern environmental justice movement because they drew attention to the ways that toxic chemicals such as DDT caused extensive harm to both humans and the environment. The health and safety clause of one UFW contract made the connection between human and environmental well-being explicit. The UFW "recognize[s] the need to protect and conserve human life, water, soil, and vegetation," the contract stated. It went on to declare that "Economic positions, when used incorrectly by a grower in agriculture in any crop, create grave dangers to farmworkers and to consumers, disrupt the earth's ecology, and do not properly serve farmers."[19] The UFW campaign to regulate pesticides can also be seen as a precursor to the modern religious environmental movement because throughout his campaigns Chavez drew heavily from his Catholic faith, using religion as a tool to motivate and organize fellow farmworkers.[20]

Building on those 1960s-era struggles for social justice, Latine activists also took leading roles in the environmental justice movement as it developed throughout the 1980s and 1990s.[21] Richard Moore, a co-director of the SouthWest Organizing Project in Albuquerque and a descendant of Puerto Rican farmworkers—co-authored an open letter to major environmental organizations in January 1990. The letter demanded accountability for racist practices such as prioritizing nonhuman nature above marginalized human communities and excluding people of color from decision-making roles in their organizations.[22] Moore's letter gained significant media attention after it was covered by the *New York Times*, and forced leaders of major environmental organizations to acknowledge their failure to consider the concerns of minoritized communities. Examples of Latine-led grassroots environmental justice campaigns also abound, including Puerto Rican community members in New York who formed coalitions with Asian Americans to protect their communities from pollutant exposure and toxic waste, and Spanish-speaking farmworkers in California's Central Valley who organized to oppose a toxic waste planned for their community.[23] In Los Angeles, Juana Gutiérrez and several other Latina mothers established the Mothers of East Los Angeles (MELA) in 1985 to oppose a state prison planned for their neighborhood. After successfully mobilizing their community in opposition to the prison, MELA organizers continued advocating for a healthy, safe community for their children by protesting an oil pipeline and toxic waste incinerator that would have negative impacts on the environment and their community's health.[24] The religious aspects of MELA are seldom discussed in the scholarship documenting this important organization, but it is noteworthy that this group held its meetings in the basement of Resurrection Catholic Church of East Los Angeles with the active support of Father John Moretta.

With a focus on the connections between social and environmental concerns, and a priority on advancing wellbeing, dignity, and justice for the entire community, Latine communities have long maintained sustainable, reciprocal relationships with the land. There is much to suggest that many of the values that scholars of Latine environmentalism have identified are connected to a sense of religion or spirituality, yet that is not a framework that has garnered significant attention in this field. Understanding the religious roots of these connections requires a turn to theology.

Contributions from Latine Eco-Theology

To the extent that Latine theologians and religious leaders have directly engaged with environmental issues, it has primarily been through a Catholic framework and has emphasized themes of relationality and interdependence.[25] Brazilian theologians Leonardo Boff and Ivone Gebara began integrating ecological concerns into the framework of Latin American liberation theology in the 1990s, drawing attention to the deep connections between environmental degradation and oppression of the poor. In *Cry of the Earth, Cry of the Poor* (1997), Boff echoes arguments made by Latine environmental justice leaders when he insists that ecological conversations must move beyond a focus on protecting endangered species to wage large-scale societal critique. "That is why the ecological argument is continually invoked in all matters having to do with the quality of life, human life in the world, and safeguarding of or threat to the totality of the planet or the cosmos," he writes.[26] Gebara also places relationality at the center of ecotheology in *Longing for Running Water* (1999), where she focuses more specifically on the twinned exploitation of women and the earth. Drawing from her many years as a Catholic nun working in impoverished neighborhoods of Brazil, Gebara offers an ecofeminist theology of everyday life. For urban women who are struggling to survive, Gebara writes, ecological interests are not driven by questions of "how to save the earth and its rain forests and rivers." Instead, such women are interested in "how to live on the land; how to love it, and how to build a house on it. It is hard to try to save the earth when ... you spend your time just wishing for a piece of it."[27] Subsequent generations of Latine ecotheologians have built on Boff and Gebara by emphasizing the importance of political economic critique. In particular, US theologian Daniel Castillo offers an "ecological theology of creation" that embraces Boff and Gebara's relational ecology while adding a priority on political responses.[28]

Within the formal institution of the Catholic Church, the Conference of Latin American Bishops (CELAM) has also advanced eco-theological conversations in Latin America. CELAM formed in 1958 based on recognition of shared cultural backgrounds and concerns among Catholic communities across Latin America and held five conferences in the ensuing fifty years. While the primary concerns of its meetings centered on justice and human rights, ecological issues increasingly garnered the bishops' attention.[29] The Latin American bishops first addressed environmental issues at its conference in Puebla, Mexico in 1979, where they discussed humans' deteriorating relationship with the earth and the human suffering that resulted from the forces of uncontrolled development.[30] In Santo Domingo in 1992, the bishops further critiqued discourses of sustainable development by observing that powerful, wealthy communities benefitted from its goals while impoverished communities paid a steep price. They also reiterated how the social doctrine of the Church taught that God intended for the goods of creation to benefit everyone, not just the rich and powerful.[31] CELAM's 2007 conference in Aparecida, Brazil engaged most directly with ecological issues and directly influenced later Catholic teachings on the environment. In particular, the bishops called for greater inclusion of Indigenous perspectives on sustainable development. While Latin America "holds one of the greatest biodiversities on the planet and a rich socio-diversity [is] represented by its peoples and cultures," the bishops note, Indigenous communities with deep knowledge of how to live sustainably in the region have been excluded from discussions of sustainable development. As a result, nature "continues to be assaulted [as] the land has been plundered" and water is treated as a commodity that can be bought and sold by powerful corporations.[32] While the bishops discussed environmental issues with an unapologetic focus on human interests, CELAM documents are significant for advancing ecological conversations from a distinctively Latin American perspective and for acknowledging the central importance of environmental issues in the social teachings of the Catholic Church.

CELAM's writings on the environment are also significant because they contributed to Pope Francis' thinking in his 2015 encyclical on climate change and the environment. In *Laudato Si: On Care for Our Common Home*, Pope Francis develops the concept of an integral ecology to emphasize how social, environmental, and economic issues are interconnected. "Since everything is closely interrelated, and today's problems call for a vision capable of taking into account every aspect of the global crisis," Francis writes, "I suggest that we now consider some elements of an integral ecology, one which clearly respects its human and social dimensions."[33] Similar to *buen vivir* philosophy, Francis insists that nonhuman nature has intrinsic value.[34] But he stops short of suggesting that the value of nature is equal to the value of humans, instead maintaining a sense of human superiority in keeping with Catholic intellectual tradition. Nevertheless, Latine Catholic churchgoers draw from a variety of sources as they develop their own ecological ethics of everyday life, and cultural, political, and familial influences can shape their values alongside the formal teachings of the Catholic Church. The next section delves into stories of lived religious environmental ethics among Latine Catholic communities in the contemporary United States.

Lived Religious Environmentalism

My own research on environmental values among Latine Catholic communities in Los Angeles conveys the complexity of those various influences. Between 2015 and 2020—in the months and years surrounding the release of *Laudato Si*—I conducted ethnographic research among Spanish-speaking Catholics in Los Angeles.[35] My interlocutors taught me that that home-based conservation measures such as cultivating backyard gardens, avoiding consumerism, and limiting waste were routinely shared among families in their communities and that these practices were connected to inherited family traditions and a sense of love and respect for God. I describe these practices as *la tierra* environmentalism, following theologian Jeanette Rodríguez's work on *la tierra* theology.[36] *La tierra* environmentalism entails a Catholic sacramental understanding that God is present in the material world, combined with an Indigenous outlook in which the human–nature boundary is porous.

A conversation that took place during a focus group among Spanish-speaking immigrants at a Los Angeles church illustrates how Catholic and Indigenous perspectives interacted in their own lived environmental ethics. When I asked the participants whether their Catholic faith had anything to say about their responsibilities toward nature or the environment, Yessenia immediately responded in the affirmative. "From the moment we believe in God and all his creation, we are already aware of nature, of the connection of humans with nature," she explained in Spanish. "From the simple fact of being Catholic and believing in God and in the Bible, we are one hundred percent conscious of nature and the environment." Roger built on Yessenia's remarks and added his own expressions of heartfelt love: "As Yessenia said, God created everything, and we have to love it ... If we believe in God, then we have to love everything that surrounds us." José agreed with Yessenia and Roger, suggesting that loving nature was a fundamental purpose of humankind. "When God created us, he first made the world. He made gardens, animals, everything," José declared. Then God realized that something was missing and created humans "to love nature."

The adult daughters and sons of immigrants were more likely to see a division between humans and the rest of nature, but they still claimed a distinct set of environmental values developed from a strong recognition of humans' dependence on the land. Luciana, whose parents had grown up on ranches in Puebla, Mexico, told me she had always know that it was important to "tak[e] care of the earth and not pollut[e] it" because her parents had relied on the earth for their survival. Firsthand experience had taught them that if the rain did not come on time, their crops would die and they would not have enough to eat. As Luciana described it, her faith did not teach specific responsibilities such as recycling or conserving water. Yet for as long as she could remember, her mother had ensured that the family embraced environmentally sustainable behaviors such as conserving energy and water, maintaining a vibrant garden, recycling, and not wasting food. These home-based conservation measures were inspired in part by her family's impoverished circumstances. The family lived on a tight budget and could not afford to waste resources. But those values also were influenced by her Catholic faith, Luciana reflected, as nature imagery and an ethic of respecting God's creation were significant elements in her religious life. While inspired in part by church teachings on caring for creation and the example of *Laudato Si*, the environmental values my interlocutors embraced were also shaped by cultural inheritances from outside of the church, embracing perspectives that placed a priority on well-being, dignity, and justice for the entire community, including both humans and the more-than-human world.

Conclusion

This survey on the history of Latine religious environmentalism has conveyed that Latine communities have long maintained sustainable, reciprocal relationships with the environment, even if they have not necessarily enacted those values through collaboration with the mainstream environmental movement. Theologians and scholars of religion have attended to Latine religious environmental expressions primarily through a focus on Catholic religious worlds, but there is need for additional research in diverse Latine communities. Protestant theologies and religious environmental activism offer one important area for future research. Organizations such as the *Por La Creación*, a faith-based project of the Hispanic Access Foundation, unite Latine Protestants in the work of caring for God's creation.[37] Future research can also investigate the prevalence of environmental spiritualities among the growing number of Latine young adults who identify as "spiritual but not religious."[38] Such research is vital not only for strengthening our understanding of earth care from a Latine perspective, but also for expanding notions of what it means to be an environmentalist.

14

Departing from the American Dream: Toward Visions of Collective Latine Human Dignity

Francisco J. García Jr.

The notion of the *American dream,* made popular during the Great Depression by historian James Truslow Adams, has permeated the national consciousness in the United States for the past century. Rooted in the idea that individuals can advance economically and find a better life through hard work and personal achievement, and that *America* is an endless *land of opportunity* for anyone that persists (or really wants it), the American dream has been a captivating and troubling metaphor engaged by scholars, politicians, and everyday people since. During the Civil Rights era, Martin Luther King used it as key backdrop for his famous "I have a dream" speech at the 1963 March on Washington for Jobs and Freedom; meanwhile, Malcolm X rejected the American dream and called it "an American nightmare." For Latines in the United States and would-be migrants from Latin America, the lure of the mythic *sueño americano* can be very real. Polls taken a few years before and just after the pandemic show that a strong majority of Latines still believe that achieving the American dream is possible.[1] And well-meaning liberal-progressive Latine elected officials such as Julian Castro—who in 2012 as Mayor of San Antonio gave the keynote at the Democratic National Convention endorsing Barack Obama for President—continue to employ the American dream metaphor as an aspirational goal.

But the reality of achieving many of the symbols of the American dream—homeownership; well-paid, meaningful work; social, economic, and political capital; access to higher education; time for rest and recreation—remains out of reach for the majority of the Latine community. In this chapter, I argue for a radical departure away from the American dream as a driving metaphor for the Latine community and for the working-class majority of Americans, and call for the exploration and development of new metaphors focused on communal material and spiritual well-being, informed by liberatory Latine religious thought, intersectional class analysis, and historic-contemporary examples of faith, labor, and community organizing in diverse Latine contexts.

Continued reliance on the concept of the American dream is harmful because it masks the pervasive and adaptable social and economic structures of neoliberal capitalism that by design are reliant on the exploitation of the working majority, including a super majority of Latine working people, so that a precious few economic and political elites can become excessively wealthy. Rather than perpetuating the largely unreachable and untenable American dream, I argue that we must search deep into liberatory Latine religious thought and lessons from Latine-led movements for social and economic justice—which often have religious roots and at times explicitly stated religious motivations—and replace the notion of the American dream with an economically cooperative vision of dignity and justice for all. Drawing on the collective strength of Latine religious thought and focus on economic justice and the dignity of all labor, I will reference the early labor organizing example of Chicana/Mexicana Emma Tenayuca in 1930s San Antonio as a precursor to the well-documented United Farm Workers struggle, and consequently, to contemporary Latine-immigrant worker organizing. These are historic and contemporary movements that point to an alternative vision of collective power building that can move us way from the individualist lure of the traditional American dream.

The American Dream in Contemporary Latine Contexts

In 2012, then San Antonio Mayor Julian Castro, a rising star in Democratic politics, gave the keynote at the Democratic National Convention in support of the reelection of President Barack Obama. He told a story of his grandmother, a working-class Mexican immigrant who labored tirelessly to give her daughter a decent life and in the hopes that someday her grandchildren would have a better life. Her daughter went on to college, cut her teeth as a Chicana Civil Rights activist, and her two grandchildren—twins Joaquin and Julian Castro—attended Ivy League schools, studied law, and became involved in regional and national political work. At the time of this speech, Julian Castro was seen with great potential as a future "Barack Obama," and his brother Joaquin was running for US Congress. He begins his speech with his humble family origins:

> The unlikely journey that brought me here tonight began many miles from this podium. My brother Joaquin and I grew up with my mother Rosie and my grandmother Victoria. My grandmother was an orphan. As a young girl, she had

> to leave her home in Mexico and move to San Antonio, where some relatives had agreed to take her in. She never made it past the fourth grade. She had to drop out and start working to help her family. My grandmother spent her whole life working as a maid, a cook and a babysitter, barely scraping by, but still working hard to give my mother, her only child, a chance in life, so that my mother could give my brother and me an even better one.[2]

Castro's speech is steeped in the mythos of the American dream, but from a Latine sensibility. To go from such modest beginnings—a poor Mexican immigrant grandmother working in the borderlands with little to no educational access or economic security to a grandson giving a keynote speech on a national political stage—indeed seems to be the stuff of dreams. Castro taps into this immigrant-generational success story to demonstrate a certain vision of "America" that rightly seeks to counter long-standing anti-immigrant, anti-Latine, and specifically anti-Mexican narratives and stereotypical tropes that have abounded in dominant US politics, culture, and economic systems since the Treaty of Guadalupe Hidalgo in the mid-1800s. Castro's counternarrative might be conceived as the following: "Immigrants—including us Latines/Mexicans—work hard, and contribute to the economic and political landscape in more ways than one. We can advance from maid to mayor in two generations!" This is essentially an American Dream narrative.

Julian Castro's speech also includes the Mexican Catholic working-class spirituality of his grandmother, as he reflects: "I can still remember her, every morning as Joaquin and I walked out the door to school, making the sign of the cross behind us, saying, "*Que Dios los bendiga.* (May God bless you.)" The notion of receiving *la bendición* as you leave your home or somewhere else—especially received from an elder—is a common practice in many Latine homes."[3] Castro closes his speech by sharing a moment when he continued this practice of offering *la bendición* to his own daughter as she went off to her first day of preschool.

Castro's speech, with some qualifications, employs the belief that the American dream is a "thing" but expands it to make it more universal. He picks up on the theme of hard work as a pathway to upward mobility and of aspirational entry into the middle class:

> And that's the middle class—the engine of our economic growth. With hard work, everybody ought to be able to get there. And with hard work, everybody ought to be able to stay there—and go beyond. The dream of raising a family in a place where hard work is rewarded is not unique to Americans. Its a human dream, one that calls across oceans and borders. The dream is universal, but America makes it possible. And our investment in opportunity makes it a reality.[4]

Here Castro focuses on the notion of the American dream as essentially good, except that there's a small problem. He speaks of his high school classmates in San Antonio as having "the same talent, the same brains, the same dreams as the folks we sat with at Stanford and Harvard." It was not a difference in ability or desire to advance.

For Castro, opportunity—seen through college prep and financial aid programs from pre-K through high school—makes all the difference.

Toward the end of his speech, Castro brings to fruition a nuanced articulation of the American dream, again, based on the experiences of his Mexican-American family. He notes:

> In the end, the American dream is not a sprint, or even a marathon, but a relay. Our families don't always cross the finish line in the span of one generation. But each generation passes on to the next the fruits of their labor. My grandmother never owned a house. She cleaned other people's houses so she could afford to rent her own. But she saw her daughter become the first in her family to graduate from college. And my mother fought hard for Civil Rights so that instead of a mop, I could hold this microphone.[5]

In this speech to the DNC, Castro articulates a Latine economic and religious sensibility steeped in the myth of the American Dream. It is a classic story of social progress. His grandmother cleaned houses. They went from "mop to microphone" in two generations. These are the kinds of stories that people love to hear about, especially in Latine and communities of color, because it demonstrates that someone like "me" made it. *And if they can make it, so can I!* While not dismissing the personal achievements within one Latine family and acknowledging their significant contributions to the San Antonio and wider Latine community, later I will return to Castro's narrative and problematize the American dream metaphor.

Origins of the American Dream and Latine Engagement

Castro's use of the American dream metaphor stems from a long-standing tradition in the twentieth century, especially in political circles. But where did it first emerge? While its antecedents come from foundational ideas of freedom as seen in the Declaration of Independence—such as the "the right to life, liberty, and the pursuit of happiness"—James Truslow Adams is widely seen as the person who popularized the term in the 1930s. In his widely read book *The Epic of America,* Adams invokes the American dream at various points, calling it a "dream of a better, richer, and happier life for all our citizens of every rank."[6] Central to Adams' thesis is a belief that through hard work, persistence, and drive, America can serve "as a land in which life should become fuller for every man, with opportunity for each according to his ability or achievement."[7] Adam's book about the idealism and possibility of advancement for all regardless of background ironically emerged as a best seller during the height of the Great Depression, and the hopeful notion of the American dream gained traction. While Adams had sympathies for the *common man,* Adams did not offer any tangible critiques of the economic system.

As Howard Schneiderman notes, "from the start ... the American dream was not about the elimination of social class distinctions, but for mobility through those ranks based on hard work."[8] The American dream was essentially about individual or familial upward social and economic mobility and progress, which fits well with other themes that emerged during the period, such as the notion of *rugged individualism* associated with frontier history.[9] Adams was not an eternal optimist, however, and just a year after his *Epic of America* book, wrote an essay speaking of America's lost opportunity.[10]

Latines have publicly engaged directly or indirectly with the American dream most readily since the Black freedom and broader Civil Rights movement emerging in the 1960s. Chicano activist and poet Corky Gonzales's poem "I am Joaquin" speaks to the ambiguity and oppressive nature of the Latine experience in the United States from his perspective as a Chicano:

I am Joaquín, lost in a world of confusion,
caught up in the whirl of a gringo society,
confused by the rules, scorned by attitudes,
suppressed by manipulation, and destroyed by modern society.
My fathers have lost the economic battle
and won the struggle of cultural survival.
And now! I must choose between the paradox of
victory of the spirit, despite physical hunger,
or to exist in the grasp of American social neurosis,
sterilization of the soul and a full stomach.
Yes, I have come a long way to nowhere,
unwillingly dragged by that monstrous, technical,
industrial giant called Progress and Anglo success.[11]

Gonzales engages with the economic and social struggles that Latines often face in the Anglo-dominant, economically exploitative society of the United States. He also engages the dream "of a better life" alongside the complicated Latine religious identity stemming from conquest and colonization, speaking of being both "Aztec prince and Christian Christ." This was the reality of Latines, mostly Mexican-Americans, in the Southwest. Puerto Ricans contended with the contradictions of colonialism and the American dream as many migrated from their island to the Northeast United States in large numbers during the "Great Migration" after the Second World War.[12] Puerto Rican author Ed Morales speaks of both "the flowering and disintegration" of that American dream for his family, which began with the initial hope of his parents, "only to see their dream fade with the bitter reality that our homeland, and possibly our culture and traditions, were slowly dying."[13] While each community, whether Cuban, Dominican, Salvadoran, or other Latines, have their own particular relationship and experience with the American dream that stems from differing political, economic, and social contexts, the economic and cultural challenges are often a shared experience.

What's Wrong with the American Dream? Latine Demographics and Structural Inequalities

Latines, like other communities that have faced historic economic, ethno-racial, and other forms of exploitation and marginalization, have wrestled with the American dream for generations. Anecdotally, if economic, social, and political status are the indicators of "having made it," then the results are mixed. A recent post-pandemic economic report from the Latine nonprofit advocacy group *UnidosUS* tries to paint a balanced picture of the overall Latine economic condition: Latines collectively contribute significant dollars to the US economy—currently (mid-2020s) over $3.2 trillion every year—and their five million businesses yield revenues of over $800 billion annually. The US Latine economy, in terms of size, would be the fifth largest in the global economy! Moreover, Latine rates of homeownership, the creation of businesses, household income, and consumer spending are also growing at a higher pace than others. Despite these indicators, Latines overall remain economically, socially, and politically more precarious than their white counterparts. Moreover, Latines are now almost one-fifth of the US population (at 19.5 percent or 65 million people) and are the largest population group aside from non-Hispanic whites, but remain severely underrepresented politically, representing just two percent of all elected officials.[14] Economically, *UnidosUS* notes that "[Latines] face significant and longstanding economic challenges. They have less wealth and lower incomes compares to white Americans, are less likely to own their homes, pay a greater share of their income on rent and mortgage payments, have fewer retirement savings, and are more likely to work in lower-paying jobs with fewer benefits."[15] As the report also notes, only about 20 percent of Latines between the ages of twenty-five to sixty-four have college degrees; what the report does not state is that a strong majority of US-born (56 percent) and foreign-born Latines (69 percent) have only a high school degree or less in education. Moreover, Latines face higher rates of poverty than other Americans.[16]

Latines, overall, are a working-class community, even accounting for those small segments that would consider themselves middle-class and the even smaller percentages that have made it into higher economic brackets. Moreover, as economist Michael Zweig notes, the so-called middle-class is really part of the working class as they do not control the means of production.[17] Sociologist Ruth Milkman notes that a majority of workers at the bottom of the labor market are Latine immigrants, working in jobs that have been deregulated, de-unionized, subcontracted, and transitioned from blue-collar to "brown-collar" jobs, low-wage jobs that have been "racially stereotyped as best suited to [Latine] immigrants."[18] Milkman's research from 2020 sadly points to a larger historic trajectory that scholars have chronicled over generations of the US Latine-immigrant experience. Carey McWilliams described conditions in the fields of California in the 1920s, where Mexican workers (alongside other immigrant workers, but Mexicans were the majority) were the most desirable workers because they were "easily exploited," they were good workers, they were largely "unorganized," and could be deported.[19] In 1979, Chicano political scientist Mario Barrera did a study analyzing racial-economic inequality from the Mexican-American War to his present moment and concluded that Chicano workers in the Southwest were kept in a "colonial labor system," "segmented along ethnic and/or racial lines … [and] systematically maintained in a subordinate position."[20] Emiliano Aguilar notes that "racial discrimination and exploitation characterize the experiences of Latina and Latino laborers during periods of expansion and economic development in the United States."[21] Amid the growing gap between the poor and the extremely rich, Latine workers, and undocumented workers in particular, have been consistently at the bottom, making the American dream largely out of reach for the majority of the Latine community. By design, the American brand of racial capitalism allows for a minority of Latines and other workers historically on the margins to "make it" so that others continue to offer their labor; such a system strips working-class communities of their economic and political democracy, requiring a majority workforce to remain as an underclass.[22] Success stories across generations like that shared by Julian Castro and his family, however wonderful for them, create the semblance of the American dream, but it remains illusory. What of the American dream for the immigrant generation? Are they relegated to the work in the dregs of exploitative jobs as sacrifice?

Alternatives to the American Dream?

There are alternatives to pursuing the American dream, and Latine religious thought coupled with movement building can help point us in that direction. Gaston Espinosa et al., in their edited volume *Latino Religions and Civic Activism in the United States*, say that "Latino religious ideology, institutions, leaders, and symbols have played a crucial role in Latino political, civic, and social action in the United States … [and] have served as the ideological glue for some of the most important struggles in the Latino community in the past 150 years."[23] Many movements since the civil rights struggles emerging in the 1960s come to mind, most notably the religiously infused organizing of the United Farm Workers (UFW) in California, replete with pilgrimages, spiritual fasts, and images of *La Virgen de Guadalupe* guiding the way. Chicano/Mexican leaders of the movement (noting that there were also notable Filipino leaders[24]) were influenced by a blend of Catholic social teaching on labor and human dignity, philosophies of nonviolence from Gandhi and Martin Luther King Jr., and Mexican cultural-religious mysticism (the penitente tradition).[25] The UFW's unique approach, especially through the mid-1970s, has greatly influenced generations of activists, organizers, and faith leaders both within and outside of the Latine community.[26]

But there were Latine labor struggle antecedents to the UFW, including in Julian Castro's San Antonio. In the 1930s, Chicana/Mexicana and lifelong Catholic Emma Tenayuca emerged as a fiery labor organizer and strike leader of pecan shellers, a workforce consisting entirely of Mexican labor. As a leader of the Workers Alliance and the local Communist Party, Tenayuca and her husband penned "The Mexican Question in the Southwest," a manifesto calling for organizing "against economic discrimination, educational and cultural inequality, and social oppression."[27] Most histories depict Tenayuca solely as a radical organizer inspired by communist ideals. But as Arlene Sánchez-Walsh notes, a faith commitment is not always expressed institutionally, especially when it comes to Latine religious expressions. Sánchez-Walsh asserts that "most Catholics lived their faith lives outside the confines of the institutional church, where folk beliefs and practices—and certainly political causes considered at odds with the Church—would only find life in a robust investment in popular religious expressions."[28] Despite facing backlash from the Catholic Archdiocese for her affiliations, Tenayuca cited her upbringing at St. Agnes, her Catholic parish, as playing an important role in keeping her family together and shaping her sense of justice. While she battled the political–economic–religious elites of her day and sought to transform living conditions for her working-class community, she was grounded in a preliberation theology ethic akin to the *preferential option for the poor* later developed by Latin American liberation theologians and revisited constantly by US Latine religious scholars.[29] This collective vision of justice and belonging flies in the face of traditional American dream metaphors rooted in limiting notions of rugged individualism, personal advancement, and economic excess.

Conclusion

The American dream, in an entrenched capitalist economy, is out of reach for the majority of Latines and for the working-class majority of Americans more broadly. Based on this dilemma, and stemming from the individualist nature of the American dream metaphor, I argue for a departure from its usage as an aspirational ideal. Rather, a more sober and structural analysis of the Latine economic condition alongside a hopeful vision for alternatives rooted in grassroots labor-community organizing, economically cooperative models, and inspired and sustained by liberatory Latine religious thought, can help propel us toward making tangible and systemic changes in people's lives that honor collective human dignity.

15

Screwing with the System

Miguel A. De La Torre

I am old enough to remember housing discrimination, witnessing my parents fight for decent housing during our time in New York City. Being Latines, being poor, we were relegated to the slums—to a roach- and rat-infected tenement building that had one bathroom per floor to be shared with three other families. When we finally moved to a low-income neighborhood that was predominately composed of poor Irish and Italians, where my father obtained the stereotypical role of the building's superintendent, I experienced the violence of the streets as classmates at my school—Blessed Sacrament—routinely made their displeasure with a Latine presence in their neighborhood physically known through beatings. While being a Latine today encompasses a certain degree of economic and physical vulnerability, living in the "belly of the beast" prior to Civil Rights legislation entailed its own endangerments.

Taught to feel shame for occupying a Latine body led to self-hatred as I swallowed the lie of my own inferiority, learning to see myself through the eyes of those who dismissed me as less-than-human. It was during my pre-teen years that I became familiar with a turf Latine street gang from Chicago that began operating in New York City who called themselves the Young Lords.[1] Since its early formation during the 1950s, the street gang evolved into a Maoist–Marxist political social movement waging a struggle for dignity, housing, and healthcare for Latines by focusing on gentrification, police brutality, and poor health services. Their conscious-raising praxis deeply influenced Latines like me who have come to believe that the space to which I was relegated by the dominant culture was both apropos and deserved. Although the Young Lords were not a religious affiliated organization, they demonstrated, more so than most Christian theologians or ethicists of that time, that incarnating what Christians claims became an act of holy rebellion which destabilizes, disrupts, and defies those who have become complicit with the oppressive status quo.

I still recall the East Harlem Garbage Offensive launched on July 27, 1969. Contrary to white supremacist stereotypes of the dirty smelly Latine, they wanted their *gente* to live in clean decent neighborhoods— so they swept the streets, collected discarded trash and neatly stacked the garbage on the corners for collection by the sanitation department. Unfortunately, services to Latine and Black New York neighborhoods were historically ignored. When the garbage failed to be collected, the Young Lords piled trash bags into a flaming five-foot-tall barricade across Third Avenue, a main thoroughfare which commuters took when departing Manhattan for the vanilla suburbs. Scuffles with law enforcement and arrests followed. In support for the Young Lords, over a thousand neighborhood residents marched to the 126th street police precinct protesting police brutality. Despite law enforcement crackdown, bad press shamed city bureaucrats to finally respond to their long-ignored responsibility of providing regular garbage collection in neighborhoods of color.[2]

Additionally, on July 14, 1970, the Young Lords occupied Lincoln Hospital in South Bronx, the only health institution—due to segregationist attitudes—serving the needs of the predominantly Latine and African American New York communities. Not surprisingly, a history of ignoring their health concerns and treatment existed. The health services provided to communities of color were so bad that locals dubbed it "the butcher shop" a slaughterhouse masquerading as healthcare. In response, for twelve hours during the evening, the Young Lords took possession of the hospital, demanding door-to-door preventive health services be conducted, maternal and childcare be provided, drug addiction care be established, senior citizens' services be expanded, and minimum wage for hospital employees be increased. Again, media exposure laid bare appalling healthcare conditions provided to disenfranchised communities of color. The takeover produced one of the first Patient's Bill of Rights impacting doctor–patient relationships nationwide.[3]

Not only did the Young Lords hold the government and agencies providing health services accountable to the rhetoric these institutions expounded, but they also held religious institutions accountable. In December 1969, they occupied *La Primera Iglesia Metodista Hispana* at Lexington Street and 111th Avenue in Spanish Harlem. A delegation of the Young Lords requested the use of available church space to provide a breakfast program for children. Although the church laid empty throughout most of the week, the pastor and the church board refused, dismissing the Young Lords delegates as *satanás*—demons. When the Young Lord delegates attempted to address the congregation during Sunday service on December 7th (a day that will live in infamy), the police were called who proceeded to brutally beat the Young Lords. A few weeks later, during the December 28th Sunday service, over a hundred Young Lord activists and sympathizers occupied the church, taking possession, expelling the pastor, and fastening the doors shut with six-inch railroad spikes. A wooden sign with red letters renaming the church *La iglesia del pueblo*—The People's Church—was raised. During eleven days of occupation, over three thousand people attended church. *La iglesia del pueblo* not only established a breakfast program for children, but also, childcare for working parents was provided, clothing drives were conducted, political education was taught, consciousness about police brutality was raised, and a concerted effort was made concerning investments in social services (like health clinics). Police retook the church on January 7, 1970, arresting 105 occupiers.[4] Thus, the church ceased being the people's church.

As could be expected, F.B.I. infiltration and political infighting led to the disintegration of the Young Lords in the early 1970s. Yet, for a brief moment in time, an indigenous Latine-based ethical methodology was in-fleshed. The Young Lords were concerned with institutions (governmental, health, and religious) that played vital roles within the Latine community but were abdicating their expressed mission and hypocritically ignoring the rhetoric they professed. Through their militant praxis, they demonstrated how those claiming to perform the task of ensuring the people's welfare were violating their social contract. In effect, they held these institutions accountable by implementing themselves the services these institutions should have been providing, shaming them to live up to their supposed mission and rhetoric. They were not engaged in civil disobedience—popularized during the Civil Rights Movement—but rather civil initiative.

An Ethics of Civil Initiative

Most eurocentric ethics operate deductively, arguing that action (praxis) is derived from truth (doctrine). Orthodoxy (correct doctrine) leads to orthopraxis (correct action). Liberative ethics turns this eurocentric deductive ethical paradigm on its head, arguing that theological and theoretical reflections are derived from praxis—orthopraxis inductively leads toward orthodoxy. The eurocentric paradigm fails because "truth," as constructed by the dominant culture, reflects the bias and prejudices of that culture which consciously or unconsciously creates an ethical worldview complicit with empire, falling short of calling for any radical changes that might threaten the possessions, power, or privileges of those for whom the dominant culture is designed to serve and protect. Liberative ethicists argue that ethics must be a grassroots endeavor, arising from disenfranchised communities reflecting on the survival-based praxis needing implementation.

For Latines, such an ethics incorporates a civil initiative—a concept developed among immigration rights groups along the US southern border, a methodology that spotlights governmental human rights violations taking place against the undocumented. Based on the praxis employed during the 1980s Sanctuary Movement, the ethical concept of civil initiative arose as a reflection of the actions implemented by houses of worship which provided haven to Central American refugees threatened due to our foreign Central American policies of supporting brutal dictatorships and our domestic immigration policies of deporting at-risk migrants to dictatorial regimes. US-sponsored civil wars in El Salvador and Guatemala gave rise to death squads that would disappear these migrants if expatriated. While employing civil disobedience sought to change laws that were bad (i.e., Jim and Jane Crow laws prior to the Civil Rights Movement), civil initiative sought to force governments and institutions (civic and religious) to live up to the mission and rhetoric they voiced.[5]

During the 1980s Sanctuary Movement, the problem was not the existing laws. It was the US government that was violating its own refugee laws, refusing to recognize those fleeing persecution. In effect, it was the government committing civil disobedience. The goal of the Sanctuary Movement was to force the government to follow the good laws that already existed. This strategy required a new term. Jim Corbett, a Quaker activist and cofounders of the Sanctuary Movement, coined the term "civil initiative" to name the praxis being employed. "Civil initiative," according to the other cofounder of the movement John Fife, "is the legal right and the moral responsibility of society to protect the victims of human rights violations when government is the violator."[6] Civil initiative is based on international law, specifically the legal argument employed during the Nuremberg trials which dismissed the often-used excuse for multitude atrocities of "simply following orders." In *United States v. Goering* (1946), the court concluded that international duties transcend individual obligations to obey national states. A moral obligation exists to render assistance to victims of human rights violations. Civil initiative is a Latine-centric ethical response developed by those doing feet-on-the-ground ethics among *nuestra gente*. Those of us traversing the desert leaving food and water are the ones in compliance with international law which states that the US government should be doing what we are doing. Our civil initiative attempts to force the government to follow the international treaties signed providing humanitarian aid to those in need and asylum to those endangered. We recognize that international duties transcend individual obligations to obey national states.

A Disruptive Ethics

Eurocentric ethics—however idealistic—operates at the service of the dominant culture whose supreme purpose and goal is to maintain social order. For Reinhold Niebuhr, inequalities are a necessity for the orderly function of society. "No complex society," he writes, "will be able to dispense with certain inequalities of privilege. Some of them are necessary for the proper performance of certain social functions."[7] He equates social order to an ethical principle with the Christian concept of love. Another prominent eurocentric social ethicist, Paul Ramsey, critiqued lunch counter sit-ins during the Civil Rights Movement as an improper social Christian action because it disrupted society's law and order.[8] For John Rawls, justice was encouraged so long as it remained constrained within the limits of a well-ordered society.[9] James Gustafson argued that the pursuit of justice is fine as long as it did not upset "a necessary equilibrium in society."[10] And finally, Stanley Hauerwas—probably the most influential contemporary ethicist—argues that as important as justice might be, "the current emphasis on justice and rights as the primary norms guiding the social witness of Christians is in fact a mistake"[11] The majority of contemporary Eurocentric ethicists argued that the preservation of the established order, even if unjust, is paramount, making the ethics of the dominant culture the moral justifier of policies detrimental to Latines and other disenfranchised groups. To employ eurocentric ethics makes one complicit with their own oppression, and as such, Latines must reject such ethics for one which disrupts and subverts the equilibrium of the dominant culture.

Who would not cherish a stable social order? But unfortunately for Latines relegated to the underside of society, poverty, inadequate housing, underemployed and unemployment, dilapidated schools, police brutality, ICE brutality, violence, incarceration, and a lack of adequate health care, societal equilibrium is prevented. For empire to function at full efficiency—as Niebuhr recognized—an undereducated, underemployable reserve army of labors is required. The economic structures of neoliberalism foundational to eurocentric ethicists' equilibrium, embedded in racism and ethnic discrimination, are beyond reform. Radical change, specifically in how the earth's resources are distributed, is required. No doubt, there are eurocentric ethicists who benefitting from the present arrangement may willingly participate in charity, but most remain unwilling to move toward any type of justice that questions or threatens their power, possessions or privilege.

The Young Lords, in response to the marginalized spaces they occupied, disrupted the social equilibrium advocated by ethicists of the dominant culture who consciously or unconsciously supported the order of things. The Young Lords' justice-based praxis led to beatings and arrest. They sought more relevant ethical paradigm rooting moral agency in the lived experiences of disenfranchised Latines. The call to burn the uncollected trash on Third Avenue was a disruptive ethical praxis that came to be because those carrying out the act were in relationship with those marginalized by the city's refusal to regularly collect trash. The issue is not if trash burning on the city's major intersections should become a universal law as per Kant's Categorical Imperative.[12] Such propositions may hold merit among Euroamerican accustomed to regular garbage collection, but it is a preposterous proposition proposed for those relegate to live amidst filth. The decision to participate in disruptive ethical acts becomes a communal-based ethics that rejected eurocentric-based ethics.

Resisting what the dominant culture has normalized and legitimized compels the moral agent to move beyond what has been constructed and defined as the good. When Latines engage in disruptive ethics which subverts and confronts normative Eurocentric definitions of the moral, said praxis will be deemed and defined as dreadful and disgusting by those engaged in eurocentric ethical analysis seeking to maintain and sustain the equilibrium of the dominant culture. Physically taking over churches and hospitals or burning trash in the streets will be viewed negatively by those seeking the preservation of a social order that protects their privileged space. Consequently, to disrupt the norm, to screw with the systems, becomes a moral imperative.

If ethics seeks to disorder the status quo, disturb the necessary equilibrium upon which the dominant culture relies to preserve their power, then the best model to emulate to bring about said disruption is probably the trickster figure, known for creating situations leading to new ways of acting within oppressive systems and structures. Because society's structures are constructed to mask oppressive systems of operation by legitimizing and normalizing the status quo; resistance to the present social order become futile as both those who benefit and those afflicted are lolled into supporting the status quo. Frontal assaults which disrupt the equilibrium designed to protect the power, privilege and possessions of those whom society is intended to protect is hopeless and deadly as the full force of the dominant culture is unleashed to safeguard their unearned station within society by whatever means necessary.

A Trickster-Based Ethics

Prevalent in eurocentric moral thought is an either/or Western rationalism demarcating the good from the bad. Usually, ethical analyses are based on a good–evil binary where your actions are either aligned with the forces for good (i.e., God) or the forces for evil (i.e., Satan). But all too often, in the fight against what has been defined as evil, greater atrocities occur in defense of the Good. In a world where the Good is defined through eurocentric ethical methodologies based on the reasoning or experience of those who get to legitimize and normalize their definition of the Good, little hope for justice or liberation of those dispossessed exists. Why? Because such ethical perspectives, derived from those for whom the center of empire is designed to privilege, usually cause more evil than good for those on the margins of the dominant culture.

Contrary to the good/bad dichotomy of the dominant eurocentric culture, how can a more ambiguous both/and be incorporated to signal the messiness of life? What Latine cultural symbols exist which moves beyond the ineffectiveness of the eurocentric good–evil dualism that can capture the equivocality of Latine existence and the moral agency ambiguity which considers the need to dispense with personal puritanical piety for the greater good of simply surviving—more importantly, survival of *la comunidad*? In effect, how do we begin to decolonize our mind, move away from the eurocentric definitions of ethics and morality, and begin to construct our own worldview based on our own cultural symbols?

Regardless of our best efforts, centuries of eurocentric supremist conditioning have colonized the minds of Latines relegated to inferiority. If we hope to see with our own eyes, absent from a eurocentric worldview which provides us with the definitions of ourselves and our faith, then we must become winemakers. The late nineteenth-century revolutionary philosopher José Martí saw the dangers of Latines relegated to the underside of the then-emerging US empire. He feared his Latin American compatriots, close to the hegemonic orbit of the colossal North, risked embracing eurocentric philosophical worldviews harmful to their very being. Liberation of the mind meant forging a new way of thinking and being based on one's indigenous roots. In response he wrote, "*El vino de plátano; y si sale agrio, ¡es nuestro vino!*"[13] Martí called for the development of a Latine way of thinking contributing to ethnically sensitive strategies based on Latine cultural symbols. And even if we get it wrong it does not matter, for they remain better than the thoughts and tactics of colonizers. Why? Because they are our own, forged from our own ingredients. We who find ourselves on the margins of Eurochristianity must choose to understand, define, and implement our ethical praxis by rejecting the dominant culture's interpretation for the sake of our own survival, sanity, and salvation.

One Latine cultural symbol often ignored which can be utilized as a methodology for ethical analysis is the ambiguous role played by the trickster. The trickster is a mythical character amalgamated within the social reality of Latines who can serve to unmask external oppressive social structures under which Latines live. Because trickster figures break rules, they allow for the suspension of strict eurocentric definitions of morality and ethical analytical paradigms, thus breaking free from the ethical standards created by a dominant culture designed to keep Latines in dominated and domesticated spaces. As consummate survivor, the trickster serves as an exemplar for Latines seeking survival strategies for the disenfranchising reality constructed for them.

By disrupting the dominant culture's equilibrium—creating compromising situations for those in power—the trickster exposes what oppressors prefer to remain hidden; thus, ripping off their artificial masks of superiority to reveal their weaknesses and phobias. Trickster's trials and tests force the powerful to consider the hypocrisy of their rhetoric while disrupting constructed norms, thus creating fresh opportunities by which to approach marginalization. Political scientist James C. Scott maintained that the trickster function within a public sphere of a group politics of disguise and anonymity intended to convey double meanings even while providing space for the powerless to speak to power with authority while shielding their identity. Tricksters may appear as harmless or comical fools, but for those whose social location is marked by oppression, their stories celebrate cunning wiles of those navigating a social structure designed for their destruction. Despite the treacherous designs of oppressors, the trickster—by scrutinizing their weaknesses and negative habits—occasionally triumphs over the more powerful through the employment of humor, deceptive methods, lies, or passive aggression.[14]

For anthropologist Victor Turner, trickster characters are "liminal" figure (from the Latin word *limen* which means threshold) that stands at the threshold of cultures, breaking down old categories to bring forth new possibilities.[15] Perceived as weaker and inferior to the dominant eurocentric culture focused on their domination, tricksters rely on deception to exploit oppressor's false sense of self-righteousness which usually masks their unsatisfying greed for power, privilege, possessions, or any combination thereof. Like Latines, the trickster straddles two worlds, whereas threshold (border) crossers are forced to breakdown the reality in which they find themselves so that they can survive, cognizant that through their deconstruction on how power operates, new liberative opportunities and possibilities can arise. Within many Latine traditions, debunking the dominant culture's so-called superiority is done with humor; hence unsurprisingly, these tricksters are typically portrayed as pranksters or jokers. Their survival against oppressive odds is accomplished while masked by a child-like or clownish demeanor. To outwit those self-defining as superior, the trickster disrupts the norm and causes chaos to reveal hypocrisy.

Implementing a trickster-based ethics radically subverts established norms designed to preserve the traditional moral values and virtues undergirding eurocentric empire. Because Latiness realizes direct challenges to the existing social structures usually lead to violence, if not termination, forms of deceptive and calculating resistance are employed to enhance chances for survival and success, thus providing Latines with a paragon to emulate. Tricksters, as jokester, can be portrayed as a mischievous child. For example, among Cubans, Pepito (Little Johnny) is portrayed as a small humble simpleton who usually confounds the more powerful through childish innocence. Among Puerto Ricans, another little boy like Pepito exists. He is called Juan Bobo (John Dummy). Similar to Pepito, Juan Bobo can make social commentaries through his childish innocence. Although consigned to inferior status, the jokesters Pepito and Juan Bobo are able—through his[16] innocent demeanor or razor-sharp wit—to switch the roles and unmask the shortcoming of those who perceive themselves to be better, or of a higher social status.

Among Mexicans, there is Don Cacahuate (Mr. Peanuts), an adult simpleton, who through humorous social entanglements manages to survive. His precursor is Pedro de Urdemalas or Pedro Ordimales, literally Peter Mischief-Maker. Pedro tales date from the late twelfth century, even though the character was popular in the early seventeenth century as illustrated by Miguel de Cervantes in his comedic writings. Well known throughout the Spanish-speaking Southwestern United States, he is a bit more *picaro* (street-smart) than Don Cacahuate. A critic of the status quo, he is constantly outwitting his supposed superiors for his own gain. Humor is used, providing the marginalized hearers needed laughter to deal with their own struggles. These jesters can question and challenge, through humor, what is accepted as normative. Jokesters' humor temporarily frees hearers from existing social restraints, as proper decorum is suspended and the social morals, values, and virtues benefitting oppressors are rejected or subverted.

These tricksters at times, occupy sacred spaces, especially when the Christian biblical text is read with Latine eyes. Reading the Bible from the margins reveals a prevalent trickster literary genre ignored by those of the dominant culture accustomed to reading the text from the eurocentric dominant social location. For example, Abraham tricked both the Egyptian Pharaoh and the King Abimelech of Gerar into believing that his wife was his sister, resulting in financial gain (Gen. 12:10-20; 20:1-18); a trick his son Isaac repeated with King Abimelech of Gerar (Gen. 26:1-14). Then there is Jacob who tricks his older brother Esau out of their father's blessings (Gen. 27:1-45). But trickster can also be tricked, as in the case of Laban, Jacob's father-in-law, who tricks Jacob out of seven years of labor and the woman he wants to marry by switching brides on the wedding night (Gen. 29:15-30).

During Egyptian captivity, the Hebrew midwives Shiphrah and Puah lie and deceive the Pharaoh to save the lives of the Hebrew babies (Exod. 1:15-21). The Hebrews are then tricked by an elaborate scheme perpetrated by the Gibeonites to enter a non-aggression treaty (Josh. 9:3-20). In the book of Judges, there is Ehud who tricks Eglon the tyrannical King of Moab into a secluded room so that he could be murdered (Judg. 3:12-30); Jael also liberates her people by providing Sisera deadly hospitality (Judg. 4:17-22); and there is Samson, who through his riddles tried to achieve personal gain only to eventually being tricked himself by his wife Delilah (Judg. 14; 16). Then there is King David who feigns madness before the King Achish of Gath to preserve his life (1 Sam. 21:11-14). And there is his son King Solomon who tricks the two women fighting over the baby to discover who is being truthful by threatening to cut the baby in half (1 Kgs. 3:16-28). These tricksters screw with the established order, engaged in deception to achieve personal gain (Jacob), survival (David), salvation of their people (Shiphrah, Puah, Jael and Ehud), or discover truth (Solomon).

Still, two biblical figures—Jesús and Satan—can also be reinterpreted as screwers of structures and systems. Jesús is a liberator who consistently screwed with the established political and religious authorities by subverting the legitimacy constructed by oppressors. For this he was crucifixion, accused of being a heretic. He screwed with those who established themselves the political and religious leaders and from their haughty positions screwed the very people they were entrusted to represent, support and protect. Cleansing the Temple becomes a liberative praxis that literally overturned established tables (Mk 11:15-18). The other biblical trickster figure worth mentioning is Satan.

Often Satan is portrayed as the ultimate manifestation of evil, neatly fitting within the cosmic good–evil binary. But what if instead of constructing Satan as evil personified, he instead is portrayed as a trickster?[17] He is more a literary ambiguous figure then simply the representation of universal evil. Satan's trickery can lead one to deeper truths or destruction. For example, read his attempt to tempt Jesús in the wilderness. Three times Satan tries to test (trick) Jesús. The first is with possessions, "command that these stones may become bread" (Mt. 4:3); then with privilege "If you are the son of God, throw yourself down" (Mt. 4:6); and finally with power "I will give all these [kingdoms] to you if you fall down and worship me" (Mt. 4:9). As trickster, Satan tests Jesús with the same temptations we all face, unearned possessions, privilege, and power; but Jesús did not succumb to these tricks, and in so doing—thanks to Satan—Jesús learned something about himself and his mission which he immediately began upon leaving the desert. Falling for the tricksters' deception can lead to ruin or create situations where the one being tested can rise to the occasion recognizing new opportunities to move forward. The consequences of the response to tricksters are not the trickster's fault, but rather, it is ours.

The tricksters found throughout the biblical text provide moral justification for the employment of deception as a means of self-preservation for those who face overwhelming odds against surviving. Tricksters as religious symbols are not restricted to Christianity. A major component of Latine identity is African culture, especially those of us whose roots are in the Caribbean. The spirituality relied upon many enslaved to survive has—over centuries—become part of the *mestizaje* of our culture. Specifically, Afro-Caribbean religious tradition contains stories concerning the quasi-deity (*orisha*) named Eshu whose origins are traced to Yoruba (present-day Nigeria). Eshu is also known as Eleggúa among followers of Santeriá, Exu in Brazilian Candomblé Legba in Caribbean vodou, and Lucero in Palo Mayombe. Of all the *orishas*, Eshu personifies the ultimate African tricksters. Because I am a child of Eleggúa, it should not be surprising that the trickster image plays a paramount role in my ethical analysis.

One of the traits common among Latine-based tricksters is their disregard for the prevailing rules and regulations. Why? Because they realize—as did the Young Lords—that the prescribed social order exists to maintain and legitimize the privileges of the few at the expense of many. When tricksters lie, cheat, joke, and deceive, they reveal deeper truths obscured by the moralistic rhetoric of the dominant culture. What eurocentric cultures define as moral, is immoral for those on their margins—and vice versa. This Latine ethics I am proposing—fully aware it is not fully embraced by all of my compatriots—is a trickster ethics operating within a realm that moves beyond good and evil, beyond what the dominant culture defines as right or wrong. Succinctly stated, the ethics which I call for is an ethics *para joder*, an ethics which f*cks with the systems!

An Ethics *para joder*

We have evolved into a society that requires obtaining a permit from the police department to picket the police department for the police brutality of the police department. Freedoms to protest exists, if it does not disrupt the social equilibrium demanded by those privileged with power—a social equilibrium morally justified by those Euroamerican ethicists who benefit from these same social structures. We created a social order where Latines inhabit Holy Saturday, a liminal space between the hopelessness of Friday's crucifixion, and the not yet possibility of Easter Sunday's resurrection. This is a space where some faint hope for Sunday's Good News is obscured by the reality and consequences of Friday's brutality. This is the space where hopelessness becomes the companion of those—like Latines—who are used and abused; where hope's audacity becomes a middle-class privilege for those protected from Friday's realities or an opium which numbs that same reality until Sunday. Regardless of the optimism professed, the disenfranchised, their children, and their children's children will more than likely continue to live in an ever-expanding poverty caused so that the few can benefit. They face a reality, regardless of who happens to be president of the empire, which remains hopeless.

When hopelessness is a given, we are left to ponder what is the ethical response to our marginalization, what becomes the Latine's moral initiative? To base our response on eurocentric paradigms is to contribute to our own oppression. Concepts like *Liberté, Egalité, and Fraternité* shouted from the streets of Paris during the French Revolution exclude their colonized people in Vietnam, Haiti, or Algiers. When Thomas Jefferson penned the immortal words—"we hold these truths to be self-evident, that all men are created equal," it was never meant for nor interfere with the continuous rape of his enslaved fourteen-year-old Sally Hemings. The high-sounding rhetoric of the dominant culture does not apply to all who fall short to the white supremacy-based worldview. The Young Lords understood that the promises of liberty in the land of the free was never meant for them. What then becomes the ethical response? I believe the Young Lords provide a model to emulate.

They f*cked with governmental agencies, health organizations, and religious institutions. Their *jodiendo* in the mean streets of New York (and Chicago) shaped what a Latine ethical paradigm could look like. To *joder* is a Spanish verb never used in polite company which usually is translated as a certain four-letter word: f*ck. The vulgarity of the word used is not what is the problem, but rather the treatments of Latines in this country are what is truly vulgar. A politer translation would be "to screw with"—not "to screw," but to "screw with," a crucial semantical difference. Coining a term describing an ethical practice that has already existed among the marginalized implies this methodology of *jodiendo* is not a new concept dreamt in my ivy tower. I am not suggesting anything new. Oppressed people have always engaged in such subversive praxis. All I am doing is naming it and rooting it within my own Latine culture. As an organic intellectual, I simply reflect on this existing praxis for the purpose of theorizing and theologizing.

This ethics *para joder*[18] f*cks with the prevailing power structures fostering an effective response to the consequences of white supremacy—the oppressive normativity of social structures. This ethical model, rooted in the Latine experience, is a proactive civil initiative whose disruptiveness is based on tactics learned from Latine trickster figures. I suggest Latines follow the lead of the Young Lords. Obviously, the term did not exist in the late 1960s nor has any members of the Young Lords ever stated they were participating in an ethics *para joder*. I am fully aware of the peril of imposing a contemporary term I coined on historic events. Nevertheless, I will argue that these events were led by individuals who refused to follow the rules that ensured their people's subjugation to the dominant culture by employing disruptive praxis akin tricksters. I argue that the only way for the powerless, the marginalized, the disenfranchised, and the dispossessed to radically counter the prevailing status quo is to *joder*.

The Young Lords were *joderones*. A *joderon* connotes an individual who purposely is a pain in the rear end, who purposely is causing trouble, who constantly disrupts the established norm, who refuses to stay in his or her place, who shouts from mountain tops that which those in power prefer kept under a bushel. Because Latines stand before the vastness of neoliberalism infused with white Christian nationalism and supremacy, little hope for radical change—especially in the era of and after Trump—exists in their lifetime. Few ethical responses to latinephobia exists. Regardless of the good intentions of some who are privileged by the dominant culture, or the praxis they employ to paternalistically save Latines, the devastating consequences of empire will only worsen as the few get wealthier while many Latines sink deeper into the despair of stomach-wrenching oppression. The dominant culture, including white liberal ethicists, may be quick to offer charity and to stand in solidarity, but few are willing to participate in the dismantling of the very structures designed to privilege them at the expense of their Others.

To *joder* creates instability within precious eurocentric social equilibrium, thus upsetting the prevailing Panopticon-based social order designed to maintain the law and order of the privileged. Instability could lead some within the dominant culture to share in the hopelessness of overcoming their complicity with neoconservative and neoliberal forces, creating an opportunity for change. No doubt, a liberative ethics *para joder* is frightening for those accustomed to their protected space which ensures their unearned possessions, power, and privileges, for hopelessness signals lack of control. Because those who benefit from the present social structures insist on control, sharing the plight of being vulnerable to forces beyond control illustrates hope's shortcomings.

History demonstrates that simply denouncing unjust social structures falls short. True, we may see some reform which might slightly lighten the burden carried by Latines; but in the final analysis, those for whom the social structures are designed to privilege will never willingly abdicate what they have come to believe is their eugenically based birthright. When those excluded from the fruits of society refuse to play by the rules established by those who provide space for orderly protest which pacifies the disenfranchised need to vent but does not change the existing power relationships within social structures; they create instability. To *joder* is to overturn traditional tables which maintains the existing oppressive social order. An ethics *pare joder* provides moral justification for the employment of deception as a means of self-preservation against the overwhelming odds of surviving. Political and social change requires going beyond the rules created by the dominant culture, moving beyond what is expected, pushing beyond universalized eurocentric experiences.

As long as established tables remain stable, opportunities for liberation remain stifle. F*cking with oppressive structures which undergirds white supremacy might lead to new possibilities. And in truth, it might not. After all, Hegel's optimistic historical dialectics upon which hope is based is but a doctrine accepted by faith. Rejecting the upward linier movement of history, the only ethical response for Latines facing insurmountable repressive social structures is to be like Jesús, overturning those tables in the *hope* of creating new opportunities through disorder and chaos. To *joder* is not a praxis where Latines engage out of a thirst for vengeance. Heaven forbids! To *joder* is an act of love toward oppressors, forcing them to live up to their rhetoric in the *hopes* of confronting their complicity with oppression, a confrontation which might lead to their salvation. Christian nationalists and white supremacists are also victims of the structures designed to privilege them, for in their complicity with the dehumanization of Latines, they lose their own humanity.

No doubt such liberative praxis will be dismissed as immoral by the dominant culture; still, tricksters are ethical, operating in a realm beyond good and evil, beyond what society defines as right or wrong. An *ethics para joder* is a liberative praxis capable of transforming society for the better, even though the ultimate utopian goal may never be realized. Still, we strive not because we hope to succeed (because we more than likely won't) or because we cling to some belief in some heavenly reward in the afterlife; we struggle for justice against all the odds because we have no other choice if we wish to live the faith we claim to possess. But more importantly, we struggle for justice if we wish to remain faithful to our humanity. We strive forward because in the crucible of struggle, we construct our identity and define our purpose. And even if some still insist on the existence of some utopian hope, then maybe, just maybe, it might be found when we say "f*ck it."

If the prevailing history that justifies the dominant social order, as argued throughout this chapter, exists to legitimize and normalize the privileges of the few at the expense of many, then *joderones* become tricksters who lie to reveal truth; cheat to create a level playing field; steal so as to feed the hungry who are denied food; joke so that the devil can be shamed; deceive so that the vulnerable can be protected; and disrupt so that new liberative opportunities might arise.

16

Sacred Texts

Jacqueline M. Hidalgo

Just as Latines encompass a complex diversity of histories and experiences rooted in a range of ethnic, national, and religious backgrounds, so too do their "texts" and verbal traditions. For Latine communities in the United States, the category of "text" is far more expansive, fluid, and contested than conventional definitions might suggest. While the Bible stands as a significant and prototypical example of a sacred text for many Latine communities, even within Jewish, Catholic, and Protestant traditions, there is no singular Bible. The texts that constitute "the Bible" vary across Latine communities, and so too do the ways people relate to them. Even in the broader Christian tradition, the Bible itself cannot be understood simply as a bounded or unified text, given the diversity of voices within it, the canonical variations between traditions, and the range of interpretive practices that shape its use.

Edwin David Aponte has shown how Latine religiosity is deeply embedded in everyday life—in food, music, dance, and ritual. For Aponte, *santo* is not just a theological category but a lived, embodied practice. It is through these practices that Latine communities construct sacred meaning, often outside the bounds of institutional religion.[1] Moreover, in describing Navajo creation narratives, Dennis Kelley notes how "religious texts" are not always written, nor are they necessarily textual in the conventional sense. They are often embodied, performed, and relational—emerging through story, land, and community. More importantly, Kelley emphasizes that religious texts function in particular ways: They orient communities, transmit memory, authorize behavior, and mediate relationships with the sacred.[2] Although many Latines descend from colonizing communities that have inflicted harm on Indigenous Latine communities, Kelley's approach clarifies how—for many communities—"religious texts" function more expansively than what is merely bound or written. His insights help us perceive how texts emerge through place, story, and community, and how they function to orient, authorize, and connect.

For Latine communities, to speak of "texts" is to speak not only of the Bible but also of murals, corridos, recipes, protest manifestos, oral stories, altars, and more. These "texts" are not merely supplementary to what we might call "scripture"; they are, in many cases, scriptures themselves—texts through which communities encounter the sacred, negotiate power, and imagine alternative worlds. This broader understanding of "texts" challenges dominant models of scripture that privilege written, bounded, and institutionally sanctioned forms of religious authority. Vincent L. Wimbush's work suggests that what we think of as "scriptures" are not static objects of mere text but dynamic processes of social power and knowledge through media deemed sacred—practices of scripturalization that are always entangled with histories of migration, enslavement, colonization, survival, resistance, and daily persistence. In this sense, scripture is not a thing but a doing: a way of making meaning, shaping identity, and contesting power.[3] While I use "texts" to refer broadly to verbal, visual, and embodied forms of meaning-making, I use "scriptures" to signal those texts—biblical or otherwise—that communities treat as sacred, authoritative, or revelatory.

This essay examines how Latine communities engage a broad range of texts as sacred, contested, and communal. Drawing on my own research on the multivalence of the Bible and other scriptures in Latine contexts, I argue that "scriptures" as "sacred texts" in Latine lived religion function as "technologies of diaspora" and "utopian homing devices"—tools for making meaning and making home in the midst of displacement. These practices are not merely interpretive; they are world-making. They are ways of reading and writing the sacred into everyday life. Yet Latine engagements with "religious texts" at large—and "scriptures" in particular—also carry with them fraught histories of use and abuse.

The Bible as Icon and Instrument of Power

As the prototypical example of a "sacred text," the Bible occupies a paradoxical position in Latine lived religion: it is at once a sacred text, a cultural icon, a colonial weapon, and a source of healing. Its multivalence—its capacity to function in contradictory ways—makes it a particularly potent example of how "texts" operate in Latine communities. As Timothy Beal has observed, the Bible is not a singular, bounded object but a compendium of diverse texts, translations, and material forms.[4] It appears as Torah scrolls, illuminated manuscripts, leather-bound books, podcasts, and even as musical theater. Yet despite this diversity, the Bible has long held a special, iconic role in the Americas, often imagined as a singular, authoritative book.

This iconicity is deeply entangled with histories of colonization. The oft-repeated story of Atahualpa and the Bible—where the Inca leader is said to have thrown down a Bible that "said nothing"—has become a symbolic narrative of the Bible's role in conquest. Whether or not the event occurred as described, its retelling, especially in Eduardo Galeano's *Memory of Fire*, has shaped the cultural memory of the Bible as a tool of imperial violence.[5] The Bible, in this imagination, is not a neutral text but an ideological arm of colonial assault. This perception was echoed in 1992 when a group identifying as "Indians of the Andes and the Americas" returned the Bible to Pope John Paul II, declaring that it belonged to the oppressors who had used it to justify conquest.[6]

Yet the Bible is not only a symbol of domination. For many Latine communities, it is also a source of healing, guidance, and homemaking that can be engaged in myriad ways. Elsewhere I have described how, in my own Roman Catholic family, the Bible was not read extensively but was present in prayers, songs, and rituals that bring people together. In Protestant communities, the Bible may be read daily, studied in depth, or used in healing rituals—for instance, laid open to Psalm 23 or touched to the body of the sick.[7] Elaine Penagos, a scholar of religion, describes how, in Santería and other Afro-diasporic traditions, biblical figures like Lazarus are syncretized with orishas like Babalú Ayé, but she also draws on her personal story to show how such syncretization takes on meaning because it becomes part of a sacred narrative of suffering and healing that her grandmother shared with her.[8] These practices show that the Bible is not always read; it is also worn, sung, touched, and lived.

To some extent, Latine engagements with the Bible reflect what Angela Parker calls the Bible's "authoritarian" versus "authoritative" functions. In authoritarian modes, the Bible is treated as a conversation-ender, a fixed text that demands submission. In authoritative modes, it becomes a conversation partner—open to interpretation, dialogue, and change.[9] Both modes exist within Latine communities, often side by side, and there are Latines who also invest no authority in their relationship with the Bible. Miguel De La Torre reminds us that the Bible has often been interpreted in ways that reinforce the status quo but that reading "from the margins" requires a hermeneutic of suspicion and survival. For De La Torre, the Bible can still be read, but it should be read *ethically*—that is, with attention to the lived realities of the oppressed.[10] Some Latines engage the Bible as a sacred guide for living in a hostile world; others reject its authority altogether, even as they draw on its language and imagery in art, protest, and storytelling.

The Bible's multivalence is not merely a matter of interpretation; it is a matter of power. As Wimbush argues, scripturalization is a process through which texts become loci of identity formation as well as social power.[11] The Bible's role in Latine communities must be understood within this framework: it is not just a text but a site of struggle. Whether embraced, contested, or reimagined, the Bible remains a central—if ambivalent—text in Latine lived religion.

Beyond the Bible: Everyday Scriptures and Lived Texts

While the Bible remains a central and contested text in many Latine communities, it is far from the only one. Sacred meaning is often mediated through a wide array of texts that are not bound, canonized, or even always written. These "everyday scriptures" include murals, corridos, protest manifestos, oral stories, recipes, and ritual practices—forms that are not merely expressive but scriptural in their own right. These texts are not marginal to religious life; they are central to how Latine communities make meaning, make home, and make the sacred present in everyday life.

In *Revelation in Aztlán*, I argued that Chicane and Latine communities have long engaged in practices of scripturalization that extend beyond the Bible. Drawing on Wimbush's framework, I understand scripturalization as a process through which texts—broadly defined—become loci of social power and identity formation. In the Chicano movement of the 1960s and 1970s, for example, texts like *El Plan Espiritual de Aztlán* and *El Plan de Santa Barbara* functioned as scriptures: they were ritually read, cited, performed, and contested.[12] They offered not only political programs but also utopian visions of belonging, identity, and sacred space.

Scripturalization, in this broader sense, is not merely about authority or tradition. It is a utopian activity: a way of envisioning and inhabiting "an-other world."[13] These everyday scriptures function as what José Esteban Muñoz might call "utopian horizons"—not static destinations, but dynamic orientations toward a better world.[14] They are not only about survival; they are about belonging and transformation. They offer a vision of the sacred that is grounded in the lives of the people, not in the authority of institutions.

These scriptural practices were not limited to written texts. As Cherríe L. Moraga and others have shown, murals, poetry, and performance also functioned as sacred texts. Moraga's notion of the "Chicano codex" expands the category of scripture to include embodied, visual, and oral forms of knowledge.[15] In this sense, a mural on a barrio wall or a grandmother's story can be as scriptural as a passage from the Bible. These sacred "texts" are technologies of diaspora—tools for making home in a world that often renders Latine communities placeless.

This view of scriptures also allows us to see how Latine communities contest the exclusions embedded in dominant religious texts. The Chicano movement's use of Aztlán was not without its problems. It often relied on heteropatriarchal and nationalist frameworks that excluded women's, LGBTQIA, AfroChicano, and Indigenous voices. Yet even these exclusions became sites of contestation. Feminist and queer critics like Moraga and Gloria Anzaldúa reimagined Aztlán as a borderlands space—a site of in-betweenness that could hold multiple identities and histories.[16] In doing so, they expanded the scriptural imagination of the movement, showing that scriptures are not fixed but always in the process of being remade.

Scripturalization, then, is not a purely liberatory act. It is a contested and ambivalent process. It can open up new worlds, but it can also close them off. It can affirm identity, but it can also enforce boundaries. What makes scripturalization utopian is not its purity but its potential—its capacity to imagine otherwise, to name what is not yet, and to call it into being. Whether in the new Jerusalem or in Aztlán, in the Bible or in barrio murals, Latine communities have used scripture to imagine "an-other world"—a world that is not yet but might be. De La Torre's hermeneutical approach to the Bible remains relevant beyond the Bible as well. Everyday scriptures are not neutral; they are forged in struggle. They are read and performed in kitchens, on street corners, in protest marches, and in healing rituals. They are not only about survival—they are about transformation. They offer a vision of the sacred that is grounded in the lives of the people, not in the authority of institutions, and all scriptures are open to conflict, contestation, and revision.

Contesting the Sacred: Latine Biblical Scholars and the Reimagining of Scriptures

Although they represent one particular window onto the work that scriptures do in Latine contexts, Latine biblical scholars have long engaged in a critical contestation of the sacred—not by rejecting scriptures outright, but by interrogating their uses, reconfiguring their meanings, and reimagining their potential for forging a better world that is more responsive to minoritized and oppressed communities. This contestation is epistemological, political, and embodied, rooted in the lived experiences of Latine peoples and their historical entanglements with colonialism, migration, and racialization. Each of the critics I highlight below demonstrate how readings informed by migration and the borderlands particularly challenge interpretive traditions that treat the text—and its depictions of God—as an authoritarian figure requiring the reader's submission.

In his work describing Latine biblical interpretations, Francisco Lozada Jr. interrogates the politics of identity and belonging in biblical texts and interpretation, particularly through the lens of language, translation, and migration. He draws at times on his own experiences as a Puerto Rican in diaspora to complicate simple meanings we might place upon identities or belonging. His work on the Lord's Prayer, for example, explores how translation is never neutral but always encodes narratives of identity and power.[17] He reframes the study of biblical translation as a practice that connects ancient texts with contemporary struggles for recognition and justice.

Similarly, scholars have taken inspiration from Latine experiences with migration to reexamine not only the meaning of biblical texts but also the moves of mainstream biblical scholarship, which has tended to presume the character of God aligns with dominating rule. For instance, in Jean-Pierre Ruiz's reading of Matthew 20:1–16, the parable of the day laborers, Ruiz resists conventional theological interpretations that cast the landowner as a figure of divine generosity. Instead, he centers the lived experiences of immigrant workers in New York. For Ruiz, the parable becomes a site of contestation where the vineyard owner's actions reflect not divine grace but economic exploitation and social control. The landowner's decision to pay all workers equally, regardless of hours worked, is not a gesture of generosity but a demonstration of power that reinforces the laborers' precarity and dependence.[18] Ruiz's reading reframes the parable as a critique of systems that devalue labor and obscure injustice under the guise of divine benevolence.

Similarly, Leticia Guardiola-Sáenz's cultural reading of Matthew 15:21–28 offers a borderlands hermeneutic that foregrounds the agency of the Canaanite woman. Reading from her own social location as an ethnically Mexican woman shaped by the US–Mexico borderlands, Guardiola-Sáenz interprets the woman's plea not as submissive faith but as a bold act of protest and reclamation. She argues that the woman crosses ideological and geographical borders to demand justice, challenging the ideology of chosenness embedded in the Matthean narrative. Guardiola-Sáenz frames the biblical text as a "borderless" or hybrid cultural text, one that is continually reinterpreted through the lived experiences of readers who have themselves been dispossessed.[19] Her work contests imperialistic interpretations and gives voice to the Other.

Offering an internal critique that challenges how crossing into both queerness and the United States from Mexico has been imagined in Latine contexts, Manuel Villalobos Mendoza, in his essay on Anzaldúa and the Ethiopian eunuch, offers a powerful example of contesting the sacred through queer, decolonial, and borderlands hermeneutics. He reads Acts 8 through the lens of Anzaldúa's concept of *nepantla*—a liminal, in-between space of transformation. Villalobos argues that the eunuch, like Anzaldúa's nepantlera, inhabits a space of radical ambiguity and potential.[20] By queering the text and centering the body of the eunuch, Villalobos challenges the heteronormative and colonial logics that have shaped traditional interpretations of scriptures, including within Latine communities as well as outside of them.

Finally, Gregory L. Cuéllar's work draws on critical biblical studies in order to read the US–Mexico border and the borderlands more broadly as sacred texts that must be challenged and reframed. In *Resacralizing the Other*, Cuéllar critiques the ways in which the state weaponizes the sacred to justify the dehumanization and criminalization of migrant bodies.[21] Drawing particularly on frameworks from Luis León and Gloria Anzaldúa, Cuéllar imagines how to resacralize the Other as a counter-hermeneutic to dehumanization. He rereads biblical traditions as well as other texts like corridos and traditions of curanderismo through the lens of border-crossers and the border-crossed, arguing that scriptures, including the sacralized boundaries of the nation, must be reinterpreted in ways that affirm the sacredness of marginalized lives. Cuéllar's work challenges biblical scholars to confront the complicity of religious discourse in state violence and to imagine new hermeneutical frameworks rooted in justice, healing, and solidarity.

Together, these scholars demonstrate that contesting the sacred is not about abandoning scriptures but about reclaiming them as sites of struggle, survival, and transformation. Their work invites us to see the Bible and other scriptures not as a static repository of divine truth, but as a living archive—one that can be reread, re-performed, and reimagined.

Conclusion

In Latine contexts, scriptures are not merely inherited texts but dynamic, contested, and communal practices. Whether through the Bible, murals, protest manifestos, or oral traditions, Latine communities engage in acts of scripturalization that are deeply rooted in histories of migration, colonization, racialization, survival, and resistance. These texts—biblical and beyond—do not simply convey sacred meaning; they make it. They orient communities, authorize behavior, and offer visions of belonging and transformation in the face of displacement and exclusion. These practices are not only interpretive but world-making. They are technologies of diaspora and utopian homing devices—tools for imagining "an-other world" in the midst of struggle.

At the same time, scriptures are not neutral. They are forged in histories of power and are often sites of exclusion. Yet Latine biblical scholars have modeled how to contest the sacred—not by discarding scriptures, but by reimagining them. In order to understand texts and words in Latine lived religious contexts, we must think expansively about what counts as scriptures and who counts as an interpreter. We must attend not only to texts but to the communities that live them. Scriptures are living, breathing practices—ones that continue to shape and be shaped by the sacred struggles of Latine life.

17

Sound, Cinema, and *Santería*: Listening to "Angelitos Negros" with Oyá

Deborah De La Torre

Sound, as moving air and vibration, animates the sensorial cinematic experience. Powered by *aché*, the energy of existence, Oyá's abilities, as *orisha* warrior of the wind and cemeteries, can become a profound auditory partner while listening to old cinematic melodramas and cultural works related to *Angelitos Negros*. In this chapter, drawing from sound studies, ethnomusicology, folklore, and film studies, I make the interdisciplinary argument that sound recording and filmmaking technologies have much to share with *Santería*. I engage with Oyá's electrified communications through three of her powerful modes—the sheer force of her persona, her *vaina* (rattle), and her shroud—which offer capacious ways of hearing and thinking about genealogical bodies of cultural production. My subjective Latine way of listening poetically invokes the phrase *de cierta manera* (a certain way) from Cuban film and literature,[1] as foundational to listening and hearing alongside Oyá, while my background as a musician relies on interpretative aesthetics and other modes of perception to (dis)assemble technical understandings about old songs, poems, and films.

Part 1: Who is Oyá?

In the pantheon of *orishas*, Oyá fans her multicolored skirt,[2] causing the wind to blow into "an enormous gale."[3] Associations include St. Teresa in Cuba, the color maroon, how fire lights candles,[4] and the color purple.[5] Her protective *elekes* (beads) comprise nine alternating white and black beads. She is, "tempestuous; violent; sensual; [and] authoritarian" while her power, or "discipline," represents "causing windstorms or electrocution."[6] Quoting one of her interlocutors, anthropologist Judith Gleason writes, "across vast inchoate air she [Oyá] comes to ground" and that she "was born in the air she plants on the earth."[7]

Oyá is married to Oggún and is the mistress of Changó, while "Elegguá may be the son of either." Metal, specifically iron, is the domain of the "war-orisha"[8] Oggún, while thunder, fire, electricity and lightning are related to Changó. Elegguá serves as communicator or messenger, passing knowledge, know-how, and "legends" among the *orishas*. Connected through *Santeriá*, these elements containing *ashé* - air, metal, electricity, and storytelling - are fundamental to sound and cinema.

Intervening as a "fellow warrior" between Oggún and Changó in their brotherly fights, Oyá's relationship with electricity is thus physically internalized: "when the winds are strongly blowing, people know that lightning is not far behind."[9] "Shango and Oya's shared sovereignty can be boisterous in the skies for all to see, though which owns lightning remains contested by partisans on both sides of the Atlantic."[10]

How did Oyá become associated with the cemetery? Anthropologist Aisha Beliso-De Jesús describes Oyá, as "owner of the cemetery. She is both the air we inhale and the lungs in our bodies." Sister to Obba, Changó's legitimate wife, and the youngest sister of Yemayá and Ochún,[11] one legend records Oya's sister Ochún originally owning the cemetery, who "cried every time she saw her children arrive," and "changed her post with Ollá [*sic*]."[12] Another version describes Yemayá tricking Oyá, making the switch.[13] "If not properly attended to, Oyá, a black feminine who is a gateway to dead spirits, can make people lose their minds."[14] For example, "If a person needed protection against death, they would make an offering to Oyá."[15] The grim reaper figure that we see in the movies, the angel of death, is represented by Ikú, "a quasi-deity whose function is to dispose of life" and who "can usually be found in the graveyard, where he abides under the jurisdiction of the *orisha* Oyá."[16] Severance and brokenness are models comprising Oyá's follower-candidate initiation requirements: "visit nine ragged sites, like broken fences, crumbling walls, abandoned houses in the process of falling down, ruins of previous settlements, dumps containing rusted car carcasses, bulldozed gardens."[17]

Oyá's Rattle, Sonidos Escondidos, Sounds Escaping

Devotees of Oyá use a *vaina*, a seed pod shaker or rattle, for addressing and sonic celebration. Gleason describes these as "'nine painted flamboyant pods' (which always adorn Oya's throne; you shake them and you hear the wind)."[18] Rainbows of painted colors, cowrie shells, elaborate ornamental designs, and encircling beads connect the *vaina* to her multicolored skirt. Gleason used "double doors"[19] to describe "new ways of looking at Oya." For me, this double-door friction resembles the *audio collision*, where sound swings off-hinge, a scraped listening meet-up. Composer Pierre

Schaefer defined hearing, *audition,* in terms of violence, as in, "to hear is to be struck by sounds."[20] I hold this particular listening resembles the sonic, puncturing, turbulent breath of Oyá's rattle and skirt, colliding with one's ears.

As the internal *sonidos escondidos* (hidden sounds) of Oyá's *vaina's* become mobilized,[21] the external, whole-sound-maker resembles the audio-viewer's[22] experience of cinema's image-sound-adherence contrasting with the movie production's "occult aesthetics"[23] (think of a horse's clip-clopping hooves realized by a backstage drummer tapping coconut shells). The "noise" of the *vaina's* secret innards is concealed,[24] akin to Schaeffer's *musique concrète,* detected by slowed-down tape recordings[25] as "vibrating and resonant bodies."[26] Rattled sounds can be heard at some distance. Oyá's rattle makes a visually trapped sound that can be pried apart in time and space through film and audio recording and editing.[27] Another way to think of the rattle's internal structuring is one that acts out simultaneous physical and sonic adhesive dislocation. The rattled sound is severed, trapped, and simultaneously escaping, capable of exceeding its permeable, wrapped containment.

Proximities to Sonidos Escondidos and Occult Aesthetics

Sometimes, the characters and stories contained within old projected films visit with us via metallically and electrically portaled, lit-up celluloid, pulsing-out sounds and portrayals of the dead through the air. I balance this technology alongside the illuminations of Santería-based natural, organic relationships, such as translucent sea-foam (*espuma del mar*), containing dissolved debris of the dead and decomposed. The activating, bubbling chemistry of sea-foam evokes the elemental chemical baths of early photography and filmmaking. Solimar Otero recalls sea-foam usefullness for "think[ing] through the shifting nature of the residual transcripts explored in relation to multiple experiences of modernity, science, spirituality, and materiality," such as "virtual existence and decentered notions of place."[28] In *Archives of Conjure: Stories of the Dead in Afrolatinx Cultures* (2020), Otero, a scholar of folklore and Afrolatinx religions, writes that *espuma del mar* "evokes memory because of the many ways we hear, feel, smell, or see it. As a rhythmic aftermath of a wave, it acts as a residual transcript."[29] Otero writes that Oyá can also participate in "a shifting amalgam," "as an example of a kind of spiritual palimpsest," in the spiritual *trabajo* (work) performed by spirit guides.[30]

Santería, as a religion of enslaved and oppressed Africans in the Caribbean and Latin America, used numerous methods to preserve beliefs and maintain practices by "mask[ing] their gods with the clothing of Catholic saints," keeping much of their rituals occluded.[31] Anthropologist Aisha M. Beliso-De Jesús observes *Santería*'s growing hegemony[32] further enabled due to technologically influenced geographical relationships of *orisha* energies intersecting politically, spiritually, and geographically dislocated places and spaces. The internet's helpful[33] ability to instantly globally disperse recorded *Santería* practices has also seen its prohibitions.[34] Oyá-circuited listening draws from Beliso-De Jesús's exploration of how metal machines relay various "electrifying spiritual currents (*los corrientes espirituales*)," expanding our understanding of what presence can be, in the here-and-now.[35] Sound studies scholar Steven Connor wrote, "Listen, says a voice: some being is giving voice."[36] For me, an Oyá-informed listening to metal-projected, electricity-powered *películas* (movies) and *canciones* (songs) hears Connor's articulation of "some being" *in a certain way*. I see that multi-representational experiences, attuned to life, death, and transformation, fulfill and extend film theorist Kevin J. Donnelly's definition of "occult aesthetics."[37] For me, Oyá-attunement hears technology and *Santería* working in tandem: the *sonidos escondidos* of *los corrientes espirituales* heard beyond their containment, carrying "some being," *de cierta manera*.

Beyond Electro-Organic-Sonic Collaborations

Engaging Schaefer and Beliso-De Jesús, I propose a widened Latine audiovisual aperture. In a certain way, *de cierta manera*, I am trying to listen more carefully, more specifically, to what is being electrically vibrated, transmitted, and carried through the air.

Schaefer wrote, "Sometimes we do not hear even though we are listening, and often we hear without listening."[38] Within *Santería*, states Beliso-De Jesús, "the electrical waves of oricha and *egun* call for a reconfiguration of anthropological understandings of media and religion."[39] She has observed "pluralized relationships with and in relation to technology, nature, and spirit—that is, active negotiations with intra-agents (alive, dead, and nonhuman) that have their own politics and life forces."[40] Beliso-De Jesús states that these "copresences also use video currents" where "the electricity of copresences are redistributed" in a manner "akin to diffraction" of light waves.[41] As "cross-spatial subjects, elements that expand and shift bodily registers," which communicate by participating within "technoritual interspaces," they point to "understanding Santería modes of feeling [and] perceiving."[42] Cuban practitioner-made videorecordings have facilitated a sense, according to Beliso-de Jesús, of being "spiritually *present* through videos."[43] The case I am making here focuses on hearing cinema and old recordings along similar lines.

Oyá and a Way of Listening to "Angelitos Negros"

An Oyá-accompanied "*Angelitos Negros*" case study of elusive currents of poetry, songs, films, *telenovelas*, visual art, and public processions is preceded by historical traumatic realities. Sounds of violence made by over ten million enslaved Africans emanating from outside and inside 36,000 slave ships across the Middle Passage, and 11,000 voyages within the Americas, were a multi-century production of the Spanish Caribbean capitalist enterprise, beginning in the mid-1500s.[44] By Abolition in 1886, sounds made by Cuba's freed Africans were repackaged in new commercial ways.

The Spanish Caribbean saw the widespread development of racialized ventriloquy and mimicry in song and dance, advancing "the process of transforming Africans into commodities, such as the Jim Crow portrayal and diction."[45] "The ventriloquy of (stereotyped) black dialect" would become commercially connected to musical performances using "further simplified black speech into a few racist phonetic scripts through equally racist dialect" writes ethnomusicologist Matthew D. Morrison.[46] Caribbean ventriloquies of racialized sound-making arrived in the Gulf of Mexico via touring groups such as "Compañia de Bufos Cubanos,"[47] contributing to the development of "Cuban comic theatre,"[48] writes ethnomusicologist Robin D. Moore. Filmmaker Ebony Marie Bailey has observed that Latine films have contained a variety of encryptions used by society to represent "codings of Blackness through blackface, the "tragic mulatto" figure, and dialogues that took away from the agency of the Black characters."[49] Connected to advertisements describing enslaved people attempting to "pass for white" while on the run from their enslavers,[50] the *Angelitos Negros*'s story of *mestizaje* and racialized rejection followed the genre and codings inherent within "Passing Films" from the 1930s to the 1940s.[51]

Interactivity: An Invitation to the Reader to Listen to Andrés Eloy Blanco Recite His Poem "Angelitos Negros"

The poem from 1936 titled, "*Pintame angelitos negros,* by light-skinned Venezuelan poet Andrés Eloy Blanco (1896–1955),[52] was written to "valorize African diasporic cultures."[53] The reader is encouraged to take a moment to listen and reflect on a publicly available recording dated 1943[54] of Blanco reciting his poem in Spanish, via the Library of Congress. The author's voice recounts a black woman's lamentation over losing her little boy. She is comforted knowing that God has placed him "as a little angel in Heaven." The authorial voice then chastises her: "*Desengáñese, comadre, que no hay angelitos negros* (*Don't be fooled, comadre, there are no little black angels*)." Attention is directed to the "Painter of saints in alcoves" who has forgotten, when painting saints and Virgins, to paint little black angels. Blanco's verses for inclusion are sorted by levels of skin pigmentation, resembling the *Casta* paintings from Colonial Mexico.[55] Reader, as you listen to Blanco's words from the poem, what images, sounds, and ideas come to mind?

Close to Blanco's age was the white Puerto Rican poet, Luis Palés Matos (1898–1959), "who introduced Afro-Caribbean rhythms, metaphors and voices to the formal Spanish-language literary consciousness," as "an exploiter of racial imagery and themes." Apart from the work of Afro-Cuban author Nicolás Guillén," Matos became credited with "initiating *poesía negra*," as well as the "geographical consciousness that he called *afroantillana*."[56] Significant is how Matos' poem "Ñañigo al Cielo," (Ñañigo [African wise one] to heaven), contradicts Blanco's theological arguments against Black salvation. "*Ha entrado un alma en el cielo, ¡y ésa es el alma del ñañigo!* (A soul has entered heaven, and that is the soul of the ñañigo!"[57]

Listening to "Angelitos Negros" as Shrouded Bodies of Cultural Production

Gleason writes, "Oya is the mistress of shrouded presentation of the ineffable."[58] I build from Gleason's incorporation of dead body coverings to consider shroud as a technology used for recording and listening "live" sounds. This type of "thick(ened) listening"[59] is one which plays on the uses of microphone windscreens. The padded or meshed mic coverings prevent external air (the wind) and internal air (bodily-made speech-air) from impacting our imagined and interpreted audio preferences. Just as windscreens hold sound accountable to certain desired ways of hearing, I hold that the genealogies of cultural production related to "*Angelitos Negros*," the poem, song, and subsequent artistic renderings, experience a shrouded form of understanding, listening, hearing, and transportation.

Shrouded Music: "Angelitos Negros" and "Ave Maria!"

While recognizing the project's numerous antecedent flows from existing Caribbean aesthetics and folkloric practices, my initial attunement to the multi-bodied project "*Angelitos Negros*" as visual artworks, soundings, and choreographed displays, was struck by the *repeated naming* of the Black child's post-death status as an *angelito*. The shock of this horrific status, I claim, has been muffled by genealogies of cultural production, in particular the popularized *bolero* with lyrics demanding justice and heaven's acceptance, leaving the child's cause of death unheard and unaccounted-for.[60]

The song's composer, Manuel Alvarez Renteria "Maciste," was born in the city of Tequila, Mexico on August 8, 1892, and he died in Mexico City on October 13, 1960. Guitarist, singer, songwriter, and director of the composition department of the Mexican Association of Filmmakers, Maciste helped to organize the Mexican Composers Society. In 1930, his radio show *Una guitarra en la noche* (A guitar in the night), aired on Mexican station XEW. Contemporary Spanish literature and music scholar Vanessa Knights determined that "*Angelitos Negros*" was a "bolero."[61] Versions of Maciste's

"*Angelitos Negros*," were published by Peer Music in New York City. The Discography of American Historical Recordings (DAHR), shows Maciste associated with twenty-three recordings, several of himself singing and playing the guitar.[62]

Sometime in 1946, Maciste published the original song in sheet music form. His 1949 piano arrangement containing Spanish and Italian lyrics, specifies the tempo as "tango," begins with eight bars from the sung refrain of "Ave Maria!", and ends by repeating three "Ave Maria!" bars in conclusion.[63] Mexican singer Antonia del Carmen Peregrino Álvarez (1912–1982), performing as Toña La Negra, recorded "*Angelitos Negros*," in 1942,[64] including the "Ave Maria!" enclosure. Recorded versions by Pedro Infante (1947), Eartha Kitt (1953) and Roberta Flack (1969), for example, do not, however, include the "Ave Maria!"[65]

Why did Maciste incorporate portions of the devotional song "Ave Maria!" by Austrian composer Franz Schubert into his musical arrangement of "*Angelitos Negros*"? Was it to exploit its well-known socio-religious capital, in hopes of securing its success? Toña La Negra's 1942 hit recording of "*Angelitos Negros*" swept all the way to Spain, rattling the ears of Cuban singer Antonio Machín who cabled his cousin in Havana the very next day to help locate the sheet music.[66] Indeed, by the time the first *Angelitos Negros* movie was released in 1948, the song, performed in the film by Mexican singer Pedro Infante, and already available as sheet music for two years, was likely to have achieved sing-along status.[67] Latine studies scholar Frances R. Aparicio writes that the song was "felt all over Latin America," as "its text denounced the colonialist, Eurocentric, and whitened paradigms in the visual arts that have prevailed throughout Latin American high culture."[68]

The *Angelitos Negros* 1948 film's title cards appear with "an imposing, heavily orchestrated version of "Angelitos negros" [which] sets the tone for the poignant story that follows,"[69] while paintings and statues of angels, cherubs, cathedrals, bridges, and Michelangelo's *La Pietà* appear on-screen. The song is heard as an accompanied solo at an important moment within the film's story (in one version on the piano, and in another on the guitar), and more somberly during the end credits. Joselito Rodriguez's name as director appears while the music strikes dramatically louder chords against a drum roll as foreshadow. In both the original and the subsequent film versions, racialized adjectives barrage the ears of the black grandmother characters, one of which sings a lullaby in racialized ventriloquism resembling *bozal*.[70] Racialized sonic mimicry is carried out in the first version's Santeria-imitative theatrical performance in blackface. In the 1969 version, there is a nightclub act, "Soul 70," of characterized blackface, and the grandmother's voice is dubbed over in imitative speech.

After *Angelitos Negros* was remade in 1969 by its director, Joselito Rodriguez, the powerful visual musical ballet *El Baquiné de los Angelitos Negros* (1971) featured music composed by New York Puerto Rican composer Willie Colon with Cuban singer Celia Cruz's voice reciting portions of the text. The Puerto Rican children's wake tradition of Baquiné has been explored through poetry by the aforementioned Puerto Rican poet Luis Palés Matos. Church murals featuring "little black angels" have been noted in Puerto Rico and Spain. Nineteenth- and twentieth-century paintings featuring children's wakes have been depicted by Francisco Oller (Puerto Rico), Arturo Gordon (Chile), and Jose Maria Lopez Mezquita (Spain).

Was the symbolic sonic embrace provided by "Ave Maria!" intended to resolve the *angelito negro's* Du Boisian problem?[71] Schubert's exclamatory work, composed in 1826 as the third song from his *Lady of the Lake* cycle, was based on the poem by Sir Walter Scott. The text, based on the Angel Gabriel's salutation and standardized after 1050,[72] is connected to mystical meanings, conceived as an *antiphon*—sung before and after prayers or scriptures, and has been set to music by numerous composers over the centuries.[73] An Oyá-troubled listening, however, different to M. De La Torre's visualized discussion of La Virgen de la Caridad/Ochún,[74] leads me to wonder whether the European-adopted Maria wrap-around has truly helped the *angelito negro*. Listening subversively with Oyá-rattled ears, how has the violence against the *angelito negro* been addressed? Or has the *angelito* been captured and tonally embraced by another Divine mother, not representing Juana, his own? Is this wrapping instead a warping set against his true journey? Had the text been accountable, what type of song would have sufficed to wrap the *angelito negro* within the comforting arms of his ancestors? How might Oyá have comforted the *angelito negro*?

While neither *Angelitos Negros* (1948) and (1969) contain a child's funeral, a child's wake was depicted in the popular Chilean-Argentinean project *Largo Viaje* (1967), containing an entirely different song performed by Chilean folklorist Violeta Parra. I propose that the genealogies of "*Angelitos Negros*" as cultural products have experienced a profound connection to historical hemispheric practices involving the child's wake, often called *velorio de angelito*, which has been studied by ethnomusicologists and folklorists.

Conclusion: (Un)shrouding the Violent Soundtrack of Angelitos Negros

Scholarly works discussing the two Mexican commercial films, *Angelitos Negros* (1948) and (1969), subsequent telenovelas, and theatrical versions, have primarily engaged with messaging involving *mesitzaje*, the use of blackface, and fugitivity regarding Black heritage. Chicana studies scholar Theresa Delgadillo has discussed the lives and work of three women who have recorded the song: Toña La Negra, Eartha Kitt, and Roberta Flack.[75] In this chapter, I have drawn from ethnomusicology and folklore to begin to describe how certain energies, roles, and abilities of Oyá are synergistic with sound studies and film studies. My own Latine audiovisual engagement considers Oyá alongside a genealogical project compelled to address Black grief, loss, and death, heard through genealogies of surround-sounded violence, and shrouded by the success of a hit song about forgetting. Standing by Oyá's fanned-out skirts and looking inward, my Caribbean sense of audio-engagement with "*Angelitos Negros*" tells me that the topic must be rattled and shaken to more clearly hear the *sonidos escondidos*.

18

"To Heal Every Little Wound": Reconnecting, Reclaiming, and Revitalizing Cultural Spiritual Traditions Among Indigenous Peoples of Mexico in the United States

Ramona Beltrán, Miriam Valdovinos, Olivia Hunte, My Ngoc To, and Tina Hulama

"Mexicans reconnecting to their Indigenous identities is not a trend, it's a prophecy." This statement comes from a widely circulated social media meme. It is part of a long-standing social and educational movement that began in the United States with the Chicano Movement. This movement has evolved to understand that Indigeneity is deeply connected to land, kinship, and Tribal sovereignty. It reflects a growing awareness of the traumas that led to genocide, enslavement, displacement, and detribalization of many Indigenous peoples of Mexico. Understanding the colonial past can facilitate engagement in repairing historical ruptures while restoring ancestral knowledge and community connections built on Indigenous ways of being and knowing.

In this chapter, we highlight how some US-based Indigenous peoples of Mexico are reconnecting with, reclaiming, and revitalizing their traditional cultural and spiritual practices as a form of resistance to colonial violence and healing deep wounds. We begin by highlighting the Doctrine of Discovery (DOD) as the first source of colonial violence which ensured Spanish dominion over what is now called Mexico and Latin America (Abya Yala).[1] After describing how Spanish invasion led to historically traumatic events through systematic destruction, exploitation, and theft of Indigenous land, labor, cultural, and spiritual sovereignty that persists today, we share findings from the Our Stories, Our Medicine Archive (OSOMA) project to illustrate how some community members are healing from these colonial legacies.

Doctrine of Discovery: An Origin of Colonial Violence

The early merging of Christianity with imperialism coalesced into a "divine entitlement to invade, reclaim, or occupy land inhabited by infidels [Muslims] and other non-Christians."[2] The premise: Christians could claim ownership of any land occupied by non-Christians, as it was considered *terra nullius* (land belonging to no one).[3] Land appropriation via *terra nullius*, tracing back to Roman law, and the idea of "discovery" took root in the early fifteenth century when a series of papal bulls were issued.[4] These Bulls became part of the basis for the DOD.[5]

Notably, in 1452, Pope Nicholas V issued *Dum Diversas*, giving Portugal's King Alfonso V permission "to invade, search out, capture, and subjugate the Saracenes, and any other unbeliever and enemies of Christ ... and to reduce [them] into perpetual servitude."[6] In 1493, Pope Alexander V issues a second influential papal bull, *Inter Caetera*, declaring that any land not inhabited by Christians was free to be "discovered," claimed, and used by Christian rulers.[7] This solidified Spain's exclusive rights and subsequent conquest of the "New World," Indigenous lands Christopher Columbus claimed to have "discovered" in 1492.[8]

Greenberg describes the DOD as a doctrine of domination, as it legitimized the subjugation and exploitation of Indigenous peoples and their lands.[9] Domination extended to the cultural and spiritual realms, establishing European Christianity as superior to all Indigenous and non-Christian belief systems, resulting in forced conversion to Christianity and violent suppression of Indigenous cultural traditions, practices, languages, and beliefs.[10] This legacy contributes to social and psychological challenges in Indigenous communities, including historical and intergenerational trauma, loss of cultural and community identity, systemic inequality, and persistent discrimination.[11] The DOD's relationship with securing exclusive rights of Spain to Abya Yala warrants its consideration as a root cause for the persistent conditions and impacts on Indigenous peoples today. Despite its repudiation by modern institutions, including the Vatican,[12] the DOD's legacy continues to influence contemporary issues faced by Indigenous communities.

Spanish Invasion and Colonial Occupation: Foundations of Susto Profundo

Indigenous and Chicane scholars describe how cultural disruptions from colonization and ongoing exposure to systematic inequity cause "*susto profundo*"[13] or profound collective trauma requiring individual and collective healing strategies.[14] *Susto profundo* aligns with the concept of historical trauma, a collective trauma experienced and passed down through generations due to large-scale destructive events targeting a community. In American Indian communities, massacres, boarding schools, and forced relocation are considered historically traumatic events[15] that are connected to poor health, mental health, and social outcomes.[16]

Emerging research with Mexican American,[17] and Mexican American Indian communities, explores colonial impacts to health and social outcomes.[18] For Mexican origin communities, the Spanish invasion in 1519 and subsequent traumatic events like foreign diseases and land dispossession significantly reduced the population[19] and established a Spanish settler-colonial state through large ranches or plantations using forced Indigenous labor.[20]

The Spanish "*sistema de castas*," a racialized caste system, implemented a complex hierarchical categorization with at least twenty-two categories based on race, blood quantum, and phenotype.[21] This caste system stratified power and shaped social norms by amplifying oppression of those identified as or appearing to be Indigenous or Black.[22] Political and economic factors, such as the government's aim to divide the colonial population and create a free wage-labor force for urban economies, haciendas, and mining complexes, also reinforced this system.[23] The Spanish caste system institutionalized Indigenous erasure and de-tribalization, persisting with the Mexican State's establishment.[24] In the mid-nineteenth and early twentieth centuries, mestizaje arose as a prominent ideological narrative of the Mexican state, forwarding the idea that Mexico's population was "mestizo," a mix of European and Indigenous ancestry.[25] Recent scholars critique mestizaje as an agenda of Indigenous erasure.[26]

Colonial oppression persists through international policies, such as North American Free Trade Agreement,[27] driving displacement and northern migration, racism and xenophobia in the United States,[28] militarization at the US–Mexico border, mass deportations, family separation,[29] and gender-based violence in both Mexico and the United States.[30] This series of events reflects how initial colonization has reverberated in iterations that sustain *susto profundo*.

"If trauma can be inherited from one generation to the next, then so can love, resilience, and wisdom"—#TLSNunavut

Despite multiple historically traumatic events, Indigenous peoples of Mexico have retained their traditional beliefs, languages, and cultural systems.[31] While colonization and ongoing oppression impact health, mental health, and social well-being in Indigenous communities, research has identified protective mechanisms that may buffer the intergenerational transmission of trauma.[32] Cultural resilience factors include enculturation,[33] engaging in spiritual and cultural traditions,[34] and feelings of connection to family, community, and the natural environment.[35]

Subsequently, we describe a community-based digital archive project that centers narratives of health and healing as evidence of the survivance, resilience, and critical hope embedded in Indigenous peoples with ancestral ties to Mexico. Specifically, we highlight how community members describe reconnecting to their Indigenous identities through grappling with the colonial past; reclaiming connections to land, language, culture, and ceremonial traditions; and revitalizing these traditions while ensuring collective preservation for future generations.

Method

The Our Stories, Our Medicine Archive is an oral history and cultural artifact documentation project focused on urban Native American and Indigenous Latine communities. The project documents, amplifies, and makes accessible remedies, cultural practices, and innovative strategies for health and healing from these communities. Fifty-one adults (18+) completed oral history interviews over three phases of the project of which the final phase focused on cultural knowledge keepers, teachers, elders, and practitioners (see demographic table (Table 18.1) for sample characteristics). In this analysis, we focus on oral histories from ten community members who identify as Indigenous Latine with ancestral or current tribal connections to Mexico.

Data Analysis

Data analysis began with immersion in oral history interview transcripts. The research team observed numerous descriptions of reconnecting, reclaiming, and revitalizing cultural and spiritual practices. After creating a first-level codebook to organize the narratives according to these three themes, additional review of transcripts coded for nuanced experiences (i.e., recognition of colonial history, a turn toward spiritual cultural

TABLE 18.1 Participant Demographic Characteristics (*N*= 51)

Age (years)	Frequency (Mean)	%
23–82	47 (48.1)	92
No response	4	8
Intersectional race/ethnicity and Indigenous or tribal identities (participants identified as Chicano/a, Indigenous/Indigena, Maya, Mexican, Native, Peruvian, Puerto Rican, and Xicana. Descriptions of Tribal heritage included Andina, Aztec, Comanche, Dine/Navajo, Genizaro Apache, Indeh, Mexica, Sl` uu Savi, Otomi, Poqomam, P'urCpecha, Taino, Tihua, Tehua, Ute, and Yaqui)		
Native American or Indigenous	24	47
Indigenous and Latine	18	35
Latine	5	10
No response	4	8
Gender		
Cis-gender women	27	53
Gender non-conforming/non-binary	7	14
Cis-gender men	6	12
Categories did not reflect their gender identity	5	10
Transgender men	1	2
Prefer not to disclose	1	2
No response	4	8

traditions, preservation of knowledge for future generations). We have edited quotes for grammar and clarity and used pseudonyms to protect confidentiality.

Reconnecting: Acknowledging the Wound and (Re)learning Traditions

Community members discussed acknowledging the traumatic inheritance from the colonial past as a key first step on the healing journey. Several emphasized the need to name colonial violence as an original source of *susto profundo*. For instance, Malinalli, educator and activist, explained,

> forms of genocide and erasure are exactly the formulations that the different nation states want...bringing in that question of mestizo and mestizaje and showing that history, that those were the ideologies imposed in Mexico for us to forget who we are and to literally de-Indigenize us.

Atekpatzin, an elder and curandero, described how long-term ramifications of colonization and white supremacy lead people to "feel like they don't belong in the world." Addressing this loss of belonging involves providing support to one another and understanding the complexity of colonization on all Indigenous peoples. Malinalli echoed this as part of her "role" and "intervention" in the community. She began by asking, "How do we [reconnect] in a way where we're not erasing or not acknowledging Native peoples?" She responded, "if we're doing this work of remembering our ancestral lineages, of doing the work to claim Indigeneity," then it's about "making space for that and not shaming and not using that guilt or even allowing for those ideas of appropriation to enter." She elaborated on the richness embedded in our own traditions:

> Yes, we need to be accountable. Of course, we're not going to appropriate other people's practices or traditions. That's not what we're here to do. In your family and in our communities, there is so much knowledge and medicine. It's just that it's been untapped or it's been undercover to survive.

Participants also described reconnecting as a spiritual turn. For several, experiences of Catholicism felt imposing and disjointed. While acknowledging the church's historical role in colonization and ongoing injustices, community members described their turn toward Indigenous traditions as a process of relearning how to pray and be in community. For example, Itzel, educator and mother, reflected, "The temazcal (sweat lodge), it's medicine in the sense that you're praying which I have had to relearn how to do because praying earlier in my life was connected to being involved in the Catholic Church." She recalled church in childhood as a "mechanical and depersonalized" obligation with "zero connection." Learning about the Catholic church's role in "colonization and genocide and destruction" of Indigenous peoples, simultaneous with reports of priests abusing children led her and her family to leave the church entirely. Itzel's connection with Chicana students at college who were practicing Mexica traditions, including temazcal, encouraged her to embrace reconnecting through relearning: "you're going in there, you're praying, which I think is really beautiful, especially if you're re-learning it, and learning in community … that's beautiful."

Simultaneous learning and relearning can be facilitated through engaging in traditional ceremonies. Several community members described ceremonies as crucial to healing. Atekpatzin defined ceremony as "a space for us to go and to reconnect and to belong to a community, to reconnect with our ancestral past, and to find the healing that we need for ourselves." Ceremony can uniquely facilitate individual and collective healing concurrently. Atekpatzin expanded with his experiences facilitating ceremony with young people experiencing suicidality: "That sense of not belonging can be addressed." He elaborated that ceremony does what therapy, parenting, or discourse cannot do, saying, "There's nothing I can say to them. Their parents can say. There's nothing anyone in the world can say, certainly not a therapist that's going to switch up and change how they feel relative to belonging in this world." Rather, the collective process of bringing young people who are suffering into ceremony is the treatment.

> When we take them into a ceremony, what are we doing? We're bringing them into community. It is the process of the entire community there focused on the well-being of that individual that heals them. It only takes one ceremony. This isn't covered by insurance, but we can take them into a ceremony. When they walk out of that ceremony, they're not suicidal anymore.

Atekpatzin's description of ceremony's healing capacity is built into its way of addressing root causes or larger collective wounds,

> because Western approaches focus on the individual … It is symptomatic of something larger, [which is a] sick community. We take the community in there and we treat the whole community, and we focus on this individual. When we're done, that individual now feels a part of that community, because the ceremony does that. It is the community that does the healing.

Reclaiming: Learning and Growing into Traditions

Following reconnection through recognition of the historical past, community members described reclaiming their Indigenous cultural and spiritual traditions by learning the practices as beginners. Malinalli, for instance, recalled meeting an elder in Mexico who helped her reclaim a ceremony that helped heal family relationships which had suffered due to historical and intergenerational trauma. Upon seeing the representation of Tlazoteotl (a Nahua divine entity) painted on an elder's adobe in Mexico, Malinalli learned about healing the umbilical connection to the earth and her family and "started to understand that she [Tlazoteotl] was the one who helped us transform and come back to our rebirth... [back then] those ideas seemed very conceptual to me." She described how experiential elements helped her "connect with the plantitas (plants) and the rocks and the fire" that helped her heal some of her "inner child traumas and connect to her mother and her father again." She elaborated, "then I understood. Tlazolteotl is here to help guide this process of connecting to our mother once again, connecting to that umbilical cord of the earth, and do the work of removing any narratives, thoughts, pathways, habits that are within our cells."

Reclaiming also unfolded in daily practices such as learning about plant medicines as tools to facilitate mindfulness embedded in prayer. Lucia, a social worker and artist, described herself as a beginner: "I'm rediscovering some medicines for myself, like burning sage and palo santo. I didn't realize that was part of my culture." As she learned, she made connections, saying, "Another way we connect to our mind, body, and spirit is through mindfulness. It's not something the church teaches when they talk about mindfulness, but it's basically what they do when you're praying." She described the process of smudging with plant medicines as mindfulness and prayer tools inherited from Indigenous ancestors, stating, "I like to burn sage, palo santo, lavender, and other things to help me reconnect ... even though it's not in the Catholic Church ... Those are my ceremonies and things I do for myself to reconnect."

Elder Atekpatzin elaborated on the mindfulness component embodied in smudge, emphasizing cultural traditions as simple and effective rather than mystical and romantic or part of an exotic Indigenous past:

> Many Indigenous communities in North America and Turtle Island ... have used smoke as a way of energetically cleansing someone or a space ... Sometimes we burn sage, sometimes we burn lavender, sometimes we burn copal, palo santo ... Forget about the mystical magical stuff. At the very least, the smell of what we're burning takes us to the place that we need to be to center ourselves—it gives us sort of a meditation, if you will. It helps us to relax and to be present. I call these artifacts. When we smudge ourselves; when we put the smoke over ourselves and cleanse ourselves energetically with the smoke. What it does is it helps to root us in some artifact that reconnects us with the sense of who we are. If there's nothing else that it does, it does that. That's enough.

An important element of learning was the individual practice of using medicines for mindfulness, prayer, and healing, and sharing those medicines with the community. Illustrating the relational processes embodied in Indigenous traditions, Quetzalli, educator and activist, described a teaching from an elder about the need to give and share, "especially around medicine." She recalled when she first started her journey, she used to "just hold onto medicine" but the elder said, 'You have to give that medicine out. You have to use that medicine; you can't hold onto it because then you're making the space for abundance and flow.' Quetzalli describes abundance as her ability to "have medicine or resources in order to pass them on."

Participants also reclaimed cultural and spiritual traditions involving movement as prayer. Yoloteotl, cultural leader and activist, recalled when she first began to include Danza Mexica (Aztec dance) in her spiritual practices. She described being welcomed into the tradition at nineteen by the lead dancer and subsequently learning that danza is a form of prayer centered on connections to the natural world. She solidified her commitment to the tradition after hearing the response, "We pray to the elements--what we have here on the earth, the animals, the fire, the water, the things that are sustaining us" after she asked an elder about prayer.

Revitalizing: Intergenerational Transmission of Cultural Traditions

Experiences related to reconnection and reclamation informed how community members revitalized cultural and spiritual practices connected to their ancestors, focusing on sharing these practices in community and intergenerationally. Olga, non-profit leader and community advocate, described a naming ceremony for her son, led by Otomi elders, who helped reestablish this ceremonial practice in the United States.

> It was the first time that we'd ever had an Otomi naming ceremony this side of the border. It was powerful. We had community come, many who maybe didn't identify quite in the same way as being Indigenous but just seeing them all show up with food and wanting to witness it and be part of it was beautiful. In that ceremony, he received his Otomi name.

Olga recalled how she was also given "the responsibility and the honor of carrying the sahumador," a traditional vessel used to burn incense, resins, and plant medicines for smudging in ceremony. The community witnessed her being recognized by her elders as a "guardiana del fuego," a keeper of the sacred fire and sacred teachings of her community. She described the ceremony, which took place in the mountains overlooking a lake at night, as giving the community pathways to learn about the meaning and importance of names and naming ceremonies within the community.

> We buried the placenta by a tree as is part of our tradition so that the tree grows strong, and our children can grow strong with it. His names come from the sky. It's that connection to the heavens and the stars. We held him, we honored him, we saluted the four directions, and we noticed there was a star moving in the four directions along with us.

She emphasized that shared experience as connected to her traditional belief systems:

> We also believe that the stars are the eyes of our ancestors, and in that moment, we felt that connection, that they were looking down upon us. We prayed that they were pleased we were continuing to preserve these traditions through our children and passing that on—that our names have meaning and power.

Subsequently, the young person whose naming ceremony is mentioned above, Nezahualcoyotl, artist and activist, described another naming ceremony that he initiated when he was transitioning to adulthood. This ceremony was reintroduced into the community and exemplifies the power of intergenerational transmission of knowledge and practices.

> People were very excited to have something like that because it, at least here [in the city], hadn't been done that we know of. Letting people see and just imagining being offered a chance to choose how they define themselves and to be accepted wholeheartedly in that choice was really beautiful.

While some people may have coming-of-age parties such as *quinceañeras*, which are often rooted in Catholic traditions, Nezahualcoyotl recalled how he and his family looked to historical Indigenous practices to recreate a ceremony that acknowledged both his gender identity and name. He described how many pre-colonial Indigenous communities let identities unfold according to the child's expressions and understanding of self.

> when a child was born, sometimes they weren't assigned a gender until they were able to express what they were to their parents. Being named, not based on something they want, but based on who you are. And because I was transitioning, I wanted everyone to know what my new identity was, what my new name was, and to be accepted in the Indigenous community here.

He detailed the ceremony as being built around five components that culminated in a community celebration of his chosen identity and name:

> There were four altars in a circle, and each one was meant to define a different place in your life and also where you wanted to go. It started with the children's area, which is what I was technically leaving, and then I would walk around to each [altar] and really assess where I wanted to be. There was an altar for the space of women, for the space of men, and for the space of queer people. I chose the queer space as being my community and even then, it's not super set because technically for me, I go everywhere. But it was choosing and then everyone celebrated and then it was also part of me becoming an adult. So, there was a cord tied to me and to my mom and then it was cut in the middle to show that I was now becoming my own person.

Turning to elders for support with remembering and preserving traditions is critical to the revitalization of intergenerational knowledge. Elder and cultural leader, Alonzo, reflected on turning to Indigenous knowledge during turbulent times. "I think ceremonies have become very busy for a lot of people, especially if we're losing our older generation. A lot of it is just the cycle of life, but we're also losing that part of our history." He highlighted that documenting elder knowledge is especially crucial during periods of widespread threats to health such as the COVID-19 pandemic, "the elders were the ones that are taking the lead in trying to calm the stress and the anxiety of our children because they don't understand. That's our duty and our responsibilities to especially our mothers and women."

Considering the importance of knowledge keepers, Lucia encouraged children to participate in healing through asking "all the questions" and viewed her decolonizing process as deeply connected to her responsibility to share her new knowledge with future generations:

> Any new knowledge I've learned to share it with the next generation so that it helps them. Even if it's things that I've learned in decolonizing my own life. If I'm trying to reconnect with my roots right now, that's part of decolonizing what I've been taught and how to ask curious questions.

She encouraged community to resist colonizing ideas of quiet and obedient children, saying "they tell us 'stop asking so many questions' and it's like 'no, keep asking all the questions!' That's how we learn. That's how we grow and transform and be better for others."

Bonifacio, social worker and father, described teaching his children how to plant and cultivate corn and beans in alignment with his Indigenous teachings. Viewing cultivation as a relationship that needs care and attention through the heart, soul, and mind, he said, "I want my kids … to [plant] corn and beans. Hopefully they're not just going to plant and just let it grow." He described the teaching from his grandfather, "Every time you do something, you move something, you think about something, there's always a purpose to it. You have to be intentional about what you're going to do. Put your heart and soul to it, your mind to it."

Through many of the oral histories, this intergenerational love and care was also illustrated through the care for self in individual practices simultaneous to critical hope and imagination for healing toward a flourishing community. Tearing up, Lucia gently offered,

> I hope others learn that healing is so beautiful and so hard, but it's worth it. To heal every little wound … because it's going to help us flourish. When we heal, we heal not just our own things. We heal the future as well and we heal the past. So, for those who are the future generations, I want them to know to dig deep, even if they feel disconnected from our culture, to dig, to find out, to stay curious … And even if

they can't, that they know that someone out there is looking out for them and trying to give them as many blessings as they can.

Discussion

In the wake of *susto profundo* inflicted by the legacy of the DOD and the subsequent violent colonization imposed by the Catholic Church and later the nation state, US-based Indigenous peoples of Mexico have safeguarded, retained, reclaimed, and revitalized many of their traditional, cultural, spiritual, and healing practices. The stories shared here illustrate how people continue to reconnect by naming the original colonial violence, addressing the disruptions to their collective sense of self and belonging, and confronting the persistent trauma often reinforced by religious principles. They describe a turn toward Indigenous spiritual and cultural traditions through learning ceremonial practices as beginners, committing to roles that create pathways toward individual and collective healing. For instance, community members described reclaiming in small intimate practices with plant medicines that they then share with their communities in a circular and non-transactional manner. They also discussed revitalization through bringing Indigenous traditions "across the border" or making something new and whole out of what was previously known only in pieces. The oral histories represented here also arc toward the promise of future generations. In a multidimensional flow of care, community members look at evidence left from ancestors, record and preserve the knowledge of their elders, and offer these teachings, and most importantly, critical hope for a beautiful future for their children and generations to come. This chapter provides a glimpse into some of the ways community members are remembering, reconnecting, and recreating pathways for reviving traditional healing and spiritual practices, cultural histories, and ancestral ways of knowing as resistance to the historically situated and traumatic inheritance of the Doctrine of Discovery. Through the intergenerational transmission of love and wisdom, community members remain steadfast in their commitment to nurturing and empowering future generations, ensuring the preservation and flourishing of their cultural heritage and ancestral knowledge.

19

Crossing Borders

Noemi Vega Quiñones

Yanaguana flows southeast from the northern springs of what is now known as the city of San Antonio to the San Antonio Bay and the Gulf of Mexico. The Payaya band of the Tāp Pīlam Coahuiltec Nation know this river as Yanaguana, the "Land of Spirt Waters."[1] Archeological records show that Coahuiltecans have cultivated the lands of South Texas and Northeast Mexico for thousands of years.[2] The first European colonial settlers arrived in the sixteenth and seventeenth centuries from Spain. Colonial settlers employ what historian Patrick Wolfe describes as a "logic of elimination," a process of cultural and physical erasures via violence, forced missionization, forced migration, imported diseases, and the loss of language.[3] Franciscan missionary, Fray Damian Massanet, and the first governor of Texas, Domingo Teran de Los Rios, changed Yanaguana's name to San Antonio de Padua on June 13, 1691, the day of the holy feast of San Antonio.

The river's name, however, is fluid like water, and indigenous communities continue to remember Spirit Waters as Yanaguana. In an act of remembrance, and perhaps resistance to erasure, David Zamora Casas created a public art painting titled *Cuentos Grotto* with the poem, "The Voices of Yanaguana." The painting is displayed in downtown San Antonio by the Hemisfair Tower. Zamora Casas likens Yanaguana's history of occupation to an "epic...based on Memory, History, and Spirit...Enchanted by Legend, Religion, Violence, Blood, Creed, Injustice, and Splendor."[4] Latine migrants come from lands whose histories, traditional ways of knowing, and names have been changed, like Yanaguana. But like "*ríos de agua viva*" and "Spirit Waters," Latine migrants draw from religious and ancestral traditions to create a network of support for survival before, during, and after crossing borders.[5] This chapter explores the fluidity of borders legislatively clothed in immutable immigration laws, the fluidity of Latine migrant's religious and gendered experiences, and the fluidity of migrant futures as Latines in the United States seek to remember and resist colonial erasures.

The Fluidity of Borders: A Brief History of Forced Border Crossings

Latines have a range of migratory experiences crossing the border and making our lives in the United States. Indigenous Latines trouble US immigration laws. Coahuiltecans, for example, as well as several indigenous tribes once sovereign or under Mexican governance, were categorized as either "Mexican" or "American," depending on which side of the geopolitical border they were on, after the Mexican American War (1846–48).[6] Families were separated then, as they continue to be separated now. While the line drawn between the United States and Mexico after the war appeared fixed and firm, never to change, communities separated by the new bordered reality continued to communicate, influence, love, celebrate, and grieve with one another.

Historian Natalia Molina describes the efforts to racialize Mexicans after the war via the racial scripts of indigeneity and whiteness. It was not enough to be on the "right side" of the border. Newly minted Americans of Latine, indigenous, and/or African descent had to be both "white" in terms of shade and "white" in terms of culture.[7] Seventeen years after the war with Mexico, the US Civil War began in 1861 and ended in 1865. Ideologies such as Manifest Destiny (a phrase coined by John Louis O'Sullivan as white American's providential rights to indigenous lands) and the Doctrine of Discovery (a set of fifteenth-century papal bulls that granted religious and political justifications for the enslavement of indigenous peoples and the transnational slave trade) were employed in the mid to late twentieth century to justify the legislative and forced theft of indigenous lands after these wars.[8] Historian Sucheng Chan categorizes the time after the US Civil War as a period of Reconstruction and a significant, yet brief, advancement of human rights with the establishment of the Thirteenth, Fourteenth, and Fifteenth Amendments in the US Constitution.[9] Laura Gomez notes that amidst US expansion, people of Mexican descent held a precarious position within white society: at times they were legally white (and afforded the privileges of being categorized as white) but at times (more often than not) they were treated as socially non-white, other, and foreign.[10] The history of US expansion indicates that Latines of indigenous ancestry experienced the border crossing *them* as a consequence of war, a violent eruption in traditional ways of knowing and connecting with their communities across geopolitically defined regions.

Several Latines at this time also willfully chose to migrate to the expanding United States due to an increase in demand for agricultural and low wage labor. The racial script of the "deportable Mexican" emerged in the 1920s after an influx of migrant laborers refused to return to their countries of origin.[11] Molina describes the period between 1924 and 1965 as the creation of the US "immigration regime" that concretized racial migrant categories such as "illegal Mexican"[12] The categorization of "legal citizen" was in flux and largely dependent on a judge's decision regarding the definition of "white."[13] Public circulations in the early 1900s such as the Los Angeles area newspaper *La Opinion* encouraged Mexican Americans to return to Mexico, further racializing "legalized" Mexican Americans as foreign.[14] The public rhetoric in the early twenty-first century indicates that the definitions of "whiteness," "citizenship," and "migrant" were changing like fluid and required a concerted effort on behalf of legislatures, public opinion, and racial optics to deem Latines, particularly darker Latines, as permanent migrants.

Latines continue to confound, trouble, and challenge the immutability of migrant and racial categories. The most recent resistors to the easy categorization of "Latine migrants" are Haitian refugees. Since 2019, Haitians have sought asylum in the United States. on the grounds of political turmoil and economic devastations due to the compounding impact of climate change. The US Citizenship and Immigration Services defines a refugee as someone who has experienced persecution or a credible "fear they will be persecuted on account of race, religion, nationality, and/or membership in a particular social group or political opinion."[15] In 2022, I walked along the Reynosa, Mexico, and McAllen, Texas, border with a Latina minister named Alma Ruth. Alma showed our group how the conditions of Haitian migrants compared with the conditions of other European migrants seeking asylum. Trump's Remain in Mexico policy devastated migrants as they were forced to wait in Reynosa and other border towns in makeshift tent cities—cooking, playing, learning, and waiting for their immigration court date amidst inhumane conditions. The racial contrast between asylum seekers waiting along the Rio Grande border on the Mexican side and those who were granted the opportunity to wait for their court date on the US side was stark and noticeable.

Yanaguana crosses geographical landscapes with native flora and fauna for over 240 miles and pours into the waters of the Gulf which eventually touch the lands of the United States, Mexico, and Cuba.[16] Yanaguana remains connected to these lands even as it migrates. Gloria Anzaldúa describes the violence of border creation in general and the US-Mexico border in particular *como una herida abierta*, an open wound that refuses to be erased. Connection is one way to heal this open wound. Several Latine ministers across faith backgrounds live, work, and serve along both sides of the US–Mexico border insisting on humane and dignified treatment of all migrants, including Sister Norma Pimentel who oversees the Catholic Charities of the Rio Grande Valley. I understand their work as a way of connecting the open wound of the border.

Crossing Borders: The Fluidity of Latine Migrant Bodies and Religious Expressions

I spent one hot day in the summer of 2012 walking along a small patch of Arizona desert dropping off water at various locations with several college students volunteering for Border Angels. We learned about the daily deaths that occurred and remained unidentified along the border. The Medical Examiner's office counted 3,634 migrant deaths between 2020 and 2022 in Pima County alone.[17] At least five migrants died in the desert each day in that period. Immigration humanitarian workers remember the dead by creating burial sites with white crosses where a person has been found or where they can be laid to rest. Placing unnamed crosses along the border is a reminder that crossing a border is a matter of life and death for many, though certainly not all, Latine migrants. To cross implies the potential to "be crossed," to die, but that risk is calculated as better than the risk of staying in one's home country. I focus this section on the experiences of Latine migrants who identify as women and the unique persecutions that they face, at times exacerbated by religious institutions.

There are over 280 million people categorized as migrants around the world.[18] Christians make up close to half of the world's migrants (47 percent), followed by Muslims (29 percent), the religiously unaffiliated (13 percent), Hindu (5 percent), Buddhist (4 percent), other religions (2 percent), and Jews (1 percent).[19] Mexico is the most common country of origin for Christian migrants and the ninth most country of origin for the religiously unaffiliated. Venezuela follows Mexico as the tenth most common country of origin for the religiously unaffiliated representing approximately 740,000 individuals. In the United States, Latines in general predominantly affiliate as Catholic (43 percent) according to one Pew survey.[20] Latine migrants in the survey identify as Catholic (52 percent), unaffiliated (21 percent), evangelical (19 percent), Protestant (4 percent), other faiths (4 percent), or did not answer (1 percent). In sum, 75 percent of the 168 Latine migrants interviewed identify with one of the main Christian traditions (Catholic, evangelical, and Protestant). The survey also found that among all Latines living in the United States regardless of immigration status, over half say that their faith is either very important to them or somewhat important to them. The same survey shows that one in four Latines in the United States change their religion. Religion is important to many Latine migrants but as the data indicate, religious affiliations shift and intermix over time, indicating an increasingly diverse array of religious expressions.

Latina/e migrants experience higher rates of physical and sexual violence than male migrants. Rosa Linda Fregoso notes that in 2002, close to three hundred women (282) were murdered along the border.[21] Women were deemed "immoral" for working in the maquiladoras and blamed for the rise in feminicide since they were breaking with traditional gender roles.[22] Shirlene Soto emphasized three prominent gender tropes in the 1980s and 1990s: La Malinche, La Virgen de Guadalupe, and La Llorona.[23] These "cultural models" pushed Latine women into strict modes of being and maintained grave social consequences for failing to embody the virginal purity of La Virgen. Rather than conforming to concretized gender expectations, Latina migrants continue to move across borders in pursuit of a life without extreme violence.

Latina/es are at risk for feminicide even after crossing the border. The Sovereign Bodies Institute (SBI) reported in 2023 that there were 259 cases of Missing and Murdered Indigenous People in forty-two of California's fifty-eight counties and that

"Two-Spirit and IndigiQueer relatives are at a disproportionate risk of violence."[24] Six of these cases represent indigenous migrant women from the Zapotec (3), Aztec (1), and Tarahumara (1) tribes. SBI interviews revealed high rates of spiritual abuse among indigenous and IndigiQueer relatives.[25] Pew analysts Stephanie Kramer and Yunping Tong note that "religion and migration are often closely connected," and that "many migrants move to escape religious persecution or to live among people who hold similar religious beliefs."[26] The case of Geovanni Hernandez-Montiel highlights the interplay between religious persecution, migration, and sexual identity. The Ninth Circuit Court of Appeals in 2000 ruled that Hernandez-Montiel could be granted asylum because as a transgender woman she belonged to a "particular social group" that experienced religious persecution in Mexico.[27] Sexual, physical, and psychological violence is prevalent in migrant (for-profit and non-profit) detention centers.[28] Artists partner with immigration rights organizations to create spaces of healing and expression for migrant children impacted by the Trump administration's family separation policies and by living in carceral facilities.[29] Latine migrants find creative ways to heal from the violence they have experienced in migration.

One way that Latines heal is through religious expression. Placing crosses along the desert as an act of remembrance is one example. Voces Sin Eco is another example. Families of missing and murdered migrant women paint crosses in public spaces as a way of claiming citizenship and belonging for their loved ones. Fregoso writes that the "use of religiosity—crosses, luminaries, vigils— is a form of indirection...for healing the trauma of the unrepresentable: death as the ultimate other."[30] Still a third example are the long-established Latine migrant communities in the United States that provide a sense of connectedness, resourcing, and spiritual support. Jonathan Calvillo notes that in Santa Ana, "religion often functioned as a primary platform of ethnic collectivism. It could provide the ethos that enabled exchange and care within the ethnic community in a broad, public sense."[31] In *Sanctuary Everywhere,* Barbara Andrea Sostaita references the US Church Sanctuary Movement that provided protected housing for undocumented migrants seeking asylum. Refusing concretized notions of sanctuary, Sostaita writes that "sanctuary travels with migrants and other fugitives as they flee captivity and confinement; it emerges alongside the smuggled, who pose a perpetual threat to the settled."[32] Latine migrants continue to practice their faith traditions, and integrate new ones, even in the process of adapting to a new place.[33] Latine migrants defy gendered, physical, religious, and mental borders that seek to repress our creative and collective healing.

Yanaguana's Song and the Fluidity of Migrant Futures

Yanaguana cries, "like the Llorona, the Weeping Woman who wanders around riverbeds in search of her lost child ... *Canta no llores Llorona, aquí estamos tus Hijos Mestizos*."

The last lines of Zamora Casa's *Cuentos Grotto* point to a future where crying will cease, and children will be found. Immigration lawyers, humanitarian organizations, and long-time activists were prepared for whatever the 2024 election reveals. They are equipped with ideas about how to respond to the threats of mass deportation, to stop the collaboration between local police and Immigration and Customs Enforcement, to uncover the capitalistic interests in maintaining and expanding crimmigration (the criminalization of and profiting from migrating), and to prepare communities for potentially more child separation policies and the reinstatement of the Remain in Mexico decree. Futures are unknown and are like a river, adaptable to changing circumstances. Latine migrants will continue to practice their ancestral wisdom of religious traditions to heal from the traumas of racialization, sexualization, and criminalization. They will draw upon their civic, religious, and social supports to confront fear tactics. Latine migrants will continue to contribute to the formation, connectedness, and remembrance of the histories and the futures of these lands.

20

Nones and Alternative Paths

José Francisco Morales Torres

The most recent Pew Research on Latine religion in the United States[1] was a fulcrum that shifted the study of Latine religion, particularly as it pertains to the growth in the non-religious or religiously unaffiliated and the precipitous drop of the Latine Catholic adherents. In roughly a decade, Latine Catholics went from 67 percent to 43 percent of the Latine demographic. US-born Latines are more likely to be unaffiliated (39 percent) than Catholic (36 percent). About half of Latine youth and young adults (ages eighteen to twenty-nine) self-identify as "religiously unaffiliated." It should be noted, moreover, that the Catholic exodus is not headed to Protestant or *evangélico* lands. The percentage of growth and total numbers of Latine Protestants is less than that of Latine nones during the same period,[2] though some scholars contend with methodological assumptions that misclassify a portion of Latine *evangélicos* as "no religion."[3] The emerging skyline of the nones' and alternate paths' "promise land" is devoid of steeples.

This essay is composed of three general areas. In the first and principal portion, I formulate working definitions for "none" and "alternate path," with exploratory annotations. Then, I articulate the ways in which nones and alternate paths are critical movements, speaking to how they resists modern definitions of religiosity and spirituality, and their political intersections and effects. Lastly, I propose that these alternate paths are not simply critical movements but also creative phenomena.

Defining the Terms: Nones and Alternate Paths

Working definitions for "nones" and "alternate paths" must be established before moving forward since both terms are contested—ambiguous at best and contentious at worst. These (a)religious manifestations, "whose boundaries are blurred," are difficult to define within the categorization of the classical study of religions. Consequently, they "put our conceptual schemes to the test."[4] Often understood and utilized nebulously, clear (or at least clearer) terms are needed.

"Nones" generally denote those who claim no confessional-*institutional* affiliation. The emphasis on the institution and its teaching, moral, and legislative authority is key because the category is broad, theologically or philosophically. Some are avowed atheism and deny any transcendence beyond the evolutionary biological. Others affirm some "higher power," "life force," or "spirit" that emanates within the biological lifeworld.[5] Some others still affirm a personal god/God (or gods) but refuse to relinquish the knowledge of or access to divinity to clerical apparati or to the "sacramental" dispensations of institutional religion.[6] Hence, "nones" range from (alternate) forms of theism to atheism. The theological therefore cannot be the centering device for grasping the contours of the nones.

What is a surer definitional ground is the nones' and alternate paths' anti-institutional orientation toward the transcendent, the spiritual, and the good. This is not simply a rejection to a particular institution, though it can be and often is. It is a rejection of institutions qua institutions with respect to the moral or spiritual life. For example, the American Humanist Association's motto is "Good Without a God." Some count the Humanists among the nones since there is no centralized "magisterium." To be sure, various philosophical accounts are needed to draw clearer, fuller contours around the "nones" moniker. Yet, at bottom, and cutting the metaphysical pluralism of the category, one finds the rejection of institutionalized dispensations of spiritual/transcendental sources and moral edification.

The term "alternate path" is an umbrella term. It even includes the nones or "spiritual-but-not-religious," but it may include other articulations of religious self-identification and other expressions of spiritual thriving not customarily found the "canonical" list of religions. As if it is often used, it signified any religious or spiritual tradition not "normatively" counted among the "world religions." Yet as Tomoko Masuzawa highlights, the "advent of 'world religions'" is a "dominant discourse … [obsessed] with the primitive and the original" in ways that universalizes the world religions while localizing (i.e., reducing to merely the local) indigenous cosmologies.[7] Although the category is useful, the Eurocentric colonial framing must be questioned. Interestingly, Humanism is often placed herein, despite its origins in the European Enlightenment.

Scholars who work with this colonial construction of world religions vis-à-vis the local /tribal "other" might include within the category of "alternate paths," for example, indigenous traditions or African diasporic religions across the Americas, to which portions of the Latine world belong. To be fair, the term "alternate" is apt *in a sense*, if one intends a religious expression of *alter*ity or the sub*altern* that resist universalizing (i.e., "whitewashing") the religious contours of the American continents. After all, reclaiming indigenous or African religious lineage is a way some push against the totalizing religious narratives of Latin America and the Latine United States as essentially Catholic or Christian.[8] As a clandestine act of resistance against the oppressors and their (Christian) religion, diasporic Africans across the Americas maintain spiritual and religious ties by practicing traditional rituals and teaching traditional beliefs.

Indigenous retrievals today in Latin America and in the Latine diasporas, dubbed *indigenismo*, is yet another mode of culturo-religious resistance that recover ritual practices, cosmologies, and even languages as denunciations to religious histories that erase the original inhabitants of the land.[9] Françoise Morin notes that this Eurocentric revisionist history is contested by the "indigenists" who seek to turn on its head this fabricated image with which the " 'colonialist' writers strive to legitimize" *la Conquista* and "to defend the historical dimension of tyranny."[10] In response to this politico-historiographical act of erasure, "Indianity" (*indianidad*) becomes for some the "political expression of the indigenous people to break with this colonial relationship and define and claim their own specificity."[11] Last, it should be noted that the retrieval of indigenity for philosophical critique and construction is not new. There are two key thinkers in the intellectual history of the Americas who appreciatively retrieve, albeit problematically, indigenous traditions and beliefs in their philosophies: José Martí of Cuba (1853–1895) and José Mariátegui (1894–1930).[12]

Nevertheless, a decolonial hermeneutic resists categorizing African diasporic and indigenous traditions in this manner. These religious movements are self-sustaining, architectonic *traditions*, and they qualify to be place alongside the so-called "world religions." An linguistic analogy is Orientalists speaking of European "languages" and West Africa "dialects."[13] Masuzawa warns that the "modern discourse on religion and religions" is, from the start, a product of a "discourse of secularization" and a "discourse of othering" uttered from the backdrop of a supposed secular, "neutral" Europe.[14] Hence, the danger is not only the distortion of religion(s) but also of "secularism" and "secularity." José Casanova concurs and rightly points out that the European pattern of secularization should neither be the norm in scholarly inquiry nor applied universally in interpretive work. Otherwise, one ignores regional and historical particularities.[15] As the matrix from which the Latine nones and alternate paths emerge, secularity cannot be defined singularly (i.e., 'Europeanly') across the globe.

One emerging, alternate path merits some attention here, namely, multiple religious participation/belonging. Multiple religious participation/belonging is a lively and ongoing preoccupation for the comparative study of religion and for comparative theology. The difference between *participation* and *belonging* is one of degree of involvement in a second tradition. The former describes those who participate in only certain acts, rituals, or praxes of the second tradition while maintaining the first tradition as primal, primordial, or centering. The often-problematic appropriation of yoga in the United States comes to mind. Multiple religious *belonging* denotes one's full or formal initiation into the second tradition (e.g., being baptized, taking a vow, or publicly affirming a creed) while maintaining one's commitment to and participation in a first tradition.

Highlighting multiple religious belonging/participation is not due to the ways this phenomenon materializes first in the United States[16] and then is appropriated by Latine peoples. Quite the contrary! There is a long tradition of multiple religious belonging, especially (though not exclusively) among the African Diaspora and Indigenous peoples in Latin America and the Caribbean.[17] Belonging to multiple religions is an usurpingly underground mode of religiocultural resistance against the oppressors and their (Christian) religion. As the progeny of Africans held captives by *peninsulares* and *criollos* across the Americas, some Afro-Latine communities maintain spiritual and religious ties by practicing traditional rituals and teaching traditional beliefs while still attending Christian worship services on Sundays, baptizing their children, and belonging to Christian communities.[18] Notably, Indigenous resistance by way of multiple religious belonging are aesthetic (e.g., use of traditional garb) and linguistic (e.g., learning the native language), though they should not be reduced to these.[19]

Lastly, the story of the *conversos*,[20] at least for some, could be defined as one of multiple religious belonging or participation. The settler project of Iberian colonial regimes in the fifteenth and sixteenth centuries coincided with *la Reconquista*, when the Spanish Catholic crown (re-)claimed the whole of Iberia for the Catholic Church, leading to expulsions or forced conversions of Jews and Muslims. To survive some Jews outwardly converted to Christianity while maintaining Jewish beliefs, practices, and laws (e.g., dietary restrictions). Scholars have noted the rise of Latine Americans, who though, raised Christian, have discovered their hidden Jewish roots.[21] Thus, any discussion on Latine multiple religious belonging/participation that assumes United Statian or North Atlantic origins is faulty from the start. The roots of Latine multiple religious belonging or participation are deep in the subaltern, religious terrain of Latin America and the Caribbean, among the forcedly displaced (Indigenous), forcedly enslaved (African), and forcedly converted (Jewish *conversos*). Latine multiple religious participation/belonging has its own Latine religious genealogy.

Nones and Alternate Paths as Critical Movements

As stated previously, an anti-institutional impetus is central to understanding nones' and alternate paths' critique of religion. Yet, this is not the sum of their critique. Humanist scholar Juhem Navarro-Rivera delineates the process of disaffection as a three-step journey of behavior, belonging, and belief. One first stops attending services or enacting rituals (e.g., praying, going to confession). Then, one no longer claims the identity that the religious institution claims for itself and for its adherents. "Eventually," he concludes, "the belief starts to go away."[22] In discussing secularization, José Casanova offers a similar pattern of criticism, namely, the "cognitive critique of traditional religious worldviews, the moral-practical critique of religious ideologies of legitimation, and the subjective-expressive critique of religious asceticism and alienation."[23] To be sure, the process Navarro-Rivera outlines does not follow this order in every case. Doubt often precedes practice, for example. Yet, the core of the nones' critique involves practices, identity, and belief, *and* the institutional claims to the authorized dispensation, enactment, and pronouncement of these.

In his seminal text on secularization, *Public Religions in the Modern World*, Casanova offers a different triadic structure of the secularist critique of religion, which is apt when discussing the emergence of Latine nones. He posits that the secularization cannot be described solely as the privatization of religion, and much less, the death of the same. This is empirically obvious. Religions have not died (some have grown), and religions have often taken on public roles, be they conservative (e.g., Christian nationalisms in Brazil and among the Latine United States[24]) or on the left (e.g., liberation theologies[25]). A simple historical survey debunks the simplistic privatization theory.

As an alternative to the stand-alone privatization theory, Casanova reformulates secularization as religious decline, as differentiation, and as privatization.[26] These are useful to understand the growth and witness of Latine nones and alternate paths. The pattern of religious diminishment applies to Latine communities in the United States as research shows steep declines in traditional religious engagement, especially with Catholicism.[27] In a dozen years (from 2010 to 2022), the number of Latine Catholics drop by about 25 percent, with 30 percent of the Latine populace identifying as religiously unaffiliated. Among Latine persons between eighteen and twenty-nine years of age, the percentage of nones are much higher, at 49 percent.[28] This surge in religious disaffiliation in Latine communities is not new, as the phenomenon was already polled, discussed, and interpreted in the 2010s.[29] Despite the rise of Latine fundamentalism in the United States (and its radical political spawn, the Latine "alt-right"[30]), data show that the growth among Latine *evangélicos* has been rivaled by the rise of religiously unaffiliated since the same decade.[31] And, Latine nones are countering the proliferation of Latine conservativism (social, political, and economic) with their overwhelmingly progressive politics.[32] Navarro-Rivera notes that "nonreligious Latinos are driving a lot of the progressive attitudes you find in Latino public opinion."[33] The act of leaving is a *critique by way of dissident abdication.*[34]

Secularization as differentiation is a *cultural* project for Latine nones and alternate paths. This areligious cohort advocates to overcome the stigma within Latine communities that nones, Humanists, and Freethinkers face for their atheism, agnosticism, or mere religious inactivity. They form networks of support and empowerment, like the Hispanic American Freethinkers and the Latinx Humanist Alliance.[35] The fear of disenfranchisement is real for Latine agnostics, atheists, and humanists. They fear "alienation from family and holiday gatherings," since they admit that "it is really difficult to divorce any form of Latinx culture [including holidays like *navidad* and religious observances like *quinceñeras*] from Christianity."[36] The nones' and alternate paths' struggle to cut off religion from cultural formation—that is, from determining what is deemed as authentic *latinidad*—is a *critique by way of divergent acculturation.*

Lastly, final critique is political as nones and alternate paths is adamant about limiting or even eliminating religio-institutional encroachment on democracy and push for delimiting religio-institutional power in political decision-making. They assert that the theocratic impulses (both subtle and overt) is a "moral danger" in that "a doctrine of faith transgresses into the life of a nonbeliever," for the "object of religious belief" is "unintelligible save through faith," and consequently is "an obstacle to the attainment of mutual understanding and the process of fruitful inquiry,"[37] two indispensable values of a true democracy. Working through a humanist pragmatist framework, Devin Fitzpatrick writes, "A basic premise of secular humanism is that whatever value is derived from commitment to supernatural doctrine can also be derived without the inhibition of inquiry or said moral danger, or bolder still, that it is a better life which inquires freely, threatens fewer, and resolutely faces its own finitude."[38] Again, Latine nones and alternate paths have a Latin American genealogy from which to draw. Ambrosio Velasco Gómez describes it as "*un humanismo hispanoamericano*" that promotes "a critical, pluralistic and emancipatory humanism, oriented by republican ideals and engaged with the defense of human rights" against "a colonialist and authoritarian tradition."[39] The critical politics of nones and alternate paths is a *critique by way of dissident advocacy*, dissenting to the implicit theocratic impulses in a democracy that explicitly constitutionalized the separation of church and state.

Nones and Alternate Paths as Creative Movements

As stated previously, the phenomena of nones and alternate paths cannot be reduced to reactionary deconstruction. Amidst the rumble of critique lays the kindling of creative fires. Something new—new though with a long genealogy—emerges. These alternate paths and unaffiliated religiosities/spiritualities are constructive enterprises among Latine peoples. They are not just critiquing; they are creating. They are not simply denouncing; they are generating. Below are two points on this matter, one philosophical/theological and the other sociological/political.

The lived experience of Latine nones and alternate paths are (new) explorations in philosophical anthropology. Meaning, they propose new vistas into what it means to be human. As experiments in anthropological construction, they offer "self-reflection of the social and cultural sciences on their biological foundations … considered in relation to determinate historical and political problems."[40] That is to say, the emerging philosophical anthropologies take as foundational—or least, take seriously—what is being learned from the life and social sciences *as to what it means to be human*. All transcendent articulations originate from the immanent, namely, the biological and the social.[41] They are experiences of "self transcendence"[42]—an anthropological transcendence that cannot be confined by religion or (in the case of multiple religious belonging) by adherence to *one* religion. In what Hans Joas (working within the pragmatist tradition) calls "the creativity of action,"[43] by which he does not mean "a single type of action called 'creative action' but to a *quality* found in all human action,"[44] nones and alternate paths are inviting not the discovery of the self, but the ongoing creation of the self. Out of this "quality" of "creative action" and out of the processes of social interaction emerges a new "self,"[45] inviting imaginative philosophical anthropologies constructed from the raw materiality and experience of nones and alternate paths.

With this, a new anthropology requires a new sociality, inviting sociologists and political theories likewise to reconsider social life in the intersecting and overlapping *poleis* in which humanity finds itself: *la patria*, *el pueblo*, *el barrio*, and *el hogar*. This might be biggest challenge to-date for Latine nones and alternate paths. What Philip Kitcher says of secular humanism can be said of these new forms of Latine (a)religion: they have not yet "succeeded in finding surrogates for institutions and ideas that religious traditions have honed over centuries or millennia." He admonishes, "Until those surrogates are more widely available, we need respect and tolerance for the doctrinally entangled."[46] Leveraging technology, groups have formed, mostly around humanist commitments, like The Latinx Humanist Alliance (affinity group of the American Humanist Association) and Hispanic American Freethinkers, as well as chapters, affinity groups, or Latine-focused outreach within organizations like Atheists United and the Freedom from Religion Foundation.[47]

However the nones and alternate paths may choose to construct themselves and their communities, the Latine cultural peculiarities demand that Latine nones and alternate paths consider a balance between continuity and discontinuity with their Latine cultures—cultures that have been constituted substantially by their longstanding religious inheritances. These emerging modes of being-religious, with their immanent, humanist and pragmatist orientations, "can make no sense of a total break with the past or an absolute end to a system, for the condition of the intelligibility of future actions is reliant upon a history of sedimented meanings."[48] The aim must not be rupture but a " 'radical interruption' of profound intensity." Only by preserving some of "condition of the intelligibility of future actions" can nones and alternate paths "continue to be a be an active source of critical reflection and an emancipatory guide in our nations."[49] To do otherwise and seek total rupture would be like cutting off one's branch from the family tree while still being perched on it.

Conclusion: Where Are We Going—Where Have We Been

Miguel A. De La Torre

Latines live under the worst form tyranny, the tyranny of an imposed history—not events that occurred in the past, but the hope held for events that supposedly will unfold in the future. This myth, rooted in a eurocentric philosophical salvation history worldview, is so ingrained in the US consciousness——that it not only shapes a United Statian sense of self—but also the Latine consciousness. Assimilating to eurocentric philosophical thought contributes to the domestication of Latine bodies and the colonization of Latine minds. The future many Latines embrace is rooted upon the methodology of the American Dream, where anyone can succeed economically in this country if they simply are smart enough and work hard. As someone who came to this country with nothing—just what could fit into a suitcase—forced to live on the margins of society well into early adulthood; to now enjoy middle-class economic privilege can on the surface provide validation for the myth of the American Dream.

I supposedly succeeded due to the depth of my street smarts and the expansiveness of my work ethics. I tell myself that I am a self-made man, beholden to no one. If I can do it, then obviously anyone can. Not surprisingly, such immigrant success stories are placed on pedestals testifying to the truth of the American Dream. But if I am honest with myself, my success had more to do with arbitrary luck than any special skills I possessed or inevitable movement of history where the sacrifices of parents place their children on an upwardly mobile economic trajectory. I am quite cognizant of how many of my former neighbors—regardless of their intelligence or work ethics—are nonetheless six-feet-under due to the violence associated with living in slums. Probably Malcolm X said it best when he noted that he did not see an American dream, but instead, an American nightmare.[1] As Francisco Garcia demonstrated in the fourteenth chapter of this book, "Departing from the American Dream," Latines, who are facing greater poverty, find elusive the belief of creating generational wealth.

Still, maintaining this myth is crucial because the flip side implies that those who fall short of the dream must mean that they are dumb and lazy. Blaming those sidelined to the margins deflects from the real causes of Latine disenfranchisement, social structures and systems undergirded by white supremacy. The simplistic Black–white dichotomy explaining US racial oppression fails to explicate the current fervent anti-Latine ethnic discrimination that has reached new sadistic heights during the first couple of decades of the twenty-first century, where even the biracial so-called liberal president resurrected the discontinued practice since 1997 of imprisoning migrant Latine children in family prisons.[2] Not surprisingly, lack of intelligence, slothfulness—coupled with lawlessness—has become the normative Latine stereotype. Who could forget when candidate Donald Trump kicked off his first presidential campaign with the villainization of Latines: "[They] have lots of problems, and they're bringing those problems with us. They're bringing drugs. They're bringing crime. They're rapists."[3] Or the glee he expressed when touring the newly built South Florida concentration camp for Latine migrants: "It's known as Alligator Alcatraz, which is very appropriate because I looked outside and that's not a place I want to go hiking ... But very soon, this facility will house some of the most menacing migrants, some of the most vicious people on the planet."[4]

Latine supposed ignorance, idleness, and illegality mask Latine disenfranchisement—a marginalization based on how we have been taught to philosophically understand the movement of history that informs our identity and our trajection into the future. Demythologization this eurocentric sense of history sets the stage—I argue—for the possibly of moving closer to something which might be considered for Latines a bit more just, a bit more liberative.

[Race]ing Toward the Future

Eurocentric thought has strain to provide some general unifying theory that could explain the movement of history. The so-called Age of Enlightenment, a product of modernity, is first and foremost a Eurocentric phenomenon that excludes those relegated to the margins of history. Metaphysical philosopher G. W. F. Hegel, seeking a God's-eye view of the direction and meaning of history, constructed a complete and full elucidation of the structures, processes, and events associated with the passage of time. Such a venture revealed the meaning and purpose of the totality of history. He argues for, "the process whereby the Spirit discovers itself and its own concept."[5] For Hegel, the movement of time toward the teleological realization of human freedom was both intelligible and rational. Through the movement of Spirit in history, human freedom is achieved, constituting the true meaning of history which is itself a process that is also fundamentally political.[6]

Basically, Hegel creates a world history narrative based on an ever-improving political evolution; a narrative undergirded by a religious philosophical metaphysic hybridizing Stoicism and German Pietism with Aristoteleanism, whose root is the mind of some divine being immanent in matter. This ultimate reality of God, which Hegel recognizes as Spirit, becomes the axis upon which the world and history turn.[7] Returning to a pre-Kantian religious-based philosophy, a traditional metaphysical interpretation of Hegel argues that we can grasp and know the Spirit through the process of pure thought.[8] For Hegel, philosophy and theology "have the Divine as their common object" sharing the same ultimate goal—understanding God.[9]

But if understanding God is the goal through the study of universal history, then both the goal and the process are inherently racialized. Hegel's maintains that the progressive evolutionary movement of world history as the unfolding of human freedom moves from East to West. He imposes a divine order upon the direction of human history with the apex of the fullest understanding of God centered in northern Europe, specifically the German Spirit, which is understood as the Spirit of the new World whose aim becomes the realization of absolute Truth as the unlimited self-determination of Freedom.[10] Hegel's entire philosophical venture of elucidating universal and transcendent truth rests on the superiority of Europeans (specifically Germans) and the inferiority of non-Europeans because the axial end of History and the Germanic-Anglo-Saxon heart of Europe is the center and end of universal history.[11]

Because Hegel's dialectical movement of Spirit and time is linked to notions of progress constituted by the evolution of human societies, his historiographical methods create a hierarchy of human development where some are fully advanced while others are stuck in a more primitive stage of development. History's march toward the European center removes Southern Europe, Africa, and Latin America from the movement of World History because they do not bear the Spirit, only Germanic Anglo-Saxons do.[12] The hierarchy he creates essentializes progress by demarcating the start of modernity with when Europeans began the global consolidation of their power over Other peoples and continents.[13] He goes so far as to provide justification for colonialism by invisibilizing them: "In contrast with this absolute right which [Europe] possesses as bearer of the present stage of the world spirit's development," Hegel argues, "the spirits of other nations are without rights, and they, like those whose epoch has passed, no longer count in world history."[14]

Historia versus Historia

Latine's salvation requires the rejection the dominant culture's official history based on the Hegelian historical dialectic which centers Germanic-Anglo-Saxons. Because these Europeans are bearers of the development of the world's Spirit, the rest of us are relegated to the margins of Eurocentric history. Eurocentric historical truth inherently inscribes shame upon our bodies, demanding assimilation as our means to salvation.

Latine memory is substituted with the fictitious story of oppressors, robbing our identity, our centered-ness, and our authenticity. Worse than physical harm, it shatters our soul, spirit, mind, and very essence. Lacking history relegates Latines to the not-yet human as rendered in Hegel's master-slave dialectic. To have one's presence noted in history is limited to when those marginalized are encountered by colonizers. Till then, they remain invisible.

Those of us who read history in Spanish understand the term *historia* can be translated as "a narrative of past events" or as "tale, fable or story." *La historia* (history) is a *historia* (story) recognizing that all *historias* (histories/stories) are fiction. Even when *historia* is based on true events, they often are romanticized, braggadocious and self-serving by how they are (re)membered. All *historias* (histories) are revisionist where objective accounts do not exist. The question before us is whose revisionist *historia* will become normative and legitimate. *La historia*, the fable, is *la historia*, the history of the transculturation of the different aspects of our locus. The early twentieth-century Cuban ethnographer Fernando Ortiz, coined "transculturation" to describe the historical process of identity fraught with conquest, silencing and resistance. All distinct aspects of marginalized cultures become deculturated under the weight of the ever-forming ethos. Rather than using the term "acculturation," the process of acquiring another culture, transculturation for Ortiz involves the loss or uprooting of the previous culture as it feeds the reproduction of the new phenomena.[15] Neglecting *la historias* (the stories) of transculturation belonging to Latines makes an accurate analysis of oppression impossible.

To construct a liberative methodology employing Hegelian philosophical paradigms is to contribute to and be complicit with one's own oppression. Rather than incorporating philosophies which purposely remove Latines from history; we require new worldviews which privileges the *historias* (stories) of those written out of *historia* (history). And while all *historias* (histories) like *historias* (stories) are revisionist, some are closer to a less falsified or romanticized *historia* (history) than others. Making a preferential historiographical option for Latines relegated to the underside of *historia* (history) requires a counterhistorical narrative closer to actual events than the *historias* (story) told to justify prevailing power structures.

Such a counterhistorical narrative can be found in the work of the Spanish philosopher Miguel de Unamuno who introduces the concept of *intrahistoria*, blending objective official statistics with the monotony of the subjective *cotidiano* (everyday) of ordinary real people. *Historia* (history or story) for Unamuno is essentially one with *intrahistoria*, becoming a dynamic unifying force bridging together the natural spirit with the individual.[16] His sense of history rejects all rational equations as he criticizes the positivism of his day that dismissed as irrelevant anything science and/or reason could not prove, where the sense of mystery is rejected in favor of eurocentric enlightenment. History for Unamuno is forged through unconscious acts absent by those whom history considered to be "nobody" not found in the history books written for future generations, those removed from the movement of World History due to their inferiority by Hegel.

Humans are not a means but an end, as per Unamuno, they are the supreme subject of history.[17] Hegel's dialectic frustrate Latines' ability of establishing a worldview which synchronizes their minoritized experience of estrangement. Fortunately, Unamuno provides a model by which to resist Eurocentric dominance by epitomizing the rejection of a Hegelian historical dialectical construct, where Northern Europe is the telos of Western civilization. He ponders if "[m]aybe the disease itself is the essential condition of what we call progress, and progress itself a disease" based on his interpretation of the Genesis creation story where progress emerges with original sin.[18] Resisting the "progress" of Northern Europe, he argues that the choice is not between Europeanization or barbarism, technology or ignorance, modernity or medievalism. For him, the kinetic principle embodied within eurocentric technological progress is not absolute but an imposition upon Spanish culture robbing her of her essence, for employing reason separates us from a God which can neither be proven nor disproven. His arguments for the rejection of the Europeanization of Spain serves Latines as a guide by which we can also resist the continuing Europeanization of our culture which is left out of Hegel's *historia* (story) due to our supposed inferiority.

Finding Jesús

Every so often, Jesús turns up on a tortilla. *Historia* (history) is a constructed illusion, an attempt to see order amidst humanity's inhumanity. Our brains are wired to construct patterns amid disorder hoping to provide meaning to the chaos we are observing. Hence, in the random contours caused when frying a tortilla, the image of Jesús at times appear.[19] Just as we see Jesús's image on a tortilla, so too do we see in Hegel's dialectical history as a linear progressive movement of history amidst the chaos of time. As enlightenment thinkers of modernity construct as their teleology progress within their *historia* (story/history), religious thinkers substitute the idea of progress for a salvation history which also discerns meaningful pattern within time—arguing that *historia* (story/history) is divinely ordained. Both propositions are an article of faith which leads humanity to an unprovable utopia. While religious interpreters characterize historical events as God's will thus giving meaning to the passage of time—regardless of the horrors which occur; enlightenment thinker, while rejecting religious interpretations, nonetheless advocate for a nontheistic salvation history.

I argue that *historias* (histories) of religious and secular metahistorians are but what they are predisposed to see in the chaotic static of movement of time. What is called *historia* (history) is but a series of unrelated and unconnected events occurring in a disjointed, nonlinear, multidimensional passage of time. Literary critic Walter Benjamin argued for a non-successive conception of the movement of time. Where we perceive a chain of events," Benjamin argued, "[the angel of time] sees one single catastrophe which keeps piling wreckage upon wreckage and hurls it in front of his feet."[20] The barbarism which the angel of time sees is not what threaten culture, for culture's so-called historical progress is already entangled with barbarism.[21] Latines who have experienced the barbarism of the United States (specifically its immigration policies), know that civilization contains domination and exploitation. And yet, for Benjamin, what historians call "progress" causes them to misinterpret *historia* (history) because this progress legitimizes and normalizes the present, despite the piles of human wreckage it produces. *Historias* (stories) are created by those possessing the power to create so that (re)membered *historia* (history) can be commodified to justify the values and social power of those civilization privileges.

Benjamin pursues a non-Hegelian, nondialectical understanding of history—a historical materialism that "annihilates within itself the idea of progress."[22] To gaze at this particular 2026 movement of time allows for an appreciation as to how grave our current situation is. Latines are witnessing the inevitability of human barbarism. *Historia* (history) is not a *historia* (story) of progression as per Hegel's imagination; it is the reality of an accumulating pile of wreckage which dialecticians label progress. Because *historia* (history) is not evolutionary—exteriority of accidents, complete reversals, and false appraisals gain value. To propose that some universal truth about human experience exists within the historical movement of time is problematic, a fallacy that universalizes contingent ethical, moral, and political commitments. If true, then the so-called arc of the moral universe is *neither* long *nor does* it necessarily bend toward justice. Because *historia* (history) lacks an arc, the universe is amoral, and an absence of salvation history means there exists no predestine bending.

Moving Forward

Rejecting eurocentric *historia* (story) means that the movement of time has no rhyme nor reason. Rejecting a eurocentric romanticized understanding of ethics based on the hope of salvation history (a doctrinal belief), means we approach the God which may or may not exist based on how the disenfranchised among Latines understand the space and time they occupy before the God of Job who chooses silence about their oppression. For many, God is the panopticon guard, or the possessor of the unblinking eye constantly staring at creation. To always be watched, unable to hide from the relentless gaze, forces us to learn how to impose our own discipline; thus, becoming our own dominatrix.

For many Latines, our marginalization is neither God's will, nor the consequent of some unknown sin, nor a means by which character is built in preparation for the eschatological future. Even many who have rejected the concept of God still blame themselves for their situation—embracing the lie they lack intelligence, will, or drive to succeed. Any attempt to look for a logical progression or some moral undergirding to *historia* (history) becomes a misguided venture. And yet, for many, salvation history is the predominant lens by which Christians and enlightenment thinkers make sense of the randomness of life. Seeking to impose order on the random chaos associated with the movement of time creates structures of oppression where liberation becomes elusive as one's *historia* (story) is constructed to reinforce oneself as the cause of one's victimization. Maybe liberation begins with the telling of one's own *historia* (story), one's own constructed *historia* (history), rejecting the legitimatized dominant *historia* (history) created to justify the status quo of Latine oppression. Some Latines do find a false liberation by embracing eurocentric thought, assimilating to the dominant culture, seeking to become ontologically white. But liberation can never be found within eurocentric thought, it arises from our Latine communities, where we learn how to strive toward a more just society by being in solidarity with disenfranchised Latines. In short, by being *¡presente!*

Notes

Introduction: How We Got Here

1 Amy S. Greenberg, *A Wicked War: Polk, Clay, Lincoln, and the 1846 U.S. Invasion of Mexico* (New York: Vintage Books/Random House, 2012); Peter Guardino, *The Dead March: A History of the Mexican-American War* (Cambridge, MA: Harvard University Press, 2017); Timothy J. Henderson, *A Glorious Defeat: Mexico and Its War with the United States* (New York: Hill and Wang, 2007).

2 Cf. Brian DeLay, *War of a Thousand Deserts: Indian Raids and the U.S. Mexican Wars* (New Haven: Yale University Press, 2008); Winston P. Erickson, *Sharing the Desert: The Tohono O'odham in History* (Tucson: University of Arizona Press, 1994); Evelyn Hu-DeHart, *Yaqui Resistance and Survival: The Struggle for Land and Autonomy, 1821–1910*, revised edition (Madison: University of Wisconsin Press, 2016); Peter Iverson, *Diné: A History of the Navajos* (Albuquerque: University of New Mexico Press, 2002); Ariel Zatarain Tumbaga, *Yaqui Indigeneity: Epistemology, Diaspora, and the Construction of Yoeme Identity* (Tucson: University of Arizona Press, 2018); Michael Steven Wilson and José Antonio Lucero, *What Side Are You On? A Tohono O'odham Life across Borders* (Chapel Hill: University of North Carolina Press, 2024).

3 Treaty of Guadalupe Hidalgo [Exchange copy]; 2/2/1848; Perfected Treaties, 1778–1945; General Records of the United States Government, Record Group 11; National Archives Building, Washington, DC. https://www.archives.gov/milestone-documents/treaty-of-guadalupe-hidalgo, accessed December 27, 2025.

4 Gloria Anzaldúa, *Borderlands/La Frontera: The New Mestiza* (San Francisco, CA: Aunt Lute Books, 1987, 1999), preface, no page number.

5 Mariana Alessandri, "Laughing in Spanish," *New Philosopher* 17 (Summer 2017): 41.

6 Cf. Roberto D. Hernández, *Coloniality of the US/Mexico Border: Power, Violence, and the Decolonial Imperative* (Tucson: University of Arizona Press, 2018).

7 See Juan Carlos Scannone, "Pope Francis and the Theology of the People," *Theological Studies* 77 (2016): 118–35; Thomas R. O'Rourke, *The Roots of Pope Francis's Social and Political Thought: From Argentina to the Vatican* (Lanham, MD: Rowman & Littlefield, 2016); Rafael Luciani, *Pope Francis and the Theology of the People* (Maryknoll, NY: Orbis Books, 2017); William McCormick, "The Populist Pope? Politics, Religion, and Pope Francis," *Politics and Religion* 14 (2021): 159–81.

8 Pope Francis, Laudato Si', *On Care for Our Common Home* (Vatican City: Vatican Publishing House, 2015), https://www.vatican.va/content/francesco/en/encyclicals/documents/papa-francesco_20150524_enciclica-laudato-si.html.

9 Homily of His Holiness Pope Francis, Ciudad Juárez Fair Grounds, Wednesday, February 17, 2016. Dicastery for Communication, The Holy See. https://www.vatican.

va/content/francesco/en/homilies/2016/documents/papa-francesco_20160217_omelia-messico-ciudad-jaurez.html.

10 To begin to name their names risks overlooking many, but here are the names of some of the Black and Brown victims racial injustice, police, and vigilante violence in the United States: George Floyd, Jr., Trayvon Martin, Breonna Taylor, Michael Brown, Carlos Ingram López, Sharonda Singleton, Eric Garner, Sean Monterrosa, Aiyona Mo'Nay Stanley-Jones, and Amadou Diallo.

11 Cf. Kyle B. T. Lambelet, *¡Presente! Nonviolent Politics and the Resurrection of the Dead* (Washington DC: Georgetown University Press, 2019); Diana Taylor, *¡Presente! The Politics of Presence* (Durham, NC: Duke University Press, 2020).

12 Nancy Tatom Ammerman, *Sacred Stories, Spiritual Tribes: Finding Religion in Everyday Life* (Oxford: Oxford University Press, 2014), 5.

13 Robert A. Orsi, *Between Heaven and Earth: The Religious Worlds People Make and the Scholars Who Study Them* (Princeton, NJ: Princeton University Press, 2005), 5, 15. A related approach is found in what is called lived theology as distinguished by Charles Marsh: "Lived religion examines practices, beliefs, and objects to understand more clearly the human phenomenon of religion, while lived theology examines practices, objects, and beliefs in order to understand God's presence in human experience. Charles Marsh, "Introduction," in *Lived Theology: New Perspectives on Method, Style, and Pedagogy*, eds. Charles Marsh, Peter Slade, and Sarah Azaransky (New York: Oxford University Press, 2017), 7.

14 Manuel A. Vásquez, *More Than Belief: A Materialist Theory of Religion* (Oxford: Oxford University Press, 2011), 254–5.

15 For more on *lo cotidiano*, see Edwin David Aponte and Miguel A. De La Torre, *Introducing Latinx Theologies Revised edition* (Maryknoll, NY: Orbis Books, 2020), 82–3.

16 Djamila Ribero, *Where We Stand*, trans. Padma Viswanathan (New Haven, CT: Yale University Press, 2024), 27.

1

1 Miguel A. De La Torre and I made earlier attempts to address this issue of naming and identity, see Edwin David Aponte, *¡Santo! Varieties of Latino/a Spirituality* (Maryknoll: Orbis Books, 2012), 57–77; Edwin David Aponte and Miguel A. De La Torre, *Introducing Latinx Theologies* (Maryknoll: Orbis Books, 2020), 1–17.

2 Marie Arana, *LatinoLand: A Portrait of America's Largest and Least Understood Minority* (New York: Simon & Schuster, 2024), xi–xii.

3 Robert Wald Sussman, *The Myth of Race: The Troubling Persistence of an Unscientific Idea* (Cambridge, MA: Harvard University Press, 2014); Michael Omi and Howard Winant, *Racial Formation in the United States*, 3rd ed. (New York: Routledge, 2015); Eduardo Bonilla-Silva, *Racism without Racists: Color-Blind Racism and the Persistence of Racial Inequality in America*, 6th ed. (Lanham, MD: Rowmsan & Littlefield, 2022).

4 Felipe Hinojosa, "Latina/o Religious Politics," in *Oxford Research Encyclopedia of American History*, ed. Jon Butler (2018), accessed September 14, 2025, https://oxfor

dre.com/americanhistory/view/10.1093/acrefore/9780199329175.001.0001/acrefore-9780199329175-e-456.

5 Felipe Hinojosa, Maggie Elmore, and Sergio M. González, "Introduction: Latino Religious Politics: Mapping the Field," in *Faith and Power: Latino Religious Politics Since 1945*, ed. Felipe Hinojosa, Maggie Elmore, and Sergio M. González (New York: New York University Press, 2022), 4.

6 Mike Davis, *Magical Urbanism: Latinos Reinvent the US City* (London: Verso, 2001), 11–12.

7 US Census Bureau, "Updates to Race/Ethnicity Standards for Our Nation," accessed September 16, 2025, https://www.census.gov/about/our-research/race-ethnicity/standards-updates.html_.

8 Jeffrey S. Passel and Jens Manuel Krogstad, "How a Coding Error Provided a Rare Glimpse into Latino Identity Among Brazilians in the U.S." Pew Research Center, accessed April 19, 2023, https://www.pewresearch.org/?p=8088.

9 Helen Marrow, "To Be or Not to Be (Hispanic or Latino): Brazilian Racial and Ethnic Identity in the United States," *Ethnicities* 3, no. 4 (2003): 427–64. See also Alan P. Marcus, "Brazilian Immigration to the United States and the Geographical Imagination," *Geographical Review* 99, no. 4 (2009): 481–98.

10 Clarisse Halpern, Zachary Austin Ward, and Hasan Aydin, " 'I'm Brazilian, Not Brazilian American': The Experiences of Second-Generation Brazilian Adolescents Preserving Their Heritage Language and Resisting Assimilation," *International Journal of Multicultural Education* 24, no. 2 (2022): 132–56. https://doi.org/10.18251/ijme.v24i2.3173.

11 Ibid., 142.

12 Catarina Fritz, "Redefining Racial Categories: The Dynamics of Identity Among Brazilian-Americans," *Immigrants and Minorities* 33, no. 1 (2015): 45–65.

13 For additional insights about Brazilians in the United States, see João B. Chaves, *Migration Religion: Context and Creativity in the Latinx Diaspora* (Waco, TX: Baylor University Press, 2021), 27–43.

14 Pew Research Center, Jeffrey S. Passel, and Jens Manuel Krogstad, "How a coding error provided a rare glimpse into Latino identity among Brazilians in the U.S." Pew Research Center, accessed April 19, 2023, https://pewrsr.ch/3ULh6mp.

15 Tatiana Seijas, *Asian Slaves in Colonial Mexico: From Chinos to Indians* (New York: Cambridge University Press, 2014).

16 Nicole CuUnjieng Aboitiz, *Asian Place, Filipino Nation: A Global Intellectual History of the Philippine Revolution, 1887–1912* (New York: Columbia University Press, 2020).

17 Steffano Montano, "Theoretical Foundations for an Intercultural, Antiracist Theological Education" (PhD diss., Boston College, 2019), 115, Boston College, eScholarship@BC (https://ur.bc.edu/islandora/theoretical-foundations-intercultural-antiracist-theological-education).

18 Michel Gobat, "The Idea of Latin America in the Nineteenth Century," in *The Routledge Hispanic Studies Companion to Nineteenth Century Latin America*, ed. Agnes Lugo-Ortiz and Graciela Montaldo (London: Routledge, 2025), 28–42. See also Paul Edison, "Latinizing America: The French Scientific Study of Mexico, 1830–1930" (PhD diss., Columbia University, 1999), 5–6.

19 Salvador Vidal-Ortiz and Juliana Martínez, "Latinx Thoughts: Latinidad with an X." *Latino Studies* 16 (2018): 384–95. https://doi.org/10.1057/s41276-018-0137-8.

20 Alexis R. Miranda, Amaya Perez-Brumer, and Brittany M. Charlton, "Latino? Latinx? Latine? A Call for Inclusive Categories in Epidemiologic Research," *American Journal of Epidemiology* 192, no. 12 (2023): 1929–32, https://pubmed.ncbi.nlm.nih.gov/37392097/; Caitlin E. Samples, "Gender-inclusive Language in Twitter," *Hispania* 107, no. 1 (2024): 139–60, https://muse.jhu.edu/pub/1/article/921466/pdf.

21 Paola Ramos, *Finding Latinx: In Search of the Voices Redefining Latino Identity* (New York: Vintage Book, 2020), 300.

22 Ed Morales, *Latinx: The New Force in American Politics and Culture* (London: Verso, 2018), 4.

23 Cristobal Salinas Jr. and Adele Lozano, "The History and Evolution of The Term Latinx," in *Handbook of Latinos and Education* (second edition), ed. E. G. Murillo, D. Delgado Bernal, S. Morales, L. Urrieta, E. Ruiz Bybee, J. Sánchez Muñoz, V. B. Saenz, D. Villanueva, M. Machado-Casas, and K. Espinoza (New York: Routledge, 2021), 249–63.

24 San Diego Pride, accessed September 14, 2025, https://sdpride.org/latine/.

25 Pew Research Center, September 12, 2024, "Latinx Awareness Has Doubled Among U.S. Hispanics Since 2019, but Only 4% Use It," https://www.pewresearch.org/race-and-ethnicity/2024/09/12/u-s-hispanics-preferences-among-pan-ethnic-terms/#fn-186651-6.

2

1 Laura Limonic, *Kugel and Frijoles: Latino Jews in the United States* (Detroit, MI: Wayne State University Press, 2019), 1–23.

2 Judith Laikin Elkin, *The Jews of Latin America*, 3rd ed. (Boulder, CO: Lynne Rienner Publishers, 2014), 1–28.

3 Laura Limonic, "The Role of Transnational Actors in the Growth of Chabad-Lubavitch among Argentine Jews," *Contemporary Jewry* 41, no. 4 (2021): 1–15.

4 Sergio DellaPergola, "World Jewish Population, 2020," in *American Jewish Year Book: The Annual Record of the North American Jewish Communities Since 1899*, ed. Arnold Dashefsky and Ira M. Sheskin (New York: Springer, 2022), 54.

5 Pew Research Center, *Jewish Americans in 2020: U.S. Jews are Culturally Engaged, Increasing Diverse, Politically Polarized and Worried about Anti-Semitism* (May 11, 2021), 37.

6 See Eric L. Goldstein, *The Price of Whiteness: Jews, Race, and American Identity* (Princeton, NJ: Princeton University Press, 2006).

7 See Karen Brodkin, *How Jews Became White Folks and What That Says About Race in America* (New Brunswick, NJ: Rutgers University Press, 1998).

8 Tobin Belzer, Tory Brundage, Vincent Calvetti, Gage Gorsky, Ari Y. Kelman, and Dalya Perez, *Beyond the Count: Perspectives and Lived Experiences of Jews of Color* (Oakland, CA: Jews of Color Initiative, 2021), 1–46.

9 Peggy Levitt, "God Needs No Passport: Trying to Define the New Boundaries of Belonging," *Harvard Divinity Bulletin* (Autumn 2006): https://bulletin.hds.harvard.edu/god-needs-no-passport/.

10 Belzer, et al., *Beyond the Count*, 1–46.

11 See Judit Bokser Liwerant, *National and Transnational Paths of Latin American Jews: Modernity, Community, Society, and the State* (Boston, MA: Brill, 2025).

3

1 bell hooks, *The Will to Change: Men, Masculinity, and Love* (New York: Washington Square Press, 2004), 17.

2 Harold D. Morales, *Latino and Muslim in America: Race, Religion, and the Making of a New Minority* (New York: Oxford Univeristy Press, 2018), 6. These statistics are taken from Gaston Espinosa, Harold Morales, and Juan Galvan, "Latino Muslims in the U.S.: Reversion, Politics, and Islamidad," *Journal of Race, Ethnicity, and Religion* 8, no. 1 (2017): 5.

3 Abbas Barzegar, "Latino Muslims in the United States: An Introduction," *Journal of the High Plains Society for Applied Anthropologists* 23, no. 2 (Fall 2003): 126.

4 Morales, *Latino and Muslim in America*, 19–20.

5 Ibid., 24.

6 Ibid., 28.

7 Ibid., 25.

8 Ala Alryyes, *A Muslim American Slave: The Life of Omar Ibn Said* (Madison: University of Wisconsin Press, 2011), 3.

9 Rahim Ocasio and Juan Galvan, *Alianza Islamica: Spanish Harlem's Islamic Odyssey* (Springfield, IL: Publishing Experts, LLC, 2024), 103.

10 Samuel P. Huntington, *The Clash of Civilizations and the Remaking of World Order* (New York: Simon & Schuster, 1996), 209–13.

11 Samuel P. Huntington, *Who Are We? The Challenges to America's National Identity* (New York: Simon & Schuster, 2004), 221–56.

12 Espinosa, Morales, and Galvan, "Latino Muslims in the U.S," 4.

13 Ibid., 153.

14 Ibid., 124.

15 Khaled Abou El Fadl, *The Prophet's Pulpit: Commentaries on the State of Islam*, Vol. 1, ed. Josef Linnhoff (Dublin, OH: Usuli Press, 2022), 102–3.

16 Ibid., 97.

17 Ocasio and Galvan, *Alianza Islamica*, 122.

18 Ibid., 130.

19 Ibid., 123.

20 Robert Stam and Ella Shohat, *Race in Translation: Culture Wars Around the Postcolonial Atlantic* (New York: New York University Press, 2012), 4, 13–17; and Ella Shohat, "The Sephardi-Moorish Atlantic: Between Orientalism and Occidentalism," in *Between the Middle East and the Americas: The Cultural Politics of Diaspora*, ed. Ella

Habib Shohat and Evelyn Azeeza Alsultany (Ann Arbor: University of Michigan Press, 2013), 42–62.

21 Ocasio and Galvan, *Alianza Islamica,* 152.

22 Ibid., 31.

23 Ibid., 115.

24 Miguel A. De La Torre, *Latina/o Social Ethics: Moving Beyond Eurocentric Moral Thinking* (Waco, TX: Baylor University Press, 2010), 5.

25 See Patricia Hill Collins and Margaret Anderson, eds., *Race, Class and Gender: An Anthology* (Boston, MA: Cengage, 2019).

26 The year 2017 marked the 30th anniversary of Alianza Islamica's incorporation. That corporation was dissolved in 2005.

27 Quoted from the landing page of: https://mosqueofislamicbrotherhood.org/.

28 Ocasio and Galvan, *Alianza Islamica,*143–4.

29 Ibid., 146.

30 See Sylvia Marcos, *Taken from the Lips: Gender and Eros in Mesoamerican Religions* (Leiden: Brill, 2006); and Oyeronke Oyewumi, *The Invention of Women: Making an African Sense of Western Gender Discourses* (Minneapolis: University of Minnesota Press, 1997).

31 Houria Bouteldja, *Whites, Jews, and Us: Towards a Politics of Revolutionary Love,* trans. Rachel Valinsky (Los Angeles: MIT Press, 2017), 73–4.

32 See Alma M. Garcia, ed., *Chicana Feminist Thought: The Basic Historical Writings* (New York: Routledge, 2014), 18–23.

33 Barzegar, "Latino Muslims in the United States," 127.

34 Ibid.

35 Ocasio and Galvan, *Alianza Islamica,* 46.

36 Ibid., 75.

37 César Domínguez, phone interview by author, October 4, 2024.

38 Abou El Fadl, *The Prophet's Pulpit*, 62.

39 Ibid.

40 Yomaira C. Figueroa-Vásquez, *Decolonizing Diasporas: Radical Mappings of Afro-Atlantic Literature* (Evanston, IL: Northwestern University Press, 2020), 120.

41 Ramón Grosfoguel, "The Structure of Knowledge in Westernized Universities: Epistemic Racism/Sexism and the Four Genocides/Epistemicides of the Long 16th Century," *Human Architecture: Journal of the Sociology of Self-Knowledge* 11, no. 1 (Fall 2013): 73–90.

42 "Leadership Team," in Masjid Anisa website: https://www.masjidanisa.org/leadership.

43 Ocasio and Galvan, *Alianza Islamica,* 74.

44 'Ali b. Ahmad Ibn Hazm, *Los Caracteres y La Conducta: Tratado de Moral Practica por Abenhazam de Cordoba,* trans. Miguel Asín Palacios (Madrid: Centro de Estudios Históricos, 1916), 31.

45 Morales, *Latino and Muslim in America*, 71.

46 Yusuf Ziya Kavakçi, interviewed by author, Istanbul, Türkiye, February 9, 2016.

47 Morales, *Latino & Muslim in America*, 3.

4

1 Throughout this chapter, the Spanish name for Jesus, Jesús, will be used when referring to a Latine understanding of Christ and the English Jesus when speaking of Anglo perspectives on Christ.

2 Edward R. Handy, ed., *Christology of the Later Fathers* (Philadelphia, PA: Westminster Press, 1954), 373.

3 Jon Sobrino, *Christology at the Crossroads*, trans. Cesar Jerez (Maryknoll, NY: Orbis Books, 1978), 3.

4 Óscar Romero, *Su pensamiento*, Vol. 6 (San Salvador, El Salvador: Publicaciones pastorales del Arzobispado, 1980–9 [December 17, 1978]), 38—my own translation.

5 Luis G. Pedraja, *Jesus Is My Uncle: Christology from a Hispanic Perspective* (Nashville, TN: Abingdon Press, 1999), 67.

6 Virgilio Elizondo, *Galilean Journey: The Mexican-American Promise*, 2nd ed. (Maryknoll, NY: Orbis Books, 2000), 49.

7 Luis G. Pedraja, *Teología: An Introduction to Hispanic Theology* (Nashville, TN: Abingdon Press, 2003), 128.

8 Ada María Isasi-Díaz, *Mujerista Theology: A Theology for the Twenty-First Century* (Maryknoll, NY: Orbis Books, 1996), 149.

9 Ada María Isasi-Díaz, "Preoccupations, Themes, and Proposals of Mujerista Theology," in *The Ties That Bind: African American and Hispanic American/Latino/a Theologies in Dialogue*, ed. Anthony B. Pinn and Benjamin Valentin (New York: Continuum, 2001), 137–8.

10 Pedraja, *Jesus Is My Uncle*, 106.

11 Ibid., 69.

12 Pedraja, *Teología*, 158.

13 Social media post by MAGA political activist Laura Loomer, defending the creation of Alligator Alcatraz while implying that all Americans of Latine heritage deserve to be imprisoned there given that 65 million is the number of Hispanics currently living in the United States according to the US Census Bureau. See "Alligator Alcatraz sparks backlash, nearly half of Americans disapprove of controversial facility," *The Economic Times*, English Edition (July 4, 2025).

14 Emma Marsden, "Trump Supporter Detained by ICE Thought Only Criminals Would Be Deported," *Newsweek* (June 27, 2025).

15 Miguel A. De La Torre, *The Politics of Jesús: A Hispanic Political Theology* (Lanham, MD: Rowman & Littlefield, 2015), 1.

16 Ibid., 2.

17 Ibid., 7 (emphasis in the original).

18 Ibid., 15.

19 Pedraja, *Jesus Is My Uncle*, 69.

20 Pedraja, *Teología*, 103.

21 See Eduardo C. Fernández, S. J., "Three Visual Images of Jesus the Christ from the Latino/a Community: God the Vulnerable; God the Broken; God the Loving," in *Jesus in the Hispanic Community: Images of Christ from Theology to Popular Religion*, ed. Harold J. Recinos and Hugo Magallanes (Louisville KY: Westminster John Knox Press, 2009), 171–89.

22 Ibid., 172.

23 Carlos F. Cardoza-Orlandi, "Qué Lindo Es Mi Cristo: The Erotic Jesus/Christ in the Caribbean, Lain American, and Latino/a Protestant Christian Music," in *Jesus in the Hispanic Community: Images of Christ from Theology to Popular Religion*, ed. Harold J. Recinos and Hugo Magallanes (Louisville: Westminster John Knox Press, 2009), 163–4.

24 Roberto S. Goizueta, *Caminemos Con Jesús: Toward a Hispanic/Latino Theology of Accompaniment* (Maryknoll, NY: Orbis Books, 1999), 8.

25 Roberto S. Goizueta, *Christ Our Companion: Toward a Theological Aesthetics of Liberation* (Maryknoll, NY: Orbis Books, 2009), 54. See also Alex García-Rivera, *St. Martin De Porres: The "Little Stories" and the Semiotics of Culture* (Maryknoll, NY: Orbis Books, 1995).

26 Goizueta, *Christ Our Companion*, 9.

27 Goizueta, *Caminemos Con Jesús*, 67.

28 Goizueta, *Christ Our Companion*, 23.

29 Cornel West, *Prophesy Deliverance! An Afro-American Revolutionary Christianity*, 20th anniversary edition (Louisville, KY: Westminster John Knox Press, 2002), 35.

30 Goizueta, *Christ Our Companion*, 2.

31 Ibid., 3.

5

1 For Hebrew Bible examples, see Judg. 14:5-6; 1 Sam. 16:12-13; and Zechariah 4:5-6. For New Testament examples, see Acts 2:33; 4:30-32; Lk 24:49; Jon. 14:16; 15:26; 16:13; and 1 Jon. 2:20.

2 For the Gifts of the Spirit, see Isa. 11:2-3; and 1 Cor. 12:7-11.

3 For the Fruits of the Spirit, see Gal. 5:16 and 22-23.

4 For more Latine Christian views of the Holy Spirit, see Emilio Alvarez, *Pentecostal Orthodoxy: Toward an Ecumenism of the Spirit* (Lisle, IL: InterVarsity Press, 2022); Gastón Espinosa, *Latino Pentecostals in America: Faith and Politics in Action* (Cambridge, MA: Harvard University Press, 2016); Néstor Medina, "Theological Musings toward a Latina/o Pneumatology" in *Wiley Blackwell Companion to Latino/a Theology*, First Edition, ed. Orlando Espín (Hoboken, NJ: Wiley, 2015), 173–89.

5 Anita de Luna, *Faith Formation and Popular Religion: Lessons from the Tejano Experience* (Lanham, MD: Rowan & Littlefield, 2002), 38.

6 Jürgen Moltmann, *The Spirit of Life: A Universal Affirmation*, trans. Margaret Kohl (Minneapolis, MN: Fortress Press, 1992), 8.

7 Veli-Matti Kärkkäinen, *Spirit and Salvation: A Constructive Christian Theology for the Pluralistic World, Vol. 4* (Grand Rapids, MI: Eerdmans, 2016), 10–11 (emphasis added).

8 Orlando O. Espín, *Pentecost at Tepeyac: Pneumatologies from the People* (Maryknoll, NY: Orbis Books, 2024), 125 (emphasis in the original).

9 Edwin David Aponte, *¡Santo!:Varieties of Latino/a Spirituality* (Maryknoll, NY: Orbis Books, 2012), 13.

10 For historical analysis of these four pneumatological characteristics in European Christianity from the twelfth to the seventeenth centuries, see Albert Hernández, *Subversive Fire: The Untold Story of Pentecost* (Lexington, KY: Emeth Press, 2010), 1–26, 253–70.

11 Justo L. González, *Mañana: Christian Theology from a Hispanic Perspective* (Nashville, TN: Abingdon, 1990), 158.

12 Justo L. González, *The Story of Christianity, Volume I: The Early Church to the Dawn of the Reformation*, revised and updated edition (New York: HarperCollins, 2010), 2.

13 Aponte, *!Santo!:Varieties of Latino/a Spirituality*, 147.

14 Kat Armas, *Abuelita Faith: What Women on the Margins Teach Us about Wisdom, Persistence, and Strength* (Grand Rapids, MI: Brazos Press, 2021), 33.

15 Jürgen Moltmann, *The Spirit of Life: A Universal Affirmation* (Minneapolis, MN: Fortress Press, 1992), 8.

6

1 Charles H. Long, *Significations: Signs, Symbols, and Images in the Interpretation of Religion* (Philadelphia, PA: Fortress Press, 1986), 7.

2 For example, see Karen McCarthy Brown, *Mama Lola: A Vodou Priestess in Brooklyn*, 3rd ed. (Berkeley: University of California Press, 2010); Mercedes Cros Sandoval, *Worldview, the Orichas, and Santería: Africa to Cuba and Beyond* (Gainesville: University of Florida Press, 2006); Thomas A. Tweed, *Our Lady of the Exile: Diasporic Religion at a Cuban Catholic Shrine in Miami* (New York: Oxford University Press, 1997); Thomas A. Tweed, *Crossing and Dwelling: A Theory of Religion* (Cambridge, MA: Harvard University Press, 2006); and Claudine Michel, "Of Worlds Seen and Unseen: The Educational Character of Haitian Vodou," *Comparative Education Review* 40, no. 3 (1996): 280–94.

3 Cros Sandoval, *Worldview, the Orichas, and Santería*, xviii.

4 Jose Bedia, personal communication with author, July 21, 2021, and John Thornton, "The Development of an African Catholic Church in the Kingdom of Kongo, 1491–1750," *The Journal of African History*, 25 (1984): 147–67.

5 Cros Sandoval uses this term to describe the process of matching the *orichas* with Catholic saints that occurred in Cuba. Cros Sandoval, *Worldview the Orichas, and Santería*, xviii.

6 See Joseph Murphy, *Botanicas: Sacred Spaces of Healing and Devotion in Urban America* (Jackson: University of Mississippi, 2015).

7 See "Text of U.S. Supreme Court Decision: Church of the Lukumi Babalú Ayé, Inc. and Ernesto Pichardo, Petitioners, v. City of Hialeah: Argued 4 November 1992–Decided 11 June 1993," *Journal of Church and State* 35, no. 3 (Summer 1993): 668–95.

8 See Kamari M. Clarke, *Mapping Yoruba Networks: Power and Agency in the Making of Transnational Communities* (Durham, NC: Duke University Press, 2004). See also Tracey E. Hucks, *Yoruba Traditions and African American Religious Nationalism* (Albuquerque: University of New Mexico Press, 2012).

9 Ennis B. Edmonds and Michelle A. Gonzalez, *Caribbean Religious History* (New York: New York University Press, 2010), 94. Scholars estimate that around the knowledge of about 30 orishas was successfully retained throughout the colonial and plantation periods in the Americas and Caribbean. This number has grown as globalization has increased Santería's transnational exchanges with the African continent which has introduced other orishas into the diasporic pantheon.

10 Miguel A. De La Torre, "Afro-Caribbean Religious Expressions," in *The Cambridge History of Religions in Latin America*, eds. Virginia Garrad-Burnett, Paul Freston, and Stephen C. Dove (New York: Cambridge University Press, 2016), 641.

11 Margarite Fernández Olmos and Lizabeth Paravisini-Gebert, *Creole Religions of the Caribbean: An Introduction, from Vodou and Santería to Obeah and Espiritismo* (New York: New York University Press, 2003), 102; and Edmonds and Gonzalez, *Caribbean Religious History*, 103.

12 Lydia Cabrera, *El Monte: Notes on the Religions, Magic, and Folklore of the Black and Creole People of Cuba*, trans. David Font-Navarrete (Durham, NC: Duke University Press, 2023), 124; and Todd R. Ochoa, "PRENDAS-NGANGAS-ENQUISOS: Turbulence and the Influence of the Dead in Cuban Kongo Material Culture," *Cultural Anthropology* 25, no. 3 (2010): 392–3.

13 Bárbaro Martínez-Ruiz, *Kongo Graphic Writing and Other Narratives of the Sign* (Philadelphia, PA: Temple University Press, 2013), 164. On microcosm, see David H. Brown, "Annotated Glossary for Fernando Ortiz's 'The Afro-Cuban Festival: Day of the Kings,' " in *Cuban Festivals: An Illustrated Anthology*, ed. Judith Bettelheim (New York: Garland, 1993), 85. See also De La Torre, "Afro-Caribbean Religious Expressions," 645; and Edmonds and Gonzalez, *Caribbean Religious History* 105.

14 See Murphy, *Botánicas*.

15 Martinez-Ruiz, *Kongo Graphic Writing*, 164.

16 Christine Ayorinde, *Afro-Cuban Religiosity, Revolution, and National Identity* (Gainesville: University Press of Florida, 2005), 20–1; and Edmonds and Gonzalez, *Caribbean Religious History*, 118.

17 Maureen Campesino and Gary E. Schwartz, "Spirituality Among Latinas/os Implications of Culture in Conceptualization and Measurement," *ANS. Advances in nursing science* 29, no. 1 (2006): 69–81.

18 Edmonds and Gonzalez, *Caribbean Religious History*, 116.

19 Diana Espírito Santo, *Developing the Dead: Mediumship and Selfhood in Cuban Espiritismo* (Gainesville: University Press of Florida, 2015), 222.

20 Ibid., 83.

7

1 Luis E. Escobedo, Lilia Cervantes, and Edward Havranek, "Barriers in Healthcare for Latinx Patients with Limited English Proficiency- A Narrative Review," *Journal of General Internal Medicine* 38, no. 5 (2023): 1265.

2 Arlene Sánchez Walsh, *Pentecostals in America* (New York: Columbia University Press, 2018), 1.

3 Pew Center Research, "Among U.S. Latinos, Catholicism Continues to Decline but Is Still the Largest Faith," April 13, 2023.

4 Heather D. Curtis, "The Global Character of Nineteenth-Century Divine Healing," in *Global Pentecostal and Charismatic Healing*, ed. Candy Gunther Brown and Harvey Gallagher Cox (Oxford: Oxford University Press, 2011), 35.

5 Candy Gunther Brown and Harvey Gallagher Cox, *Global Pentecostal and Charismatic Healing*, ed. Candy Gunther Brown and Harvey Gallagher (Oxford: Oxford University Press, 2011), 5.

6 Walsh, *Pentecostals in America*, 3.

7 Joseph W. Williams, *Spirit Cure: A History of Pentecostal Healing*, 1st ed. (Oxford: Oxford University Press, 2012), 31.

8 Gastón Espinosa, *Latino Pentecostals in America: Faith and Politics in Action* (Cambridge, MA: Harvard University Press, 2014), 22.

9 Ibid., 78.

10 Gary J. Hale, "Migrant Caravans: A Deep Dive into Mass Migration Through Mexico and the Effects of Immigration Policy," Houston: Baker Institute for Public Policy, March 2, 2023.

11 Pew Research Center. "Among U.S. Latinos," April 13, 2023.

12 Jonathan Calvillo, *The Saints of Santa Ana: Faith and Ethnicity in a Mexican Majority City* (New York: Oxford University Press, 2020), 142.

13 Joseph M. Murphy, *Botánicas: Sacred Spaces of Healing and Devotion in Urban America* (Jackson: University Press of Mississippi, 2015), 21.

14 Brian McNeill and Joseph Michael Cervantes, *Latina/o Healing Practices: Mestizo and Indigenous Perspectives* (New York: Routledge, 2008), 272.

15 Sylvia Marcos, *Taken from the Lips: Gender and Eros in Mesoamerican Religions* (Boston, MA: BRILL, 2005), 2.

16 Robert T. Trotter, Juan Antonio Chavira, and Luis D. León, *Curanderismo: Mexican American Folk Healing* (Athens: University of Georgia Press, 1997), 36.

17 Angela A. Sanchez, "An examination of the folk healing practice of Curanderismo in the Hispanic community," *Journal of Community Health Nursing* 35, no. 3 (2018): 148–61.

18 Maria L. Cruz, Samantha Christie, Estrella Allen, Erika Meza, Anna María Nápoles, and Kala M. Mehta, "Traditional Healers as Health Care Providers for the Latine Community in the United States, a Systematic Review," *Health Equity* 6, no. 1 (2022): 412–26.

19 Brian McNeill et al., *Latina/o Healing Practices*, 284.

20 Ibid., 272.

21 Trotter et al., *Curanderismo*, 34.

22 Ibid., 35.

23 Murphy, *Botánicas*, 16.

24 Jacob K. Olupona, "Rethinking the Study of African Indigenous Religions," *Harvard Divinity Bulletin*, Spring/Summer 2021.

25 Mary Ann Clark, *Santeria: Correcting the Myths and Uncovering the Realities of a Growing Religion* (Westport, CT: Praeger, 2007), 84.

26 Philip A. Howard, *Changing History: Afro-Cuban Cabildos and Societies of Color in the Nineteenth Century* (Baton Rouge: Louisiana State University Press, 1998), 25.

27 Michelle Gonzalez Maldonado, "Cuba," in *The Oxford Handbook of Latinx Christianities in the United States*, ed. Kristy Nabhan-Warren (Oxford: Oxford University Press, 2022), 220.

28 Robert F. Thompson and John F. Szwed, "Foreword: Forest as Moral Document," in *El Monte: Notes on the Religions, Magic, and Folklore of the Black and Creole People of Cuba*, 1st ed., trans. David Font-Navarrete (Durham, NC: Duke University Press, 2023), xiii.

29 Clark, *Santeria*, 85.

30 Ibid., 87.

31 Ibid., 89.

8

1 National Disability Institute, "Race, Ethnicity and Disability: The Financial Impact of Systemic Inequality and Intersectionality" (August 2020), 4.

2 Ibid., 5.

3 Laurin Bixby, Stacey Bevan, and Courtney Boen, "The Links Between Disability, Incarceration, and Social Exclusion," *Health Affairs* 41, 10 (2022): 1462.

4 Erika Harrell, "Crime Against Persons with Disabilities, 2009–2019 – Statistical Tables," U.S. Department of Justice: Bureau of Justice Statistics (November 2021), 5.

5 Julie Avril Minich, "Enabling Whom? Critical Disability Studies Now," in *Lateral: Journal of the Cultural Studies Association* 5, no. 1 (Spring 2016): 3.

6 Ibid.

7 Dan Goodley, *Disability Studies: An Interdisciplinary Introduction*, 2nd edition (Thousand Oaks, CA: Sage, 2016), 191.

8 Mia Mingus, "Changing the Framework: Disability Justice," *RESIST Newsletter*, 2010.

9 Christopher D. Tirres, *Liberating Spiritualities: Reimagining Faith in the Américas* (New York: Fordham University Press, 2024), 17.

10 Ibid.

11 Colin Barnes, "Understanding the Social Model of Disability: Past, Present and Future," in *Routledge Handbook of Disability Studies*, 2nd ed., ed. Nick Watson and Simo Vehmas (London: Routledge, 2020), 20.

12 Kristen Salkas, Sandy Magaña, Isabela Marques, and Mansha Mirza, "Spirituality in Latino Families of Children with Autism Spectrum Disorder," *Journal of Family Social Work* 19, no. 1 (2016): 38–55.

13 Ibid., 48.

14 Amy Kenny, *My Body Is Not a Prayer Request: Disability Justice in the Church* (Grand Rapids, MI: Brazos Press, 2022), 16.

15 Rhoda Olkin, *What Psychotherapists Should Know about Disability* (New York: Guilford Press, 1999), 25.

16 "Autistic Boy Dies During Exorcism," *CBS News*, August 25, 2003.

17 My conceptualization of the eugenics model is informed by A. J. Withers' construction of the eugenics model in A. J. Withers, *Disability Politics and Theory* (Halifax, NS: Fernwood Publishing, 2012).

18 Withers, *Disability Politics and Theory*, 15.

19 Kim E. Nielsen, *A Disability History of the United States* (Boston, MA: Beacon Press, 2012), 103.

20 Natalia Molina, "Medicalizing the Mexican: Immigration, Race, and Disability in the Early-Twentieth-Century United States," *Radical History Review* 94 (2006): 29.

21 Ibid.

22 Nicole L. Novak et al., "Disproportionate Sterilization of Latinos Under California's Eugenic Sterilization Program, 1920–1945," *American Journal of Public Health (1971)* 108, no. 5 (2018): 611.

23 Natalie Lira, *Laboratory of Deficiency: Sterilization and Confinement in California, 1900–1950s* (Oakland: University of California Press, 2022), xiv.

24 Novak et al., "Disproportionate Sterilization of Latinos," 612.

25 Lira, *Laboratory of Deficiency*, 10.

26 Lennard J. Davis, "Introduction," in *Beginning with Disability: A Primer*, ed. Lennard J. Davis et al. (New York: Routledge, 2018), 12.

27 Deborah Beth Creamer, *Disability and Christian Theology: Embodied Limits and Constructive Possibilities* (Oxford: Oxford University Press, 2009), 24.

28 Rudolph P. Reyes II, "Prophetic Temptation of Ecological Disgust," in *Gonna Trouble the Water: Ecojustice, Water, and Environmental Racism*, ed. Miguel A. De La Torre (Cleveland, OH: Pilgrim Press, 2021), 94.

29 Marno Retief and Rantoa Letšosa, "Models of Disability: A Brief Overview," *HTS Teologiese Studies / Theological Studies* 74, no. 1 (2018): 1–8

30 Mia Mingus, "Moving Toward the Ugly: A Politic Beyond Desirability," in *Beginning with Disability: A Primer*, ed. Lennard J. Davis et al. (New York: Routledge, 2018), 138.

31 Ibid., 139.

32 I follow Colin Barnes's emphasis on the disability/impairment distinction as a pragmatic distinction. Barnes, "Understanding the Social Model of Disability," 25.

33 Creamer, *Disability and Christian Theology*, 96.

34 Susan Wendell, "Unhealthy Disabled: Treating Chronic Illnesses as Disabilities," *Hypatia* 16, no. 4 (2001): 18.

9

1 The authors have chosen the term "Latin America" to signify all the peoples who travers the lands of America who have different relationships with national boundaries but carry their Marian devotions across these boundaries.

2 The authors are using "Latine" for consistency of this volume while also acknowledging that this term is contested and not often used outside of academic settings. Furthermore, most people who fall under this broad umbrella in the United States still use the term closest to their country of origin or family's country of origin or terms derived from their relationship with the oppressive political structures of the United States instead.

3 "Mary of the Americas," a cross-disciplinary project between religious studies and engineering students at the University of Dayton: www.MaryAPParitions.org.

4 Special thanks to Aneudy De Jesus, Luis F. Russe Gonzalez, Courtney M. Ware, Mary T. Landry, Scott A. Vater, and Anne E. Keefe for their contributions to the initial research.

5 See Jeanette Favrot Peterson, "The Virgin of Guadalupe: Symbol of Conquest or Liberation?," *Art Journal* 51, no. 4 (1992): 34–5; Mina García Soormally, "The Image of a Miracle: The Virgin of Guadalupe and the Context of the Apparitions," *Chasqui* 44, no. 2 (2015): 185; and Eric R Wolf, "The Virgin of Guadalupe: A Mexican National Symbol," *The Journal of American Folklore* 71, no. 279 (1958): 34–5.

6 Jean-Pierre Ruiz, "The Bible and U.S. Hispanic Theological Discourse: Lessons from a Non-Innocent History," in *From the Heart of Our People: Latino/a Explorations in Catholic Systematic Theology*, ed. Orlando O. Espín and Miguel H. Díaz (Maryknoll, NY: Orbis Books, 1999), 105.

7 Soormally, "The Virgin of Guadalupe," 177.

8 Joseph Kroger and Patrizia Granziera, *Aztec Goddesses and Christian Madonnas: Images of the Divine Feminine in Mexico* (Farnham, UK: Ashgate, 2012), 228–9.

9 Wolf, "The Virgin of Guadalupe," 35. For more research on Guadalupe by Latine scholars see Jeanette Rodriguez, *Our Lady of Guadalupe: Faith and Empowerment among Mexican-American Women* (Austin: University of Texas, 1994); David A. Sanchez, *From Patmos to the Barrio: Subverting Imperial Myths* (Minneapolis, MN: Fortress Press, 2008); María del Socorro, *Castañeda, Our Lady of Everyday Life* (Oxford: Oxford University Press, 2018); and Orlando O. Espín, *Pentecost at Tepeyac? Pneumatologies from the People* (Maryknoll, NY: Orbis Books, 2024).

10 Kroger and Granziera, *Aztec Goddesses and Christian Madonnas*, 229.

11 Wolf, "The Virgin of Guadalupe," 37.

12 Peterson, "The Virgin of Guadalupe," 42.

13 "Pro-Life Prayers," St. Peter Catholic Church: https://stpeterparish.com/pro-life-prayers.

14 Katherine Dugan, "Fatima Family Shrine: Reinterpreting Mary on the South Dakota Prairie," in *American Patroness: Marian Shrines and the Making of US Catholicism*, ed. Katherine Dugan and Karen E. Park (New York: Fordham, 2024), 125; and "Unborn Children Memorial Services at the Shrine in La Crosse, WI," Shrine of Our Lady of Guadalupe: https://guadalupeshrine.org/memorial-to-the-unborn/.

15 "Our Billboards," Our Lady of Guadalupe for Life: https://olgfl.org/billboards.

16 Ramón Lugo Lovatón, "Nuestra Señora de de Las Mercedes En La Isla de Santo Domingo," *Journal of Interamerican Studies and World Affairs* 13, no. 1 (1971): 57.

17 Juan F. Pepén, *Donde florecio el naranjo: la Altagracia, origen y significado de su culto* (Santo Domingo: Amigo del Hogar, 1984), 25–9.

18 Stephen Holler, "The Origins of Marian Devotion in Latin American Cultures in the United States," *Marian Studies* 46, no. 11 (1995): 110; see also Kroger and Granziera, *Aztec Goddesses and Christian Madonnas.*

19 Ibid.

20 Frank Moya Pons, *Manual de historia dominicana* (Santo Domingo: Universidad Católica Madre y Maestra, 1980), 29.

21 Pope Paul III, *Sublimis Deus on the Enslavement and Evangelization of Indians*, May 29, 1537.

22 Moya Pons, *Manual de historia dominicana*, 95.

23 Thomas Weyr, *Hispanic U.S.A.: Breaking the Melting Pot* (New York: Harper & Row, 1988), 206.

24 Ibid.

25 Armando Machado, "Our Lady of Altagracia Mass Celebrated at St. Patrick's Cathedral," The Good Newsroom (blog), January 17, 2024: https://thegoodnewsroom.org/our-lady-of-altagracia-mass-celebrated-at-st-patricks-cathedral-2024.

26 Asunción Lavrin, "Nuestra Señora de la Divina Providencia," in *Latinas in the United States: A Historical Encyclopedia*, ed. Vicki L. Ruiz and Virginia Sánchez Korrol (Bloomington: Indiana University Press, 2006), 528–9.

27 "Nuestra Señora de Providence," University of Dayton: https://udayton.edu/marianlibrary/all-about-mary-update.php.

28 Lavrin, "Nuestra Señora de la Divina Providencia," 528.

29 There are various dates given for the apparition; 1612, 1627, 1628, and 1635 are the most widely cited.

30 I. A. Wright, "Our Lady of Charity," *The Hispanic American Historical Review* 5, no. 4 (1922): 709.

31 Redemptorist Pastoral Publication, *Mary Throughout Latin America* (Liguori, MO: Liguori Publications, 2005), 14.

32 Miguel A. De La Torre, "Ochún: (N)Either the (M)Other of All Cubans (n)or the Bleached Virgin," *Journal of the American Academy of Religion* 69, no. 4 (2001): 838.

33 Ibid., 850.

34 Ana Celia Perera Pintado, "Religion and Cuban Identity in a Transnational Context," *Latin American Perspectives* 32, no. 1 (2005): 150.

35 Ibid., 156.

36 Ibid., 157.

37 Thomas A. Tweed, *Our Lady of the Exile: Diasporic Religion at a Cuban Catholic Shrine in Miami* (Oxford: Oxford University Press, 1997), 1–21.

38 Matthew J Geiger, *Mission of Nombre de Dios Shrine of Our Lady of La Leche St. Augustine, Florida: A Brief History* (St. Augustine: Mission Nombre de Dios Gift Shop, 2003), 23.

39 Małgorzata Oleszkiewicz-Peralba, *The Black Madonna in Latin America and Europe* (Albuquerque: University of New Mexico Press, 2007), 119; and Nicholas Joseph Santoro, *Mary in Our Life: Atlas of the Names and Titles of Mary, the Mother of Jesus* (Bloomington, IN: iUniverse Publishing, 2011), 140.

40 "Latin American Titles of Mary," University of Dayton: https://udayton.edu/marianlibrary/all-about-mary-update.php#anchor4.

41 Ibid.

42 Rafael Shoji, "The Failed Prophecy of Shinto Nationalism and the Rise of Japanese Brazilian Catholicism," *Japanese Journal of Religious Studies* 35, no. 1 (2008): 35–6.

43 Marc Meistrich Gidal, "Catholic Music in Lusophone New Jersey: Circum-Atlantic Music, Intergroup Dynamics, and Immigrant Struggles in Transnational Communities," *American Music* 34, no. 2 (2016): 184.

44 Ibid., 185.

45 See Nancy Pineda-Madrid, *Suffering and Salvation in Ciudad Juárez* (Minneapolis, MN: Fortress Press, 2011); Laura Victoria Villarreal, "Addressing Marianismo within the United States: Latinx and Xicanas," *Labyrinth* 3 (Spring, 2018): 6–15; Martinque K. Jones and Melissa Briones, "The Impact of Marianismo on the Association Between Intersectional Discrimination and Depressive Symptoms among Latina Women: A Profile Analysis," *Journal of Latinx Psychology* 10, no. 4 (2022): 304–21; and Norma J. Fuller Osores, "En torno a la polaridad machismo-marianismo," *Anuario de hojas de Warmi* (1996): 11–18.

46 Alicia Nuñez, et al., "Machismo, Marianismo, and Negative Cognitive-Emotional Factors: Findings From the Hispanic Community Health Study/Study of Latinos Sociocultural Ancillary Study," *Journal of Latina/o Psychology* 4, no. 4 (2016): 202–17; Monica L. Gallegos and Chris and Segrin, "Exploring the Role of Marianismo and Loneliness in Latinas' Physical and Mental Well-Being," *Health Communication* 39, no. 12 (2024): 2884–95.

47 Nuñez, et al., "Machismo, Marianismo, and Negative Cognitive-Emotional Factors," 9.

48 Ibid., 10.

49 Gallegos and Segrin, "Exploring the Role of Marianismo," 2885.

50 Ibid., 2890.

10

1 A dedication to the particularities of my social location clarifies that I am writing about my experience as a light-skinned Latina with significant Euro-American heritage, making my experiences of oppression utterly distinct from dark-skinned Latinas, Afro Latinas, Black Latinas, and Indigenous experiences of oppression.

2 Ada María Isasi-Díaz, "Mujerista Discourse: A Platform for Latinas' Subjugated Knowledge," in *Decolonizing Epistemologies*, ed. Ada María Isasi-Díaz and Eduardo Mendieta (New York: Fordham University Press, 2012), 44.

3 Ada María Isasi-Díaz, *Mujerista Theology: A Theology for the Twenty-First Century* (Maryknoll, NY: Orbis Books, 1996), 61.

4 *The Mujerista, Instagram Profile*, accessed January 23, 2025, https://www.instagram.com/themujerista/.

5 Isasi-Díaz, *Mujerista Theology*, 62.

6 Ibid., 64.

7 See Miguel A. De La Torre, "Rethinking Mulatez," in *Rethinking Latino(a) Religion and Identity*, ed. Miguel A. De La Torre and Gastón Espinosa (Cleveland, OH: The Pilgrim Press, 2006), 159–63, where De La Torre offers this specific critique and expands on the racist and sexist implications of using *mulatez* as a signifier.

8 Isasi-Díaz, *Mujerista Theology*, 69.

9 See W.E.B. Du Bois, *The Souls of Black Folk* (Chicago: A.C. McClurg,1903), 2, where he defines double-consciousness as "this sense of always looking at one's self through the eyes of others, of measuring one's soul by the tape of a world that looks on in amused contempt and pity."

10 Isasi-Díaz, "Mujerista Discourse," 46.

11 Ibid., 50.

12 Ibid., 56.

13 Ada María Isasi-Díaz, "Hispanic Women: Prophetic Voice in the Church," in *Hispanic Women: Prophetic Voice in the Church*, ed. Ada María Isasi-Díaz and Yolanda Tarango (San Francisco, CA: Harper & Row, 1988), 1–20.

14 Ibid.

15 María Pilar Aquino, "Introduction," in *A Reader in Latina Feminist Theology*, ed. María Pilar Aquino, Daisy L. Machado, and Jeanette Rodriguez (Austin: University of Texas Press, 2002), xvi.

16 Ibid.

17 María Pilar Aquino, "Latina Feminist Theology: Central Features," in *A Reader in Latina Feminist Theology*, ed. María Pilar Aquino, Daisy L. Machado, and Jeanette Rodriguez (Austin: University of Texas Press, 2002), 134.

18 Ibid., 138.

19 Ibid., 139.

20 See Alma M. García, "Introduction," in *Chicana Feminist Thought: The Basic Historical Writings*, ed. Alma M. García (New York: Routledge, 1997), 7, where she writes on the origins of Chicana feminist discourse and its development within the Chicano movement as a result of internal community gender oppression and articulates Chicana feminism as a feminist ideology based on the specific lived experiences of women of color within the Chicano movement.

21 Nancy Pineda-Madrid, "Notes Toward a Chicanafeminist Epistemology (And Why It Is Important for Latina Feminist Theologies)," in *A Reader in Latina Feminist Theology*, ed. María Pilar Aquino, Daisy L. Machado, and Jeanette Rodriguez (Austin: University of Texas Press, 2002), 242.

22 Aquino, "Introduction," xv.

23 Pineda-Madrid, "Chicanafeminist Epistemology," 261.

24 Ibid.

25 Xhercis Méndez, "Decolonial Feminist Movidas: A Caribeña (Re)thinks 'Privilege,' the Wages of Gender, and Building Complex Coalitions," in *Theories of the Flesh: Latinx and Latin American Feminisms, Transformation, and Resistance*, ed. Andrea J. Pitts, Mariana Ortega, and José Medina (New York: Oxford University of Press, 2020), 75.

26 Ibid.

27 Ibid.

28 Ibid., 76.

29 Ibid.

30 Ibid., 77.

31 Ibid., 79.

32 Ibid.

33 Ibid., 81.

34 See Miguel A. De La Torre, *Santería: The Beliefs and Rituals of a Growing Religion in America* (Grand Rapids, MI: Eerdmans, 2004), where De La Torre characterizes Santería as an Afro-Cuban religion that is a product of enslaved Yoruba people in Cuba having been forced to assimilate and practice Catholicism in a colonial context. More than a hybrid religious expression, De La Torre argues that Santería is an ever-changing lived tradition, encapsulating colonial struggle, resistance, and the ongoing negotiation of identity and spirituality in a diasporic context.

35 Méndez, "Decolonial Feminist Movidas," 88.

36 See Gloria Anzaldúa, *Borderlands/La Frontera: The New Mestiza* (San Francisco, CA: Aunt Lute Books, 1987), where Anzaldúa writes on the symbolism of Aztlán as a reference to Aztec homeland. While there is no exact geographical pinpoint of Aztlán, Anzaldúa writes on its cultural significance for Chicanos as it functions as a site of memory, identity, and resistance in a colonial context.

37 Cherríe Moraga, "Queer Aztlán: The Reformation of Chicano Tribe," in *The Last Generation: Prose and Poetry*, ed. Cherríe Moraga (Boston, MA: South End Press, 1993), 4.

38 Ibid.

39 Ibid., 6.

40 Ibid., 4.

41 Ibid., 8.

42 Ibid., 12.

43 Ibid.

44 Mariana Ortega, "Cámara Queer: Longing, the Photograph, and Queer Latinidad," in *Theories of the Flesh: Latinx and Latin American Feminisms, Transformation, and Resistance*, ed. Andrea J. Pitts, Mariana Ortega, and José Medina (New York: Oxford University of Press, 2020), 266.

45 See Ortega, "Cámara Queer," 277–8, where Ortega writes on "melancholic longing" by referencing Jose Esteban Muñoz's work and pushing it further to acknowledge the loss of Latina desire, reiterating her own mourning of multiple erasures. She writes, "Latina desire for women has been erased from dominant culture and dominant culture's artistic production; it has also been minimized from gay/lesbian culture but also from queer culture/history/art as the latter centers the experience of the queer white male and sometimes the queer male of color."

46 Jose Esteban Muñoz, *Cruising Utopia: The Then and There of Queer Futurity* (Durham, NC: Duke University Press, 2009), 28.

47 Ortega, "Cámara Queer," 268.

48 Ibid., 270.

49 Ibid.

50 Ibid.

51 Ibid., 278.

52 See Gloria Anzaldúa, "La Prieta," in *This Bridge Called My Back: Writings by Radical Women of Color*, ed. Cherríe Moraga and Gloria Anzaldúa (Albany, NY: State University of New York Press, 2015), 198–209, where she writes on negotiating her identity as a gay, feminist Chicana and highlights the lack of acceptance of her multiplicity she experiences in each of the three identity groupings.

53 Francisco J. Galarte, "Transgender Chican@ Poetics: Contesting, Interrogating, and Transforming Chicano/a Studies," *Chicana/Latina Studies* 13, no. 2 (2014): 120.

54 Ibid.

55 Ibid.

56 Ibid., 121.

57 Cherríe Moraga, *A Xicana Codex of Changing Consciousness: Writings, 2000–2010* (Durham: Duke University Press, 2011), 189.

58 Galarte, "Transgender Chican@ Poetics," 131.

59 Ibid., 134.

60 Ibid.

11

1 Linda M. Burton, Eduardo Bonilla-Silva, Victor Ray, Rose Buckelew, and Elizabeth Hordge Freeman, "Critical Race Theories, Colorism, and the Decade's Research on Families of Color," *Journal of Marriage and Family* 71 (2010): 440.

2 Ibid.

3 Refer to the Decolonial work of Anibal Quijano and Michael Ennis. "Coloniality of Power, Eurocentrism, and Latin America," *Nepantla: Views from South* 1, no. 3 (2000): 533–80; Walter Mignolo, "The Geopolitics of Knowledge and the Colonial Difference," *The South Atlantic Quarterly* 101, no. 1 (2002): 57–96; Nelson Maldonado-Torres, "On the Coloniality of Beign: Contributions to the Development of a Concept," *Cultural Studies (London, England)* 21, no. 2–3 (2007): 240–70; and María Lugones, "Heterosexualism and the Colonial/Modern Gender System," *Hypatia* 22, no. 1 (2007): 186–219.

4 Burton, et al., "Critical Race Theories," 444.

5 Ibid., 442.

6 Kamilah M. Woodson, ed. *Colorism: With implications for Research, Policy, and Practice* (Santa Barbara, CA: Fielding University Press, 2020), 89.

7 Ibid., 26.

8 Guillermo D. López-Prieto, "Puerto Rico y Estados Unidos: (des)encuentro entre dos sistemas de organización y clasificación racial," *Romance Notes* 61, no. 3 (2021): 437.

9 Janneil Charles, "Colorism and the Afro-Latinx Experience: A Review of the Literature," *Hispanic Journal Behavioral Sciences* 43, nos. 1–2 (2021): 9.

10 Alicia Pousada "The Dynamic of Language in Puerto Rico," in *English Department, Collage of Humanities in the University of Puerto Rico* (San Juan: University of Puerto Rico, Río Piedras Campus 2012), 20–9.

11 Nayeli Y. Chavez-Dueñas, Hector Y. Adam, and Kurt C. Organista, "Skin-color Prejudice and Within-group Racial discrimination," *Hispanic Journal of Behavioral Science* 36, no. 1 (2014): 16.

12 Ibid., 18.

13 Nelson Maldonado-Torres. "Sobre la Colonialidad del Ser," in *Giro Decolonial: Reflexiones para Una Diversidad Epistémica Más Allá del Capitalismo Global*, ed. Santiago Castro-Gómez and Ramón Grosfoguel (Bogotá: Siglo del Hombre Editores, 2007), 133.

14 Tuhiwai Smith, *Decolonizing Methodologies*, 29.

15 Burton, et al., "Critical Race Theories," 445.

16 The following description was given as a demographic description of the residents of the island, and which could not be further from the truth: "The population of Puerto Rico is roughly 3.2 million. Most of the population, 75.8 percent, is white, followed by African Americans, 12.4 percent, while other ethnicities like American Indians, Native Hawaiians, and other Pacific Islanders make up the rest." See more about 2010 P.R. census in: accessed October 21, 2022, https://www2.census.gov/geo/maps/dc10_thematic/2010_Profile/2010_Profile_Map_Puerto_Rico.pdf.

17 See more about 2022 P.R. census in: accessed October 21, 2022, https://worldpopulationreview.com/states/puerto-rico-population.

18 Peter Wade, "Race in Latin America," in *A Companion to Latin American Anthropology*, ed. Debora Poole (Oxford: Blackwell Publishing, 2008), 178.

19 Robert. L. Reece, "Genesis of U.S. Colorism and Skin Tone Stratification: Slavery, Freedom, and Mulatto-Black Occupational Inequality in the Late 19th Century," *The Review of Black Political Economy* 45, no. 1 (2018): 6.

20 Edward Telles, *Pigmentocracies: Ethnicity, Race, and Color in Latin America* (North Carolina: University of North Carolina Press, 2014), 11

21 Guillermo D. López-Prieto, "Puerto Rico y Estados Unidos: (des)encuentro entre dos sistemas de organización y clasificación racial," *Romance Notes* 61, no. 3 (2021): 433.

22 Wade, Race in Latin America, 179.

23 Ibid.

24 J. Kevin Coyle, *Manicheism and its Legacy* (Boston, MA: Leiden, 2009), xiv.

25 Some examples are Isa 1:18: "Come now, let us reason together, says the Lord: though your sins are like scarlet, they shall be as white as snow; though they are red like crimson, they shall become like wool;" and Rev. 7:14: "I said to him, 'Sir, you know.' And he said, 'These are the ones coming out of the great tribulation. They have washed their robes and made them white in the blood of the Lamb.' "

26 An English translation of Angrelo's song would be: "If God were Black, my friend, everything would change—our race, my friend, would be the one in power. The Pope would be Black, and so would the minister, Black angels, and a Black Jesus Christ, my friend." *Letras*, 2023, accessed December 2024, https://www.letras.com/el-gran-combo/si-dios-fuera-negro/english.html#google vignette.

27 Willem H. Oliver, "Reconsidering the Skin Colour (Race) of Jesus and his Ancestors," *Journal of Early Christian History* 4, no. 2 (2014): 4.

28 Gonzalo Meza, "El Cristo Negro de Esquipulas, la devoción más allá de Guatemala," *Omnes*, January 9, 2024.

29 Sarah L. Webb, ed., *Colorism: Essays and Poems* (Self Published, 2017), iii.

30 Woodson, *Colorism*, 26.

31 Frantz Fanon spoke about atmospheric violence to denote that colonialism was in all aspects of our lives, including the pattern of our breathing which symbolizes the somatized effect of the everyday colonial violence.

32 Charles, "Colorism and the Afro-Latinx Experience," 9.

12

1 Rubén Darío, *Azul* (Madrid: Linkgua, 2011), 46, "Palomas blancas y garzas morenas," Digitalia, https://www-digitaliapublishing-com.du.idm.oclc.org/a/13494.

2 Joan Corominas, *Breve diccionario etimológico de la lengua castellana*, 3rd ed. (Madrid: Gredos, 1987), 497.

3 The vignette that opens this chapter is a fictional narrative that illustrates the challenges and idiosyncrasies of an immigrant transgender woman who navigates life between the Global North and the Global South. While the story is not based on a specific individual, it draws on recurring themes, patterns, and testimonies shared by trans communities across diasporic contexts. See Sylvia Rivera, "Queens in Exile, The Forgotten Ones," in *Gender Queer: Voices from Beyond the Sexual Binary*, ed. Joan Nestle, Clare Howell, and Riki Anne Wilchins (Los Angeles: Alyson Books, 2002), 67–85; Arnaldo Cruz-Malavé, *Queer Latino Testimonio, Keith Haring, and Juanito Xtravaganza: Hard Tails* (New York: Palgrave Macmillan, 2007); Lawrence La Fountain-Stokes, "Boricuas cruzando fronteras: autobiografías y testimonios trans puertorriqueños," *Clepsydra: Revista de Estudios de Género y Teoría Feminista* 21 (2021): 95–116.

I recognize the ethical implications of representing marginalized identities through fictionalized storytelling and do so not to appropriate or generalize but to highlight the transformative potential of narrative as a method of radical imagination. As scholars such as Gloria Anzaldúa, José Esteban Muñoz, and Kai Cheng Thom have shown, storytelling—especially when rooted in queer and trans epistemologies—can open space to envision otherwise: to imagine new presents and more just futures. Fiction, in this light, becomes not a diversion from truth but a companion to it, offering forms of contextualization that statistics and theory alone cannot provide. I approach this imaginative work with humility, aiming not to substitute for lived experience but to create conditions for empathy, critical reflection, and the emergence of alternative queer worlds.

4 A note on the use of LGBTQ+, LGBTQ, and queer. In this chapter, I use the terms queer, LGBTQ, and LGBTQ+ as interchangeable to describe identities, people, and ways of living and understanding sexual orientation, gender, and ethos that challenge traditional norms.

5 See Francisco Vázquez García and Richard Cleminson, *"Los Invisibles": Una historia de la homosexualidad masculina en España, 1850–1939* (Granada: Editorial Comares,

2011); Piro Subrat, *Invertidos y rompepatrias: Marxismo, anarquismo y desobediencia sexual y de género en el Estado español - 1868–1982*, 1st ed. (Madrid: Imperdible, 2019); Geoffroy Huard, *Los gais durante el franquismo: Discursos, subculturas y reivindicaciones – 1939–1977* (Barcelona: Egales Editorial, 2021); and Melissa M. Wilcox, *Queer Religiosities: An Introduction to Queer and Transgender Studies in Religion* (Lanham, MD: Rowman & Littlefield, 2021), 249.

6 André Sidnei Musskopf, "Explorando nuestro presente queer," in *Mysterium Liberationis Queer: Ensayos sobre teologías queer de la liberación en las Américas*, Vol. I, ed. Hugo Córdova Quero, Miguel H. Díaz, Anderson Fabián Santos Meza, and Cristian Mor (Nashua, NH: Institute Sophia Press, 2024), 444.

7 Musskopf, "Explorando nuestro presente queer," 445.

8 Muxe is a Zapotec word that refers to both individuals assigned male at birth who do not identify with that gender ("muxes gunaa" or "muxe women" in English), and those individuals who do ("muxes nguiiu" or "muxe men"). The term implies that the individuals identified as muxes (1) perform "femininity" in their daily lives, (2) carry out social roles commonly attributed to women, (3) engage in erotic-affective relationships exclusively with "masculine" men considered heterosexual ("mayates"), and (4) traditionally perform "passive" sexual roles during intercourse. Nowadays, these traditional narratives are being challenged by the muxe community. See Lorena Edith Cruz Vásquez, "El (hetero) cistema de sexualidad, género y deseo en Juchitán como marco para entender la identidad muxe," *Quaderns de Ciències Socials* (2022): 29–59.

9 In Andean cosmology, every living organism has a complementary partner which creates a complete being. See Marianela Agar Diaz Carrasco, "Desarrollo y chacha-warmi: Lógicas de género en el mundo aymara," *Revista Casa de las Américas*, no. 259 (2010): 13.

In the Aymaran language the term chacha-warrmi reflects a complementary coexistence that transcends the binary man/woman. Rocío Guerrero Aylin and María Sol Román Moreno, "*'Chacha-Warmi' y género: Términos en disputa*" (La Plata, AR: paper presented at the *2019 Jornada de Investigación Docencia Extensión y Ejercicio Profesional: Disputas por el Estado, la democracia y las políticas públicas. Concentración de la riqueza y poder popular*, September 2019), 5. This situates the relationship between partners as one without asymmetries. See Ivonne Farah H. and Carmen Sánchez G., eds., *Perfil de género Bolivia* (La Paz, BO: CIDES-UMSA / Viceministerio de Género y Asuntos Generacionales, 2008), 89.

The term chacha-warmi translates as man-woman and represents the union of opposites that is crucial in Andean and Aymaran cosmologies. See Kate Maclean, "Chachawarmi: Rhetorics and Lived Realities," *Bulletin of Latin American Research* 33, no. 1 (2014): 76–90. Thus, chacha-warmi represents a concept of gender that lives outside of the Western binary of opposition or hierarchy. Chacha-warmi understands that men (chacha) and women (warmi) are independent counterparts whose union represents a complementarity of individuals, communities, and ecosystems.

10 Greek τραῦμα wound. Oxford English Dictionary, "trauma (n.), Etymology."

11 Bessel van der Kolk, *The Body Keeps the Score: Brain, Mind, and Body in the Healing of Trauma* (New York: Penguin, 2014), 39.

12 For many migrants from Latin America and the Caribbean, the displacement from Spanish, Portuguese or Indigenous languages to English—or to another dominant tongue—can rupture the intimate link between language and belonging. The loss or forced reshaping of linguistic identity often results in cultural dislocation, internalized shame, or silencing. However, while language is deeply tied to identity, it should not be treated as a gatekeeper. English-dominant Latine individuals, many of whom are born or raised in the United States, also carry layered experiences of migration, cultural memory, racialization, and resistance. The inclusion of an individual in a Latine community is not conditional upon linguistic mastery or ability. Rather, linguistic diversity invites us to embrace a broader and more fluid understanding of what it means to be Latine—an identity not rooted solely or mainly in language, but in shared histories, solidarities, and struggles for recognition.

13 Johan Galtung, "Violence, Peace, and Peace Research," *Journal of Peace Research* 6, no. 3 (1969): 167–91.

14 See Judith Lewis Herman, *Trauma and Recovery: The Aftermath of Violence—from Domestic Abuse to Political Terror*, 4th trade paperback ed. (New York: Basic Books, 2022).

15 See Vivian M. May, *Pursuing Intersectionality, Unsettling Dominant Imaginaries* (New York: Routledge, 2015).

16 Gloria Anzaldúa, *Borderlands/La Frontera: The New Mestiza*, 5th ed. (San Francisco, CA: Aunt Lute Books, 2021), 89–104.

17 See Marcella Althaus-Reid, *Indecent Theology: Theological Perversions in Sex, Gender and Politics* (London: Routledge, 2000).

18 Melissa V. Harris-Perry, *Sister Citizen: Shame, Stereotypes, and Black Women in America* (New Haven, CT: Yale University Press, 2011), 221–65.

19 bell hooks, *Ain't I a Woman: Black Women and Feminism* (Oxford: Taylor & Francis Group, 2014).

20 Cathy Caruth, *Unclaimed Experience: Trauma, Narrative, and History*, 20th Anniversary ed. (Baltimore, MD: Johns Hopkins University Press, 2016), 4, 8, 17.

21 Wendy Doniger, *Other Peoples' Myths: The Cave of Echoes* (Chicago: University of Chicago Press, 1995), 1–7.

22 One example is the story of the *Three Sisters* of the Iroquois (Haudenosaunee) people of North America. In this tradition, The Three Sisters—corn, beans, and squash—are considered spirit-being or siblings who live and grow together, sustaining the people. The story of the Three Sisters was passed down as an oral tradition for centuries. Nowadays, different variations of the story exist. However, in the Iroquois tradition, the most accepted version of the legend sustains that "Sky Woman"—an Iroquois sky goddess— planted three sacred plants on her daughter's grave who had died while giving birth. The growing plants—corn, beans, and squash— provided sustenance to Sky Woman's grandchildren, and later, to the entire humanity ensuring the survival of the Haudenosaunee people.

23 Audre Geraldine Lorde, *A Burst of Light: Essays* (Ithaca: Firebrand Books, 1988), 125.

24 Hermandad (Spanish) (n.): neutral term for brotherhood, sisterhood, and siblinghood.

25 Anderson Fabián Meza Santos, "Resistencia queer: Mística, política y diversidad," *Religión e Incidencia Pública* 9 (2021): 88.

26 Ibid., 92.

27 Ibid.

28 Ibid.

29 Althaus-Reid, *Indecent Theology*, 18.

30 Meza Santos, "Resistencia queer," 90.

31 "We define complex psychological trauma as involving traumatic stressors that (1) are repetitive or prolonged; (2) involve direct harm and/or neglect and abandonment by caregivers or ostensibly responsible adults; (3) occur at developmentally vulnerable times in the victim's life, such as early childhood; and (4) have great potential to compromise severely a child's development. The sequelae of such exposure are equally complex and include states, features, conditions, and phenomenology, including severe problems with emotion dysregulation, dissociation, somatic distress, and identity and relational disturbance and spiritual alienation." Christine A. Courtois and Julian D. Ford, eds., *Treating Complex Traumatic Stress Disorders: An Evidence-Based Guide* (New York: Guilford Press, 2009), 1.

13

1 Mihnea Tanasescu, "The Rights of Nature in Ecuador: The Making of an Idea," *International Journal of Environmental Studies* 70, no. 6 (2013): 856.

2 Ibid.

3 The Ecuadorian Constitution does so by expressly celebrating nature, "the Pacha Mama (Mother Earth), of which we are a part, and which is vital to our existence." See *Constitution of the Republic of Ecuador*, 2008: https://pdba.georgetown.edu/Constitutions/Ecuador/english08.html.

4 Ibid.

5 See Sarah D. Wald, David J. Vazquez, Priscialla Solis Ybarra, and Sarah Jaquette Ray, eds., *Latinx Environmentalisms: Place, Justice, and the Decolonial* (Philadelphia, PA: Temple University Press, 2019); Randy J. Ontiveros, *In the Spirit of a New People: The Cultural Politics of the Chicano Movement* (New York: New York University Press, 2014); Devon G. Peña, *Mexican Americans and the Environment: Tierra y Vida* (Tuscon: University of Arizona Press, 2005); and Amanda J. Baugh, *Falling in Love with Nature: The Values of Latinx Catholic Environmentalism* (New York: New York University Press, 2024).

6 Eduardo Gudynas, "Buen Vivir: Today's Tomorrow," *Development* 54, no. 4 (2011): 441.

7 Sara Caria and Rafael Domínguez, "Ecuador's 'Buen vivir': A New Ideology for Development," *Latin American Perspectives* 43, no. 1 (2016): 19.

8 Eduardo Gudynas, "Religion and Cosmovisions Within Environmental Conflicts and the Challenge of Ontological Openings," *Church, Cosmovision and the Environment: Religion and Social Conflict in Contemporary Latin America*, ed. Evan Berry and Robert Albro (New York: Routledge, 2018), 231.

9 Robert Albro, "Bolivia's Indigenous Foreign Policy: Vivir Bien and Global Climate Change Ethics," in *Church, Cosmovision and the Environment: Religion and Social Conflict in Contemporary Latin America*, ed. Evan Berry and Robert Albro (New York: Routledge, 2018), 101.

10 Theresa Yugar, "Buen Vivir: Historical Narrative of Environmental Resisters in the United States and Latin America," *Perspectivas*, no. 19 (2022): 58.

11 Priscilla Solis Ybarra, *Writing the Goodlife: Mexican American Literature and the Environment* (Tuscon: University of Arizona Press, 2016), 7. Goodlife writing takes its name from a 1949 book by Fabiola Cabeza de Baca, *The Good Life: New Mexico Traditions and Food* (Santa Fe: Museum of New Mexico Press, 2006), in where Cabeza de Baca describes a "rich but simple" life lived off the land.

12 Sara C. Fingal, "Latinx Environmentalism," in *Oxford Research Encyclopedia of American History* (Oxford: Oxford University Press, 2019), 2–3; and Theodore Steinberg, *Down to Earth: Nature's Role in American History*, 3rd ed. (Oxford: Oxford University Press, 2012), 136–54. https://doi.org/10.1093/acrefore/9780199329175.013.421.

13 Dina Gilio-Whitaker, *As Long as Grass Grows: The Indigenous Fight for Environmental Justice from Colonization to Standing Rock* (Boston, MA: Beacon Press, 2019), 92–5; see also Mark David Spence, *Dispossessing the Wilderness: Indian Removal and the Making of the National Parks* (New York: Oxford University Press, 1999), 55–70.

14 Fingal, "Latinx Environmentalism," 3.

15 Ontiveros, *In the Spirit of a New People*, 88.

16 Luis Valdez and Stan Steiner, eds, "El Plan Espiritual de Aztlán," in *Aztlan: An Anthology of Mexican American Literature* (New York: Knopf, 1972), 402–3.

17 Ontiveros, *In the Spirit of a New People*, 97.

18 Ibid.

19 Quoted in Laura Pulido, *Environmentalism and Economic Justice: Two Chicano Struggles in the Southwest* (Tucson: University of Arizona Press, 1996), 118.

20 Kevin J. O'Brien, " 'La Causa' and Environmental Justice: Cesar Chavez as a Resource for Christian Ecological Ethics," *Journal of the Society of Christian Ethics* 32, no. 1 (2012): 153; and Jacques E. Levy and Cesar Chavez, *Cesar Chavez: Autobiography of La Causa* (Minneapolis: University of Minnesota Press, 2007), 27.

21 Fingal, "Latinx Environmentalism," 7–10.

22 Ibid., 8; and Luke W. Cole and Sheila R. Foster, *From the Ground Up: Environmental Racism and the Rise of the Environmental Justice Movement*, 1st ed. (New York: New York University Press, 2001), 31.

23 Fingal, "Latinx Environmentalism," 87; Cole and Foster, *From the Ground Up*, 1–9; and Julie Sze, *Noxious New York: The Racial Politics of Urban Health and Environmental Justice* (Cambridge, MA: MIT Press, 2006), 84–8.

24 Fingal, "Latinx Environmentalism," 8.

25 Nichole M. Flores, "Latine Perspectives on Care for Creation," in *The Wiley Blackwell Companion to Latino/a/x Theology*, ed. Orlando O. Espín (Hoboken, NY: John Wiley & Sons, 2023), 347–9.

26 Leonardo Boff, *Cry of the Earth, Cry of the Poor* (Maryknoll, NY: Orbis Books, 1997), 4.

27 Ivone Gebara, *Longing for Running Water: Ecofeminism and Liberation* (Minneapolis, MN: Fortress Press, 1999), 4–5.

28 Daniel Patrick Castillo, *An Ecological Theology of Liberation: Salvation and Political Ecology* (Maryknoll, NY: Orbis Books, 2019); Flores, "Latine Perspectives on Care for Creation," 3–38.

29 Guillermo Kerber, "Church Advocacy in Latin America: Integrating Environment in the Struggle for Justice and Human Rights," in *Cosmovision and the*

Environment: Religion and Social Conflict in Contemporary Latin America Church, ed. Evan Berry Robert Albro (New York: Routledge, 2018), 21.

30 Kerber, "Church Advocacy in Latin America," 25.

31 Ibid.

32 CELAM, "Aparecida Document," in *Documento Aparecida: V Conferencia General del Episcopado Latinoamericano y del Caribe, Documento Conclusivo* (Bogota: CELAM, 2007), Line 83.

33 Pope Francis, *Laudato Si: On Care for Our Common Home* (May 24, 2015): par. 137.

34 Ibid., par. 140.

35 See Amanda J. Baugh, *Falling in Love With Nature: The Values of Latinx Catholic Environmentalism* (New York: New York University Press, 2024).

36 Jeanette Rodriguez, "La Tierra Theologies' Contribution to Creation Theologies," in *In Our Own Voices: Latino/a Renditions of Theology*, ed. Benjamín Valentín (Maryknoll, NY: Orbis Books, 2010), 21–40.

37 *Por La Creación Faith Based Alliance*: https://www.hispanicaccess.org/what-we-do/por-la-creacion-faith-based-alliance

38 Pew Research Center, "Among U.S. Latinos, Catholicism Continues to Decline but Is Still the Largest Faith," April 2023.

14

1 Pew Research Center, Mark Hugo Lopez, Ana Gonzalez-Barrera, and Jens Manuel Krogstad, "Latinos are More Likely to Believe in the American Dream, but Most Say it is Hard to Achieve," September 11, 2018: https://www.pewresearch.org/short-reads/2018/09/11/latinos-are-more-likely-to-believe-in-the-american-dream-but-most-say-it-is-hard-to-achieve/; and Russell Contreras, "Exclusive poll: Most Latinos Believe in the American dream," *Axios, Politics and Policy*, March 24, 2022: https://www.axios.com/2022/03/24/axios-ipsos-poll-american-dream-latinos-politics.

2 Transcript: "Julian Castro's DNC Keynote Address," *NPR*, September 4, 2012: https://www.npr.org/2012/09/04/160574895/transcript-julian-castros-dnc-keynote-address.

3 Ida Miranda., "Faith Formation with Hispanic/Latino Families," in *Lifelong Faith Journal* 1.2 (Summer 2007): 22–3.

4 Transcript: "Julian Castro's DNC Keynote Address."

5 Transcript: "Julian Castro's DNC Keynote Address."

6 James Truslow Adams, *The Epic of America* (New York: Transaction Publishers, [1931] 2012), xx.

7 Ibid., 404.

8 Howard Schneiderman, "Introduction to the Transaction Edition: James Truslow Adams and the American Dream," in *The Epic of America*, ed. James Truslow Adams (New York: Transaction Publishers, [1931] 2012), xiii.

9 Samuel Bazzi, Martin Fiszbein, and Maximiliano Garcia, "The Moral Values of 'Rugged Individualism'," in *Working Paper 32433*, National Bureau of Economic Research (May 2024): 2–4.

10 James Truslow Adams, "America's Opportunity: How We Lost It and How We May Regain It" (New York: Charles Scribner's Sons, 1932).

11 Rodolfo "Corky" Gonzales, "I am Joaquin: An Epic Poem," in *Looking Out, Looking In: An Anthology of Latino Poetry*, ed. William Luis (Houston, TX: Arte Público Press, 2012), 99.

12 Juan Gonzalez, *Harvest of Empire: A History of Latinos in America* (New York: Penguin Books, 2022), 354–5.

13 Ed Morales, *Fantasy Island: Colonialism, Exploitation, and the Betrayal of Puerto Rico* (New York: Bold Type Books, 2019), 17–18.

14 Juliana Phan, "10 Facts About Latino Representation in Congress," UCLA Latino Policy and Politics Institute, October 28, 2024: https://latino.ucla.edu/research/latino-representation-in-congress/.

15 "Latino Economic Report—From the Pandemic to the Present: Forging a Path from Recovery to Prosperity," *UnidosUS*, July 2024.

16 Pew Research Center, Mohamad Moslimani, and Luis Noe-Bustamante, *Facts on Latinos in the U.S.*, August 16, 2023.

17 Michael Zweig, *The Working Class Majority: America's Best Kept Secret*, 2nd Edition (Ithaca: ILR Press/Cornell University Press, 2012), 2–3; 9–10.

18 Ruth Milkman, *Immigrant Labor and the New Precariat* (Cambridge, UK: Polity Press, 2020), 20–1.

19 Carey McWilliams, *Factories in the Fields: The Story of Migratory Labor in California* (Boston, MA: Little, Brown, and Company, 1950), 125.

20 Mario Barrera, *Race and Class in the Southwest: A Theory of Racial Inequality* (Notre Dame: University of Notre Dame Press, 1979), 39.

21 Emiliano Aguilar, "Latino Workers," in *Oxford Research Encyclopedias, American History* (Oxford: Oxford University Press, 2021), 2.

22 For a discussion of economic and political democracy, see Joerg Rieger, *Theology in the Capitalocene: Ecology, Identity, Class, and Solidarity* (Minneapolis, MN: Fortress Press, 2022), 72–4.

23 Gaston Espinosa, Virgilio Elizondo, and Jesse Miranda, *Latino Religions and Civic Activism in the United States* (New York: Oxford University Press, 2005), 5.

24 Notable Filipino labor leaders in the UFW include Philip Vera Cruz and Larry Itliong. Filipino organizers and farm workers initiated the historic 1965 Delano grape strike. See John Gregory Dunne, *Delano: The Story of the California Grape Strike* (Berkeley: University of California Press, 2008).

25 Frederick John Dalton, *The Moral Vision of César Chávez* (Maryknoll, NY: Orbis Books, 2003), 46, 85, 130, 137. Just before publication of this work, news broke regarding serious and troubling allegations of sexual abuse committed by UFW co-founder and leader César Chávez, which involved an extensive multi-year investigation by the *New York Times* and a testimony by co-founder Dolores Huerta of her own experience of abuse by Chávez. The repercussions of these developments will be felt for years to come. Prior to this, much work has been done by scholars about Chávez's problematic leadership behaviors and the internal problems that resulted in the UFW in the 1970s-80s. See Matt García, *From the Jaws of Victory: The Triumph and Tragedy of César Chávez and the Farm Worker Movement* (Berkeley: University of California

Press, 2012). My use of the United Farm Workers example has to do with the spirit of the movement at its height in the 1960s and early 1970s, which, while influenced significantly by Chávez, would not be possible without the faith, tenacity, and organizing of farm workers, their families, leaders like Dolores Huerta and countless other organizers and volunteers. These elements and the gains achieved belong to the movement and transcend any one leader.

26 Randy Shaw, *Beyond the Fields; César Chávez, The UFW, and the Struggle for Justice in the 21st Century* (Berkeley: University of California Press, 2008), 268–94.

27 Gabriela González, "Carolina Munguía and Emma Tenayuca: The Politics of Benevolence and Radical Reform," *Frontiers: A Journal of Women Studies* 24, no. 23 (2003): 220.

28 Arlene Sanchez-Walsh, "Tenayuca, Elites, and the Pecan-Shellers' Strike," in *The Pew and the Picket Line: Christianity and the American Working Class*, ed. Christopher D. Cantwell, Heath W. Carter, and Janine Giordano Drake (Champaign: University of Illinois Press, 2016), 149.

29 See Gustavo Gutiérrez, "Option for the Poor," in *Mysterium Liberationis: Fundamental Concepts of Liberation Theology*, ed. Ignacio Ellacuría and Jon Sobrino (Maryknoll, NY: Orbis Books, 1993), 235–50. There are numerous US Latine religious scholars who have engaged with the concept of economic justice issues in their work. Here I will reference Ada María Isasi-Díaz's *En La Lucha: Elaborating a Mujerista Theology* (Minneapolis, MN: Fortress Press, 2004) and Miguel A. De La Torre's *Latina/o Social Ethics: Moving Beyond Eurocentric Moral Thinking* (Waco, TX: Baylor University Press, 2010) and *The Politics of Jesús: A Hispanic Political Theology* (Lanham, MD: Rowman & Littlefield, 2015) as two key examples. However, more contemporary work needs to be done to deepen the intersections between Latine religious thought and class analysis.

15

1 For a detailed understanding of the Young Lords, see Elias Ortega-Aponte, "Young Lords Party," in *Encyclopedia on Hispanic American Religious Culture*, Vol. 2, ed. Miguel A. De La Torre (Santa Barbara, CA: ABC-CLIO, 2009), 583–5.

2 Daniel José Older, "Garbage Fires for Freedom: When Puerto Rican Activists Took Over New York's Streets," *New York Times*, October 31, 2019.

3 Emma Francis-Snyder, "The Hospital Occupation That Changed Public Health Care," *New York Times*, October 12, 2021.

4 Daniel Parra, "Young Lords reflexionan sobre protestas, racismo y violencia policial en Nueva York," *City Limits*, June 17, 2020.

5 I am grateful to Reverend John Fife, pastor emeritus of Southside Presbyterian Church, who taught me this concept as we walked the migrant trails providing food and medical attention to the undocumented. Fife is a co-founder of *No More Deaths* and was one of the founding members of the 1980s Sanctuary Movement.

6 John Fife, "Civil Initiative," in *Trails of Hope and Terror: Testimonies on Immigration*, ed. Miguel A. De La Torre (Maryknoll, NY: Orbis, 2009), 172.

7 Reinhold Niebuhr, *Moral Man and Immoral Society: A Study in Ethics and Politics* (New York: Scribner, 1932), 128.

8 Paul Ramsey, *Christian Ethics and the Sit-In* (New York: Association, 1961), 48–9.

9 John Rawls, *A Theory of Justice* (Cambridge, MA: Belknap Press of Harvard University Press, 1971), 453–7.

10 James M. Gustafson, *Can Ethics Be Christian?* (Chicago: University of Chicago Press, 1975), 119–20.

11 Stanley Hauerwas, *After Christendom? How the Church Is to Behave if Freedom, Justice, and a Christian Nation Are Bad Ideas* (Nashville, TN: Abingdon, 1991), 45.

12 "Act according to that maxim which thou couldst at the same time will an universal law." See Immanuel Kant, *The Metaphysics of Ethics*, trans. J. W. Semple (Edinburgh: Thomas Clark, 1836 [1785]), 54.

13 "Our wine from plantains; and if it turns out sour it's our wine!" José Martí, "Nuestra América," *El Partido Liberal*, January 30, 1891 (*Obras Completa* 6:20).

14 James C. Scott, *Domination and the Arts of Resistance* (New Haven, CT: Yale University Press, 1990), 162–6.

15 Victor W. Turner, *The Ritual Process: Structure and Anti-Structure* (Chicago: Aldine, 1969), 125–8.

16 Important to note that most trickster figures are portrayed as male, even though trickery and deceit are not limited to one gender—no doubt a historical and/or cultural sexist implication might be that women, as female tricksters, are unable to outwit others.

17 This is the argument I make in an earlier book. See Miguel A De La Torre and Albert Hernández, *The Quest for the Historical Satan* (Minneapolis, MN: Fortress Press, 2011), 198–214.

18 For over a decade I have been calling for an *ethics para joder*. For a fuller understanding of this ethical paradigm, see Miguel A. De La Torre, *Latina/o Social Ethics: Moving Beyond Eurocentric Moral Thinking* (Waco, TX: Baylor University Press, 2010); and De La Torre, *Embracing Hopelessness* (Minneapolis, MN: Fortress Press, 2017).

16

1 Edwin David Aponte, *¡Santo!: Varieties of Latino/a Spirituality* (Maryknoll, NY: Orbis Books, 2012), 45.

2 Dennis Kelley, "How are Indigenous Narratives and Oral Traditions Like Texts?" in *Indigenous Religious Traditions in Five Minutes*, ed. Molly H. Bassett and Natalie Avalos (Bristol, CT: Equinox Publishing, 2022), 226–8.

3 Vincent L. Wimbush, *White Men's Magic: Scripturalization as Slavery* (New York: Oxford University Press, 2012), 3.

4 See Timothy Beal, *The Rise and Fall of the Bible: The Unexpected History of an Accidental Book* (Boston, MI: Houghton Mifflin Harcourt, 2011).

5 Eduardo Galeano, *Memory of Fire: Genesis*, trans. Cedric Belfrage (New York: W.W. Norton, 1985), 41.

6 Pablo Richard, "Hermenútica biblica india: Revelacíon de Dios en las religiones indígenas y en la Biblia (Después de 500 años de dominación)," in *Sentido histórico del V Centenario (1492–1992)*, ed. G. Meléndez (San José, Costa Rica: CEHILA-DEI, 1992), 45–6; and Elsa Tamez, "The Bible and the Five Hundred Years of Conquest," in *Voices form the Margin: Interpreting the Bible in the Third World*, ed. R. S. Sugirtharajah, rev. ed. (Maryknoll, NY: Orbis Books, 2006), 18.

7 Pablo A. Jiménez "The Bible: A Hispanic Perspective," in *Teología En Conjunto: A Collaborative Hispanic Protestant Theology*, ed. J. D. Rodríguez and L. I. Martell-Otero (Louisville, KY: Westminster/John Knox, 1997), 67.

8 Elaine Penagos, "How We Heal: Genealogical Narratives of Healing among San Lázaro Devotees," *Genealogy* 5, no. 1 (2021): 18.

9 Angela Parker, *If God Still Breathes, Why Can't I?: Black Lives Matter and Biblical Authority* (Grand Rapids, MI: Eerdmans, 2021), 22.

10 Miguel A. De La Torre, *Reading the Bible from the Margins* (Maryknoll, NY: Orbis Books, 2002), 15.

11 Wimbush, *White Men's Magic*, 42.

12 See Jacqueline M. Hidalgo, *Revelation in Aztlán: Scriptures, Utopias, and the Chicano Movement* (New York: Palgrave Macmillan, 2016).

13 Charles H. Long, *Significations: Signs, Symbols, and Images in the Interpretation of Religion* (Philadelphia, PA: Fortress Press, 1986), 78.

14 José Esteban Muñoz, *Cruising Utopia: The Then and There of Queer Futurity* (New York: New York University Press, 2009), 1.

15 Cherríe Moraga, ed., *The Last Generation: Prose and Poetry* (Boston, MI: South End Press, 1993), 190.

16 Ibid., 150; Gloria Anzaldúa, *Borderlands/La Frontera: The New Mestiza*, 4th ed. (San Francisco, CA: Aunt Lute Books, 2012), 19.

17 Francisco Lozada, Jr., *Towards a Latino/a Biblical Interpretation* (Atlanta, GA: Society of Biblical Literature Press, 2017), 113–16.

18 Jean-Pierre Ruiz, *Readings from the Edges: The Bible and the People on the Move* (Maryknoll, NY: Orbis Books, 2011), 115–22.

19 Leticia Guardiola-Sáenz, "Borderless Women and the Word: A Cultural Reading of Matthew 15:21–28," *Semeia* 78 (1997): 57–73.

20 Manuel Villalobos Mendoza, "Anzaldúa and the Ethiopian Eunuch: Border-Crossing and the Reimagining of Sacred Texts," in *Bible Trouble: Queer Reading at the Boundaries of Biblical Scholarship*, ed. Teresa J. Hornsby and Ken Stone (Atlanta, GA: Society of Biblical Literature Press, 2011), 215–30.

21 Gregory L. Cuéllar, *Resacralizing the Other at the US-Mexico Border: A Borderland Hermeneutic* (New York: Routledge, 2020), 5.

17

1 I primarily refer to the film *De cierta manera* (1974) by Sara Gómez and the literary work of Antonio Benitez-Rojo, *The Repeating Island: The Caribbean and the Postmodern Perspective, 2nd Edition* (Durham, NC: Duke University Press, 1996).

2 Judith Gleason, "Oya in the Company of Saints," *Journal of the American Academy of Religion* 68, no. 2 (2000): 270.

3 Miguel A. De La Torre, *Santería: The Beliefs and Rituals of a Growing Religion in America* (Grand Rapids, MI: Wm. B. Eerdmans, 2004), 130.

4 Ibid., 53, 77.

5 Aisha M. Beliso-De Jesús, *Electric Santería: Racial and Sexual Assemblages of Transnational Religion* (New York: Columbia University Press, 2015), 92, 134.

6 M. De La Torre, *Santería*, 49, 52,109.

7 Gleason, "Oya in the Company of Saints," 273, 275.

8 M. De La Torre, *Santería*, 13, 59.

9 Ibid., 65, 75, 76, 233.

10 Gleason, "Oya in the Company of Saints," 276.

11 M. De La Torre, *Santería*, 76, 83; Beliso-De Jesús, *Electric Santeria*, 92.

12 Solimar Otero, *Archives of Conjure: Stories of the Dead in Afrolatinx Cultures* (New York: Columbia University Press, 2020), 13.

13 Beliso-De Jesús *Santería*, 76.

14 Beliso-de Jesús, *Electric Santería*, 144.

15 M. De La Torre, *Santería*, 20.

16 Ibid., 23.

17 Gleason, "Oya in the Company of Saints," 275.

18 Ibid., 275.

19 Ibid., 266.

20 Pierre Schaeffer, *Treatise on Musical Objects: An Essay Across Disciplines* (Oakland: University of California Press), 73.

21 Michel Chion, *Audio-Vision: Sound on Screen*, Second Edition (New York: New York University Press, 2017), 10.

22 Michel Chion, *Film: A Sound Art*, trans. Claudia Gorbman (New York: Columbia University Press, 2009), 468. "A term more accurate than viewer or spectator to emphasize that the experience of films, television, or other audiovisual texts involves sigh and hearing in interaction."

23 See Kevin J. Donnelly, *Occult Aesthetics: Synchronization in Sound Film* (New York: Oxford University Press, 2014).

24 Schaeffer, *Treatise on Musical Objects*, 13, 90.

25 Pierre Schaeffer, "Acousmatics," in *Audio Culture: Readings in Modern Music*, ed. Cristoph Cox and Daniel Warner (New York: Continuum International Publishing Group, 2006), 80.

26 Schaeffer, *Treatise on Musical Objects*, 90.

27 Gilles Deleuze, *Cinema 2: The Time-Image*. Translated by Hugh Tomlinson and Robert Galeta (Minneapolis: University of Minnesota Press, 1989), 278.

28 Otero, *Archives of Conjure*, 24, 178.

29 Ibid.

30 Ibid., 80–1.

31 M. De La Torre, *Santería*, 3.

32 Beliso-De Jesús, *Electric Santería*, 4.

33 Ibid., 53, 54.

34 Ibid., 45.

35 Ibid., 2.

36 Steven Connor, *Dumbstruck: A Cultural History of Ventriloquism* (New York: Oxford University Press, 2000), 4.

37 Donnelly, *Occult Aesthetics*, 70.

38 Schaeffer, *Treatise on Musical Objects*, 73.

39 Beliso-De Jesús, *Electric Santería*, 43.

40 Ibid., 78.

41 Ibid., 43, 48.

42 Ibid., 24, 42, 65.

43 Ibid., 61.

44 Statistics provided by Slavevoyages.org, accessed July 29, 2025.

45 Katrina Dyonne Thompson, *Ring Shout, Wheel About: The Racial Politics of Music and Dance in North American Slavery* (Urbana: University of Illinois Press, 2014), 48, 169.

46 Matthew D. Morrison, *Blacksound: Making Race and Popular Music in the United States* (Berkeley: University of California Press, 2024), 30.

47 Jacqueline A. Avila, *Cinesonidos: Film Music and National Identity During Mexico's Época de Oro* (New York: Oxford University Press, 2019), 41 quoting Alejandro Madrid; and Robin D. Moore, *Nationalizing Blackness: Afrocubanismo and Artistic Revolution in Havana*, 1920–1940 (Pittsburgh, PA: University of Pittsburgh Press, 1997), 42.

48 Moore, *Nationalizing Blackness*, 42.

49 Ebony Marie Bailey, "Codings of Blackness in Mexican Cinema: An Analysis of *La Negrada*," *Publication of the Afro-Latin/American Research Association (PALARA)* 23, no. 8 (2019): 1–9.

50 Allyson Hobbs, "Passing," in *Keywords for African American Studies*, ed. Erica R. Edwards, Roderick A. Ferguson, and Jeffrey O.G. Ogbar (New York: New York University Press, 2018), 133–5.

51 Karen M. Bowdre, "Passing Films and the Illusion of Racial Equality," *Black Camera* 5, no. 2 (2014): 21–43.

52 The back page of an event program from the *Exposición Bibliografica Iconografica: Andrés Eloy Blanco En el XXV Aniversario de su Muerte*, 21 de Mayo de 1980 features a reproduction of the poem in Blanco's apparent handwriting, signed by the author with the date "1936." Appearing beneath is the following dedication: "*Copia para Estrella Girón Cordialmente en Caracas 7 de diciembre 1938 Andre Eloy Blanco.*"

53 Arvelo (n.d.), in Delgadillo, "Singing 'Angelitos Negros," 410.

54 Andrés Eloy Blanco, "*Pintame angelitos negros*" appears as the fifth poem on the recording, from the collection "La Juanbimbada": https://lccn.loc.gov/93842789.

55 Bailey, "Codings of Blackness in Mexican Cinema," 1–9.

56 Julio Marzán, "Introduction: In the Mingling Grain," in *Selected Poems / Poesía Selecta: Luis Palés Matos*, ed. and trans. Julio Marzán (Houston, TX: Arte Público Press, 2000), xi, xiv.

57 Luis Palés Matos, "Ñañigo al Cielo," in *Selected Poems / Poesía Selecta: Luis Palés Matos*, ed. and trans. Julio Marzán (Houston, TX: Arte Público Press, 2000), 41.

58 Gleason, "Oya in the Company of Saints," 274.

59 I, am riffing on Clifford Geertz' *The Interpretation of Cultures: Selected Essays* (New York: Basic Books, 1973).

60 Blanco's poem graphically states that the boy wasted away.

61 Vanessa Knights, "Modernity, Modernization and Melodrama: The Bolero in Mexico in the 1930s and 1940s," in *Contemporary Latin American Cultural Studies*, ed. Stephen Hart and Richard Young (London: Routledge, 2014), 132. Knights describes the song as "the famous bolero 'Angelitos negros' [Little Black Angels]."

62 The Discography of American Historical Recordings (DAHR) is part of the American Discography Project, funded by the National Endowment for the Humanities, the University of California Santa Barbara Library, and the William R. Moran Fund for Recorded Sound. https://adp.library.ucsb.edu/index.php.

63 Manuel Alvarez Maciste, *Angelitos Negros (Angeli Negri): Canción Moruna*, Italian text by Larici-Testoni, original text by Andrés Eloy Blanco (Milano, IT: Edizioni Southern Music, 1949), 4.

64 Aparicio, *Listening to Salsa*, 175.

65 Delgadillo, "Singing "Angelitos Negros," 407–30.

66 Pedro Heredia, *Antonio Machin* (Barcelona: Editorial Miguel Arimany S.A., 1976), 99.

67 Mark Pedelty, "The Bolero: The Birth, Life, and Decline of Mexican Modernity," *Latin American Music Review* 20, no. 1 (1999): 41.

68 Frances R. Aparicio, *Listening to Salsa: Gender, Latin Popular Music, and Puerto Rican Cultures* (Hanover, NH: Wesleyan University Press, 1998), 175.

69 Marilyn Miller, "The Soul Has No Color" But the Skin Does: Angelitos Negros and the Uses of Blackface on the Mexican Silver Screen, ca. 1950," in *Global Soundtracks: Worlds of Film Music*, ed. Mark Slobin (Middletown, CT: Wesleyan University Press, 2008), 245.

70 Puerto Rican musician and poet Fortunato Vizcarrondo described the question powerfully in "*Y tu abuela donde 'eta?*"—And where is your grandmother? (1942) a poem demanding to sonically reveal how the question would be answered with the eye.

71 W.E.B. Du Bois, *The Souls of Black Folk* (Greenwich, CT: Fawcett Publications, [1903] 1961), 12.

72 Herbert Thurston, "Hail Mary," in *The Catholic Encyclopedia* (New York: Robert Appleton, 1910).

73 J, "Antiphon." in *The Catholic Encyclopedia* (New York: Robert Appleton, 1907).

74 Miguel A. De La Torre, "Ochún: (N)Either the (M)Other of All Cubans (n)or the Bleached Virgin," *Journal of the American Academy of Religion* 69, no. 4 (2001): 837–61.

75 See Theresa Delgadillo, *Geographies of Relation: Diasporas and Borderlands in the Americas* (Ann Arbor: University of Michigan Press, 2024); Theresa Delgadillo,

"Singing 'Angelitos Negros;" and Idem, " 'Angelitos Negros' and Transnational Racial Identifications."

18

1 The term "Abya Yala" is a Kuna Tule word, which translates to "land in its full maturity." It has been used since the 1980s as a unifying Indigenous term to describe the American continent. See Emilio del Valle Escalante, "Self-Determination: A Perspective from Abya Yala," in *Restoring Indigenous Self-Determination: Theoretical and Practical Approaches*, ed. Marc Woons (Bristol, GB: E-International Relations, 2014), 101.

2 See Nestor Medina, "The Doctrine of Discovery, LatinXo Theoethics, and Human Rights," *Journal of Hispanic/Latino Theology* 21, no. 2 (2019): 4–10.

3 See Tony Castanha, "The Doctrine of Discovery: The Legacy and Continuing Impact of Christian "Discovery" on American Indian Populations," *American Indian Culture and Research Journal* 39, no. 3 (2015): 43–5; See Joy H. Greenberg, "The Doctrine of Discovery as a Doctrine of Domination," *Journal for the Study of Religion, Nature & Culture* 10, no. 2 (2016): 228–35; and Nestor Medina, "The Doctrine of Discovery, LatinXo Theoethics, and Human Rights," *Journal of Hispanic/Latino Theology* 21, no. 2 (2019): 4–10.

4 Castanha, "The Doctrine of Discovery," 43–5

5 See Castanha, "The Doctrine of Discovery," 43–5; Greenberg, "The Doctrine of Discovery as a Doctrine of Domination," 228–35; Ali Friedberg, "Reconsidering the Doctrine of Discovery: Spanish Land Acquisition in Mexico (1521–1821)" *Wisconsin International Law Journal* 17 (1999): 87; and Robert J. Miller, "The Doctrine of Discovery: The International Law of Colonialism," *Indigenous Peoples' Journal of Law, Culture & Resistance* 5, no. 1 (2019): 35–7.

6 Pope Nicholas V, *Dum Diversas*, June 18, 1452—as quoted in Medina, "The Doctrine of Discovery, LatinXo Theoethics," 62.

7 Castanha, "The Doctrine of Discovery," 43–5; Medina, "The Doctrine of Discovery, LatinXo Theoethics," 4–10; and Miller, "The Doctrine of Discovery," 35–7.

8 Castanha, "The Doctrine of Discovery," 43–5.

9 See Greenberg, "The Doctrine of Discovery as a Doctrine of Domination," 228–35.

10 See Castanha, "The Doctrine of Discovery," 41–64; Greenberg, "The Doctrine of Discovery as a Doctrine of Domination," 236–7; Ali Friedberg, "Reconsidering the Doctrine of Discovery"; and Tonya Gonnelia Frichner, "The 'Preliminary Study' on the Doctrine of Discovery," *Pace Environmental Law Review* 28, no. 1 (2010): 339.

11 Ramona Beltrán, et al., "Salud, Cultura, Tradición: Preliminary Findings from an Alcohol and Other Drugs and HIV Needs Assessment in Urban 'Mexican American Indian' Communities," *Journal of Ethnic & Cultural Diversity in Social Work* 30, no. 1–2 (2020): 3–6; and Susy J. Zepeda, *Queering Mesoamerican Diasporas: Remembering Xicana Indígena Ancestries* (Champaign: University of Illinois Press, 2022).

12 See Assembly of First Nations, "Dismantling the Doctrine of Discovery." (Ottawa, ON: Assembly of First Nations, January 2018); and also Holy See Press Office Bulletin Summary, "Joint Statement of the Dicasteries for Culture and Education and for

Promoting Integral Human Development on the 'Doctrine of Discovery'" (Vatican City: Vatican, March 30, 2023).

13 Susto is a Spanish word that literally translates to English as "fright," "fear," "scare," or "shock." It has been explored by many disciplines from health to social sciences, and while there is not a singular shared definition or description of susto, there is general understanding of the term to describe multiple levels of acute or complex traumas that impact health and well-being. The DSM-5 defines susto as "a cultural explanation of distress and misfortune in Latin America that refers to an illness attributed to a terrifying event that causes the soul to leave the body and leads to unhappiness and illness, as well as difficulties in performing key social functions." See Fanny Beatriz Martínez-Radl, Devon Emerson Hinton, and Ulrich Stangier, "Susto as a Cultural Conceptualization of Distress: Existing Research and Aspects to Consider for Future Investigations," *Transcultural Psychiatry* 60, no. 4 (2023): 690. It has also been described in collective terms to describe trauma and particularly profound, unresolved intergenerational trauma. Particularly, the term "susto profundo" has been used to describe this collective trauma in Indigenous Latine communities. See Susy Zepeda, "Decolonizing Xicana/x Studies: Healing the Susto of De-Indigenization," *Aztlán: A Journal of Chicano Studies* 45, no. 1 (2020): 225–41.

For more explorations of susto and susto profundo, see Elena Avila and Joy Parker, *Woman Who Glows in the Dark: A Curandera Reveals Traditional Aztec Secrets of Physical and Spiritual Health* (New York: Penguin, 2000); David Atekpatzin Young, *A Magic Feather: The Science and Theory of Chicano Traditional Healing Practices of Aztlán* (Boulder, CO: Calmecaztlan Press, 2020), 193–230; Zepeda, *Queering Mesoamerican Diasporas*, 3–10; and Zepeda, *Decolonizing Xicana/x Studies*, 226.

14 See Avila and Parker, *Woman Who Glows in the Dark*; Young, *A Magic Feather*, 193; Zepeda, Decolonizing Xicana/x Studies; Saraliza Anzaldúa, *Monsters and Mestizos: Mestizaje as White Supremacy and the Monsterization of Indigeneity* (Los Angeles: University of California, 2023), 225–41; and Patrisia Gonzales, *Red Medicine: Traditional Indigenous Rites of Birthing and Healing* (Tucson: University of Arizona Press, 2012).

15 See Maria Yellow Horse Brave Heart, "The Return to the Sacred Path: Healing the Historical Trauma and Historical Unresolved Grief Response among the Lakota through a Psychoeducational Group Intervention," *Smith College Studies in Social Work* 68, no. 3 (1998): 287–305; Teresa Evans-Campbell, "Historical Trauma in American Indian/Native Alaska Communities: A Multilevel Framework for Exploring Impacts on Individuals, Families, and Communities," *Journal of Interpersonal Violence* 23, no. 3 (March 2008): 316–38; and Karina L. Walters, Jane M. Simoni, and Teresa Evans-Campbell, "Substance Use Among American Indians and Alaska Natives: Incorporating Culture in an 'Indigenist' Stress-Coping Paradigm," *Public Health Reports* 117, Suppl 1 (2002): S104–17.

16 See Maria Yellow Horse Brave Heart, "The Return to the Sacred Path"; Evans-Campbell, "Historical Trauma in American Indian/Native Alaska Communities," 287–305; Eduardo Duran, et al., "Healing the American Indian Soul Wound," in *International Handbook of Multigenerational Legacies of Trauma*, ed. Yael Danieli (New York: Plenum Press, 1998): 341–54; and See Karina L Walters and Jane M. Simoni, "Reconceptualizing Native Women's Health: An 'Indigenist' Stress-Coping Model," *American Journal of Public Health* 92, no. 4 (April 2002): 520–4.

17 See Antonio Estrada, "Mexican-Americans and Historical Trauma Theory: A Theoretical Perspective," *Journal of Ethnicity in Substance Abuse* 8, no. 3 (2009): 330–40.

18 See Ramona Beltrán, Antonia Rose-Garriga Alvarez, and Angela R. Fernandez. "I See Myself Strong: A Description of An Expressive Poetic Method to Amplify Two-Spirit, Lesbian, Gay, Bisexual, Trans, Queer Indigenous Youth Experiences in a Culture-Centered HIV Prevention Curriculum," *Genealogy* 7, no. 3 (2023): 55–71; and Angela Fernandez and Ramona Beltran, " 'Wherever I Go, I Have It Inside of Me': Indigenous Cultural Dance Narratives as Substance Abuse and HIV Prevention in an Urban Danza Mexica Community," *Frontiers in Public Health* 9 (2022): 1–16.

19 See Roxanne Dunbar-Ortiz, *An Indigenous People's History of the United States* (Boston: Beacon Press, 2014); and Justyna Olko, Language Attitudes and Educational Opportunities: Challenging a History of Oppression and Assimilation Among Indigenous Communities in Mexico," *Sámi dutkansearvvi journála* 1 (2019): 3–8.

20 See Estrada, "Mexican-Americans and Historical Trauma Theory," 330–40; Manuel Barajas, "Colonial Dislocations and Incorporation of Indigenous Migrants from Mexico to the United States," *American Behavioral Scientist* 58, no. 1 (2014): 330–40; and Shannon Speed, "Structures of Settler Capitalism in Abya Yala," *American Quarterly* 69, no. 4 (December 2017): 783–90.

21 See Martínez, "The Language, Genealogy, and Classification of 'Race' in Colonial Mexico"; Zepeda, "Decolonizing Xicana/x Studies," 225–41; and Michelle Garcia-Olp, *How Colonization Impacts Identity Through the Generations: A Closer Look at Historical Trauma and Education*, dissertation (Denver: University of Denver, 2018), 56–77.

22 See Dunbar-Ortiz, *An Indigenous People's History of the United States*; Martínez, "The Language, Genealogy, and Classification of 'Race' in Colonial Mexico"; and Zepeda, "Decolonizing Xicana/x Studies," 225–41.

23 See Friedberg, "Reconsidering the Doctrine of Discovery," 87–89; and Martínez, "The Language, Genealogy, and Classification of 'Race' in Colonial Mexico."

24 See Zepeda, "Decolonizing Xicana/x Studies," 225–41.

25 See Zepeda, "Decolonizing Xicana/x Studies," 225–41; Mónica G. Moreno Figueroa, "Naming Ourselves: Recognising Racism and Mestizaje in Mexico," in *Contesting Recognition: Culture, Identity and Citizenship*, ed. Janice McLaughlin, Peter Phillimore, and Diane Richardson (London: Palgrave Macmillan, 2011), 122–43; Jill Fleuriet, "Health and Health Care Problems Among the Kumiai of San Antonio Necua and Their Indigenous Relatives in Baja California: Reflections of Poverty, Marginality, and a History of Colonization," *California Journal of Health Promotion* 1, no. 1 (2003): 140–57; and Susan Deans-Smith and Ilona Katzew, "Introduction: The Alchemy of Race in Mexican America," in *Race Classification: The Case of Mexican America*, ed. Susan Deans-Smith and Ilona Katzew (Stanford, CA: Stanford University Press, 2009), 1–24.

26 See Saraliza Anzaldúa, *Monsters and Mestizos*; and Zepeda, "Decolonizing Xicana/x Studies," 225–41.

27 See Saskias Casanova, Brendan H. O'Connor, and Vanessa Anthony-Stevens, "Ecologies of Adaptation for Mexican Indigenous Im/Migrant Children and Families in the United States: Implications for Latino Studies," *Latino Studies* 14 (July 2016): 192–213.

28 See Alfonso Gonzales, *Reform Without Justice: Latino Migrant Politics and the Homeland Security State* (New York: Oxford University Press, 2013).

29 See Miguel Antonio Levario, *Militarizing the Border: When Mexicans Became the Enemy* (College Station: Texas A&M University Press, 2012); Nicholas P. De Genova and Nathalie Peutz, *The Deportation Regime: Sovereignty, Space, and the Freedom* *of Movement* (Durham, NC: Duke University Press, 2010); Randy Capps, et al., *Implications of Immigration Enforcement Activities for the Well-Being of Children in Immigrant Families* (Washington, DC: Urban Institute and Migration Policy Institute, 2015); and Ariel G. Ruiz Soto, Colleen Putzel-Kavanaugh, and Doris Meissner, *Shifting Realities at the U.S.-Mexico Border: Immigration Enforcement and Control in a Fast-Evolving Landscape* (Washington, DC: Migration Policy Institute, 2024).

30 See Ramona Beltrán, et al., "I See Myself Strong," 55–71; Alfredo Mirandé, "Hombres Mujeres: An Indigenous Third Gender," *Men and Masculinities* 19, no. 4 (2016): 384–409: and Rosa-Linda Fregoso and Cynthia Bejarano, eds., *Terrorizing Women: Feminicide in the Americas* (Durham, NC: Duke University Press, 2010).

31 See James Lockhart, *The Nahuas After the Conquest: A Social and Cultural History of the Indians of Central Mexico, Sixteenth Through Eighteenth Centuries* (Stanford, CA: Stanford University Press, 1994); Ramón Antonio Martínez and Melissa Mesinas, "Linguistic Motherwork in the Zapotec Diaspora: Zapoteca Mothers' Perspectives on Indigenous Language Maintenance," *Association of Mexican American Educators Journal* 13, no. 2 (June 2019): 122–44; and Cueponcaxochtl D. Sandoval, et al., "Warrior Butterflies Walking with the Ancestors: A Longitudinal Study of Indigenous Youth Becoming Leaders of Social Justice," in *Decolonial Feminist Praxis: Centering Knowledge & Resistance at the Margins*, ed. A. I. Fukushima and K. M. Quick Hall (Champaign: University of Illinois Press, at Press).

32 See Walters and Simoni, "Reconceptualizing Native Women's Health," 520–4; Walters, et al., "Substance Use Among American Indians and Alaska Natives," S104–17; and Evans-Campbell, "Historical Trauma in American Indian/Native Alaska Communities," 316–38.

33 See Walters, et al., "Substance Use Among American Indians and Alaska Natives," S104–17.

34 See Beltrán, et al., "Salud, Cultura, Tradición," 62–79; Fernandez and Beltran, "Wherever I Go, I Have It Inside of Me," 1–16; and Walters, et al., "Substance Use Among American Indians and Alaska Natives," S104–17.

35 Evans-Campbell, "Historical Trauma in American Indian/Native Alaska Communities," 316–38; Nathaniel V. Mohatt, et al., "Assessment of Awareness of Connectedness as a Culturally-Based Protective Factor for Alaska Native Youth," *Cultural Diversity & Ethnic Minority Psychology* 17, no. 4 (October 2011): 444–55; and Jessica Saniguq Ullrich, "For The Love of Our Children: An Indigenous Connectedness Framework," *AlterNative: An International Journal of Indigenous Peoples* 15, no. 2 (2019): 121–30.

19

1 "Indigenous Tribes of San Antonio, Texas," American Library Association: www.ala.org/aboutala/indigenous-tribes-san-antonio-texas.

2 "Historical Timeline," Tāp Pīlam Coahuiltecan Nation: https://tappilam.org/our-history/.

3 Patrick Wolfe, "Settler Colonialism and the Elimination of the Native," *Journal of Genocide Research* 8, no. 4 (2006): 387.

4 David Zamora Casas, *Cuentos Grotto,* 2007, paint mural, 15′ × 11′ × 3′, Downtown Public Art, San Antonio, TX. For further reflection about the fluidity of Latine identities and borders, see María Del Socorro Castañeda-Liles, *Our Lady of Everyday Life: La Virgen de Guadalupe and the Catholic Imagination of Mexican Women in America* (Oxford: Oxford University Press, 2018).

5 "Ríos de agua viva" is an adaptation of a line in a well-known Spanish Pentecostal *corito* titled, "Yo tengo gozo en mi alma," source unknown.

6 Gloria E. Chacón, "Example of Indigenous Erasure Among Latinx Community," *Latino Studies* 15, no. 2 (2017): 183.

7 Natalia Molina, *How Race is Made in America: Immigration, Citizenship, and the Historical Power of Racial Scripts* (Berkeley: University of California Press, 2014), 23–6, 66.

8 Ibid., 26.

9 Sucheng Chan, *Asian American Studies Now: A Critical Reader* (New Brunswick, NJ: Rutgers University Press), 214.

10 Molina, *How Race is Made,* 26.

11 Ibid., 34.

12 Ibid., 5.

13 Ian Haney Lopez, *White by Law: The Legal Construction of Race* (New York: New York University Press, 2006).

14 Lisa A. Flores, "Constructing Rhetorical Borders: Peons, Illegal Aliens, and Competing Narratives of Immigration," *Critical Studies in Media Communication* 20, no. 4 (2003): 364.

15 "Refugees and Asylum," U.S. Citizenship and Immigration Services: www.uscis.gov/humanitarian/refugees-asylum.

16 "Water Facts & Impacts," Remember the River Office of Equity in San Antonio, TX": https://www.sanantonio.gov/Remember-the-River/Get-the-Facts/Water-Facts-and-Impacts.

17 Albinson Linares, "Invisible and Unaccounted for: Why Some Migrant Deaths on the Border Aren't Recorded," *NBC News*, December 4, 2024.

18 Pew Research Center, Stephanie Kramer and Yunping Tong, *The Religious Composition of the World's Migrants*, August 19, 2024.

19 Ibid. Pew Research sourced these numbers from the United Nations' "International Migrant Stock 2020" Report and the Pew religious estimates based on the U.S. 2020 Census and a survey of 270 participants.

20 Pew Research Center, Jens Manuel Krogstad, and Joshua Alvarado, *Among U.S. Latinos, Catholicism Continues to Decline but Is Still the Largest Faith*, April 13, 2023.

21 See Rosa Linda Fregoso, "Toward a Planetary Civil Society," in *Women and Migration in the U.S.-Mexico Borderlands: A Reader,* ed. Denise A. Segura and Patricia Zavella (Durham, NC: Duke University Press, 2007), 35.

22 Ibid., 53.

23 Shirlene Soto, "Tres Modelos Culturales: La Virgen de Guadalupe, La Malinche, y La Llorona," *Fem* 48 (1986): 13–16.

24 Annita Lucchesi, *Taaqtam Müüy'müy'k - Hidden Bodies: MMIWG2 and MMIP of Central and Southern California* (Arcata, CA: Sovereign Bodies Institute, in partnership with the San Manuel Band of Mission Indians, 2023), 46.

25 Ibid., 41.

26 Pew Research Center, Kramer and Tong, *Religious Composition.*

27 Transgender Law Center, *Report on Human Rights Conditions of Transgender Women in Mexico* (Ithaca, NY: Cornell University Law School LGBT Clinic, 2016), 5, 22–3.

28 Ibid., 28. See also See Duaa Eldeib, Jodi S. Cohen, and Melissa Sanchez, "Records Reveal 'Lax' Supervision, Sexual Activity at Chicago-Area Shelters Housing Immigrant Children," ProPublica, August 2, 2018: https://www.propublica.org/article/heartland-chicago-immigration-shelters-lax-supervision-sexual-activity.

29 "UNCAGED ART," UTEP Institute of Oral History, April 13, 2019–December 14, 2019, https://www.utep.edu/centennial-museum/museum/past-exhibits/uncaged-art.html.

30 Fregoso, *Toward a Planetary Society,* 54.

31 Jonathan E. Calvillo, *The Saints of Santa Ana: Faith and Ethnicity in a Mexican Majority City* (Oxford: Oxford University Press, 2020), 10.

32 Barbara Andrea Sostaita, *Sanctuary Everywhere: The Fugitive Sacred in the Sonoran Desert* (Durham, NC: Duke University Press, 2024), 168.

33 Luis Ferré-Sadurní, "8 Months Inside New York's Migrant Shelters: Fear, Joy and Hope." *The New York Times*, December 23, 2024.

20

1 Pew Research Center, "Among U.S. Latinos, Catholicism Continues to Decline but Is Still the Largest Faith," April 2023.

2 Robert P. Jones, Daniel Cox, and Juhem Navarro-Rivera, "The 2013 Hispanic Values Survey: How Shifting Religious Identities and Experiences are Influencing Hispanic Approaches to Politics," *Public Religion Research Institute*, September 27, 2013.

3 Gastón Espinosa, "Nones, No Religious Preference, No Religion and the Misclassification of Latino Religious Identity," *Religions* 14, no. 3 (2023): 420. Gastón Espinosa contends, for example, that among the surveyed who selected "no religion" or "none" are Latine Pentecostals and *evangélicos* who have a negative association with the word "religion."

4 Viola Teisenhoffer, "De la 'Nebulosa Místico-Esotérica' al circuito alternativo," in *Raíces en Movimiento: prácticas religiosas tradicionales en contextos translocales*, ed. Kali Argyriadis, Renée de la Torre, Cristina Gutiérrez Zuñiga, and Aguilar Ros (Ciudad de Mexico: Centro de estudios mexicanos y centroamericanos, 2008), 45.

5 Pew Research Center, "Religious 'Nones' in America: Who They Are and What They Believe," January 2024.

6 Ibid.; cf. Russell Contreras, "Latino atheists, non-religious grow," *Axios*, August 25, 2022.

7 Tomoko Masuzawa, *The Invention of World Religions: Or, How European Universalism Was Preserved in the Language of Pluralism* (Chicago: University of Chicago Press, 2005), 27.

8 Françoise Morin, "Conclusión: Indianidad y Estado," in *Indianidad, etnocidio e indigenismo en América latina*, ed. Instituto Indigenista Interamericano (Ciudad de Mexico: Centro de estudios mexicanos y centroamericanos, 2019), loc 6434ff.

9 See: Bruce Albert et al., *Indianidad, etnocidio e indigenismo en América latina*, ed. Instituto Indigenista Interamericano (Ciudad de Mexico: Centro de estudios mexicanos y centroamericanos, 2019); Jacques Galinier, "Indio de estado versus indio nacional en la mesoamérica moderna," in *Raíces en Movimiento: prácticas religiosas tradicionales en contextos translocales*, ed. Kali Argyriadis, et al. (Ciudad de Mexico: Centro de estudios mexicanos y centroamericanos, 2008); Julia González, "El 12 de octubre, Latinoamerica se viste de indígena (con orgullo)," *Público* (October 11, 2017); and Kristen Martinez-Gugerli, "A New 'Indigenismo'? The Revival of Indigenous Culture and Pride in Latin America," *Panoramas* (March 27, 2018).

10 Françoise Morin, "Conclusión: Indianidad y Estado," loc. 6451–6561 [Translation from Spanish mine].

11 Ibid.

12 For Mariátegui, see Lilian Calles Barger, *The World Come of Age: An Intellectual History of Liberation Theology* (New York: Oxford University Press, 2018), 204–5; Maura Brighenti, "Disputando la tierra: El indigenismo de Mariátegui entre crítica de la colonialidad y búsqueda de lo común," *Intersticios de la política y la cultura: intervenciones latinoamericanas, Revista de la Cátedra de Filosofía Argentina y Latinoamericana, Escuela de Filosofía* 5, no. 10 (2016): 51–75; Eugenio Chang-Rodríguez, "José Carlos Mariátegui y la polémica del indigenismo," *América Sin Nombre*, nos. 13–14 (2009): 103; Sergio Armando Gallegos-Ordorica, "Decolonizing Mariátegui as a Prelude to Decolonizing Latin American Philosophy," in *Decolonizing American Philosophy*, ed. Corey McCall and Phillip McReynolds (Albany: State University of New York Press, 2021), 229–50. For Martí, see Miguel A. De La Torre, *José Martí's Liberative Political Theology* (Nashville, TN: Vanderbilt University Press, 2021), 115–20; *Reading José Martí from the Margins* (Lanham, MD: Rowman & Littlefield, 2024); Jacoby Adeshei Carter, "Alain Locke, José Vasconcelos, and José Martí, on Race, Nationality, and Cosmopolitanism," in *Philosophizing the Americas*, ed. Jacoby Adeshei Carter and Hernando A. Estévez (New York: Fordham University Press, 2024), 235–60.

13 Cf. Judith T. Irvine, "Subjected Words: African Linguistics and the Colonial Encounter," *Language & Communication* 28, no. 4 (2008): 323–43.

14 Tomoko Masuzawa, *The Invention of World Religions: Or, How European Universalism Was Preserved in the Language of Pluralism* (Chicago: University of Chicago Press, 2005), 28, 36.

15 José Casanova, *Public Religions in the Modern World* (Chicago: University of Chicago Press, 1994), 6.

16 For scholarship on multiple religious participation/belonging, see: Paul F. Knitter, *Without Buddha I Could Not Be a Christian* (London: Oneworld, 2013); Duane R. Bidwell, *When One Religion Isn't Enough: The Lives of Spiritually Fluid People* (Boston: Beacon Press, 2018).

17 Cf. Miguel A. De La Torre, *Santería: The Beliefs and Rituals of a Growing Religion in America* (Grand Rapids, MI: Wm. B. Eerdmans, 2004), xvii ff.; "Consultation

Explores Multiple Religious Belonging in Latin American Context," in World Council of Churches, December 21, 2021; and Dale Bisnauth, *History of Religions in the Caribbean* (Trenton, NJ: Africa World Press, 1996), 165 ff.

18 De La Torre, *Santería*, xiv; Bisnauth, *History of Religions in the Caribbean*, 165 ff.; also see Muamba Tujibikile, *La resistencia del negro en América Latina: lógica ancestral y celebración de la vida* (San José: Editorial DEI, 1990).

19 See Sybille de Pury Toumi, "El náhuatl: ¿dialecto o 'lengua civilizada' " in *Indianidad, etnocidio e indigenismo en América latina*, loc 3036 ff.; Jon Landaburu, "Los indigenas de Colombia: perspectiva de su situación lingüistica y educativa," in *Indianidad, etnocidio e indigenismo en América latina*, loc 2829 ff.; and Alberto Escobar, "Situación multilingüe y planteamiento lingüístico en el Perú," in *Indianidad, etnocidio e indigenismo en América latina*, loc 2594 ff.

20 '*Converso*' was the term used by the Catholic authorities in Iberia and in the Americas for those who converted from Judaism to Catholicism in Spain or Portugal during the fourteenth and fifteenth centuries—instead of being simply calling them "Christian" or "Catholic." This was due to authorities being suspicious or doubting the authenticity of their conversations. It was way of otherizing Jewish converts to Catholicism. Descendents of these were also called *conversos*. The suspicions were not entirely unfounded, as there were and are stories of *conversos* maintaining Jewish practices, rituals, and beliefs in private, while remaining active in their Catholic parishes.

21 Cf. Marie-Theresa Hernández, *The Virgin of Guadalupe and the Conversos: Uncovering Hidden Influences from Spain to Mexico* (New Brunswick, NJ: Rutgers University Press, 2014); David L. Graizbord, *Souls in Dispute: Converso Identities in Iberia and the Jewish Diaspora, 1580–1700* (Philadelphia: University of Pennsylvania Press, 2011); and Dalia Kandiyoti, *The Converso's Return: Conversion and Sephardi History in Contemporary Literature and Culture* (Redwood City, CA: Stanford University Press, 2020).

22 Alejandra Molina, "1 in 5 Latino Americans have no religion, the Latinx Humanist Alliances says," *Religion News Service*, April 1, 2021.

23 Casanova, *Public Religions in the Modern World*, 233.

24 See Paola Ramos, *Defectors: The Rise of the Latino Far Right and What It Means for America* (NewYork: Pantheon Books, 2024); Elle Hardy, *Beyond Belief: How Pentecostal Christianity is Taking Over the World* (London: Hurst, 2024); Hardy, "Prosperity versus liberation: How Pentecostalism's prosperity gospel replaced Catholic liberation theology in Latin American life," ed. Sam Haselby, *Aeon*, January 23, 2025.

25 Cf. Raúl E. Zegarra, *A Revolutionary Faith: Liberation Theology Between Public Religion and Public Reason* (Redwood City, CA: Stanford University Press, 2023); and Barger, *The World Come of Age*.

26 Casanova, *Public Religions in the Modern World*, 19.

27 Pew Research Center, April 2023, "Among U.S. Latinos, Catholicism Continues to Decline but Is Still the Largest Faith"; Cf. Contreras, "Latino atheists, non-religious grow"; and Luis Andrés Henao, "Poll: Among U.S. Latinos, Catholicism still largest faith," *AP News*, April 23, 2023.

28 Pew, "Among U.S. Latinos, Catholicism Continues to Decline but Is Still the Largest Faith."

29 Pew Research Center, "The Shifting Religious Identity of Latinos in the United States," May 7, 2014; and Frank DiMaria, "Catholic Church: Losing Its Share of Hispanics," *The Hispanic Outlook in Higher Education* 24, no. 22 (2014): 6–8.

30 Cf. Ramos, *Defectors*; Hardy, *Beyond Belief*; Hardy, "Prosperity versus liberation: How Pentecostalism's prosperity gospel replaced Catholic liberation theology in Latin American life," edited Sam Haselby, *Aeon*, January 23, 2025.

31 Cf. Jones, Cox, and Navarro-Rivera, "The 2013 Hispanic Values Survey"; also, Kimberly Winston, "Hispanics increasingly identify as 'nones'," Religion News Service, October 17, 2013.

32 Juhem Navarro-Rivera and Yazmin A. Garcia Trejo, "Secularism, Race, and Political Affiliation in America," in *The Oxford Handbook on Secularism* (Oxford University Press, 2017), 444–5; Molina, "1 in 5 Latino Americans have no religion."

33 Molina, "1 in 5 Latino Americans have no religion."

34 An important aside, data also show that the Latine Catholics, who remain active in the religion, are more progressive than is conventionally assumed. Paul Elie notes that "even those who aren't [leaving the faith] are defying convention and stereotypes." He adds, "Hispanics are actually the group within the Catholic Church in the United States most eager for change. Of all the groups surveyed, only among Hispanic Catholics was there a majority (fifty-six per cent) that wished for more leaders of color. How about more women leaders? Sixty-four percent of Hispanic Catholics surveyed want this (the highest of any group). More L.G.B.T.Q.+ leaders? Thirty-nine percent of Hispanic Catholics want this (the highest of any group). Trans rights? A third want this (the highest). Open discussion of political divisions in the United States? Three-tenths want this (again, the highest). So, Hispanics who remain Catholic are, by a clear margin, the progressive wing of the Church." See Paul Elie, "More Latino American Are Losing Their Faith," *The New Yorker*, March 29, 2023. The ambivalent (non-) acquiesce to the Catholic magisterium by Latine Catholics is not new. Two examples are the rise of liberation theologies in the Americas (which was challenged by the Vatican) and (a lesser-known story) the account of Padre [Antonio José] Martínez (1793–1867) and *los hermanos penitentes* in New Mexico. Padre Martínez and his Catholic followers resisted the leadership of Bishop Jean Baptiste Lamy of France, who had been placed there by Vatican officials to confront Padre Martínez' and the *penitentes*' dogmatic innovations and incalcitrant behavior toward the ecclesiastical authority. Cf. Ray John de Aragon, *Penitentes of New Mexico: Hermanos de La Luz, Brothers of the Light* (Santa Fe, NM: Sunstone Press, 2006).

35 "FFRF is elated that Latino 'Nones' are increasing," Freedom from Religion Foundation (April 14, 2023; Molina, "1 in 5 Latino Americans have no religion." Also see: Daniel Cox, Robert P. Jones, and Juhem Navarro-Rivera, "Nonreligious Tolerance: American Attitudes toward Atheists, America's Most Unpopular Religious Group" in *Religion and Political Tolerance in America: Advances in the State of the Art*, ed. Paul Djupe (Philadelphia, PA: Temple University Press, 2015),133–50.

36 Russell Contreras, "Latino atheists, non-religious grow," *Axios*.

37 Devin Fitzpatrick, "Realism and Receptivity: The Role of the Transcendent in Pragmatism," in *Transactions of the Charles S. Peirce Society* 50, no. 1 (Winter 2014): 14.

38 Fitzpatrick, "Realism and Receptivity," 14.

39 Ambrosio Velasco Gómez, "Humanismo hispanoamericano," *Revista de Hispanismo Filosófico*, no. 13 (2008): 13.

40 Axel Honneth and Hans Joas, *Social Action and Human Nature* (New York: Cambridge University Press, 1988), 9.

41 Juhem Navarro-Rivera, "Humanism and Political Identity," *The Oxford Handbook of Humanism*, ed. Anthony B. Pinn (New York: Oxford Academic, October 4, 2019), 448–64.

42 Daniel Chernilo, *Debating Humanity: Towards a Philosophical Sociology* (New York: Cambridge University Press, 2016), 64–86.

43 Cf. Hans Joas, *The Creativity of Action* (Chicago: University of Chicago Press, 1996).

44 Hans Joas, *The Power of the Sacred: An Alternative to the Narrative of Disenchantment*, trans. Alex Skinner (New York: Oxford University Press, 2021), 238. [Italics added for emphasis.]

45 Cf. Joas, *The Creativity of Action,* 240.

46 Philip Kitcher, *Preludes to Pragmatism* (New York: Oxford University Press, 2012), 301. Quoted in Fitzpatrick, "Realism and Receptivity," 14.

47 See: https://americanhumanist.org/; https://www.hafree.org/; https://www.atheistsunited.org/; https://ffrf.org/. Cf. Molina, "1 in 5 Latino Americans have no religion"; "FFRF is elated that Latino 'Nones' are increasing," Freedom from Religion Foundation.

48 Fitzpatrick, "Realism and Receptivity," 15.

49 Velasco Gómez, "Humanismo hispanoamericano," 30. [Translation from Spanish mine.]

Conclusion: Where Are We Going—Where Have We Been

1 Malcolm X, *Malcolm X Speaks: Selected Speeches and Statements*, ed. George Breitman (New York: Grove Press, 1965), 26.

2 Claudio J. Perez, "How U.S. Policy Has Failed Immigrant Children: Family Separation in the Obama and Trump Eras," *Family Law Quarterly* 54, no. 1/2 (2020): 40.

3 Philip Elliott, "Both Sides Won When Donald Trump Was Fired," *Time*, June 29, 2015.

4 Maria Briceño, Louis Jacobson, and Amy Sherman, "Fact-checking Trump's Remarks at 'Alligator Alcatraz' on Immigration and Medicaid," *PBS News*, July 1, 2025.

5 Georg Wilhelm Friedrich Hegel, *Lectures on the Philosophy of World History*, trans. H. B. Nisbet (Cambridge: Cambridge University Press, 1975 [1857]), 62.

6 Georg Wilhelm Friedrich Hegel, *The Philosophy of History*, trans. J. Sibree (New York: Colonial, 1900 [1824]), 332–3.

7 Ibid., 319.

8 Ibid., 16.

9 Ibid., 397.

10 Ibid., 341.

11 Ibid., 103.

12 Ibid., 81–2, 96.

13 Ibid., 99.

14 Idem, *Elements of the Philosophy of Right*, trans. H. B. Nisbet and ed. Allen W. Wood (Cambridge: Cambridge University Press, 1991 [1820]), § 347.

15 Fernando Ortiz, *Contrapunteo cubano del tabaco y el azúcar* (La Habana: Dirección de Publicaciones Universidad Central de Las Villas, 1963), 98–104.

16 Peter G. Earle, "Unamuno and the Theme of History," *Hispanic Review* 32, no. 4 (October 1964): 323.

17 Miguel de Unamuno, "Del sentimiento trágico de la vida," in *Filosofia* ed. Manuel García Morente (Madrid: Akal Ediciones, [1912] 1996), 67.

18 Ibid., 73–4.

19 For just a few example, see Kevin O'Keeffe, "Beeville Man Sees Jesus in Breakfast Taco," *Texas Monthly*, January 21, 2013; Shannon Carney, "Man Sees Jesus in Tortilla," *NBC- 24News*, July 23, 2015; Matt Roper, " 'Tortilla Jesus' Draws Hundreds of Pilgrims to Family's Home," *New York Post*, June 23, 2017; Uriel J. Garcia, " 'Tortilla Miracle Brought Hope and Mockery to N.M. Family," *The New Mexican*, July 8, 2017; Tyler White, "Central Texas Man Selling Tortilla He Claims has Jesus Face on It," *San Antonio Express-News*, February 25, 2015; and Shauntae Lymas, "Mexican Woman Says Jesus Appeared to Her in a Tortilla, *ABC – 12News*, June 29, 2015.

20 Walter Benjamin, "Thesis on the Philosophy of History," in *Illuminations*, trans. Harry Zohn and ed. Hannah Arendt (New York: Schocken, 1968 [1940]), 257§ IX.

21 Walter Benjamin, *The Arcades Project*, trans. Howard Eiland and Kevin McLaughlin (Cambridge, MA: Belknap, 1999 [published posthumously]), 167–8 N5a, 7.

22 Ibid., 460 N2, 2

Bibliography

Aboitiz, Nicole CuUnjieng. *Asian Place, Filipino Nation: A Global Intellectual History of the Philippine Revolution, 1887–1912*. New York: Columbia University Press, 2020.

Abou El Fadl, Khaled. *The Prophet's Pulpit: Commentaries on the State of Islam*, Vol. 1, edited by Josef Linnhoff. Dublin: Usuli Press, 2022.

Adams, James Truslow. *America's Opportunity: How We Lost It and How We May Regain It*. New York: Charles Scribner's Sons, 1932.

Adams, James Truslow. *The Epic of America*. Reprint. New York: Transaction Publishers, [1931] 2012.

Agar Diaz Carrasco, Marianela. "Desarrollo y chacha-warmi: Lógicas de género en el mundo aymara." *Revista Casa de las Américas*, no 259 (2010): 10–24.

Aguilar, Emiliano. "Latino Workers." In *Oxford Research Encyclopedias, American History*. Oxford: Oxford University Press, 2021: https://oxfordre.com/americanhistory/display/10.1093/acrefore/9780199329175.001.0001/acrefore-9780199329175-e-650

Albert, Bruce, et al. *Indianidad, etnocidio e indigenismo en América latina*, edited by Instituto Indigenista Interamericano. Cuidad de México: Centro de estudios mexicanos y centroamericanos, 2019.

Albro, Robert. "Bolivia's Indigenous Foreign Policy: Vivir Bien and Global Climate Change Ethics." In *Church, Cosmovision and the Environment: Religion and Social Conflict in Contemporary Latin America*, edited by Evan Berry and Robert Albro. New York: Routledge, 2018.

Alessandri, Mariana. "Laughing in Spanish," *New Philosopher* 17 (Summer 2017): 40–1.

Althaus-Reid, Marcella. *Indecent Theology: Theological Perversions in Sex, Gender and Politics*. London: Routledge, 2000.

Alryyes, Ala. *A Muslim American Slave: The Life of Omar Ibn Said*. Madison, WI: Wisconsin Studies in Autobiography, University of Wisconsin Press, 2011.

Alvarez, Emilio. *Pentecost: A Day of Power for All People*. The Fullness of Time Series. Lisle, IL: InterVarsity Press, 2023.

Ammerman, Nancy Tatom. *Sacred Stories, Spiritual Tribes: Finding Religion in Everyday Life*. Oxford: Oxford University Press, 2014.

Anzaldúa, Gloria. *Borderlands/La Frontera: The New Mestiza*. San Francisco, CA: Aunt Lute Books, [1987] 2021.

Anzaldúa, Gloria. "La Prieta." In *This Bridge Called My Back: Writings by Radical Women of Color*, edited by Cherríe Moraga and Gloria Anzaldúa. Albany: State University of New York Press, 2015.

Anzaldúa, Saraliza. *Monsters and Mestizos: Mestizaje as White Supremacy and the Monsterization of Indigeneity*. Los Angeles: University of California, 2023.

Aparicio, Frances R. *Listening to Salsa: Gender, Latin Popular Music, and Puerto Rican Cultures*. Hanover, NH: Wesleyan University Press, 1998.

Aponte, Edwin David. *¡Santo!: Varieties of Latino/a Spirituality*. Maryknoll, NY: Orbis Books, 2012.

Aponte, Edwin David, and Miguel A. De La Torre. *Introducing Latinx Theologies Revised edition*. Maryknoll, NY: Orbis Books, 2020.

Aquino, María Pilar. "Introduction." In *A Reader in Latina Feminist Theology*, edited by María Pilar Aquino, Daisy L. Machado, and Jeanette Rodriguez. Austin: University of Texas Press, 2002.

Aquino, María Pilar. "Latina Feminist Theology: Central Features." In *A Reader in Latina Feminist Theology*, edited by María Pilar Aquino, Daisy L. Machado, and Jeanette Rodriguez, 134–9. Austin: University of Texas Press, 2002.

Arana, Marie. *LatinoLand: A Portrait of America's Largest and Least Understood Minority*. New York: Simon & Schuster, 2024.

Argyriadis, Kali, Renée de la Torre, Cristina Gutiérrez Zuñiga, and Aguilar Ros, editors. *Raíces en Movimiento: prácticas religiosas tradicionales en contextos translocales*. Cuidad de México: Centro de estudios mexicanos y centroamericanos, 2008.

Armas, Kat. *Abuelita Faith: What Women on the Margins Teach Us about Wisdom, Persistence, and Strength*. Grand Rapids, MI: Brazos Press, 2021.

Assembly of First Nations. "Dismantling the Doctrine of Discovery." Ottawa, ON: Assembly of First Nations (January 2018): 1–7.

Avila, Elena, and Joy Parker. *Woman Who Glows in the Dark: A Curandera Reveals Traditional Aztec Secrets of Physical and Spiritual Health*. New York: Penguin, 2000.

Avila, Jacqueline A. *Cinesonidos: Film Music and National Identity During Mexico's Época de Oro*. New York: Oxford University Press, 2019.

Ayorinde, Christine. *Afro-Cuban Religiosity, Revolution, and National Identity*. Gainesville: University Press of Florida, 2005.

Bailey, Ebony Marie. "Codings of Blackness in Mexican Cinema: An Analysis of *La Negrada," in Publication of the Afro-Latin/American Research Association (PALARA)* 23, No. 8 (2019): 1–9.

Barajas, Manuel. "Colonial Dislocations and Incorporation of Indigenous Migrants from Mexico to the United States." *American Behavioral Scientist* 58, no 1 (2014): 53–63.

Barger, Lilian Calles. *The World Come of Age: An Intellectual History of Liberation Theology*. New York: Oxford University Press, 2018.

Barnes, Colin. "Understanding the Social Model of Disability: Past, Present and Future." In *Routledge Handbook of Disability Studies*, 2nd edition, edited by Nick Watson and Simo Vehmas. London: Routledge, 2020.

Barrera, Mario. *Race and Class in the Southwest: A Theory of Racial Inequality*. Notre Dame: University of Notre Dame Press, 1979.

Barzegar, Abbas. "Latino Muslims in the United States: An Introduction." *Journal of the High Plains Society for Applied Anthropologists* 23, no 2 (Fall 2003): 125–9.

Baugh, Amanda J. *Falling in Love with Nature: The Values of Latinx Catholic Environmentalism*. New York: New York University Press, 2024.

Bazzi, Samuel, Martin Fiszbein, and Maximiliano Garcia. "The Moral Values of 'Rugged Individualism.'" *Working Paper 32433*, National Bureau of Economic Research (May 2024): 1–34.

Beal, Timothy. *The Rise and Fall of the Bible: The Unexpected History of an Accidental Book*. Boston, MA: Houghton Mifflin Harcourt, 2011.

Beliso-De Jesús, Aisha M. *Electric Santería: Racial and Sexual Assemblages of Transnational Religion*. New York: Columbia University Press, 2015.

Beltrán, Ramona, Antonia Rose-Garriga Alvarez, and Angela R. Fernandez. "I See Myself Strong: A Description of An Expressive Poetic Method to Amplify Two-Spirit, Lesbian, Gay, Bisexual, Trans, Queer Indigenous Youth Experiences in a Culture-Centered HIV Prevention Curriculum. *Genealogy* 7, no 3 (2023): 55–71.

Beltrán, Ramona, Antonia R. G. Alvarez, Angela R. Fernandez, Lisa Colón, and Xochilt Alamillo. "Salud, Cultura, Tradición: Preliminary Findings from an Alcohol and Other Drugs and HIV Needs Assessment in Urban 'Mexican American Indian' Communities." *Journal of Ethnic & Cultural Diversity in Social Work* 30, no 1–2 (2020): 62–79.

Belzer, Tobin, Tory Brundage, Vincent Calvetti, Gage Gorsky, Ari Y. Kelman, and Dalya Perez. *Beyond the Count: Perspectives and Lived Experiences of Jews of Color*. Oakland, CA: Jews of Color Initiative, 2021.

Benjamin, Walter. *The Arcades Project*, translated by Howard Eiland and Kevin McLaughlin. Cambridge, MA: Belknap, 1999 [published posthumously].

Benitez-Rojo, Antonio. *The Repeating Island: The Caribbean and the Postmodern Perspective, Second Edition*. Durham: Duke University Press, 1996.

Benjamin, Walter. "Thesis on the Philosophy of History." In *Illuminations*, translated by Harry Zohn, edited by Hannah Arendt. New York: Schocken, [1940] 1968.

Bidwell, Duane R. *When One Religion Isn't Enough: The Lives of Spiritually Fluid People*. Boston, MA: Beacon Press, 2018.

Bisnauth, Dale. *History of Religions in the Caribbean*. Trenton, NJ: Africa World Press, 1996.

Bixby, Laurin, Stacey Bevan, and Courtney Boen. "The Links Between Disability, Incarceration, And Social Exclusion." *Health Affairs* 41, no 10 (2022): 1460–9.

Blanco, Andrés Eloy. "*Pintame angelitos negros.*" In, *La Juan Bimbada*. Editorial Cordillera. Venezuela, [1936] 1960.

Blanco, Andrés Eloy. "*Pintame angelitos negros.*" Vocal recording from the collection "La Juanbimbada," 1943. PALABRA Archive. *United States Library of Congress*. https://lccn.loc.gov/93842789.

Boff, Leonardo. *Cry of the Earth, Cry of the Poor*. Maryknoll, NY: Orbis Books, 1997.

Bonilla-Silva, Eduardo. *Racism without Racists: Color-Blind Racism and the Persistence of Racial Inequality in America*, 6th edition. Lanham, MD: Rowman & Littlefield, 2022.

Bouteldja, Houria. *Whites, Jews, and Us: Towards a Politics of Revolutionary Love*, translated by Rachel Valinsky. Los Angeles: MIT Press, 2017.

Bowdre, Karen M. "Passing Films and the Illusion of Racial Equality." In *Black Camera* 5, No. 2 (2014): 21–43.

Brave Heart, Maria Yellow Horse. "The Return to the Sacred Path: Healing the Historical Trauma and Historical Unresolved Grief Response among the Lakota through a Psychoeducational Group Intervention." *Smith College Studies in Social Work* 68, no 3 (1998): 287–305.

Brighenti, Maura. "Disputando la tierra: El indigenismo de Mariátegui entre crítica de la colonialidad y búsqueda de lo común." *Intersticios de la política y la cultura: intervenciones latinoamericanas, Revista de la Cátedra de Filosofía Argentina y Latinoamericana, Escuela de Filosofía* 5, no 10 (2016): 51–75.

Brodkin, Karen. *How Jews Became White Folks and What That Says about Race in America*. New Brunswick, NJ: Rutgers University Press, 1998.

Brown, Candy Gunther, and Harvey Gallagher Cox. *Global Pentecostal and Charismatic Healing*, edited by Candy Gunther Brown and Harvey Gallagher Cox. Oxford: Oxford University Press, 2011.

Brown, David H. "Annotated Glossary for Fernando Ortiz's The Afro-Cuban Festival 'Day of the Kings'." In *Cuban Festivals: An Illustrated Anthology*, edited by Judith Bettelheim. New York: Garland Publishing, Inc., 1993.

Burton, Linda M., Eduardo Bonilla-Silva, Victor. Ray, Rose Buckelew, Elizabeth Hordge Freeman. "Critical Race Theories, Colorism, and the Decade's Research on Families of Color." *Journal of Marriage and Family* 71 (2010): 440–59.

Cabeza de Baca, Fabiola. *The Good Life: New Mexico Traditions and Food.* Santa Fe: Museum of New Mexico Press, 2006.
Cabrera, Lydia. *El Monte: Notes on the Religions, Magic, and Folklore of the Black and Creole People of Cuba*, translated by David Font-Navarrete. Durham, NC: Duke University Press, 2023.
Calvillo, Jonathan. *The Saints of Santa Ana: Faith and Ethnicity in a Mexican Majority City.* New York: Oxford University Press, 2020.
Campesino, Maureen, and Gary E. Schwartz. "Spirituality Among Latinas/os Implications of Culture in Conceptualization and Measurement." *ANS. Advances in Nursing Science* 29, no 1 (2006): 69–81.
Capps, Randy, Heather Koball, Andrea Campetella, Krista Perreira, Sarah Hooker, and Juan Manuel Pedroza. *Implications of Immigration Enforcement Activities for the Well-Being of Children in Immigrant Families.* Washington, DC: Urban Institute and Migration Policy Institute, 2015.
Cardoza-Orlandi, Carlos F. "Qué Lindo Es Mi Cristo: The Erotic Jesus/Christ in the Caribbean, Lain American, and Latino/a Protestant Christian Music." In *Jesus in the Hispanic Community: Images of Christ from Popular Theology to Popular Religion*, edited by Harold J. Recinos and Hugo Magallanes. Louisville, KY: Westminster John Knox Press, 2009.
Caria, Sara, and Rafael Domínguez. "Ecuador's 'Buen vivir': A New Ideology for Development," *Latin American Perspectives* 43, no. 1 (2016): 18–33.
Carter, Jacoby Adeshei, and Hernando A. Estévez, editors. *Philosophizing the Americas.* New York: Fordham University Press, 2024.
Caruth, Cathy. *Unclaimed Experience: Trauma, Narrative, and History*, 20th anniversary edition. Baltimore, MD: Johns Hopkins University Press, 2016.
Casanova, José. *Public Religions in the Modern World.* Chicago: University of Chicago Press, 1994.
Casanova, Saskias, Brendan H. O'Connor, and Vanessa Anthony-Stevens. Ecologies of Adaptation for Mexican Indigenous Im/Migrant Children and Families in the United States: Implications for Latino Studies." *Latino Studies* 14 (2016): 192–213.
Castanha, Tony. "The Doctrine of Discovery: The Legacy and Continuing Impact of Christian "Discovery" on American Indian Populations." *American Indian Culture and Research Journal* 39, no 3 (2015): 41–64.
Castañeda-Liles, María Del Socorro. *Our Lady of Everyday Life: La Virgen de Guadalupe and the Catholic Imagination of Mexican Women in America.* Oxford: Oxford University Press, 2018.
Castillo, Daniel Patrick. *An Ecological Theology of Liberation: Salvation and Political Ecology.* Maryknoll, NY: Orbis Books, 2019.
Chacón, Gloria E. "Example of Indigenous Erasure Among Latinx Community." *Latino Studies* 15, no 2 (2017): 182–200.
Chan, Sucheng. *Asian American Studies Now: A Critical Reader.* New Brunswick, NJ: Rutgers University Press, 2010.
Chang-Rodríguez, Eugenio. "José Carlos Mariátegui y la polémica del indigenismo." *América Sin Nombre*, no 13–14 (2009): 103–12.
Charles, Janneil. "Colorism and the Afro-Latinx Experience: A Review of the Literature." *Hispanic Journal of Behavioral Sciences* 43, no 1–2 (2021): 9–31.
Chaves, João B. *Migration Religion: Context and Creativity in the Latinx Diaspora.* Waco, TX: Baylor University Press, 2021.
Chavez-Dueñas, Nayeli Y., Hector Y. Adames, and Kurt C. Organista. "Skin-Color Prejudice and Within-Group Racial Discrimination." *Hispanic Journal of Behavioral Sciences* 36, no 1 (2014): 3–26.

Chernilo, Daniel. *Debating Humanity: Towards a Philosophical Sociology.* New York: Cambridge University Press, 2016.
Chion, Michel. *Film: A Sound Art.* Translated by Claudia Gorbman. New York: Columbia University Press, 2009.
Chion, Michel. *Audio-Vision: Sound on Screen*, Second Edition. New York: New York University Press, 2017.
Clarke, Kamari M. *Mapping Yoruba Networks: Power and Agency in the Making of Transnational Communities.* Durham, NC: Duke University Press, 2004.
Clark, Mary Ann. *Santeria: Correcting the Myths and Uncovering the Realities of a Growing Religion.* Westport, CT: Praeger Publishers, 2007.
Cole, Luke W., and Sheila R. Foster. *From the Ground Up: Environmental Racism and the Rise of the Environmental Justice Movement*, 1st edition. New York: New York University Press, 2001.
Collins, Patricia Hill, and Margaret Anderson, editors. *Race, Class and Gender: An Anthology.* Boston, MA: Cengage, 2019.
Conference of Latin American Bishops (CELAM). "Aparecida Document." In *Documento Aparecida: V Conferencia General del Episcopado Latinoamericano y del Caribe, Documento Conclusivo.* Bogota: CELAM, 2007.
Creamer, Deborah Beth. *Disability and Christian Theology: Embodied Limits and Constructive Possibilities.* Oxford: Oxford University Press, 2009.
Colón, Willie. *El Baquiné De Angelitos Negros.* New York: Fania Records, [1977] 2006.
Connor, Steven. *Dumbstruck: A Cultural History of Ventriloquism.* New York: Oxford University Press, 2000.
Corominas, Joan. *Breve diccionario etimológico de la lengua castellana*, 3rd edition. Madrid: Gredos, 1987.
Courtois, Christine A., and Julian D. Ford, editors. *Treating Complex Traumatic Stress Disorders: An Evidence-Based Guide.* New York: Guilford Press, 2009.
Coyle, Kevin J. *Manicheism and its Legacy.* Boston, MA: Leiden, 2009.
Cros Sandoval, Mercedes. *Worldview, the Orichas, and Santería: Africa to Cuba and Beyond.* Gainesville: University of Florida Press, 2006.
Cuesta, Michael. *El Baquiné de angelitos negros.* New York: Latino TV Broadcasting Service. (1977), 21 min.
Cruz-Malavé, Arnaldo. *Queer Latino Testimonio, Keith Haring, and Juanito Xtravaganza: Hard Tails.* New York: Palgrave Macmillan, 2007.
Cruz, Maria L., Samantha Christie, Estrella Allen, Erika Meza, Anna María Nápoles, and Kala M. Mehta. "Traditional Healers as Health Care Providers for the Latine Community in the United States, a Systematic Review." *Health Equity* 6, no 1 (2022): 412–26.
Cruz Vásquez, Lorena Edith. "El (hetero) cistema de sexualidad, género y deseo en Juchitán como marco para entender la identidad muxe." *Quaderns de Ciències Socials*, no 48 (2022): 28–59.
Cuéllar, Gregory L. *Resacralizing the Other at the US-Mexico Border: A Borderland Hermeneutic.* New York: Routledge, 2020.
Curtis, Heather D. "The Global Character of Nineteenth-Century Divine Healing." In *Global Pentecostal and Charismatic Healing*, edited by Candy Gunther Brown and Harvey Gallagher Cox. Oxford: Oxford University Press, 2011.
Dalton, Frederick John. *The Moral Vision of César Chávez.* Maryknoll, NY: Orbis Books, 2003.
Davis, Lennard J. "Introduction." In *Beginning with Disability: A Primer*, edited by Lennard J. Davis, Jay Dolmage, Nirmala Erevelles, Sarah Parker Harris, Alexander Luft, Susan M. (Susan Marie) Schweik, and Linda P. Ware. New York: Routledge, 2018.

Davis, Mike. *Magical Urbanism: Latinos Reinvent the US City*. London: Verso, 2001.
Deans-Smith, Susan, and Ilona Katzew. "Introduction: The Alchemy of Race in Mexican America." In *Race Classification: The Case of Mexican America*, edited by Susan Deans-Smith and Ilona Katzew. Stanford, CA: Stanford University Press, 2009.
de Aragon, Ray John. *Penitentes of New Mexico: Hermanos de La Luz, Brothers of the Light*. Santa Fe, NM: Sunstone Press, 2006.
De Genova, Nicholas P., and Nathalie Peutz. *The Deportation Regime: Sovereignty, Space, and the Freedom of Movement*. Durham, NC: Duke University Press, 2010.
De La Torre, Miguel A. *Reading José Martí from the Margins*. Lanham, MD: Rowman & Littlefield, 2024.
De La Torre, Miguel A. *José Martí's Liberative Political Theology*. Nashville, TN: Vanderbilt University Press, 2021.
De La Torre, Miguel A. *Embracing Hopelessness*. Minneapolis, MN: Fortress Press, 2017.
De La Torre, Miguel A. "Afro-Caribbean Religious Expressions." In *The Cambridge History of Religions in Latin America*, edited by Virginia Garrad-Burnett, Paul Freston, and Stephen C. Dove. New York: Cambridge University Press, 2016.
De La Torre, Miguel A. *The Politics of Jesús: A Hispanic Political Theology*. Lanham, MD: Rowman & Littlefield, 2015.
De La Torre, Miguel A. *Latina/o Social Ethics: Moving Beyond Eurocentric Moral Thinking* Waco: Baylor University Press, 2010.
De La Torre, Miguel A. "Rethinking Mulatez." In *Rethinking Latino(a) Identity*, edited byMiguel A. De La Torre and Gastón Espinoza. Cleveland, OH: Pilgrim Press, 2006.
De La Torre, Miguel A. *Santería: The Beliefs and Rituals of a Growing Religion in America*. Grand Rapids, MI: Wm. B. Eerdmans, 2004.
De La Torre, Miguel A. *Reading the Bible from the Margins*. Maryknoll, NY: Orbis Books, 2002.
De La Torre, Miguel A. "Ochún: (N)Either the (M)Other of All Cubans (n)or the Bleached Virgin." *Journal of the American Academy of Religion* 69, no 4 (2001): 837–61.
De La Torre, Miguel A., and Albert Hernández. *The Quest for the Historical Satan*. Minneapolis, MN: Fortress Press, 2011.
Deleuze, Gilles. *Cinema 2: The Time-Image*, translated by Hugh Tomlinson and Robert Galeta. Minneapolis: University of Minnesota Press, 1989.
Delgadillo, Theresa. "Toña La Negra's Performance of Mexicanidad and Black Diaspora Consciousness." In, *Geographies of Relation: Diasporas and Borderlands in the Americas*. Ann Arbor: University of Michigan Press, 2024.
Delgadillo, Theresa. "Singing "Angelitos Negros": African Diaspora Meets Mestizaje in the Americas. In American Quarterly 58, No, 2 (2006): 407–430.
Delgadillo, Theresa. "'Angelitos Negros' and Transnational Racial Identifications." In *Rebellious Reading: The Dynamics of Chicana/o Cultural Literacy*, edited by Carl Gutiérrez-Jones. Santa Barbara: University of California, 2004.
DellaPergola, Sergio. "World Jewish Population, 2020." In *American Jewish Year Book: The Annual Record of the North American Jewish Communities Since 1899*, edited by Arnold Dashefsky and Ira M. Sheskin. New York: Springer, 2022.
del Socorro, María. *Castañeda, Our Lady of Everyday Life*. Oxford: Oxford University Press, 2018.
de Luna, Anita. *Faith Formation and Popular Religion: Lessons from the Tejano Experience*. Lanham, MD: Rowan & Littlefield, 2002.
del Valle Escalante, Emilio. "Self-Determination: A Perspective from Abya Yala." In *Restoring Indigenous Self-Determination: Theoretical and Practical Approaches*, edited by Marc Woons. Bristol, GB: E-International Relations, 2014.

de Unamuno, Miguel. "Del sentimiento trágico de la vida." In *Filosofia*, edited by Manuel García Morente. Madrid: Akal Ediciones, [1912] 1996.

DiMaria, Frank. "Catholic Church: Losing Its Share of Hispanics." *The Hispanic Outlook in Higher Education* 24, no 22 (2014): 6–8.

Djupe, Paul. *Religion and Political Tolerance in America: Advances in the State of the Art.* Philadelphia, PA: Temple University Press, 2015.

Doniger, Wendy. *Other Peoples' Myths: The Cave of Echoes.* Chicago: University of Chicago Press, 1995.

Donnelly, Kevin J. *Occult Aesthetics: Synchronization in Sound Film.* New York: Oxford University Press, 2014.

Du Bois, W.E.B. *The Souls of Black Folk.* Chicago: A.C. McClurg & Co., 1903.

Dugan, Katherine. "Fatima Family Shrine: Reinterpreting Mary on the South Dakota Prairie." In *American Patroness: Marian Shrines and the Making of US Catholicism*, edited by Katherine Dugan and Karen E. Park. New York: Fordham, 2024.

Dunbar-Ortiz, Roxanne. *An Indigenous People's History of the United States.* Boston, MA: Beacon Press, 2014.

Duran, Eduardo, Bonnie Duran, Maria Yellow Horse Brave Heart, and Susan Yellow Horse-Davis. "Healing the American Indian Soul Wound." In *International Handbook of Multigenerational Legacies of Trauma*, edited by Yael Danieli. New York: Plenum Press, 1998: 341–54.

Earle, Peter G. "Unamuno and the Theme of History." *Hispanic Review* 32, no 4 (October 1964): 319–39.

Edison, Paul. "Latinizing America: The French Scientific Study of Mexico, 1830–1930." PhD diss., Columbia University, New York, 1999.

Edmonds, Ennis B., and Gonzalez, Michelle A. *Caribbean Religious History.* New York: New York University Press, 2010.

Elizondo, Virgilio. *Galilean Journey: The Mexican-American Promise*, 2nd edition. Maryknoll, NY: Orbis Books, 2000.

Elkin, Judith Laikin. *The Jews of Latin America.* 3rd edition. Boulder, CO: Lynne Rienner Publishers, 2014.

Escobedo, Luis E., Lilia Cervantes, and Edward Havranek. "Barriers in Healthcare for Latinx Patients with Limited English Proficiency-a Narrative Review." *Journal of General Internal Medicine* 38, no 5 (2023): 1264–71.

Espín, Orlando. *Pentecost at Tepeyac? Pneumatologies from the People.* Maryknoll, NY: Orbis Books, 2024.

Espín, Orlando O., and Miguel H. Díaz, editors. *From the Heart of Our People: Latino/a Explorations in Catholic Systematic Theology.* Maryknoll, NY: Orbis Books, 1999.

Espinosa, Gastón. "Nones, No Religious Preference, No Religion and the Misclassification of Latino Religious Identity." *Religions* 14, no 3 (2023): 420–41.

Espinosa, Gastón. *Latino Pentecostals in America: Faith and Politics in Action.* Cambridge, MA: Harvard University Press, [2014] 2016.

Espinosa, Gaston, Harold Morales, and Juan Galvan. "Latino Muslims in the U.S.: Reversion, Politics, and Islamidad." *Journal of Race, Ethnicity, and Religion* 8, no 1 (June 2017): 1–48.

Espinosa, Gastón, Virgilio Elizondo, and Jesse Miranda, editors. *Latino Religions and Civic Activism in the United States.* Madison, NY: Oxford University Press, 2005.

Espírito Santo, Diana. *Developing the Dead: Mediumship and Selfhood in Cuban Espiritismo.* Gainesville: University Press of Florida, 2015.

Estrada, Antonio. "Mexican-Americans and Historical Trauma Theory: A Theoretical Perspective." *Journal of Ethnicity in Substance Abuse* 8, no 3 (2009): 330–40.

Evans-Campbell, Teresa. "Historical Trauma in American Indian/Native Alaska Communities: A Multilevel Framework for Exploring Impacts on Individuals, Families, and Communities." *Journal of Interpersonal Violence* 23, no 3 (March 2008): 316–38.

Farah H., Ivonne, and Carmen Sánchez G., editors. *Perfil de género Bolivia*. La Paz: CIDES-UMSA / Viceministerio de Género y Asuntos Generacionales, 2008.

Fernandez, Angela, and Romona Beltran. " 'Wherever I Go, I Have It Inside of Me': Indigenous Cultural Dance Narratives as Substance Abuse and HIV Prevention in an Urban Danza Mexica Community." *Frontiers in Public Health* 9 (2022): 1–16.

Fernández, S. J., Eduardo C. "Three Visual Images of Jesus the Christ from the Latino/a Community: God the Vulnerable; God the Broken; God the Loving." In *Jesus in the Hispanic Community: Images of Christ from Popular Theology to Popular Religion*, edited by Harold J. Recinos and Hugo Magallanes. Louisville, KY: Westminster John Knox Press, 2009.

Fernández Olmos, Margarite, and Lizabeth Paravisini-Gebert. *Creole Religions of the Caribbean: An Introduction, from Vodou and Santería to Obeah and Espiritismo*. New York: New York University Press, 2003.

Fife, John. "Civil Initiative." In *Trails of Hope and Terror: Testimonies on Immigration*, edited by Miguel A. De La Torre. Maryknoll, NY: Orbis, 2009.

Figueroa, Mónica G. Moreno "Naming Ourselves: Recognising Racism and Mestizaje in Mexico." In *Contesting Recognition: Culture, Identity and Citizenship*, edited by Janice McLaughlin, Peter Phillimore, and Diane Richardson. London: Palgrave Macmillan, 2011.

Figueroa-Vásquez, Yomaira C. *Decolonizing Diasporas: Radical Mappings of Afro-Atlantic Literature*. Evanston, IL: Northwestern University Press, 2020.

Fingal, Sara C. "Latinx Environmentalism." In *Oxford Research Encyclopedia of American History*. Oxford and New York: Oxford University Press, 2019.

Fitzpatrick, Devin. Realism and Receptivity: The Role of the Transcendent in Pragmatism. *Transactions of the Charles S. Peirce Society* 50, no 1, A Collaborative Critical Conversation on Philip Kitcher's *Preludes to Pragmatism* (Winter 2014): 9–17.

Fleuriet, Jill. "Health and Health Care Problems Among the Kumiai of San Antonio Necua and Their Indigenous Relatives in Baja California: Reflections of Poverty, Marginality, and a History of Colonization." *California Journal of Health Promotion* 1, no 1 (2003):140–57.

Flores, Lisa A. "Constructing Rhetorical Borders: Peons, Illegal Aliens, and Competing Narratives of Immigration." *Critical Studies in Media Communication* 20, no 4 (2003): 362–87.

Flores, Nichole M. "Latine Perspectives on Care for Creation." In *The Wiley Blackwell Companion to Latino/a/X Theology*, edited by Orlando O. Espín. Hoboken, NJ: John Wiley & Sons, 2023.

Francis, Pope. *Laudato Si: On Care for our Common Home*. Vatican City: Vatican Publishing House, 2015, https://www.vatican.va/content/francesco/en/encyclicals/documents/papa-francesco_20150524_enciclica-laudato-si.html.

Francis, Pope. Homily of His Holiness Pope Francis, Ciudad Juárez Fair Grounds, Wednesday, February 17, 2016. Dicastery for Communication, The Holy See. https://www.vatican.va/content/francesco/en/homilies/2016/documents/papa-francesco_20160217_omelia-messico-ciudad-jaurez.html.

Fregoso, Rosa Linda. "Toward a Planetary Civil Society." In *Women and Migration in the U.S.-Mexico Borderlands: A Reader*, edited by Denise A. Segura and Patricia Zavella. Durham, NC: Duke University Press, 2007.

Frichner, Tonya Gonnelia. "The 'Preliminary Study' on the Doctrine of Discovery." In *Pace Environmental Law Review* 28, no 1 (2010): 339–45.

Friedberg, Ali. "Reconsidering the Doctrine of Discovery: Spanish Land Acquisition in Mexico (1521–1821)." *Wisconsin International Law Journal* 17 (1999): 87–108.
Fritz, Catarina. "Redefining Racial Categories: The Dynamics of Identity Among Brazilian-Americans." *Immigrants and Minorities* 33, no 1 (2015): 45–65.
Fuller Osores, Norma J. "En torno a la polaridad machismo-marianismo." *Anuario de hojas de Warmi* (1996): 11–18.
Galarte, Francisco J. "Transgender Chican@ Poetics: Contesting, Interrogating, and Transforming Chicano/a Studies." *Chicana/Latina Studies* 13, no 2 (2014): 120–34.
Galeano, Eduardo. *Memory of Fire: Genesis*, translated by Cedric Belfrage. New York: W.W. Norton, 1985.
Gallegos, Monica L., and Chris and Segrin. "Exploring the Role of Marianismo and Loneliness in Latinas' Physical and Mental Well-Being." *Health Communication* 39, no 12 (October 14, 2024): 2884–95.
Galtung, Johan. "Violence, Peace, and Peace Research." *Journal of Peace Research* 6, no 3 (1969): 167–91.
Garcia, Alma M., editor. *Chicana Feminist Thought: The Basic Historical Writings.* New York: Routledge, [1997] 2014.
García, Matt. *From the Jaws of Victory: The Triumph and Tragedy of César Chávez and the Farm Worker Movement.* Berkeley: University of California Press, 2012.
Garcia-Olp, Michelle. *How Colonization Impacts Identity Through the Generations: A Closer Look at Historical Trauma and Education.* Dissertation. University of Denver, Denver, 2018.
Gebara, Ivone. *Longing for Running Water: Ecofeminism and Liberation.* Minneapolis, MN: Fortress Press, 1999.
Geertz, Clifford. *The Interpretation of Cultures: Selected Essays.* New York: Basic Books, 1973.
Geiger, Matthew J. *Mission of Nombre de Dios Shrine of Our Lady of La Leche St. Augustine, Florida: A Brief History.* St. Augustine: Mission Nombre de Dios Gift Shop, 2003.
Gidal, Marc Meistrich. "Catholic Music in Lusophone New Jersey: Circum-Atlantic Music, Intergroup Dynamics, and Immigrant Struggles in Transnational Communities." *American Music* 34, no 2 (2016): 180–217.
Gilio-Whitaker, Dina. *As Long as Grass Grows: The Indigenous Fight for Environmental Justice from Colonization to Standing Rock.* Boston, MA: Beacon Press, 2019.
Gleason, Judith. "Oya in the Company of Saints." In *Journal of the American Academy of Religion* 68, No. 2 (2000): 265–91.
Goldstein, Eric L. *The Price of Whiteness: Jews, Race, and American Identity.* Princeton, NJ: Princeton University Press, 2006.
Gobat, Michel. "The Idea of Latin America in the Nineteenth Century." In *The Routledge Hispanic Studies Companion to Nineteenth Century Latin America*, edited by Agnes Lugo-Ortiz and Graciela Montaldo. London: Routledge, 2025.
Goizueta, Roberto S. *Christ Our Companion: Toward a Theological Aesthetics of Liberation.* Maryknoll, NY: Orbis Books, 2009.
Goizueta, Roberto S. *Caminemos Con Jesús: Toward a Hispanic/Latino Theology of Accompaniment.* Maryknoll, NY: Orbis Books, 1999.
Goizueta, Roberto S. *Caminemos Con Jesús: Toward a Hispanic/Latino Theology of Accompaniment.* Maryknoll, NY: Orbis Books, 1999.
Gómez, Sara. *De cierta manera.* ICAIC. 79 min. Black/White. Spanish, 1974.
Gonzales, Alfonso. *Reform Without justice: Latino Migrant Politics and the Homeland Security State.* New York: Oxford University Press, 2013.
Gonzales, Patrisia. *Red Medicine: Traditional Indigenous Rites of Birthing and Healing.* Tucson: University of Arizona Press, 2012.

Gonzales, Rodolfo "Corky." "I am Joaquin: An Epic Poem." In *Looking Out, Looking In: An Anthology of Latino Poetry*, edited by William Luis. Houston, TX: Arte Público Press, 2012.

González, Gabriela. "Carolina Munguia and Emma Tenayuca: The Politics of Benevolence and Radical Reform." *Frontiers: A Journal of Women Studies* 24, no 23 (2003): 220–29.

González, Juan. *Harvest of Empire: A History of Latinos in America*. New York: Penguin Books, 2022.

González, Justo L. *The Story of Christianity, Volume I: The Early Church to the Dawn of the Reformation*, revised and updated edition. New York: HarperCollins, 2010.

González, Justo L. *Mañana: Christian Theology from a Hispanic Perspective*. Nashville TN: Abingdon, 1990.

Gonzalez Maldonado, Michelle. "Cuba." In *The Oxford Handbook of Latinx Christianities in the United States*, 1st edition, edited by Kristy Nabhan-Warren. Oxford: Oxford University Press, 2022.

Goodley, Dan. *Disability Studies: An Interdisciplinary Introduction*, 2nd edition. Thousand Oaks, CA: Sage Ltd, 2016.

Gordon, Arturo. *El velorio del angelito*. 54.5 x 6.5.5 cm., oil on canvas, 1909.

Graizbord, David L. *Souls in Dispute: Converso Identities in Iberia and the Jewish Diaspora, 1580–1700*. Philadelphia: University of Pennsylvania Press, 2011.

Greenberg, Joy H. "The Doctrine of Discovery as a Doctrine of Domination." *Journal for the Study of Religion, Nature & Culture* 10, no 2 (2016): 228–35.

Grosfoguel, Ramón."The Structure of Knowledge in Westernized Universities: Epistemic Racism/Sexism and the Four Genocides/Epistemicides of the Long 16th Century." In *Human Architecture: Journal of the Sociology of Self-Knowledge* 11, no 1 (Fall 2013): 73–90.

Guardiola-Sáenz, Leticia. "Borderless Women and the Word: A Cultural Reading of Matthew 15:21–28." *Semeia* 78 (1997): 57–73.

Gudynas, Eduardo. "Religion and Cosmovisions within Environmental Conflicts and the Challenge of Ontological Openings." In *Church, Cosmovision and the Environment: Religion and Social Conflict in Contemporary Latin America*, edited by Evan Berry and Robert Albro. New York: Routledge, 2018.

Gudynas, Eduardo. "Buen Vivir: Today's Tomorrow." *Development* 54, no 4 (2011): 441–7.

Gustafson, James M. *Can Ethics Be Christian?*. Chicago: University of Chicago Press, 1975.

Gutiérrez, Gustavo. "Option for the Poor." In *Mysterium Liberationis: Fundamental Concepts of Liberation Theology*, edited by Ignacio Ellacuría and Jon Sobrino. Maryknoll, NY: Orbis Books, 1993.

Hale, Gary J. "Migrant Caravans: A Deep Dive into Mass Migration through Mexico and the Effects of Immigration Policy." Houston, TX: Baker Institute for Public Policy. March 2, 2023.

Halpern, Clarisse, Zachary Austin Ward, and Hasan Aydin. " 'I'm Brazilian, Not Brazilian American': The Experiences of Second-Generation Brazilian Adolescents Preserving Their Heritage Language and Resisting Assimilation". *International Journal of Multicultural Education* 24, no 2 (2022):132–56. https://doi.org/10.18251/ijme.v24i2.3173.

Haney Lopez, Ian. *White by Law: 10th Anniversary Edition: The Legal Construction of Race*. New York: New York University Press, 2006.

Handy, Edward R., editor. *Christology of the Later Fathers*. Philadelphia, PA: Westminster Press, 1954.

Hardy, Elle. *Beyond Belief: How Pentecostal Christianity Is Taking Over the World.* London: Hurst, 2024.
Harrell, Erika. "Crime Against Persons with Disabilities, 2009–2019 – Statistical Tables." *U.S. Department of Justice: Bureau of Justice Statistics* (November 2021): 1–18.
Harris-Perry, Melissa V. *Sister Citizen: Shame, Stereotypes, and Black Women in America.* New Haven, CT: Yale University Press, 2011.
Hauerwas, Stanley. *After Christendom? How the Church Is to Behave If Freedom, Justice, and a Christian Nation Are Bad Ideas.* Nashville, TN: Abingdon, 1991.
Hegel, Georg Wilhelm Friedrich. *Lectures on the Philosophy of World History*, translated by H. B. Nisbet. Cambridge, MA: Cambridge University Press, [1857] 1975.
Hegel, Georg Wilhelm Friedrich. *The Philosophy of History.* Trans. J. Sibree. New York: Colonial, [1824] 1900.
Hegel, Georg Wilhelm Friedrich. *Elements of the Philosophy of Right*, translated by H. B. Nisbet, edited byAllen W. Wood. Cambridge, MA: Cambridge University Press, [1820] 1991.
Heredia, Pedro. *Antonio Machin. Barcelona*: Editorial Miguel Arimany S.A. (1976) 99.
Herman, Judith Lewis. *Trauma and Recovery: The Aftermath of Violence - from Domestic Abuse to Political Terror*, 4th trade paperback edition. New York: Basic Books, 2022.
Hernández, Albert. *Subversive Fire: The Untold Story of Pentecost.* Lexington, KY: Emeth Press, 2010.
Hernández, Marie-Theresa. *The Virgin of Guadalupe and the Conversos: Uncovering Hidden Influences from Spain to Mexico.* New Brunswick, NJ: Rutgers University Press, 2014.
Hernández, Roberto D. *Coloniality of the US/Mexico Border: Power, Violence, and the Decolonial Imperative.* Tucson: University of Arizona Press, 2018.
Hidalgo, Jacqueline M. *Revelation in Aztlán: Scriptures, Utopias, and the Chicano Movement.* New York: Palgrave Macmillan, 2016.
Hinojosa, Felipe. "Latina/o Religious Politics." In *Oxford Research Encyclopedia of American History.* Jon Butler, gen. ed. April 26, 2018, accessed September 14 2025, https://oxfordre.com/americanhistory/view/10.1093/acrefore/9780199329175.001.0001/acrefore-9780199329175-e-456.
Hinojosa, Felipe, Maggie Elmore, and Sergio M. González. "Introduction: Latino Religious Politics: Mapping the Field." In *Faith and Power: Latino Religious Politics Since 1945*, edited by Felipe Hinojosa, Maggie Elmore, and Sergio M. González. New York: New York University Press, 2022.
Hobbs, Allyson. "Passing," In *Keywords for African American Studies*, edited by Erica R. Edwards, Roderick A. Ferguson, and Jeffrey O.G. Ogbar. New York: New York University Press, 2018.
Holler, Stephen. "The Origins of Marian Devotion in Latin American Cultures in the United States." *Marian Studies* 46, no 11 (1995): 108–27.
Holy See Press Office Bulletin Summary. "Joint Statement of the Dicasteries for Culture and Education and for Promoting Integral Human Development on the 'Doctrine of Discovery'." Vatican City: Vatican, March 30, 2023.
Honneth, Axel, and Hans Joas. *Social Action and Human Nature.* New York: Cambridge University Press, 1988.
hooks, bell. *Ain't I a Woman: Black Women and Feminism.* Oxford: Taylor & Francis Group, 2014.
hooks, bell. *Belonging: A Culture of Place.* Oxford: Taylor & Francis Group, 2008.
hooks, bell. *The Will to Change: Men, Masculinity, and Love.* New York: Washington Square Press, 2004.

Howard, Philip A. *Changing History: Afro-Cuban Cabildos and Societies of Color in the Nineteenth Century*. Baton Rouge, LS: Louisiana State University Press, 1998.

Huard, Geoffroy. *Los Gais Durante el Franquismo: Discursos, Subculturas y Reivindicaciones - 1939–1977*. Barcelona: Egales Editorial, 2021.

Hucks, Tracey E. *Yoruba Traditions and African American Religious Nationalism*. Albuquerque: University of New Mexico Press, 2012.

Huntington, Samuel P. *Who Are We? The Challenges to America's National Identity*. New York: Simon & Schuster, 2004.

Huntington, Samuel P. *The Clash of Civilizations and the Remaking of World Order*. New York: Simon & Schuster, 1996.

Ibn Hazm, ʿAli b. Ahmad. *Los Caracteres y La Conducta: Tratado de Moral Practica por Abenhazam de Cordoba*, translated by Miguel Así Palacios. Madrid: Centro de Estudios Históricos, 1916.

Irvine, Judith T. Subjected Words: African Linguistics and the Colonial Encounter. *Language & Communication* 28, no 4 (2008): 323–43.

Isasi-Díaz, Ada María. "Mujerista Discourse: A Platform for Latinas' Subjugated Knowledge." In *Decolonizing Epistemologies*, edited by Ada María Isasi-Díaz and Eduardo Mendieta. New York: Fordham University Press, 2012.

Isasi-Díaz, Ada María. *En La Lucha: Elaborating a Mujerista Theology*. Minneapolis, MN: Fortress Press, 2004.

Isasi-Díaz, Ada María. "Preoccupations, Themes, and Proposals of Mujerista Theology." In *The Ties That Bind: African American and Hispanic American/ Latino/a Theologies in Dialogue*, edited by Anthony B. Pinn and Benjamin Valentin. New York: Continuum, 2001.

Isasi-Díaz, Ada María. *Mujerista Theology: A Theology for the Twenty-First Century*. Maryknoll, NY: Orbis Books, 1996.

Isasi-Díaz, Ada María. "Hispanic Women: Prophetic Voice in the Church." In *Hispanic Women: Prophetic Voice in the Church*, edited by Ada María Isasi-Díaz and Yolanda Tarango. San Francisco, CA: Harper & Row, 1988.

Jiménez, Pablo A. "The Bible: A Hispanic Perspective." In *Teología En Conjunto: A Collaborative Hispanic Protestant Theology*, edited by José D. Rodríguez and Loida I. Martell-Otero, 67–78. Louisville, KY: Westminster John Knox Press, 1997.

Joas, Hans. *The Creativity of Action*. Chicago: University of Chicago Press, 1996.

Joas, Hans. *The Power of the Sacred: An Alternative to the Narrative of Disenchantment*, translated by Alex Skinner. New York: Oxford University Press, 2021.

Jones, Martinque K., and Melissa Briones. "The Impact of Marianismo on the Association between Intersectional Discrimination and Depressive Symptoms among Latina Women: A Profile Analysis." *Journal of Latinx Psychology* 10, no 4 (2022): 304–21.

Jones, Robert P., Daniel Cox, and Juhem Navarro-Rivera. "The 2013 Hispanic Values Survey: How Shifting Religious Identities and Experiences are Influencing Hispanic Approaches to Politics." *Public Religion Research Institute*, September 27, 2013.

Kandiyoti, Dalia. *The Converso's Return: Conversion and Sephardi History in Contemporary Literature and Culture*. Stanford, CA: Stanford University Press, 2020.

Kant, Immanuel. *The Metaphysics of Ethics*, translated by J.W. Semple. Edinburgh: Thomas Clark, [1785] 1836.

Kärkkäinen, Veli-Matti. *Spirit and Salvation: A Constructive Christian Theology for the Pluralistic World, Vol. 4*. Grand Rapids, MI: Eerdmans, 2016.

Kaulen, Patrick. *Largo viaje*. 88 min. black & white, 1967.

Kelley, Dennis. "How are Indigenous Narratives and Oral Traditions Like Texts?" In *Indigenous Religious Traditions in Five Minutes*, edited by Molly H. Bassett and Natalie Avalos, 226–228. Bristol, CT: Equinox Publishing, 2022.

Kenny, Amy. *My Body Is Not a Prayer Request: Disability Justice in the Church.* Grand Rapids, MI: Brazos Press, 2022.

Kerber, Guillermo. "Church Advocacy in Latin America: Integrating Environment in the Struggle for Justice and Human Rights." In *Cosmovision and the Environment: Religion and Social Conflict in Contemporary Latin America Church*, edited by Evan Berry Robert Albro. New York: Routledge, 2018.

Kitcher, Philip. *Preludes to Pragmatism.* New York: Oxford University Press, 2012.

Knights, Vanessa. "Modernity, Modernization and Melodrama: The Bolero in Mexico in the 1930s and 1940s." In *Contemporary Latin American Cultural Studies*, edited by Stephen Hart and Richard Young. London: Routledge, 2014.

Knitter, Paul F. *Without Buddha I Could Not Be a Christian.* Richmond: Oneworld, 2013.

Kroger, Joseph, and Patrizia Granziera. *Aztec Goddesses and Christian Madonnas: Images of the Divine Feminine in Mexico.* Farnham, UK: Ashgate, 2012.

La Fountain-Stokes, Lawrence. "Boricuas cruzando fronteras: autobiografías y testimonios trans puertorriqueños." *Clepsydra: Revista de Estudios de Género y Teoría Feminista* 21 (2021): 95–116.

Lambelet, Kyle B.T. *¡Presente! Nonviolent Politics and the Resurrection of the Dead.* Washington DC: Georgetown University Press, 2019.

Lavrin, Asunción. "Nuestra Señora de la Divina Providencia." In *Latinas in the United States: A Historical Encyclopedia.* edited byVicki L. Ruiz and Virginia Sánchez Korrol. Bloomington: Indiana University Press, 2006.

Levitt, Peggy. "God Needs No Passport: Trying to Define the New Boundaries of Belonging." *Harvard Divinity Bulletin* (Autumn, 2006): https://bulletin.hds.harvard.edu/god-needs-no-passport/.

Levario, Miguel Antonio. *Militarizing the Border: When Mexicans Became the Enemy.* College Station: Texas A&M University Press, 2012.

Levy, Jacques E., and Cesar Chavez. *Cesar Chavez: Autobiography of La Causa.* Minneapolis: University of Minnesota Press, 2008.

Limonic, Laura. "The Role of Transnational Actors in the Growth of Chabad-Lubavitch among Argentine Jews." *Contemporary Jewry* 41, no 4 (December 2021): 843–57.

Limonic, Laura. *Kugel and Frijoles: Latino Jews in the United States.* Detroit, MI: Wayne State University Press, 2019.

Lira, Natalie. *Laboratory of Deficiency: Sterilization and Confinement in California, 1900–1950s.* Oakland: University of California Press, 2022.

Liwerant, Judit Bokser. *National and Transnational Paths of Latin American Jews: Modernity, Community, Society, and the State.* Boston, MA: Brill, 2025.

Lockhart, James. *The Nahuas After the Conquest: A Social and Cultural History of the Indians of Central Mexico, Sixteenth Through Eighteenth Centuries.* Stanford, CA: Stanford University Press, 1994.

Long, Charles H. *Significations: Signs, Symbols, and Images in the Interpretation of Religion.* Philadelphia, PA: Fortress Press, 1986.

López Mezquita, *José Maria. El velatorio.* 200 x 300 c.m, oil on canvas, 1910.

López-Prieto, Guillermo D. "Puerto Rico y Estados Unidos: (des)encuentro entre dos sistemas de organización y clasificación racial." *Romance Notes* 61, no 3 (2021): 429–40.

Lorde, Audre Geraldine. *A Burst of Light: Essays.* Ithaca: Firebrand Books, 1988.

Lovatón, Ramón Lugo. "Nuestra Señora de Las Mercedes en la Isla de Santo Domingo." *Journal of Interamerican Studies and World Affairs* 13, no 1 (1971): 53–61.

Lozada Jr., Francisco Jr. *Towards a Latino/a Biblical Interpretation*. Atlanta, GA: Society of Biblical Literature Press, 2017.

Lucchesi, Annita. *Taaqtam Müüy'müy'k - Hidden Bodies: MMIWG2 and MMIP of Central and Southern California*. Arcata, CA: Sovereign Bodies Institute, in partnership with the San Manuel Band of Mission Indians, 2023.

Luciani, Rafael. *Pope Francis and the Theology of the People*. Maryknoll, NY: Orbis Books, 2017.

Maciste, Manuel Alvarez. "Angelitos Negros (Angeli Negri): Canción Moruna." Italian text by Larici-Testoni. Original text by Andrés Eloy Blanco. Milano, IT: Edizioni Southern Music, 1949.

Maclean, Kate. "Chachawarmi: Rhetorics and Lived Realities." *Bulletin of Latin American Research* 33, no 1 (2014): 76–90.

Malcolm X. *Malcolm X Speaks: Selected Speeches and Statements*, edited by George Breitman. New York: Grove Press, 1965.

Marcos, Sylvia. *Taken from the Lips: Gender and Eros in Mesoamerican Religions*. Boston/ Leiden: Brill, [2005] 2006.

Marcus, Alan P. "Brazilian Immigration to the United States and the Geographical Imagination." *Geographical Review* 99, no 4 (2009): 481–98.

Marrow, Helen. "To Be or Not to Be (Hispanic or Latino): Brazilian Racial and Ethnic Identity in the United States." *Ethnicities* 3, no 4 (2003): 427–64.

Marsh, Charles, Peter Slade, and Sarah Azaransky, editors. *Lived Theology: New Perspectives on Method, Style, and Pedagogy*. New York: Oxford University Press, 2017.

Martínez, María Elena. "The Language, Genealogy, and Classification of 'Race' in Colonial Mexico." In *Race and Classification: The Case of Mexican America*, edited by Ilona Katzew and Susan Deans-Smith. Redwood City, CA: Stanford University Press, 2009.

Martínez, Ramón Antonio, and Melissa Mesinas. "Linguistic Motherwork in the Zapotec Diaspora: Zapoteca Mothers' Perspectives on Indigenous Language Maintenance." *Association of Mexican American Educators Journal* 13, no 2 (June 2019): 122–44.

Martínez-Ruiz, Bárbaro. *Kongo Graphic Writing and Other Narratives of the Sign*. Philadelphia, PA: Temple University Press, 2013.

Marzán, Julio. "Introduction in the Mingling Grain." In, *Selected Poems / Poesía Selecta, Luis Palés Matos*. Houston: Arte Público Press. 2000.

Masuzawa, Tomoko. *The Invention of World Religions: Or, How European Universalism Was Preserved in the Language of Pluralism*. Chicago: University of Chicago Press, 2005.

May, Vivian M. *Pursuing Intersectionality, Unsettling Dominant Imaginaries*. New York: Routledge, 2015.

McCall, Corey, and Phillip McReynolds, editors. *Decolonizing American Philosophy*. Albany: State University of New York Press, 2021.

McCarthy Brown, Karen. *Mama Lola: A Vodou Priestess in Brooklyn*. Berkeley: University of California Press, 1991.

McCormick, William. "The Populist Pope?: Politics, Religion, and Pope Francis." *Politics and Religion* 14(2021): 159–181.

McNeill, Brian, and Joseph Michael Cervantes. *Latina/o Healing Practices: Mestizo and Indigenous Perspectives*. New York: Routledge, 2008.

McWilliams, Carey. *Factories in the Fields: The Story of Migratory Labor in California*. Boston, MA: Little, Brown, and Company, 1940.

Medina, Néstor. "The Doctrine of Discovery, LatinXo Theoethics, and Human Rights." *Journal of Hispanic/Latino Theology* 21, no 2 (2019): 157–73.

Medina, Néstor. "Theological Musings toward a Latina/o Pneumatology." In *The Wiley Blackwell Companion to Latino/a Theology*, 1st Edition, edited by Orlando O. Espín. Hoboken, NJ: Wiley, 2015.

Méndez, Xhercis. "Decolonial Feminist Movidas: A Caribeña (Re)thinks 'Privilege,' the Wages of Gender, and Building Complex Coalitions." In *Theories of the Flesh: Latinx and Latin American Feminisms, Transformation, and Resistance*, edited by Andrea J. Pitts, Mariana Ortega, and José Medina. New York: Oxford University Press, 2020.

Meza Santos, Anderson Fabián. "Resistencia Queer: Mística, Política y Diversidad." *Religión e Incidencia Pública* 9 (2021): 83–106.

Michel, Claudine. "Of Worlds Seen and Unseen: The Educational Character of Haitian Vodou." *Comparative Education Review* 40, no 3 (1996): 280–94.

Milkman, Ruth. *Immigrant Labor and the New Precariat*. Cambridge, UK: Polity Press, 2020.

Miller, Marilyn. "The Soul Has No Color" But the Skin Does: Angelitos Negros and the Uses of Blackface on the Mexican Silver Screen, ca. 1950." In *Global Soundtracks: Worlds of Film Music*, edited by Mark Slobin. Middletown: Wesleyan University Press, 2008.

Miller, Robert J. "The Doctrine of Discovery: The International Law of Colonialism." *Indigenous Peoples' Journal of Law, Culture & Resistance* 5, no 1 (2019): 35–42.

Mingus, Mia. "Changing the Framework: Disability Justice." In *RESIST Newsletter*, November 2010.

Mingus, Mia. "Moving Toward the Ugly: A Politic Beyond Desirability." In *Beginning with Disability: A Primer*, edited by Lennard J. Davis, Jay Dolmage, Nirmala Erevelles, Sarah Parker Harris, Alexander Luft, and Susan Marie Schweik, and Linda P. Ware. New York: Routledge, 2018.

Minich, Julie Avril. "Enabling Whom? Critical Disability Studies Now." *Lateral: Journal of the Cultural Studies Association* 5, no 1 (Spring 2016): 1–7.

Miranda, Alexis R., Amaya Perez-Brumer, Brittany M. Charlton. "Latino? Latinx? Latine? A Call for Inclusive Categories in Epidemiologic Research" *American Journal of Epidemiology*, 192, no. 12 (2023):1929–1932, https://pubmed.ncbi.nlm.nih.gov/37392097/.

Miranda, Ida. "Faith Formation with Hispanic/Latino Families." *Lifelong Faith* (Summer 2007): 1–9.

Mirandé, Alfredo. "Hombres Mujeres: An Indigenous Third Gender." *Men and Masculinities* 19, no 4 (2016): 384–409.

Mohatt, Nathaniel V., Carlotta Ching Ting Fok, Rebekah Burket, David Henry, and James Allen. "Assessment of Awareness of Connectedness as a Culturally-Based Protective Factor for Alaska Native Youth." *Cultural Diversity & Ethnic Minority Psychology* 17, no 4 (October 2011): 444–55.

Molina, Natalia. *How Race is Made in America: Immigration, Citizenship, and the Historical Power of Racial Scripts*. Berkeley: University of California Press, 2014.

Molina, Natalia. "Medicalizing the Mexican: Immigration, Race, and Disability in the Early-Twentieth-Century United States." *Radical History Review* 94 (2006): 22–37.

Moltmann, Jürgen. *The Spirit of Life: A Universal Affirmation*, translated by M. Kohl. Minneapolis, MN: Fortress Press, 1992.

Montano, Steffano. "Theoretical Foundations for an Intercultural, Antiracist Theological Education, 115." PhD diss., Boston College, MA, 2019, eScholarship@BC (https://ur.bc.edu/islandora/theoretical-foundations-intercultural-antiracist-theological-education).

Moraga, Cherríe. *A Xicana Codex of Changing Consciousness: Writings, 2000–2010.* Durham, NC: Duke University Press, 2011.
Moore, Robin D. *Nationalizing Blackness: Afrocubanismo and Artistic Revolution in Havana, 1920–1940.* Pittsburgh: University of Pittsburgh Press, 1997.
Moraga, Cherríe, editor. *The Last Generation: Prose and Poetry.* Boston, MA: South End Press, 1993.
Morales, Ed. *Latinx: The New Force in American Politics and Culture.* London: Verso, 2018.
Morales, Ed. *Fantasy Island: Colonialism, Exploitation, and the Betrayal of Puerto Rico.* New York: Bold Type Books, 2019.
Morales, Harold D. *Latino and Muslim in America: Race, Religion, and the Making of a New Minority.* New York: Oxford Univeristy Press, 2018.
Morrison, Matthew D. *Blacksound: Making Race and Popular Music in the United States.* Berkeley: University of California Press, 2024.
Moya Pons, Frank. *Manual de historia dominicana.* Santo Domingo: Universidad Católica Madre y Maestra, 1980.
Muñoz, José Esteban. *Cruising Utopia: The Then and There of Queer Futurity.* New York: New York University Press, 2009.
Murphy, Joseph. *Botanicas: Sacred Spaces of Healing and Devotion in Urban America.* Jackson: University of Mississippi, 2015.
Musskopf, André Sidnei. "Explorando nuestro presente queer." In *Mysterium Liberationis Queer: Ensayos sobre teologías queer de la liberación en las Américas*, Volume I, edited by Hugo Córdova Quero, Miguel H. Díaz, Anderson Fabián Santos Meza, and Cristian Mor. Nashua, NH: Institute Sophia Press, 2024.
National Disability Institute. "Race, Ethnicity and Disability: The Financial Impact of Systemic Inequality and Intersectionality" (August 2020): 1–11.
Nicholas V, Pope. *Dum Diversas.* June 18, 1452.
Niebuhr, Reinhold. *Moral Man and Immoral Society: A Study in Ethics and Politics.* New York: Scribner, 1932.
Nielsen, Kim E. *A Disability History of the United States.* Boston, MA: Beacon Press, 2012.
Novak, Nicole L., Natalie Lira, Kate E. O'Connor, Siobán D. Harlow, Sharon L. R. Kardia, and Alexandra Minna Stern. "Disproportionate Sterilization of Latinos Under California's Eugenic Sterilization Program, 1920–1945." *American Journal of Public Health (1971)* 108, no 5 (April 4, 2018): 611–3.
Nuñez, Alicia, Patricia González, Gregory A. Talavera, Lisa Sanchez-Johnsen, Scott C. Roesch, Sonia M. Davis, William Arguelles, Veronica Y. Womack, Natania W. Ostrovsky, Lizette Ojeda, Frank J. Penedo, and Linda C. Gallo. "Machismo, Marianismo, and Negative Cognitive-Emotional Factors: Findings From the Hispanic Community Health Study/Study of Latinos Sociocultural Ancillary Study." *Journal of Latina/O Psychology* 4, no 4 (November 2016): 202–17.
O'Brien, Kevin J. " 'La Causa' and Environmental Justice: Cesar Chavez as a Resource for Christian Ecological Ethics." *Journal of the Society of Christian Ethics* 32, no 1 (2012): 151–68.
Ocasio, Rahim, and Juan Galvan. *Alianza Islamica: Spanish Harlem's Islamic Odyssey.* Springfield, IL: Publishing Experts, 2024.
Ochoa, Todd R. "PRENDAS-NGANGAS-ENQUISOS: Turbulence and the Influence of the Dead in Cuban Kongo Material Culture." *Cultural Anthropology*, 25, no 3 (2010): 387–420.
Oleszkiewicz-Peralba, Małgorzata. *The Black Madonna in Latin America and Europe.* Albuquerque: University of New Mexico Press, 2007.

Oliver, Willem H. "Reconsidering the Skin Colour (Race) of Jesus and his Ancestors." *Journal of Early Christian History* 4, no 2 (2014): 96–115.

Olkin, Rhoda. *What Psychotherapists Should Know about Disability*. New York: Guilford Press, 1999.

Olko, Justyna. Language Attitudes and Educational Opportunities: Challenging a History of Oppression and Assimilation Among Indigenous Communities in Mexico." *Sámi dutkansearvvi journála* 1 (2019): 1–37.

Oller, Francisco. *El Velorio*. 1893. 10 x 15, oil on canvas.

Omi, Michael, and Howard Winant. *Racial Formation in the United States*, 3rd edition. New York: Routledge, 2015.

Ontiveros, Randy J. *In the Spirit of a New People: The Cultural Politics of the Chicano Movement*. New York: New York University Press, 2014.

O'Rourke, Thomas R. *The Roots of Pope Francis's Social and Political Thought: From Argentina to the Vatican*. Lanham, MD: Rowman & Littlefield, 2016.

Orsi, Robert A. *Between Heaven and Earth: The Religious Worlds People Make and the Scholars Who Study Them*. Princeton, NJ: Princeton University Press, 2005.

Ortega, Mariana. "Cámara Queer: Longing, the Photograph, and Queer Latinidad." In *Theories of the Flesh: Latinx and Latin American Feminisms, Transformation, and Resistance*, edited byAndrea J. Pitts, Mariana Ortega, and José Medina. New York: Oxford University Press, 2020.

Ortega-Aponte, Elias. "Young Lords Party." In *Encyclopedia on Hispanic American Religious Culture*, Vol. 2, edited by Miguel A. De La Torre. Santa Barbara, CA: ABC-CLIO, 2009.

Otero, Solimar. *Archives of Conjure: Stories of the Dead in Afrolatinx Cultures*. New York: Columbia University Press, 2020.

Oyěwùmí, OyOyěwOyùmèrónké. *The Invention of Women: Making and African Sense of Western Gender Discourses*. Minneapolis, MN: University of Minnesota Press, 1997.

Palés Matos, Luis. "Ñañigo al Cielo," in *Selected Poems / Poesía Selecta: Luis Palés Matos*, edited and translated Julio Marzán. Houston, TX: Arte Público Press, 2000.

Parker, Angela. *If God Still Breathes, Why Can't I?: Black Lives Matter and Biblical Authority*. Grand Rapids, MI: Eerdmans, 2021.

Passel, Jeffrey S. and Jens Manuel Krogstad. "How a Coding Error Provided a Rare Glimpse into Latino Identity among Brazilians in the U.S." Pew Research Center, April 19, 2023.

Paul III, Pope. *Sublimis Deus on the Enslavement and Evangelization of Indians*. May 29, 1537.

Pedelty, Mark. "The Bolero: The Birth, Life, and Decline of Mexican Modernity." In *Latin American Music Review* 20, No. 1 (1999): 30–58.

Pedraja, Luis G. *Teología: An Introduction to Hispanic Theology*. Nashville, TN: Abingdon Press, 2003.

Pedraja, Luis G. *Jesus Is My Uncle: Christology from a Hispanic Perspective*. Nashville, TN: Abingdon Press, 1999.

Penagos, Elaine. "How We Heal: Genealogical Narratives of Healing among San Lázaro Devotees." *Genealogy* 5, no 1 (2021): 18.

Peña, Devon G. *Mexican Americans and the Environment: Tierra Y Vida*. Tuscon, AZ: University of Arizona Press, 2005.

Pepén, Juan F. *Donde florecio el naranjo: la Altagracia, origen y significado de su culto*. Santo Domingo: Amigo del Hogar, 1984.

Perez, Claudio J. "How U.S. Policy Has Failed Immigrant Children: Family Separation in the Obama and Trump Eras." *Family Law Quarterly*, 54, no 1/2 (2020): 37–66.

Peterson, Jeanette Favros. "The Virgin of Guadalupe: Symbol of Conquest or Liberation?." *Art Journal* 51, no 4 (1992): 34–47.

Pew Research Center. Stephanie Kramer and Yunping Tong. *The Religious Composition of the World's Migrants.* August 19, 2024.

Pew Research Center. "Latinx Awareness Has Doubled Among U.S. Hispanics Since 2019, but Only 4% Use It," https://www.pewresearch.org/race-and-ethnicity/2024/09/12/u-s-hispanics-preferences-among-pan-ethnic-terms/#fn-186651-6, September 12, 2024.

Pew Research Center. *Religious 'Nones' in America: Who They Are and What They Believe.* January 24, 2024.

Pew Research Center. Mohamad Moslimani and Luis Noe-Bustamante. *Facts on Latinos in the U.S.* August 16, 2023.

Pew Research Center. Jens Manuel Krogstad and Joshua Alvarado. *Among U.S. Latinos, Catholicism Continues to Decline but Is Still the Largest Faith.* April 13, 2023.

Pew Research Center. *Among U.S. Latinos, Catholicism Continues to Decline but Is Still the Largest Faith.* April 13, 2023.

Pew Research Center. Jeffrey S. Passel and Jens Manuel Krogstad. "How a coding error provided a rare glimpse into Latino identity among Brazilians in the U.S." April 19, 2023, https://pewrsr.ch/3ULh6mp., https://pewrsr.ch/3ULh6mp.

Pew Research Center. *Jewish Americans in 2020: U.S. Jews are Culturally Engaged, Increasing Diverse, Politically Polarized and Worried about Anti-Semitism.* May 11, 2021.

Pew Research Center. Mark Hugo Lopez, Ana Gonzalez-Barrera, and Jens Manuel Krogstad. *Latinos are More Likely to Believe in the American Dream, but Most Say it is Hard to Achieve*, September 11, 2018.

Pew Research Center. *The Shifting Religious Identity of Latinos in the United States.* May 7, 2014.

Pineda-Madrid, Nancy. *Suffering and Salvation in Ciudad Juárez.* Minneapolis, MN: Fortress Press, 2011.

Pew Research Center. "Notes Toward a Chicanafeminist Epistemology (And Why It Is Important for Latina Feminist Theologies)." In *A Reader in Latina Feminist Theology*, edited by María Pilar Aquino, Daisy L. Machado, and Jeanette Rodriguez. Austin: University of Texas Press, 2002.

Pinn, Anthony B., editor. *The Oxford Handbook of Humanism.* New York: Oxford Academic, 2019.

Pintado, Ana Celia Perera. "Religion and Cuban Identity in a Transnational Context." *Latin American Perspectives* 32, no 1 (2005): 147–73.

Pulido, Laura. *Environmentalism and Economic Justice: Two Chicano Struggles in the Southwest.* Tucson: University of Arizona Press, 1996.

Ramos, Paola. *Defectors: The Rise of the Latino Far Right and What It Means for America.* New York: Pantheon Books, 2024.

Ramsey, Paul. *Christian Ethics and the Sit-In.* New York: Association, 1961.

Rawls, John. *A Theory of Justice.* Cambridge, MA: Belknap Press of Harvard University Press, 1971.

Richard, Pablo. "Hermenútica bíblica india: Revelación de Dios en las religiones indígenas y en la Biblia (Después de 500 años de dominación)." In *Sentido histórico del V Centenario (1492–1992)*, edited by G. Meléndez. San José, Costa Rica: CEHILA-DEI, 1992.

Rivera, Sylvia. "Queens in Exile, The Forgotten Ones." In *Gender Queer: Voices from Beyond the Sexual Binary*, edited by Joan Nestle, Clare Howell, and Riki Anne Wilchins. Los Angeles: Alyson Books, 2002.

Redemptorist Pastoral Publication. *Mary Throughout Latin America.* Liguori, MO: Liguori Publications, 2005.

Reece, Robert. L. "Genesis of U.S. Colorism and Skin Tone Stratification: Slavery, Freedom, and Mulatto-Black Occupational Inequality in the Late 19th Century." *The Review of Black Political Economy* 45, no 1 (2018): 3–21.

Retief, Marno, and Rantoa Letšosa. "Models of Disability: A Brief Overview." In *HTS Teologiese Studies / Theological Studies* 74, no 1 (March 6, 2018): 1–8.

Reyes II, Rudolph P. "Prophetic Temptation of Ecological Disgust." In *Gonna Trouble the Water: Ecojustice, Water, and Environmental Racism*, edited by Miguel A. De La Torre. Cleveland, OH: Pilgrim Press, 2021.

Rodriguez, Jeanette. "La Tierra Theologies' Contribution to Creation Theologies." *In Our Own Voices: Latino/a Renditions of Theology*, edited by Benjamín Valentín. Maryknoll, NY: Orbis Books, 2010.

Rodriguez, Jeanette. *Our Lady of Guadalupe: Faith and Empowerment among Mexican-American Women*. Austin: University of Texas, 1994.

Rodriguez, Joselito. *Angelitos Negros*. Peliculas Rodríguez y Cinematografia, México,D.F.: World Media Marketing, Editorial Clio., 1948, 1 hr. 40 min.

Rodriguez, Joselito. *Angelitos Negros*. México,D.F.: On Screen Films: Televisa Home Entertainment, 2008, 110 min.

Ruiz Soto, Ariel G., Colleen Putzel-Kavanaugh, and Doris Meissner. *Shifting Realities at the U.S.-Mexico Border: Immigration Enforcement and Control in a Fast-Evolving Landscape*. Washington, DC: Migration Policy Institute, 2024.

Ruiz, Jean-Pierre. *Readings from the Edges: The Bible and the People on the Move*. Maryknoll, NY: Orbis Books, 2011.

Ruiz, Jean-Pierre. "The Bible and U.S. Hispanic Theological Discourse: Lessons from a Non-Innocent History." In *From the Heart of Our People: Latino/a Explorations in Catholic Systematic Theology*, edited by Orlando O. Espín and Miguel H. Díaz. Maryknoll, NY: Orbis Books, 1999.

Salinas, Cristobal Salinas Jr., and Adele Lozano. "The History and Evolution of The Term Latinx." In *Handbook of Latinos and Education*, 2nd edition, edited by E. G. Murillo, D. Delgado Bernal, S. Morales, L. Urrieta, E. Ruiz Bybee, J. Sánchez Muñoz, V. B. Saenz, D. Villanueva, M. Machado-Casas, and K. Espinoza. New York: Routledge, 2021.

Salkas, Kristen, Sandy Magaña, Isabela Marques, and Mansha Mirza. "Spirituality in Latino Families of Children with Autism Spectrum Disorder." *Journal of Family Social Work* 19, no 1 (January 21, 2016): 38–55.

Samples, Caitlin E. "Gender-inclusive Language in Twitter." *Hispania* 107, no 1 (2024): 139–60, https://muse.jhu.edu/pub/1/article/921466/pdf.

Sanchez, David A. *From Patmos to the Barrio: Subverting Imperial Myths*. Minneapolis, MN: Fortress Press, 2008.

Sanchez-Walsh, Arlene. "An examination of the folk healing practice of Curanderismo in the Hispanic community." *Journal of Community Health Nursing*35, no 3 (2018): 148–61.

Sanchez-Walsh, Arlene. "Tenayuca, Elites, and the Pecan-Shellers' Strike." In *The Pew and the Picket Line: Christianity and the American Working Class*, edited by Christopher D. Cantwell, Heath W. Carter, and Janine Giordano Drake. Champaign: University of Illinois Press, 2016.

San Diego Pride, accessed September 14, 2025, https://sdpride.org/latine/.

Sandoval, Cueponcaxochtl, Moreno, Miriam Georgina Valdovinos, Elisa Contreras, and Xochitl López Andrade. "Warrior Butterflies Walking with the Ancestors: A Longitudinal Study of Indigenous Youth Becoming Leaders of Social Justice." In *Decolonial Feminist Praxis: Centering Knowledge & Resistance at the Margins*, edited by A. I. Fukushima and K. M. Quick Hall. Champaign: University of Illinois Press (In Press).

Santoro, Nicholas Joseph. *Mary in Our Life: Atlas of the Names and Titles of Mary, the Mother of Jesus*. Bloomington, IN: iUniverse Publishing, 2011.
Scannone, Juan Carlos. "Pope Francis and the Theology of the People." *Theological Studies* 77 (2016): 118–35.
Schaeffer, Pierre. "Acousmatics." In *Audio Culture: Readings in Modern Music*. Edited by Cristoph Cox and Daniel Warner. New York: Continuum International Publishing Group, 2006.
Schaeffer, Pierre. *Treatise on Musical Objects: An Essay across Disciplines*. Oakland: University of California Press, 2017.
Schneiderman, Howard. "Introduction to the Transaction Edition: James Truslow Adams and the American Dream." In *The Epic of America*. New York: Transaction Publishers, [1931] 2012.
Schubert, Franz. 1826. "Ave Maria!" Op. 52/6 in Bb. From Ellens Gesang III (Hymne an die Jungfrau). Scott, trans. Storck.
Scott, James C. *Domination and the Arts of Resistance*. New Haven, CT: Yale University Press, 1990.
Seijas, Tatiana. *Asian Slaves in Colonial Mexico: From Chinos to Indians*. New York: Cambridge University Press, 2014.
Shaw, Randy. *Beyond the Fields: César Chávez, The UFW, and Struggle for Justice in the 21st Century*. Berkeley: University of California Press, 2008.
Shohat, Ella. "The Sephardi-Moorish Atlantic: Between Orientalism and Occidentalism." In *Between the Middle East and the Americas: The Cultural Politics of Diaspora*, edited by Ella Habib Shohat and Evelyn Azeeza Alsultany. Ann Arbor, MI: University of Michigan Press, 2013.
Stam, Robert, and Ella Shohat. *Race in Translation: Culture Wars Around the Postcolonial Atlantic*. New York: New York University Press, 2012.
Shoji, Rafael. "The Failed Prophecy of Shinto Nationalism and the Rise of Japanese Brazilian Catholicism." *Japanese Journal of Religious Studies* 35, no 1 (2008): 13–38.
Sobrino, Jon. *Christology at the Crossroads*, translated by Cesar Jerez. Maryknoll, NY: Orbis Books, 1978.
Soormally, Mina García. "The Image of a Miracle: The Virgin of Guadalupe and the Context of the Apparitions." *Chasqui* 44, no 2 (2015): 175–90.
Sostaita, Barbara Andrea. *Sanctuary Everywhere: The Fugitive Sacred in the Sonoran Desert*. Durham, NC: Duke University Press, 2024.
Soto, Shirlene. "Tres Modelos Culturales: La Virgen de Guadalupe, La Malinche, y La Llorona." *Fem* 48 (1986): 13–16.
Speed, Shannon. "Structures of Settler Capitalism in Abya Yala." *American Quarterly* 69, no 4 (December 2017): 783–90.
Spence, Mark David. *Dispossessing the Wilderness: Indian Removal and the Making of the National Parks*. New York: Oxford University Press, 1999.
Steinberg, Theodore. *Down to Earth: Nature's Role in American History*, 3rd Edition. Oxford: Oxford University Press, 2012.
Subrat, Piro. *Invertidos y Rompepatrias: Marxismo, Anarquismo y Desobediencia Sexual y de Género en el Estado Español - 1868–1982*, 1st edition. Madrid: Imperdible, 2019.
Sussman, Robert Wald. *The Myth of Race: The Troubling Persistence of an Unscientific Idea*. Cambridge, MA: Harvard University Press, 2014.
Sze, Julie. *Noxious New York: The Racial Politics of Urban Health and Environmental Justice*. Cambridge, MA: MIT Press, 2006.
Tamez, Elsa. "The Bible and the Five Hundred Years of Conquest." In *Voices from the Margin: Interpreting the Bible in the Third World*, edited by R. S. Sugirtharajah, Rev. ed. Maryknoll, NY: Orbis Books, 2006.

Tanasescu, Mihnea. "The Rights of Nature in Ecuador: The Making of an Idea." *International Journal of Environmental Studies* 70, no 6 (2013): 846–61.
Taylor, Diana. *¡Presente! The Politics of Presence.* Durham, NC: Duke University Press, 2020.
Teisenhoffer, Viola. "De la 'Nebulosa Místico-Esotérica' al circuito alternativo." In *Raíces en Movimiento: prácticas religiosas tradicionales en contextos translocales*, edited by Kali Argyriadis, Renée de la Torre, Cristina Gutiérrez Zuñiga, and Aguilar Ros. Centro de estudios mexicanos y centroamericanos, 2008.
Telles, Edward. *Pigmentocracies: Ethnicity, Race, and Color in Latin America.* North Carolina: University of North Carolina Press, 2014.
Thompson, Katrina Dyonne. *Ring Shout, Wheel About: The Racial Politics of Music and Dance in North American Slavery.* Urbana: University of Illinois Press, 2014.
Thompson, Robert F., and John F. Szwed. "Foreword: Forest as Moral Document." In *El Monte: Notes on the Religions, Magic, and Folklore of the Black and Creole People of Cuba*, 1st edition , edited by Lydia Cabrera, translated by David Font-Navarrete. Durham, NC: Duke University Press, 2023.
Thornton, John. "The Development of an African Catholic Church in the Kingdom of Kongo, 1491–1750." *The Journal of African History* 25, no 2 (1984): 147–67.
Thurston, Herbert. "Hail Mary." *The Catholic Encyclopedia.* New York: Robert Appleton Company, 1910.
Tirres, Christopher D. *Liberating Spiritualities: Reimagining Faith in the Américas.* New York: Fordham University Press, 2024.
Transgender Law Center and Cornell University Law School LGBT Clinic. *Report on Human Rights Conditions of Transgender Women in Mexico.* Ithaca, NY: Cornell University Law School LGBT Clinic, 2016.
Trotter, Robert T, and Juan Antonio Chavira. *Curanderismo: Mexican American Folk Healing.* Athens: University of Georgia Press, 1997.
Tujibikile, Muamba. *La resistencia del negro en América Latina: lógica ancestral y celebración de la vida.* San José, CA: Editorial DEI, 1990.
Turner, Victor W. *The Ritual Process: Structure and Anti-Structure.* Chicago: Aldine, 1969.
Tweed, Thomas A. *Crossing and Dwelling: A Theory of Religion.* Cambridge, MA: Harvard University Press, 2006.
Tweed, Thomas A. *Our Lady of the Exile: Diasporic Religion at a Cuban Catholic Shrine in Miami.* New York: Oxford University Press, 1997.
Ullrich, Jessica Saniguq. "For The Love of Our Children: An Indigenous Connectedness Framework." *AlterNative: An International Journal of Indigenous Peoples* 15, no 2 (2019): 121–30.
US Census Bureau. "Updates to Race/Ethnicity Standards for Our Nation," accessed September 16, 2025, https://www.census.gov/about/our-research/race-ethnicity/standards-updates.html_.
Valdez, Luis, and Stan Steiner, editors. "El Plan Espiritual de Aztlán." In *Aztlan: An Anthology of Mexican American Literature.* New York: Knopf, 1972.
van der Kolk, Bessel. *The Body Keeps the Score: Brain, Mind, and Body in the Healing of Trauma.* New York: Penguin, 2014.
Vázquez García, Francisco, and Richard Cleminson. *"Los Invisibles": Una Historia de la Homosexualidad Masculina en España, 1850–1939.* Granada: Editorial Comares, 2011.
Vásquez, Manuel A. *More Than Belief: A Materialist Theory of Religion.* Oxford: Oxford University Press, 2011.
Velasco Gómez, Ambrosio. Humanismo hispanoamericano. *Revista de Hispanismo Filosófico*, no. 13 (2008): 13–30.

Vidal-Ortiz, Salvador, and Juliana Martínez. "Latinx thoughts: Latinidad with an X." *Latino Studies* 16 (2018): 384–95. https://doi.org/10.1057/s41276-018-0137-8.
Villalobos Mendoza, Manuel. "Anzaldúa and the Ethiopian Eunuch: Border-Crossing and the Reimagining of Sacred Texts." In *Bible Trouble: Queer Reading at the Boundaries of Biblical Scholarship*, edited by Teresa J. Hornsby and Ken Stone. Atlanta, GA: Society of Biblical Literature Press, 2011.
Villarreal, Laura Victoria. "Addressing Marianismo within the United States: Latinx and Xicanas." *Labyrinth* 3 (Spring 2018): 6–15.
Wade, Peter. "Race in Latin America." *A Companion to Latin American Anthropology*, edited by Debora Poole. Oxford: Blackwell Publishing, 2008.
Wald, Sarah D., David J. Vazquez, Priscialla Solis Ybarra, and Sarah Jaquette Ray, editors. *Latinx Environmentalisms: Place, Justice, and the Decolonial*. Philadelphia, PA: Temple University Press, 2019.
Walsh, Arlene Sánchez. *Pentecostals in America*. New York: Columbia University Press, 2018.
Walters, Karina L., and Jane M. Simoni. "Reconceptualizing Native Women's Health: An 'Indigenist' Stress-Coping Model. *American Journal of Public Health* 92, no 4 (April 2002): 520–24.
Walters, Karina L., Jane M. Simoni, and Teresa Evans-Campbell. "Substance Use Among American Indians and Alaska Natives: Incorporating Culture in an 'Indigenist' Stress-Coping Paradigm." *Public Health Reports* 117, Suppl 1 (2002): S104–17.
Webb, Sarah L., editor, *Colorism: Essays and Poems*, Self-Published, 2017.
Wendell, Susan. "Unhealthy Disabled: Treating Chronic Illnesses as Disabilities." *Hypatia* 16, no 4 (2001): 17–33.
West, Cornel. *Prophesy Deliverance! An Afro-American Revolutionary Christianity*, 20th anniversary edition. Louisville, KY: Westminster John Knox Press, 2002.
Weyr, Thomas. *Hispanic U.S.A.: Breaking the Melting Pot*. New York: Harper & Row, 1988.
Wilcox, Melissa M. *Queer Religiosities: An Introduction to Queer and Transgender Studies in Religion*. Lanham, MD: Rowman & Littlefield, 2021.
Williams, Joseph W. *Spirit Cure: A History of Pentecostal Healing*, 1st edition. Oxford: Oxford University Press, 2012.
Wimbush, Vincent L. *White Men's Magic: Scripturalization as Slavery*. New York: Oxford University Press, 2012.
Withers, A. J. *Disability Politics and Theory*. Halifax, Nova Scotia: Fernwood Publishing, 2012.
Wright, I. A. "Our Lady of Charity." *The Hispanic American Historical Review* 5, no 4 (1922): 709–17.
Wolf, Eric R. "The Virgin of Guadalupe: A Mexican National Symbol." *The Journal of American Folklore* 71, no 279 (1958): 34–39.
Wolfe, Patrick. "Settler Colonialism and the Elimination of the Native." *Journal of Genocide Research* 8, no 4 (2006): 387–409.
Woodson, Kamilah Marie. *Colorism: Investigating a Global Phenomenon*. Santa Barbara, CA: Fielding University Press, 2020.
World Council of Churches. "Consultation Explores Multiple Religious Belonging in Latin American Context." *World Council of Churches*, December 21, 2021.
Ybarra, Priscilla Solis. *Writing the Goodlife: Mexican American Literature and the Environment*. Tuscon: University of Arizona Press, 2016.
Young, David Atekpatzin. *A Magic Feather: The Science and Theory of Chicano Traditional Healing Practices of Aztlán*. Boulder, CO: Calmecaztlan Press, 2020.

Yugar, Theresa. "Buen Vivir: Historical Narrative of Environmental Resisters in the United States and Latin America." *Perspectivas*, no 19 (2022): 55–74

Zegarra, Raúl E. *A Revolutionary Faith: Liberation Theology Between Public Religion and Public Reason*. Stanford, CA: Stanford University Press, 2023.

Zepeda, Susy. *Queering Mesoamerican Diasporas: Remembering Xicana Indígena Ancestries*. Champaign, IL: University of Illinois Press, 2022.

Zepeda, Susy. "Decolonizing Xicana/x Studies: Healing the Susto of De-Indigenization." *Aztlán: A Journal of Chicano Studies* 45, no 1 (2020): 225–41.

Zuckerman, Phil, and John Shook, editors. *The Oxford Handbook on Secularism*. New York: Oxford University Press, 2017.

Zweig, Michael. *The Working Class Majority: America's Best Kept Secret*. Ithaca: ILR Press/Cornell University Press, 2012.

Note on Contributors

Edwin David Aponte is Dean of the Theological School and Professor of Religion and Culture at Drew University in Madison, New Jersey. He is a cultural historian focusing on lived religions and spirituality, Latine religions and spirituality, and religion and politics. Previously, Aponte served as executive director of the Louisville Institute, a granting agency funded by Lilly Endowment Inc. Aponte received a Doctor of Theology, *honoris causa* from The Catholic Theological Union at Chicago. He is president of the Religious Research Association. Aponte's publications include *¡Santo! Varieties of Latino/a Spirituality* (2012); *Introducing Latinx Theologies*, co-authored with Miguel A. De La Torre (Orbis Books, 2020); and "Popular Culture and Caribbean Religions" in the *Oxford Handbook of Caribbean Religions* (2024).

Amanda J. Baugh is a scholar of the environmental humanities working at the intersection of religion, race, and environmental justice. She is the author of *Falling in Love With Nature: The Values of Latinx Catholic Enviornmetnalism* (2024) and *God and the Green Divide: Religious Environmentalism in Black and White* (2016). Baugh is a professor and the Associate Chair of Religious Studies and Director of the MA Program in Sustainability at California State University, Northridge.

Ramona Beltrán is an associate professor and Associate Dean of Research and Faculty Development at University of Denver Graduate School of Social Work. In her twenty years of professional and academic experience, spanning the United States to New Zealand, she has worked alongside Indigenous and Latine communities, spotlighting solutions that are present in our creative and cultural-driven modalities. Dr. Beltrán is a fiercely loving mother of three and is a multiracial Chicana of Indigenous descent. She acknowledges that all the earth has an Indigenous name and a community meant to steward it.

Neomi De Anda is the executive director of the International Marian Research Institute and Professor of religious studies at the University of Dayton. She actively publishes public scholarship and regularly works with media outlets regarding her research interests including Mary and breast milk, chisme, LatinoXa Christology, and migrations in conjunction with the Marianist Social Justice Collaborative Immigrant Justice Team. She maintains a commitment to a border theology at the intersections of the environment, migrations, labor, and women because of her roots in El Paso, Texas. Dr. De Anda serves on the Louisville Institute Advisory Board and as a mentor for the Hispanic Theological Initiative.

Deborah De La Torre is currently a PhD candidate in Ethnomusicology with a minor in Latine Studies, in the Department of Folklore & Ethnomusicology, at Indiana University, Bloomington. She holds a Master of Business Administration from Regis University in Denver, Colorado, and a Bachelor of Music from the University of Miami, Coral Gables, Florida. Her background includes music performance and composition and and recording original music; teaching music and Latine film studies; church music, cultural arts management, and founding and managing an international Latina/o art and film festival. Her scholarly interests include interdisciplinary approaches to Latine and AfroLatine cultural production, historical Ethnomusicology, Caribbean cultures, Iberian death ritual practices, film, sound, economics, and aging.

Miguel A. De La Torre is an international scholar, documentarian, novelist, academic author, and scholar activist. Since obtaining his doctoral in 1999, he has authored over a hundred articles and published fifty books (six of which won national awards). He presently serves as Professor of Social Ethics and Latine Studies at the Iliff School of Theology in Denver, Colorado. A Fulbright scholar, he has served as the 2012 president of the *Society of Christian Ethics*. He is the recipient of the 2020 AAR Excellence in Teaching Award and the 2021 Martin E. Marty Public Understanding of Religion Award. Recently, he wrote the screenplay to a documentary on immigration which has won over seven awards. Additionally, he has written an autofiction magical realism novel.

Jibreel 'Biel' A. Delgado Trabal is a writer, educator, artist, and activist with a background in American Studies and Middle Eastern/North African Studies. A Fulbright scholar, his research has taken him across Southwest Asia, North Africa, Spain, Puerto Rico, the Caribbean, and the United States. Currently a PhD candidate in Ethnic Studies and Religious Studies, he has worked as a humanities consultant, conference organizer, and exhibition curator for several Latine-rooted cultural and research centers in the San Francisco Bay Area.

Damien Pascal Domenack is a social ethicist and PhD candidate in Religion & Society at Drew University. He is a Lukumí omolorisha and a candidate for ordination in the Unitarian Universalist tradition. His research examines practices of care through liberative theologies and philosophies, Latine lived religion, Black Atlantic religious traditions, and Indigenous spiritual praxis, approaching religion as a generative ground for intersectional hospitality and coalitional life. His writing has appeared in *CrossCurrents*, *QTR: A Journal of Trans and Queer Studies in Religion*, and *Journal of the Society of Christian Ethics*.

Francisco J. García Jr. is an Episcopal priest, organizer, and theological educator. He completed his doctorate in theology, ethics, and action at Vanderbilt University. He teaches at the Church Divinity School of the Pacific, and is the convener and co-chair of Sacred Resistance, an immigrant rights and social justice ministry in the Episcopal Diocese of Los Angeles. He will soon be working on his first book stemming from his doctoral research, which involves the development of social movement-oriented ecclesiologies outside of formal church structures, through an exploration of faith practices among Latine immigrant workers organizing in their workplaces and communities.

Albert Hernández is Associate Professor of the History of Christianity at Iliff School of Theology and Core Faculty in Iliff's Joint Doctoral Program with the University of Denver. He was born and raised in Miami's Cuban exile community with strong ties to northern New Jersey's Cuban communities. He holds a masters and doctoral degrees from Drew University's Caspersen School of Graduate Studies and is a Fellow of the Hispanic Theological Initiative at Princeton Theological Seminary. His teaching and research areas include pneumatology and healing traditions, medieval and early modern Spain, the Italian Renaissance, and the history of mysticism.

Jacqueline M. Hidalgo is currently a Professor of Theology and Religious Studies at the University of San Diego. She presently serves as general editor of the *Semeia Studies* series with the Society of Biblical Literature and has held various leadership positions including serving as a past president for the Academy of Catholic Hispanic Theologians of the United States as well as a past president of the New England/Eastern Canada region of the Society of Biblical Literature. She is the author of *Latina/o/x Studies and Biblical Studies* (2020) and *Revelation in Aztlán: Scriptures, Utopias, and the Chicano Movement* (2016) as well as numerous articles and essays; she has also co-edited a number of volumes related to biblical studies as well as Latine religions.

Kristina Hulama is a PhD candidate at the University of Denver's Graduate School of Social Work. A Native Hawaiian-Pacific Islander scholar, she conducts community-engaged research with Indigenous women, amplifying their voices and holding oppressive healthcare systems accountable. Her scholarship is dedicated to justice, healing, collective care, and systemic transformation.

Olivia Hunte is a PhD candidate at University of Denver Graduate School of Social Work and is a graduate research assistant with the Our Stories, Our Medicine Archive (OSOMA). Olivia engages in community-centered research to develop liberatory theoretical and practice frameworks in their doctoral education.

Laura Limonic is an Associate Professor in Sociology at SUNY Old Westbury. Her research is in the area of Latine immigration to the United States, Jewish migration and race and ethnicity. Her current work examines the role of subethnic identity formation and community building among among Latin Sephardic Jews in the United States.

Sudabée Lotfian-Mena is affiliated with the University of Valladolid where her area of study is philosophy of aesthetics. She also attends the University of Dayton, where her work centers around colonization and the ravages of 1492. She has lately co-authored *Filosofía de la Religión* (2025). She is devoted to teaching theology, her latest course being "Faith and Justice," a look at Catholic Social Doctrine through the lens of Liberation.

José Francisco Morales Torres is the Associate Professor of Comparative Theology and Philosophy at Chicago Theological Seminary. His areas of interest include comparative methods in theology and philosophy, philosophies of race and theological anthropologies, and history of Latin American philosophy. His first book, *Wonder as a New Starting Point for Theological Anthropology: Opened by the World* (2023), proposes a new theological anthropology informed by the experience of wonder.

Elaine Penagos is an assistant professor at Trinity University's Department of Religion, where she teaches classes on Africana religious cultures. She is a scholar of African heritage religions, especially Regla de Ocha, known popularly as Santería. Her research utilizes art, cultural aesthetic productions, and popular culture to examine how practitioners of Afro-Cuban religions engage in their (re)making of religion. Her writing has appeared in *Genealogy*, *Practical Matters*, the Wabash Center, the Hispanic Theological Initiative's Open Plaza, and the *Oxford Handbook of Caribbean Religions*.

Grego Peña-Camprubí is an academic researcher and consultant specializing in the anthropology of religion, lived religion, and LGBTQ+ Catholicism, with focus on Spain. He is a Postdoctoral Research Fellow at the Hartford Institute for Religion Research (HIRR team), and a research consultant with the Association of Theological Schools (ATS), focusing on quality assessement in theological education. A dedicated LGBT+ Catholic advocate, he serves as Chair of Empty Chairs, a nonprofit committed to creating spaces for LGBT+ indivuals within the Roman Catholic Church.

Noemi Vega Quiñones is a PhD candidate in Religious Ethics at Southern Methodist University. Her research on the intersections of race, gender, migration, and religious faith is made possible by the SMU Mustang Fellowship, the Hispanic Theological Initiative, and the Louisville Institute as well as several family, friends, and community partners on both sides of the border.

Rudolph P. Reyes II is a visiting scholar at Graduate Theological Union. Previously, Reyes was a faculty member at Garrett-Evangelical Theological Seminary. He is a multiply neurodivergent Latino social ethicist whose research focuses on how theology and ethics influences the intersection of race, gender, class, sexuality, and disability oppression from a liberative ethical perspective.

Alexandra Rosado-Román is an Afro-Caribbean social ethicist whose research interests span Feminist Decolonial Theories, Diaspora Studies, and Spiritualities. As a scholar-activist, she's committed to unraveling the intricate workings of colonial constructs—race, class, gender, sexuality, ethnicity, and citizenship—and their impact on racialized women in Puerto Rico and the Caribbean. Rosado-Román is a professor and mentor whose teaching and community work bridge academic spaces with embodied decolonial practices. She is also the founder of Bámbula Studio, a creative and educational space dedicated to the practice and preservation of bomba—an Indigenous and Afro-Puerto Rican music and dance tradition—and to nurturing Afro-Caribbean cultural expression as a tool for healing, resistance, and collective memory..

Isabela Leonor Rosales is a PhD candidate in Latine Social Ethics whose work explores queer lived experience, cultural iconography, and the everyday moral frameworks that sustain Latine communities. Their dissertation examines how queer and trans individuals reinterpret religious and cultural figures—such as La Virgen de Guadalupe—as sites of belonging, resilience, and intergenerational ethics. She has worked extensively in reproductive justice and immigrant rights advocacy across the US Southwest and South. Currently, they serve as the popular education manager at the Tennessee Immigrant and Refugee Rights Coalition (TIRRC), where she bridges scholarly inquiry and grassroots organizing to demand liberatory futures grounded in consciousness-raising and relational care.

Rubén Rosario Rodríguez is Professor of Systematic Theology at Saint Louis University in Missouri. His teaching and research interests range from comparative religious ethics to theological anthropology, to liberation and political theologies. His most recent publications include *Theological Fragments: Confessing What We Know and Cannot Know About an Infinite God* (2023) and *Calvin for the World: The Enduring Relevance of His Political, Social, and Economic Theology* (2024).

My Ngoc To is an assistant professor at the School of Social Work at Colorado State University. She draws from over eight years of mindfulness teaching and practice to conduct community-centered contemplative research on collective healing among contemporary diasporic communities.

Miriam G. Valdovinos is an associate professor at the Graduate School of Social Work at the University of Denver. Over twenty years of social work practice informs her commitment to advocate for culturally responsive services that will address the issues that interpersonal violence has on Latine families.

Index

abuelita theology 58
accompaniment, theology of 49
activism
  disability 82–3
  environmental 128, 130–5
  faith-based 138, 143–4
  LGBTQ+ 119
  social and political 34, 36, 53, 56
African
  Afro-Latine 20, 57–8, 60, 74, 88, 102, 113, 153, 196
  American 5, 19, 37, 40, 58, 60, 63, 70, 77, 112–15, 146, 155, 228n.16
  anti-Blackness and racism 2, 6–7, 19, 22, 31, 36, 38, 47, 53, 56, 77, 80–2, 97, 99–103, 106–16, 120–1, 128–9, 143, 149, 177
  Black Theology 115
  continent 5, 26, 28, 35, 39, 41–2, 55, 63–4, 74, 195, 203, 218n.9
  descendant communities 2, 17–18, 20–2, 37–8, 41, 62, 74, 109–15, 171, 188, 194–5
  diasporic spiritualities ix, 4, 6, 9–10, 16, 55, 57–8, 60–9, 73–5, 103, 153–4, 161, 167–74, 194–5, 218n.9, 226n.34
  enslavement 6, 15–16, 35, 37–8, 40, 57, 60–4, 74, 102, 153, 155, 160, 169–71, 175, 188, 196, 226n.34
  Moro heritage 5, 37–41
  Yoruba 55, 61–8, 74, 154, 218n.9, 226n.34
agency 13, 56, 61, 98, 120, 123, 128, 149–50, 163–4, 171
Alexander V, Pope 176
Alfonso V, King 176
Alianza Islamica 36–9, 41–2, 214n.26
Althaus-Reid, Marcella 121, 124
American Dream 5, 8, 10, 137–44, 201–2
Angelitos Negros 9, 167, 170–4
Anglo-American/Euroamerican
  Black binary 17, 115–16, 202
  categorize as 18, 31, 112–13, 188–9, 207, 228n.16
  feminism 39–42, 98, 100–4, 106–7
  hierarchy 7, 20, 36, 39, 42–3, 47, 49, 53, 58, 80, 97–8, 103–5, 110, 112, 141–2, 149, 154–6, 188, 236n.45
  immigrants 19
  interracial 17, 98
  movements 36, 129
  passing 5, 19, 25, 31–3, 36, 110, 171, 188, 207
  supremacy 8, 10, 35, 38–9, 42, 53, 58, 98, 102, 113–16, 146, 151–2, 155–7, 176, 180, 202–3
Anzaldúa, Gloria 2, 106, 121, 162, 164, 189, 226n.36, 227n.52, 229n.3
Aponte, Edwin David 54, 58, 159, 210n.1
Aquino, María Pilar 100–1
Argentina 2, 26–7, 29–30, 94, 174
ashé 63–4
assimilation 10, 19, 25–6, 31, 41, 97, 115, 201, 203, 207
Aztlán 103–6, 130, 162, 226n.36
Azusa Street Revival 55, 70

barriers
  biomedical care 69–70, 82
  structural 7, 70, 82–3, 102
Beliso-De Jesús, Aisha 168–70
belonging 4, 18, 25–34, 58, 70–1, 75, 98, 104, 109, 111, 144, 162–5, 180–1, 186, 191, 196–8, 204
bendición, la 139
Benedict XIV, Pope 89
Benjamin, Walter 10, 205–6
Bergoglio, Jorge Mario, *see* Francis, Pope

Bible
book 3, 44–5, 52, 98, 152–3, 159–65
Christology 44–7
Hebrew 3, 44
murals as 160, 162
New Testament 44–5, 51
responsibilities toward nature 133–4
sacred text 46, 70, 133–4, 159–65
teachings and interpretations 9, 46–7, 52, 56, 70–1, 73, 161, 163–4
trickster figures in 8, 152–3
as weapon 115, 160–1
Biden, Joseph 37
Blanco, Andrés Eloy 171–2, 240n.42, 241n.60
Boff, Leonardo 131–2
Bolivia 94, 128
borderlands
borders 1–3, 117–21, 139, 187–92
fluidity of 118–20, 187–92
as in-between space 1–3, 9–11, 121, 162–4
migration and 187–92
as open wound 121, 189
US–Mexican 1–5, 9–11, 37, 80, 117–21, 130, 138–9, 163–5, 177, 188–92
Borderlands/La Frontera 2, 121, 162, 164, 189, 226n.36
botánicas 62, 65, 67, 73
bóvedas 66–7, 75
Brazil 7, 11, 15–19, 26, 37, 60, 92–3, 131–2, 154, 197
Buddhism 93, 190
buen vivir 8, 127–30, 133
Bush, George W. 37

Cabrera, Lydia 74
Candomble 4, 154
capitalism 8, 128, 130, 138, 143–4, 149, 155–6, 171, 192
Casanova, José 195–7
caste systems 19, 115, 177
Castro, Julian 137–40, 143
Catholicism
Augustinians 56
Carmelites 56
charismatic movements 6, 55–6, 70
church 2, 27, 48–9, 60, 73, 86–93, 128, 131–3, 144, 173, 180–2, 186, 196, 250n.34
colonialism and 53, 56–7, 62–3, 71, 86, 88, 180–1, 186, 196, 226n.34, 249n.20
Council of Chalcedon 44
and Crown 196
Dominicans 56
folk 4, 6, 46–9, 53, 67, 73–4, 85, 87–93
Franciscans 58, 86, 187
Jesuits 55–6, 58, 72
Latine 5, 8, 10, 25, 49, 51, 53–6, 62, 70–1, 91, 93, 133, 139, 143, 159, 190, 193, 197, 250n.34
martyrs 45
missionaries 18, 53, 72, 86, 91, 187
as religion 1–10, 18, 25–6, 40, 48–9, 51–8, 60–7, 70–4, 86–8, 91–3, 128, 130–5, 139, 143–4, 159, 161, 169, 180–6, 190, 193–7, 226n.34, 249n.20, 249n.24, 250n.34
saints 18, 55–7, 61–5, 67, 70, 73–4, 86, 92, 169, 171, 217n.5
Second Vatican Council 48
social teachings 132–4, 143
CELAM (Conference of Latin American Bishops) 132–3
Chavez, César 130, 235n.25
Chavez, Hugo 28
Chicana feminism 7, 101–7, 225n.20
Chicano Movement 36, 101–7, 127–34, 162, 175, 225n.20
Chile 22, 94, 173–4
Church of the Lukumi Babalú Ayé v. City of Hialeah 62
civil initiative 147–9, 155
civil rights 5, 36, 82, 129–31, 137–48
Columbia 14, 95
Colombus, Christopher 35, 176
Colon, Willie 173
colonialism
erasure 26, 105–6, 121, 177, 180, 187–8, 195
and naming/identity 4, 11, 16, 18, 20
race categories 102–3
and *susto profundo* 177–80, 186, 243n.13
See Doctrine of Discovery (DOD)
community
counteridentification 102
healing and belonging 4–5, 23, 26, 29, 34, 36, 39, 47, 68, 70–1, 75, 120, 123, 128, 131

la comunidad 22, 58, 150
as site of sacred meaning 61–4, 67, 93–4, 159–60, 165
support networks 62, 103, 106, 187, 191–2
Cone, James H. 47, 115
Conquista, la 56, 110, 196
consciousness
critical 78, 84, 107, 171–2
of the dead 59
dominant 117, 201
double 99, 225n.9
female 107
Latine 201
multiple 54
new *mestiza* 121
raise 82, 146–7
conversos 26, 196, 249n.20
Corbett, Jim 148
Costa Rica 26, 95
cotidianidad and *lo cotidiano* 5, 99–100, 110–11
COVID-19 185
Creamer, Debbie 83
Cuban
Afro- 60, 62, 64, 74, 103, 171, 173, 226n.34
-American 57, 60, 62, 73, 91
culture 9, 61–2, 74, 152, 167, 171, 173
Euro- 74
faith traditions 6–7, 55, 57, 60–4, 66, 69, 73–4, 90–1, 103, 170
island 26, 28, 30, 35, 56–7, 60–1, 66, 74, 90–2, 167, 171, 189, 195, 204
Jews 28–9, 32
people identity 7, 14–16, 19, 22, 28–9, 57, 60, 62, 64, 73–4, 90–1, 101, 103, 141, 171, 173, 226n.34
Revolution 28, 57, 62, 90
Cuéllar, Gregory L. 164

Danza Mexica 9, 183
decolonial
decoloniality 23, 37, 88–94, 150
hermeneutics 9, 164, 195
methods 7, 98, 102–4, 106–7, 109
process(es) 7, 38, 40, 120, 185
De La Torre, Miguel A. 8–10, 22, 39, 47, 90, 161–2, 174, 210n.1, 226n.34
Día de los Muertos 60, 125
diaspora 7, 9, 16, 25, 29–34, 37–8, 65–6, 73–4, 88–9, 120, 124, 160–5, 171, 194–5
disability
ableism 7, 77–8, 81–4
critical studies 7, 77–84
eugenics model 80–1
identity 7, 82–3
Individuals with Disability Education Act (IDEA) 82
justice 78
medical model 81–2
and race 77–8, 83–4
religious model 7, 79–80
social model 7, 82–4
dismembering/re-membering 122–5
Doctrine of Discovery (DOD) 176–7, 186, 188
Dominican
-Americans 88–9
faith traditions 7, 60, 87–8
island 26, 35, 87–8
people identity 14, 16, 22, 60, 88–9, 141
Du Bois, W.E.B. 99, 174, 225n.9
Dum Diversas 176

Ecuador 8, 95, 127–8
Elizondo, Virgilio 46
El Plan Espiritual de Aztlán 130, 162
El Salvador 16, 22, 95, 141, 147
England
Anglo-Saxons 20, 36, 42, 57, 203
colonizer 20, 42, 53, 91, 112
culture 141
language 1, 4, 13–15, 20, 22–3, 33, 40, 43, 69, 104, 112, 120, 115n.1, 230n.12, 228n.26, 230n.8, 230n.12, 243n.13
environmental
commodification 127
degradation 2–3, 72, 127–8, 130–1
harmony 120
-ism 8, 127–35
racism 8, 82, 128–32
tierra, la 133–5
epistemology 70, 99–101, 118–20, 129, 198
Espín, Orlando 54
Espinosa, Gaston 143
Espiritismo ix, 6, 60–1, 64, 66–9, 73
espíritus de luz 67–8, 74

ethics
  disruptive 148–50
  ecological 8, 128, 133
  eurocentric 39, 147–50, 201, 206
  Islamic 39
  liberative 56, 147, 151, 156
  para joder 8, 150–7, 237n.18
  praxis 48, 98, 153, 156
  social 39
  trickster 8, 149–57, 237n.16

family
  and colorism 110–11
  dynamics 6–8, 14, 39, 53, 57, 67, 74, 79, 94, 133–4, 138–44, 161, 178, 180–4, 197, 199, 222n.2
  immigration separation 177, 191, 202
  -ism 6, 39–42
  of nations 20
  queer 107, 119, 125
  transnational Jewish ties 31–2
  upward mobility narrative 8, 138–40
Fanon, Frantz 116
feminicide 10, 190
feminism
  critique of white 39–42, 98, 100–4, 106–7
  Latina and Chicana 6–7, 97–104, 106–7, 225n.20
Fernández, Eduardo 48
Fife, John 148, 236n.5
forced sterilization 80–1
France
  colonizer 20, 37, 39, 53
  country 20, 66, 70, 250n.34
  language 13–14, 20–1, 23
  Revolution 154
  war with Spain 55, 88
Francis, Pope 1–3, 10, 92, 133–4
Francis of Assisi, Saint 55–6, 58, 63

Galarte, Francisco J. 106–7
García Jr., Francisco J. 8, 201
García-Rivera, Alejandro 48
Gebara, Ivone 131–2
gender
  cis- 106, 124–5, 179, 190
  colonial construction of 39, 94, 101–3
  fluidity 8, 117–25, 184, 188, 230n.8
  identity 102–3, 179, 184, 191
  inclusivity ix, 20–3, 98, 100, 106, 119, 229n.4, 230n.9, 237n.16
  migrant experiences of 187–8, 190–1
  patriarchy 7, 23, 35, 39–40, 42, 54, 97–107, 124, 162
  sexism 4, 7, 19–20, 39, 56, 81, 94, 97, 100–3, 107, 114, 121, 125, 225n.20, 230n.9
  trans- 7, 104, 106–7, 117–18, 179, 191, 229n.3, 250n.34
  violence 56, 102, 110, 177, 190–1
  wages of 102–3
genocide 118, 122, 175–7, 180–1
German
  language 119
  Nazism 53, 148
  people 203
  thought and theology 54, 203
Gleason, Judith 168, 172
Goizueta, Roberto 48–9
Gonzales, Corky 141
González, Justo 56–7
Gonzalez Maldonado, Michelle 67
Gramsci, Antonio 4
gran familia puertorriqueña, la 111, 113
Guadalupe Hidalgo, Treaty of 1–2, 71, 129, 139
Guardiola-Sáenz, Leticia 163–4
Guatemala 16, 95, 115, 147
Guillén, Nicolás 172
Gustafson, James 148

Hauerwas, Stanley 148
healing
  by African traditions 61, 65–9, 74
  ceremony 87, 181
  and community 8–10, 75, 97, 109, 160–4, 176–8, 180–6, 191
  by *curanderismo* 6, 57, 61, 69, 71–3, 129, 164, 180
  disability 79–80
  divine 6, 53, 57, 61, 69–71
  by *Espiritismo* 60, 66–9, 73–5
  by folk medicine 6, 69, 71–5
  Indigenous 71–5, 180–3
  Pentecostal 57, 69–71, 75
  by plant medicines 72, 74, 182–3
  trauma 8, 97, 118–25, 180–6, 191–2
Hegel, G.W.F. 10, 156, 202–6
Hinduism 190

historia and *intrahistoria* 10–11, 203–7
HIV-AIDS 38
Holy Spirit 6, 48, 51–9, 70
Honduras 95
Huerta, Dolores 130, 235n.25
humanism 103, 130, 194, 197–9
Huntington, Samuel P. 35, 37, 42
hybridity 1–2, 6, 14, 25–6, 30, 33–4, 53–8, 121, 164, 203, 226n.34

identity
Brazilian 17
Cuban 7, 14–16, 19, 22, 28–9, 57, 60, 62, 64, 73–4, 90–1, 101, 103, 141, 171, 173, 226n.34
disability 7, 82–3
Dominican 14, 16, 22, 60, 88–9, 141
Euro 17, 20, 113, 120
gender 102–3, 179, 184, 191
imposed 5, 14, 19, 107, 204–6, 230n.12, 232n.31
Indigenous 2, 6, 9–10, 22, 67, 103–4, 176, 178, 183, 230n.12
Islamic 37, 39, 41–2
Jewish 5, 25–34
Latine ix, 1–11, 14–19, 20, 25–34, 37–9, 41–2, 47, 51–4, 57–8, 68, 71, 88, 90–1, 93, 98–9, 104–6, 111–12, 121, 123, 127–9, 137–9, 141, 152–3, 159–65, 171, 177, 180, 189–92, 202, 226n.34
naming debates and 13–23
pan-ethnic 15–16, 21–2, 30
Puerto Rican 14–16, 22, 36–8, 60, 101, 111–13, 179
queer 8, 102, 102–7, 117–19, 179, 191, 227n.52
racialized 1–2, 7, 9, 15, 17–19, 98, 112–16
transnational 25, 29–34, 71, 74, 226n.34
immigration 1–3, 16–9, 22, 29–30, 36–7, 47, 62, 69–71, 80–2, 97, 117–21, 138–9, 142–3, 147–8, 163–5, 177, 187–92
Indigenous peoples
ceremony and healing 71–5, 180–3
colonial violence against 57, 60, 88, 91–2, 110, 113, 115, 120, 129, 159, 176–80, 186, 188, 190, 196, 224n.1, 230n.12, 243n.13
epistemology 6, 8–10, 56, 71–5, 86, 88, 104, 118, 127, 132–3, 147, 150, 175–7, 180–6, 194–5, 242n.1
identity 2, 6, 9–10, 16–18, 20, 22, 38, 57, 67, 71, 88, 98, 103–4, 111–12, 121, 153, 163, 171, 176–8, 180, 183, 189–92, 230n.12
indigenismo 195
of Latin America 16–18, 35, 40, 57, 71–2, 88, 128, 132, 195–6
of Mexico 1, 9, 18, 71–2, 86, 104, 175–86, 191
naming ceremonies, Indigenous 183–4
OSOMA project (Our Stories, Our Medicine Archive) 178–85
queer 104, 162, 190–1
Quetzalli 182–3
reclaiming traditions 104, 124–5, 128, 175–83, 187–8, 194–6
tribal sovereignty 175, 188
of the US 2, 9, 104, 113, 183, 188
See Doctrine of Discovery (DOD)
See mestizaje
Inter Caetera 176
Irland 22, 145
Irving, T. B. (Al-Hajj Ta'lim 'Ali) 36
Isasi-Díaz, Ada María 46, 48, 98–101
Islam ix, 5, 26, 35–42, 56, 58, 115, 176, 190, 196
IslamInSpanish 41–2
Italy 2, 22, 89, 92, 145, 173

Jesus/*Jesús* 6, 43–55, 57, 70, 79, 91–2, 115, 122, 153, 156, 205–6, 215n.1, 228n.26
Jim Crow 147, 171
John Paul II 161
Johnson-Reed Immigration Act (1924) 26
Juan Diego 86, 73, 85
Judaism
Argentina 27, 29–30
Ashkenazi 5, 25, 27–8, 30–4
Cuba 28
European 5, 26–8
Jews of Color Initiative 31–2
Latin American 25–34
Latine 5, 25–34
Mexico 27–30, 34
persecution of 26–8, 35, 38, 40, 53, 115
and race 31–3
religion ix, 5, 25–34, 44–6, 52–3, 115, 159, 190, 196, 249n.20
Sephardic 26–8, 32

Venezuela 28
US 5, 25, 29–34

Kant, Immanuel/Kantian 149, 203
Kardec, Allan 66–7, 73–5
Kardecian Spiritism 60, 63, 66, 73–5
Kärkkäinen, Veli-Matti 54
Kimpungulu 60, 65–6
King, Martin Luther Jr. 137, 143
Kongo religion 61–2, 64–5, 74

labor
within capitalism 1, 138, 140, 142–3, 149, 163, 176–7, 188
migrant 70, 80, 138, 142, 163, 188
organizing 8, 130–1, 138, 143–4
LALMA (*La Asociación Latino Musulmana de América*) 40–2
language
African 74
Dutch 21
English 1, 4, 13–15, 20, 22–3, 33, 40, 43, 69, 104, 112, 120, 115n.1, 230n.12, 228n.26, 230n.8, 230n.12, 243n.13
French (Creole) 13–14, 20–1, 23
Germanic 119
Glossolalia (Pentecost) 70–1
Hebrew 30, 32–4
Indigenous 16–17, 23, 86, 120, 176, 178, 187, 195–6, 230n.9, 230n.12
Ladino 30
Latin 53, 119
Portuguese 17, 19, 23, 120, 230n.12
Spanglish 21, 23
Spanish 3, 5, 14–23, 25–6, 30, 32, 34, 40–2, 52–3, 57, 66–7, 69–71, 100, 117, 120, 122, 128, 131, 133, 152, 155, 171–3, 204, 215n.1, 230n.12, 231n.24, 243n.13, 246n.5
Latine
anti-Latine racism and discrimination 5, 8, 36–7, 42, 47, 81–2, 97–9, 106, 109–12, 114, 116, 120, 139, 143–5, 149, 202
Christianity 51–8
Christology 43–50
colorism 109–12, 114, 116
Cuban 7, 14–16, 19, 22, 28–9, 57, 60, 62, 64, 73–4, 90–1, 101, 103, 141, 171, 173, 226n.34
Dominican 14, 16, 22, 60, 88–9, 141
faith 40, 43–4, 46–50, 101, 121, 139, 143–4, 150, 156–7, 164
identity ix, 1–11, 14–20, 25–34, 37–42, 47, 51–4, 57–8, 68, 71, 88, 90–1, 93, 98–9, 104–6, 111–12, 121, 123, 127–9, 137–9, 141, 152–3, 159–65, 163, 171, 177, 180, 189–92, 202, 226n.34
Jews 25–34
Mexican 1, 3, 9, 18, 14–16, 20, 22, 27–30, 34, 36–7, 53–4, 60, 71–3, 80–1, 86–7, 97, 101, 104, 115, 117, 119, 121, 129–30, 138–44, 164, 175–89, 191–2
Muslims 35–42
Pentecostalism 53, 55, 57, 69–71
Puerto Rican 14–16, 22, 36–8, 60, 101, 111–13, 179
queerness 7–8, 20–2, 80, 98, 103–7, 117–25, 162, 164, 179, 190–1, 226n.45, 227n.52, 229n.3, 230n.8, 250n.34
religious environmentalism 127–35
religious thought 52, 68, 138, 121–5, 143–4
spirituality 3–5, 40, 49, 53–4, 56–8, 77–8, 84, 121, 123–4, 127, 131, 139, 153–4, 169, 193
terms 13–23, 29, 41, 46–8, 58, 100, 113, 142, 197, 199
workers 70, 80, 130–1, 138, 142–3, 163, 188
See feminism
Latinidad 5, 17, 25, 35–6, 38–9, 42, 47, 104–6, 113, 197
Laudato Si' 3, 133–4
León, Luis 164
liberation theology 4, 6, 44–6, 49, 98–101, 115, 131–2, 144, 197, 250n.34
limpieza de sangre 115
lived religion 4–5, 9, 15, 53–5, 57–8, 160–1
Long, Charles H. 60
Lorde, Audre 123
Loyola, Ignatius, Saint 55
Lozada Jr., Francisco 163

Machín, Antonio 173
Magritte, René 13, 15, 23
Malcolm X 37–9, 137, 201
Manifest Destiny 1, 53, 188

Marian
devotions 85–95
marianismo 85, 93–4
Nossa Senhora da Conceição Aparecida 7, 92–3
Nuestra Señora de Guadalupe 7, 54, 73, 85–7, 93–4, 105, 143, 190
Nuestra Señora de Luján 94
Nuestra Señora de la Altagracia 7, 87–9
Nuestra Señora de la Caridad del Cobre 7, 57, 90–1
Nuestra Señora de la Divina Providencia 7, 89, 93
Nuestra Señora de la Leche y Buen Parto 7, 91–2
Virgin Mary 54–6, 87
Martí, José 150, 195
Marxism 38, 145
Matos, Luis Palés 171–3
Maximilian, Emperor 20
Méndez, Xhercis 102–3, 106
mestizaje 2, 16–18, 20, 38, 57, 71, 88, 98, 104, 111–12, 121, 153, 163, 171, 177, 180, 189–92
Mexican
-American 1, 20, 22, 53–4, 60, 71–3, 81, 87, 115, 129–30, 138, 140–4, 177, 184, 188–9
border 1–5, 9–11, 37, 80, 117–21, 130, 138–9, 163–5, 177, 188–92
colonial 171
country 1, 3, 7, 16, 18–20, 26–7, 29–30, 37, 86–7, 104, 132, 134, 172, 175–6, 188–9
culture 8–9, 30, 34, 87, 128–9, 152, 172–4, 181, 183
faith tradition 7, 54, 71, 73, 85–7, 139, 143, 181–2, 190–1
immigrant 3, 30, 36–7, 80–1, 97, 138–9, 142–3, 187–9, 191–2
Indigenous 1, 9, 18, 86, 104, 175–86
Jews 27–30, 34
Muslim 36
people identity 1, 3, 9, 18, 14–16, 20, 22, 27–30, 34, 36–7, 53–4, 60, 71–3, 80–1, 86–7, 97, 101, 104, 115, 117, 119, 121, 129–30, 138–44, 164, 175–89, 191–2
queer 117, 119, 121, 164
Revolution 27
war with US 1, 71, 104, 129, 143, 188
Molina, Natalia 80–1, 188
Moltmann, Jürgen 54, 58
Moraga, Cherríe 103–7, 162
Mothers of East Los Angeles (MELA) 131
muertos oscuros 67–8
Mujerista theology 7, 46, 97–107
Muñoz, José Esteban 104–6, 162, 226n.45, 229n.3
mysticism 8, 40, 52, 63, 80, 123–5, 143, 174, 182, 277

Napoleon III, Emperor 20
nature 6, 8, 40, 55, 58–60, 63, 65, 127–35, 170
Navarro-Rivera, Juhem 196–7
Nepantla 2, 164
Nicaragua 95
Nicholas V, Pope 176
Nixon, Richard M. 16
nones/alternate paths 10, 193–9

Obama, Barack 37, 137–8
ontology 119–20
orishas
Babalú Ayé 62, 161
Chango/Shangó 63, 168
as deities 60–5, 154, 161, 167–8
Elegguá/Eshu 8, 63, 154, 168
Obatalá 63
Ogún/Oggún 63, 168
Olodumare 63
Olofi 63
Olorun 63
Orula 55, 63
Oshún 63
Seven African Powers/*las siete potencias Africanas* 55, 63
Yemayá 63, 168
See Oyá
Orsi, Robert 4, 210n.13
Ortega, Mariana 104–6
orthodoxy 115, 147
orthopraxis 147
Ortiz, Fernando 204
Otero, Solimar 169
Our Stories, Our Medicine Archive (OSOMA) 176, 178–9
Oyá
and Angelitos Negros 170–4
attributes of 167–8

Orisha 9, 167–74
rattle (*vaina*) of 168–70
sound and cinema and 167, 169–71

pain, communal and embodied 49–50, 123
Palo
faith tradition 6, 60–8, 73–4, 154, 182
nfumbe 60, 65, 68
nganga 64–5, 68
Panamá 95
Paraguay 95
Paul III, Pope 88
Paul VI, Pope 89
Pedraja, Luis 47–8, 50
Penagos, Elaine 6, 161
Pentecost and Feast of 6, 51–2, 54–8, 70
Pentecostalism
Assemblies of God 70–1
divine healing in 6, 69–71, 75
faith 4, 6, 52, 56, 69–70, 247n.3
growth of 55, 70–1
Latine 53, 55, 57–8, 69–71, 247n.3
See Azusa Street Revival
permeability of worlds 59–60, 68
Peru 14, 18, 26, 95, 100, 128, 179
Philippine 18–19
pilgrimage 86–8, 93, 143
Pineda-Madrid, Nancy 101
Pius XII, Pope 93
plant medicines 72, 74, 182–3, 186
plural cosmology 54
pneumatology 6, 51–8
poesía negra 171–2
popular religion 4, 6, 46, 48–9, 53, 60–1, 63–4, 85, 87–95, 144
Portugal
colonizer 15–16, 18–20, 40, 62, 94, 176
faith 93
language 16–17, 19, 23, 66, 120, 230n.12
persecutor 26, 40, 249n.24
poverty 2–3, 6–8, 35, 37, 44–6, 56–8, 71, 77, 83, 119, 131, 139, 141–5, 149, 154, 177, 201–2
praxis 7–9, 44, 46–9, 78, 84, 102–3, 145, 147–9, 151, 153, 155–7, 202
preferential option
historiographical for Latines 204
for Latinas 98–9
for the oppressed 99
for the poor 144
Primera Iglesia Metodista Hispana 146–7
Protestant
Baptist 56, 58
Evangelicals 56, 69–71, 190, 193, 197, 247n.3
faith 6, 48, 51–3, 56–8, 69–71, 134, 146–7, 159, 161, 190, 193, 197, 236n.5, 247n.3
Latine 48, 134, 159, 193, 197
Lutheran 54
Methodists 56–8, 146–7
Presbyterian 236n.5
Quaker 148
Wesleyan holiness 58
Puerto Rican
Afro- 113
colonization of 111–13, 141
culture 115, 141, 152, 171, 173
faith traditions 7, 66, 71, 89, 163
Indigenous 113, 179
island 26, 35, 89, 102, 111
Muslim 36–8
people identity 14–16, 22, 36–8, 60, 101, 111–13, 179
in US 36–8, 71, 113, 131, 163

queer
bisexual 22
community 10, 107, 119, 125
futurity 105–6
gay 22, 104–6, 119, 226n.45, 227n.52
hermeneutics 9, 105, 164
identity 7–8, 20–2, 80, 102–7, 117–21, 123–5, 162, 164, 179, 184, 190–1, 226n.45, 227n.52, 229n.4, 230n.8
Indigenous 103–4, 162, 190–1
Latin America 117, 119, 121, 164
Latine 7–8, 20–2, 80, 98, 103–7, 117–25, 162, 164, 179, 190–1, 226n.45, 227n.52, 229n.3, 230n.8, 250n.34
lesbian 22, 104–6, 119, 226n.45
LGBTQ+ 8, 20–2, 80, 105, 118–21, 123–5, 162, 229n.4
muxes 119, 121, 230n.8
mysticism 124–5
non-binary 20–1, 104, 179
thought and theology 101, 103, 107, 118–21, 123–5, 162, 164, 226n.45

trans 7, 104, 106–7, 117–18, 179, 191, 229n.3, 250n.34
Two-Spirit and IndigiQueer 104, 191
US culture 105, 106, 164
youth 21

racialization 2–3, 5, 7, 10, 15–16, 19–20, 25, 28, 30–3, 37–8, 42, 53, 56–8, 78, 81–4, 102–3, 106–9, 115–16, 163, 165, 171, 173, 177, 188–92, 203, 211n.12
Ramsey, Paul 148
Rawls, Paul 148
reclaiming traditions 41, 71–2, 113, 118, 130, 164, 175–83
Reconquista 196
recordar 117, 122–5
Regla de Ocha, *see* Santería
Renteria, Manuel Alvarez (Maciste) 172–3
resurrection 47–8, 52, 70, 122, 154
Rodriguez, Jeanette 100, 133
Romero, Óscar, Archbishop 45
Roosevelt, Theodore 129
Ruiz, Jean-Pierre 163

salvation history 201, 205–6
Sánchez-Walsh, Arlene 144
Sanctuary Movement 147–8, 191
Santería
and animal sacrifice 62
egún (ancestors) 60, 64, 74, 170
Ifá oracle 62
ilés (religious houses) 62, 68
initiation (kariocha) 62, 64
moyugba 64
origins in Cuba 61–2
religion ix, 4, 6, 9–10, 16, 55, 57–8, 60–9, 73–5, 103, 153–4, 161, 167–74, 194–5, 218n.9, 226n.34
See Yoruba
scripturalization 160–5
settler colonialism 102, 177, 187, 196
Seymour, William, J. 70
Sobrino, Jon 44
solidarity 4, 6–8, 10–11, 17, 21, 30, 36, 38, 44, 107, 109, 111, 114–16, 123, 143–4, 155–6, 164, 207
sonidos escondidos 168–70, 174
sound 9, 21, 167–74
Spain
colonizer and *conquistadors* 14, 16, 18–20, 26, 37, 40, 53, 56–8, 61, 74, 85–8, 94, 104, 171, 176–7, 187, 196
country 41, 56–7, 86–7, 92, 173
culture 7, 13, 16–17, 19, 36, 40, 53, 71, 88, 172–3, 205
expelled Jews and Muslims 35, 38, 41, 249n.20
Inquisition 26, 38, 40
Islamic *al-Andalus* 5, 36–7, 40–2
language 3, 5, 14–23, 25–6, 30, 32, 34, 40–2, 52–3, 57, 66–7, 69–71, 100, 117, 120, 122, 128, 131, 133, 152, 155, 171–3, 204, 215n.1, 230n.12, 231n.24, 243n.13, 246n.5
missionary 86
war with France 55, 88
spirits 59–68
Sublimis Deus 88
supremacy
Anglo and Euroamerican 58, 115, 151–2, 176, 203
Christian 53, 58, 155–6, 176, 197
Germanic 203
Nordic 53
white 8, 10, 35, 38–9, 42, 53, 58, 98, 102, 113–16, 146, 155–7, 180, 202
syncretism 60–2, 71, 74, 86–7, 125, 161

temazcal (sweat lodge) 9, 180–1
Tenayuca, Emma 138, 143–4
terra nullius 176
theodicy 49–50
Tirres, Christopher D. 78
Tlazoteotl (a Nahua divine entity) 182
Tonantzin (Mother Goddess) 86
Toña la Negra 173–4
trauma 8–9, 53, 71–2, 119–25, 125, 170, 175–8, 180–2, 186, 191–2, 230n.10, 232n.31, 243n.13
Trump, Donald J. 37, 47, 81, 155, 189, 191, 202
Turner, Victor 151

Unamuno, Miguel de 10, 204–5
United Farm Workers (UFW) 130, 138, 143, 236n.25

upward mobility 8, 27–9, 31, 112, 116, 137, 139–42
Uruguay 95, 128

Venezuela 22, 28–30, 32, 60, 95, 171, 190
violence
  anti-Latine 3, 36–7, 42, 81–2, 145–6, 152, 155, 201
  colonial 9, 57, 60, 88, 91–2, 110, 112–13, 115–16, 120, 129, 152, 159–61, 170–1, 175–80, 186–8, 190, 196, 224n.1, 229n.31, 230n.12, 243n.13
  fled political violence 29, 71
  immigrant 3, 10, 71, 111, 149, 189–91
  non- 143
  racial 3, 56–7, 111, 116, 170, 174, 210n.10
  state and structural 3–4, 38, 53, 99, 149, 152, 164, 169, 201
  toward disabled Latines 7, 77, 82
  See gendered violence
visible and invisible
  Latine experiences 7, 10, 14–15, 18, 20, 31, 33, 79, 82, 109–10, 121, 204
  spiritual realms 50, 59–60, 64, 67–8, 73–5
Voces Sin Eco 191
Vodou 61, 63, 154

Wesley, Charles and John 57
West, Cornel 49
Wimbush, Vincent L. 160–2

Yanaguana (San Antonio River) 9–10, 187, 189, 191–2
Ybarra, Priscilla Solis 128–9
Yoruba religion 55, 61–8, 74, 154, 218n.9, 226n.34
Young Lords 8, 38, 145–7, 149, 154–5
Yugar, Theresa 128

Zamora Casas, David 187, 192